Pearson Edexcel GCSE (9–1)
Mathematics

Purposeful
Practice Book

Foundation

◆ **Skills practice**   ◆ **Problem-solving practice**   ◆ **Exam practice**

Series Editors:
Dr Naomi Norman
Katherine Pate

Published by Pearson Education Limited, 80 Strand, London, WC2R 0RL.

www.pearsonschoolsandfecolleges.co.uk

Text © Pearson Education Limited 2019
Edited by Haremi Ltd.
Typeset by CSC
Cover design by Pearson Education Limited 2018
Cover photo/illustration © Sahua D/Shutterstock and Ozz Design/Shutterstock

The rights of Naran Gorsia, Peter Hall, Mark Heslop, Caroline Locke, Martin Noon, Dr Naomi Norman, Diane Oliver and Katherine Pate to be identified as authors of this work has been asserted by them in accordance with the Copyright, Designs and Patents Act 1988.

First published 2019

22 21 20
10 9 8 7 6 5 4

British Library Cataloguing in Publication Data

A catalogue record for this book is available from the British Library

ISBN 978 1 292 27371 6

Printed in Italy by LEGO S.p.A

Acknowledgements

Pearson Education: Adapted from 1MA1/1F, June 2018, November 2017, Specimen Papers , June 2017, May 2017, May 2018, Autumn 2016, Spring 2017, 1, 2, 3, 4, 5, 6, 7, 8, 9, 10, 11, 12, 13, 15, 16, 17, 18, 19, Mixed problem-solving practice A; Pearson Education: Adapted from 1MA1/3F, Specimen Papers , November 2017, June 2018, June 2017, Spring 2017, Autumn 2017, Spring 2017, Mock Set 3, 1, 2, 3, 4, 5, 6, 7, 8, 9, 10, 11, 12, 13, 15, 17, 18, 19, Mixed problem-solving practice A; Pearson Education: Adapted from 1MA1/2F, May 2018, June 2018, Specimen Papers, June 2017, November 2017, June 2018, November 2018, Spring 2017, 1, 2, 3, 4, 5, 6, 7, 8, 9, 10, 11, 12, 15, 16, 17, 18, 19, Mixed problem-solving practice A; Pearson Education: Adapted from 1MA0/1F, Nov 2016, May 2017, 5, 6; Pearson Education: Adapted from 1MA0/1H, June 2013, 6; Pearson Education: Adapted from 1MA0/2F, November 2012, June 2013, June 2017, June 2015, 5, 11, 14, 16; Pearson Education: Edexcel GCSE (9-1) Mathematics: Foundation Student Book,Pearson Education Limited (February 3, 2015) 6, 8, 10, 12, 15, 17.

Note from the publisher

Pearson has robust editorial processes, including answer and fact checks, to ensure the accuracy of the content in this publication, and every effort is made to ensure this publication is free of errors. We are, however, only human, and occasionally errors do occur. Pearson is not liable for any misunderstandings that arise as a result of errors in this publication, but it is our priority to ensure that the content is accurate. If you spot an error, please do contact us at resourcescorrections@pearson.com so we can make sure it is corrected.

Contents

Visit www.pearsonschools.co.uk for more information about the Pearson Edexcel GCSE (9-1) Mathematics course.

Pearson Edexcel GCSE (9–1) Mathematics Purposeful Practice Book:
Foundation

8 key messages from Series Editors Dr Naomi Norman and Katherine Pate

These GCSE Mathematics Purposeful Practice books offer:

1 Lots of practice – you can never have too much!

2 Practice that develops mathematical confidence.

3 Purposeful practice questions that lead students on a path to understanding. These questions:
   - cannot be answered mechanically, by rote
   - make connections to prior knowledge
   - develop thinking skills
   - target specific concepts

4 Reflect and reason questions to:
   - make students aware of their understanding
   - show teachers what students do (or don't yet!) understand
   - encourage students to think about the underlying mathematical patterns

5 Problem-solving practice to:
   - allow students to apply their understanding to problem-solving questions and contexts
   - practice problem-solving strategies
   - prepare for GCSE exams

6 GCSE exam-style questions with:
   - real exam feedback
   - evidence-informed grade indicators, informed by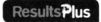

7 Designed with the help of UK teachers so you can use it flexibly alongside your current resources, in class or for independent study.

8 Purposeful practice, problem-solving practice and exam practice all in one book – the first of its kind.

Key Features of this Purposeful Practice Book:

△ **Purposeful practice** has been embedded in 3 different ways:

1. **Variation**

Carefully crafted questions that are minimally varied throughout an exercise.
As students work out the answers, they are exposed to what stays the same and what changes, from question to question. In doing so, by the end of the exercise, students deepen their understanding of the mathematical patterns, structures and relationships that underlie concepts.

2. **Variation and progression**

A mixture of minimally varied questions, along with small-stepped questions that get incrementally harder. These exercises are designed to both deepen understanding and move students on.

3. **Progression**

Questions where the skills required become incrementally harder. These small-stepped questions mean there are no uncomfortable jumps, and help to build students' confidence.

Reflect and reason

Metacognition (reflection) is a powerful tool that is used to help students become aware of their own understanding. Reasoning is a key part of the GCSE (9–1), so we've included lots of opportunities for students to show what they do (or don't yet!) understand.

⊠ **Problem-solving practice** is where the skill(s) from each sub-unit can be demonstrated and applied. These problem-solving activities will be a mixture of contextualised problems, 'working backwards' problems, and synoptic problems, ensuring that the skills practised in each sub-unit are fully embedded in new and interesting ways to build confidence.

✦ **Exam practice** is the final part of the sub-unit. Here the students will work with modified versions of real exam questions. These will follow a similar level, structure and concept to the *Purposeful practice* and *Problem-solving practice* sections, giving students the opportunity to answer exam questions with confidence.

Exam feedback   Results**Plus**

We've used ResultsPlus live data to provide grade indicators for each exam-style question, where possible. Using the full cohort for each exam sitting, we've looked at the average score of students from across the grade range. If it is more than 65% of the available marks, we've identified it as 'answered well' by that cohort at that grade range.

Note: For some exam paper questions (e.g. November sittings) the cohort is too small to provide an indication of grade. In this case, we have provided meaningful examiner report information.

Get to know your Purposeful Practice Book

Key points

Key points to remind students what they need to know.

◬ Purposeful practice

The Purposeful Practice Books start with short practice questions, carefully crafted to lead students on a path to understanding the mathematics.

⊠ Problem-solving practice

These questions lead on from Purposeful practice, allowing students to apply the skills they have learnt in different contexts where the steps aren't obvious and they must apply different strategies.

---

1 Number

1.1 Calculations

Key points

- The priority of operations is: Brackets, Indices, Division and Multiplication, Addition and Subtraction.
- Adding and subtracting are inverse operations; multiplying and dividing are inverse operations. You can use inverse operations to check answers.
- Finding the square root is the inverse of finding the square.
- Finding the cube root is the inverse of finding the cube.

◬ Purposeful practice 1

Calculate

1 $2 \times 4 + 8$ 2 $8 + 2 \times 4$ 3 $(8 + 2) \times 4$

4 $(8 - 2) \times 4$ 5 $8 - 2 \times 4$ 6 $-2 \times 4 + 8$

7 $\frac{8 \times 4}{2}$ 8 $\frac{8}{2} \times 4$ 9 $8 \times \frac{4}{2}$

10 $\frac{8}{2} \times \frac{4}{2}$ 11 $\frac{8}{4} \times \frac{4}{2}$ 12 $\frac{8}{4} \times \frac{4}{4}$

Reflect and reason

Why do **Q7–9** have a different answer?

◬ Purposeful practice 2

Calculate

1 $5 + 2 - 2$ 2 $5 \times 2 - 2$ 3 $5 \times 2 + 2$

4 $5^2 + 2$ 5 $5^2 + 5$ 6 $\sqrt{5^2}$

Reflect and reason

Why do **Q1** and **Q3** give the same answer?
Does it matter if you replace the 5 in each calculation with a different number? Explain.

◬ Purposeful practice 3

Write a calculation using the inverse operation to check

1 $11 \times 3 = 33$ 2 $11^3 = 1331$ 3 $11^3 + 3 = 1334$

4 $(11 + 3)^3 = 2744$ 5 $11^3 \times 3 = 3993$ 6 $\frac{11^3 \times 3}{11} = 363$

Reflect and reason

Did you use your answer to **Q2** to check the answer to **Q3**? How?
Did you use your answer to **Q5** to check the answer to **Q6**? How?

1

⊠ Problem-solving practice

1 Use all the numbers 1, 2, 3, 4, 5, brackets and the operations + and ×. Write one calculation that gives the answer 29.

2 $7 + 5 \times 3 + 8 = 30$.
Insert a pair of brackets to change the answer to 62.

3 Copy this 3 × 3 grid.
Write the numbers −4, −3, −2, −1, 0, 1, 2, 3, 4 into the grid.
Every row, column and diagonal should total 0.

4 Here are three poles.
Pole A is equal in length to the sum of poles B and C.
A is 18 m long. C is half the length of B.
What is the length of C?

   A
   B   C

5 Place the numbers 1, 7 and 8 in the boxes to make the calculation correct.
$\frac{2 \times (11 - \square)}{\square} = \square$

6 Sarah wants to find out how much it will cost to decorate her kitchen.
A tin of paint costs £4. She needs 80 tins of paint.
She says the paint will cost £20 because 80 ÷ £4 is £20.
Is Sarah correct? Show your method.

7 Use the numbers 3, 4, 5 and 6 to create two calculations that give the same answer.
How many ways can you do this?

✵ Exam practice

1 Claire and four friends go on a weekend holiday.
The five friends will share the costs for the holiday equally.
Here are the costs for the holiday.
   £430 for the hotel
   £1075 for the flights
   £75 for the cost of airport transfers
   Work out how much Claire has to pay for her share of the costs.   (3 marks)
   Adapted from 1MA1/1F, June 2018, Q10

2 Work out $5 + 3 \times 11$ (1 mark)
   Adapted from 1MA1/1F, November 2017, Q2

Exam feedback   Results**Plus**
Q1: Most students who achieved a **Grade 2** or above answered a similar question well.
Q2: Whilst this question tested the priority of operations, many students gave an answer of 88 and did not follow the rules of arithmetic.

Unit 1 Calculations   2

Reflect and reason

Thought provoking questions that encourage students to articulate a mathematical pattern, structure or relationship.

Results**Plus**

ResultsPlus evidence-informed grades to give insight into how well the cohort achieved nationally at this particular question type.

✵ Exam practice

Students will have the chance to answer exam-style questions related to the skills they have just learnt to help prepare for the GCSE (9–1) exam.

Mixed exercises

Mixed problem-solving practice A

1 Jordan has £10 to spend on chocolate bars.
   Each chocolate bar costs 64p.
   Jordan buys as many chocolate bars as possible.
   Work out how much money Jordan has left.

2 Insert the missing term to complete the equation.
   $2x \times \square = 10x^2$

3 a Work out the value of y when $a^3 \times a^4 = a^{\square}$
   b Work out the value of y when $(5^4)^y = 5^8$

4 Tia substitutes $u = 10$, $a = 4$ and $t = 5$ into the formula $v = u + at$
   She writes
      $v = 10 + 45$
      $v = 55$
   Explain what Tia has done wrong.

5 Kamil wants to buy 55 key rings.
   Each key ring costs £3.80.
   Kamil does the calculation 60 × 4 = 240 to estimate the cost of 55 key rings.
   a Explain how Kamil's calculation shows the actual cost will be less than £240.
      There is a special offer
      'Buy 50 or more key rings, get 20% off'
   b Work out the actual cost of buying 55 key rings using the special offer.

Mixed exercises

Every 4 units, there will be 4 pages of Mixed exercises, where students can bring topics together to encourage them to make links between the mathematical concepts they have studied previously. This is to ensure that the mathematical concepts are not learnt in isolation.

vii

1 Number

1.1 Calculations

Key points

- The priority of operations is: Brackets, Indices, Division and Multiplication, Addition and Subtraction.
- Adding and subtracting are inverse operations; multiplying and dividing are inverse operations. You can use inverse operations to check answers.
- Finding the square root is the inverse of finding the square.
- Finding the cube root is the inverse of finding the cube.

Purposeful practice 1

Calculate

1 $2 \times 4 + 8 = 16$
2 $8 + 2 \times 4$ 16
3 $(8 + 2) \times 4$ 40
4 $(8 - 2) \times 4 = 24$
5 $8 - 2 \times 4$ 0
6 $-2 \times 4 + 8$ 0
7 $\dfrac{8 \times 4}{2}$ 16
8 $\dfrac{8}{2} \times 4$ 16
9 $8 \times \dfrac{4}{2}$ 16
10 $\dfrac{8}{2} \times \dfrac{4}{2}$ $\dfrac{32}{4}$
11 $\dfrac{8}{4} \times \dfrac{4}{2}$ $\dfrac{32}{8}$
12 $\dfrac{8}{4} \times \dfrac{4}{4}$ $\dfrac{32}{16}$ 2

Reflect and reason

Why do **Q7–9** have the same answer? Same question changed order?

Purposeful practice 2

Calculate

1 $5 + 2 - 2 = 5$
2 $5 \times 2 - 2 = 8$
3 $5 \times 2 \div 2 = 5$
4 $5^2 \div 2 = 12.5$
5 $5^2 \div 5 = 5$
6 $\sqrt{5^2} = 5$

Reflect and reason

Why do **Q1** and **Q3** give the same answer?
Does it matter if you replace the 5 in each calculation with a different number? Explain.

Purposeful practice 3

Write a calculation using the inverse operation to check

1 $11 \times 3 = 33$ $\dfrac{33}{3} = 11$
2 $11^3 = 1331$ $\sqrt[3]{11^3} = 1331$
3 $11^3 + 3 = 1334$
4 $(11 + 3)^3 = 2744$
5 $11^3 \times 3 = 3993$
6 $\dfrac{11^3 \times 3}{11} = 363$

Reflect and reason

Did you use your answer to **Q2** to check the answer to **Q3**? How?
Did you use your answer to **Q5** to check the answer to **Q6**? How?

⊠ Problem-solving practice

(handwritten: $(5 \times 9 + (1 + 2 \times 3)$ $(5 \times 4) = 20$ $(5 \times 4) + (2H$ $2 \not L = 7$)

1 Use all the numbers 1, 2, 3, 4, 5, brackets and the operations + and ×.
   Write one calculation that gives the answer 29.

2 $7 + 5 \times 3 + 8 = 30$. *(handwritten brackets around 5 × 3)*
   Insert a pair of brackets to change the answer to 62.

3 Copy this 3 × 3 grid.
   Write the numbers −4, −3, −2, −1, 0, 1, 2, 3, 4 into the grid.
   Every row, column and diagonal should total 0.

4 Here are three poles.
   Pole A is equal in length to the sum of poles B and C.
   A is 18 m long. C is half the length of B.
   What is the length of C?

5 Place the numbers 1, 7 and 8 in the boxes to make the calculation correct.
   $$\frac{2 \times (11 - \square)}{\square} = \square$$

6 Sarah wants to find out how much it will cost to decorate her kitchen.
   A tin of paint costs £4. She needs 80 tins of paint.
   She says the paint will cost £20 because 80 ÷ £4 is £20.
   Is Sarah correct? Show your method.

7 Use the numbers 3, 4, 5 and 6 to create two calculations that give the same answer.
   How many ways can you do this?

✺ Exam practice

1 Claire and four friends go on a weekend holiday.
   The five friends will share the costs for the holiday equally.
   Here are the costs for the holiday.

   £430 for the hotel
   £1075 for the flights
   £75 for the cost of airport transfers

   Work out how much Claire has to pay for her share of the costs.   **(3 marks)**

   Adapted from 1MA1/1F, June 2018, Q10

2 Work out $5 + 3 \times 11$ **(1 mark)**

   Adapted from 1MA1/1F, November 2017, Q2

Exam feedback   Results**Plus**

Q1: Most students who achieved a **Grade 2** or above answered a similar question well.

Q2: Whilst this question tested the priority of operations, many students gave an answer of 88 and did not follow the rules of arithmetic.

Key points

- To divide by a decimal, multiply both numbers by powers of 10 (10, 100, ...) until you have a whole number to divide by. Then work out the division.
- To round a number to 1 decimal place (1 d.p.), look at the digit in the 2nd decimal place. If it is 5 or more, round up.

◬ Purposeful practice 1

Calculate

1	15×20	**2**	15×2	**3**	15×0.2	**4**	15×0.02
5	1.5×0.02	**6**	15×0.002	**7**	$15 \div 5$	**8**	$15 \div 0.5$
9	$15 \div 0.05$	**10**	$1.5 \div 0.05$	**11**	$0.15 \div 0.05$	**12**	$0.015 \div 0.05$

Reflect and reason

Which calculations from **Q7–12** give the same answer? Why?

◬ Purposeful practice 2

Calculate

1	$10 \div 5$	**2**	10×0.5	**3**	10×0.2	**4**	$10 \div 2$
5	$20 \div 5$	**6**	20×0.5	**7**	20×0.2	**8**	$20 \div 2$
9	4×0.25	**10**	4×0.4	**11**	$4 \div 4$	**12**	$4 \div 0.4$
13	$4 \div 0.04$	**14**	4×25	**15**	$1 \div 0.04$	**16**	1×25
17	$0.1 \div 0.04$	**18**	$0.1 \div 0.05$				

Reflect and reason

Which calculations form pairs that give the same answer?
Rewrite the decimals as fractions in these calculations. What pattern do you notice?

◬ Purposeful practice 3

Round these numbers to 1 decimal place.

1	3.45	**2**	3.54	**3**	3.545	**4**	11.545
5	0.545	**6**	3.78	**7**	3.88	**8**	3.98
9	10.98	**10**	0.98	**11**	0.098	**12**	0.0098
13	9.80	**14**	9.08	**15**	19.98		

Reflect and reason

Jack says that the answer to **Q3** is 3.6. What mistake has he made?
Did you change the units digit in **Q8**, **Q9** or **Q10**? Explain.

1. Harry buys a pizza for £18.68. Harry shares the pizza equally with three of his friends.

    a   How much should they each pay?

    b   They want to give a tip worth 0.1 of the price of the pizza. How much should they each pay as a tip? Round your answer to the nearest penny.

2. A number rounded to 1 decimal place is 3.8.

    a   What is the largest number it could be?

    b   What is the smallest number it could be?

3. Which of these divisions will give the same answer as $864 \div 12$?

    A $86.4 \div 12$ **B** $864 \div 1.2$ **C** $86.4 \div 1.2$ **D** $8.64 \div 0.12$
    E $8.64 \div 1.2$ **F** $0.864 \div 0.12$ **G** $86.4 \div 0.12$

4. Bill says that multiplying always makes a number bigger. Write a calculation to show that Bill is incorrect.

5. A horse needs 1.5 acres of land to graze.
   Each acre of land costs £40.50 per month to rent.
   Kris has 5 horses.
   How much will Kris pay each month for the land for his 5 horses?

6. To convert a number from pounds to kilograms, divide by 2.2.
   Advaith has 33 pounds of flour. He needs 20 kg of flour to bake his cupcakes.
   Does he have enough flour?

7. Penny wants to buy some packs of football stickers.
   Each pack costs £1.45. Penny has £30.
   What is the largest number of packs of football stickers Penny can buy?

8. Sam makes some strawberry tarts.
   Each tart costs £1.18 to make.
   Sam sells 20 tarts for £1.50 each. How much money does Sam make?

1. Write 4.18 correct to 1 decimal place.   **(1 mark)**

   Adapted from 1MA1/2F, May 2018, Q2

2. Work out 62.5×3.4 **(3 marks)**

   Adapted from 1MA1/1F, June 2017, Q23

Exam feedback   ResultsPlus

Q1: Most students who achieved a Grade 3 or above answered a similar question well.

Q2: Most students who achieved a Grade 5 or above answered a similar question well.

1.3 Place value

Key points

- The first significant figure (s.f.) is the one with the highest place value.
- Rounded numbers must have the same place value as the original number.
  For numbers greater than zero, this means you may need to put in zeros as 'place fillers'.
- To estimate the answer to a calculation, you can round every number to 1 s.f.

⚠ Purposeful practice 1

Round

1 127 to 1 s.f.	**2** 172 to 1 s.f.	**3** 1270 to 1 s.f.
4 1279 to 1 s.f.	**5** 1.27 to 1 s.f.	**6** 0.127 to 1 s.f.
7 0.00127 to 1 s.f.	**8** 0.00172 to 1 s.f.	**9** 0.00172 to 2 s.f.
10 0.001072 to 2 s.f.	**11** 0.00102 to 2 s.f.	**12** 3.00172 to 2 s.f.

Reflect and reason

Round the numbers in **Q5–12** to 1 decimal place. Do you get the same answers?
In **Q10**, which zero is significant? Why is this zero significant?

⚠ Purposeful practice 2

Estimate

1 127×172

2 $172 \div 12$

3 $1279 \div 1270$

4 $\dfrac{1270}{1.72}$

5 $\dfrac{1270 + 172}{1.27}$

6 $\dfrac{1270 \times 1.27}{1.72}$

7 $\dfrac{1720 \times 1.72}{1.27}$

8 $\dfrac{1270 + 172}{1.27 + 0.00102}$

9 $\dfrac{1270 + 172}{1.27 + 3.00172}$

Reflect and reason

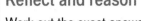

Work out the exact answers to **Q6** and **Q7**. For each answer, is your estimate an overestimate or underestimate? Why?

⚠ Purposeful practice 3

1 Use the information that $32 \times 27 = 864$ to work out the missing numbers.

    a $320 \times 27 = \square$ **b** $32 \times \square = 8640$ **c** $3.2 \times 27 = \square$ **d** $32 \times \square = 86.4$

    e $3.2 \times \square = 864$ **f** $864 \div 32 = \square$ **g** $864 \div \square = 32$ **h** $86.4 \div \square = 32$

2 Use the information that $60 \times 5 = 300$ to work out the value of

    a 59×5 **b** 59×6 **c** 59×4 **d** 6×50

Reflect and reason

Were you able to use the same strategy in **Q2** that you used in **Q1**? Explain.

1 Max has 12 months to save £5775 before he goes to university.

 a Estimate how much Max should save each month.

 b If Max saves as much as you estimated in part a, will he save enough? Explain.

2 Carrie earns £2140 a month and Arjun earns £1389.94 a month.
 They want to buy a house worth £210 985.
 They can afford it if it costs less than five times their yearly earnings.

 a Estimate whether they can afford the house. Show your working.

 b Is your answer to part a an overestimate or an underestimate? Give reasons.

3 One cup of flour weighs 4.25 ounces. Reyan needs 3.2 cups of flour to bake a cake.

 a Estimate how many ounces of flour Reyan needs.

 b Is your answer an overestimate or an underestimate? Explain.

 c Reyan finds out that his type of flour weighs more than 4.25 ounces.
 One cup weighs 4.7 ounces. How does this change your answer to part a?

4 Given that $54 \times 87 = 4698$, write a calculation with the answer 4.698.

5 Sam estimates $\frac{378 \times 56}{0.5}$ by finding 400×60 and halving the answer. Sam is wrong.
 What should Sam have done?

6 Shan can swim 82.3 metres in 98.76 seconds.
 Estimate how many minutes it would take Shan to swim 1000 metres.

⊗ Exam practice

1 Billy and Sarah use a calculator to work out $\dfrac{236}{3.72^2 + 4.06}$

 Billy's answer is 13.1855
 Sarah's answer is 131.855
 One of these answers is correct.
 Use approximations to find out which answer is correct. **(3 marks)**

 Adapted from, 1MA1/1F, November 2017, Q20

2 Write 86.573 correct to one significant figure. **(1 mark)**

 Adapted from 1MA1/2F, June 2017, Q2

Exam feedback
Results**Plus**

Q1: A similar question was answered in a variety of ways. An approximation was required but some students tried to work out the actual calculation.

Q2: In a similar question, many students gave an answer of 86.6, rounding to 1 decimal place instead of 1 significant figure.

Key points

- A prime number has exactly two factors, itself and 1.
- The highest common factor (HCF) of two numbers is the largest number that is a factor of both numbers.
- The lowest common multiple (LCM) of two numbers is the smallest number that is a multiple of both numbers.

Purposeful practice 1

1 20, 21, 22, 23, 24, 25, 26, 27, 28, 29, 30.

Which of these numbers are

   a multiples of 2 (in the 2 times table)   **b** multiples of 3

   c multiples of 5   **d** multiples of 7

   e multiples of 11   **f** prime numbers

2 List the prime numbers between 30 and 40.

3 List the prime numbers between 40 and 50.

Reflect and reason

In **Q1**, how can you use the answers to parts **a–e** to help you answer part **f**? Explain.

Purposeful practice 2

1 List all the factors of

   a 6   **b** 5   **c** 30   **d** 60   **e** 45

2 List the first five multiples of

   a 6   **b** 5   **c** 30   **d** 60   **e** 45

Reflect and reason

In **Q1**, what do you notice about the factors of 5 and 6 compared with the factors of 30?

In **Q2**, is it possible to list all the multiples of each number? Explain.

Purposeful practice 3

1 Use your answers from **Q1** of Purposeful practice 2 to find the HCF of

   a 30 and 45   **b** 30 and 6   **c** 30 and 60   **d** 5 and 6   **e** 30, 45 and 60

2 Use your answers from **Q2** of Purposeful practice 2 to find the LCM of

   a 30 and 45   **b** 30 and 6   **c** 30 and 60   **d** 5 and 6   **e** 30, 45 and 60

Reflect and reason

In **Q1** and **Q2**, how can you use the answers to parts **a–c** to answer part **e**? Explain.

1   Write two numbers with a HCF of 6. Is there more than one answer?

2   The HCF of two numbers is 10. The LCM is 120. What could the two numbers be?

3   Jamie says that 6 is a factor of 45. How do you know Jamie is wrong?

4   Tom says that if you square a prime number, the answer is always odd.
    Is Tom right? Give an example.

5   Is 8 a factor of 254? Show how you know.

6   Is 678 a multiple of 3? Show how you know.

7   There is a bus to Doncaster every 20 minutes.
    A bus to Sheffield leaves from the same stop every 15 minutes.
    A bus to Doncaster and a bus to Sheffield both leave at 8 am.
    What is the next time both buses will leave together?

8   Veggie burgers come in packs of 8. Each pack of veggie burgers costs £3.
    Buns come in packs of 12. Each pack of buns costs £2.
    How much would you need to spend to buy an equal number of buns and veggie burgers?

9   Luca is 1.5 times as old as Paul. The LCM of their ages is 90. How old are Luca and Paul?

10 Mr Hunt prepares fruit boxes for a school trip. He wants each box to be the same
    with no fruit left over.
    Mr Hunt has 40 apples and 90 strawberries.
    What is the greatest number of boxes he can prepare?

✦ Exam practice

1   Here is a list of numbers

    1, 2, 4, 9, 16, 17, 18, 24, 25

    a   From the numbers in the list, write down a number that is a multiple
        of both 3 and 8.

    b   Write down all the prime numbers in the list.   **(2 marks)**

    Adapted from 1MA1/2F, June 2017, Q8b and Q8c

2   Maja adds together two different prime numbers.
    Her answer is a multiple of 6.
    Find two prime numbers that Maja could have used.   **(2 marks)**

    Adapted from 1MA1/3F, November 2017, Q9

Exam feedback   Results**Plus**

Q1a: Most students who achieved a **Grade 1** or above answered a similar question well.

Q1b: Most students who achieved a **Grade 5** answered a similar question well.

Q2: In a similar question, many students incorrectly gave 1 as one of the two prime numbers.

Key points

- Expressions with square roots like $3\sqrt{2}$ are in surd form.
- $3\sqrt{2}$ means $3 \times \sqrt{2}$.
- An answer in surd form is an exact value (it has not been rounded up or down).

△ Purposeful practice 1

Evaluate

1 2^2	2 3^2	3 4^2	4 $(-2)^2$	5 $(-3)^2$	6 -3^2	7 $(-4)^2$
8 2^3	9 3^3	10 4^3	11 $(-2)^3$	12 $(-3)^3$	13 $(-4)^3$	14 -4^3

Reflect and reason

What happens to the sign when you square a negative number? What about when you cube it? Why?

△ Purposeful practice 2

1 Evaluate

     a $\sqrt{4}$ **b** $\pm\sqrt{4}$ **c** $\pm\sqrt{9}$ **d** $\pm\sqrt{16}$ **e** $\sqrt[3]{27}$ **f** $\sqrt[3]{-27}$

2 Evaluate

     a $\sqrt{1.6}$ to 3 s.f.   **b** $\sqrt{0.16}$ **c** $\sqrt[3]{2.7}$ to 3 s.f.   **d** $\sqrt[3]{0.27}$ to 3 s.f.

     e $\sqrt[3]{0.027}$ **f** $\sqrt[3]{0.000027}$ **g** $\sqrt{2.5}$ to 3 s.f.   **h** $\sqrt{0.25}$

     i $\sqrt{0.025}$ to 3 s.f.   **j** $\sqrt[3]{8}$ **k** $\sqrt[3]{0.08}$ to 3 s.f   **l** $\sqrt[3]{0.008}$

Reflect and reason

How many possible answers are there for **Q1e**?
Predict the number that gives the answer 0.04 when square rooted.
Check your prediction on a calculator.

△ Purposeful practice 3

Work out these. Give your answers in surd form.

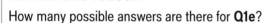

1 $\sqrt{9} + \sqrt{16}$	2 $\sqrt{9 + 16}$	3 $\sqrt{9} \times \sqrt{9}$	4 $\sqrt{3} \times \sqrt{3}$	5 $\sqrt{3} + \sqrt{3}$
6 $\sqrt{12} + \sqrt{3}$	7 $\sqrt{12} - \sqrt{3}$	8 $\sqrt{12} \times \sqrt{3}$	9 $\sqrt{12} \div \sqrt{3}$	10 $\sqrt{4} \times \sqrt{3}$

Reflect and reason

Use your calculator to convert your answers to decimals. Why might surd form be more useful when you are working out the answers to calculations?

1 The cube root and the square root of a number are the same.
   What is the number?

2 The length of one side of a square is 4.6 cm.
   What is the area of the square?

3 The area of a square is 36 cm^2.
   What is the perimeter of the square?

4 A rectangle measures 2 cm by 8 cm.
   What is the side length of a square with the same area?

5 Two consecutive numbers are squared.
   The difference between their squares is 7.
   What are the two original numbers?

6 Two consecutive numbers are squared.
   The square root of the difference between the two square numbers is 3.
   What are the two original numbers?

7 Fill in the box: $6^2 + 8^2 = \Box^2$

8 The area of one square is 49 cm^2.
   The area of another square is 0.49 cm^2.
   How many times longer is each side of the larger square?

9 Lexie says that the cube of a number will always be greater than the square of the same number.
   Give an example to prove Lexie wrong.

10 Freda says, 'Square rooting a number makes it smaller'.
   Give an example to prove Freda wrong.

✵ Exam practice

1 Work out 3^3 **(1 mark)**

Adapted from 1MA1/1F, May 2017, Q1

2 Here are three numbers.

   15   11   23

   Jordan says that the sum of the three numbers is a square number. Is Jordan correct?
   You must show how you get your answer. **(2 marks)**

Adapted from 1MA1/3F, Specimen Papers, Set 1, Q12

3 Work out $(-5)^3$ **(1 mark)**

Adapted from 1MA1/1F, Specimen Papers, Set 1, Q5

Exam feedback   ResultsPlus

Q1: Most students who achieved a **Grade 3** or above answered a similar question well.

Key points

- In index notation, the number that is being multiplied by itself is called the base.
  The number written above the base is called the index or the power.
  The index tells you the number of times that the base must be multiplied by itself.

  $$\text{base} \rightarrow a^{n} \nearrow^{\text{index or power}}$$

- To multiply powers of the same number, add the indices.
- To divide powers of the same number, subtract the indices.

△ Purposeful practice 1

Write each product using powers.

1 $3 \times 3 \times 3 \times 3$

2 $3 \times 3 \times 3 \times 3 \times 5 \times 5$

3 $3 \times 5 \times 3 \times 3 \times 5 \times 3$

4 $3 \times 3 \times 3 \times 3 \times 5 \times 5 \times 5 \times 5$

5 $3 \times 5 \times 3 \times 5 \times 3 \times 5 \times 3 \times 5$

Reflect and reason

Can you write **Q2–5** as a power with a single base? Explain.

△ Purposeful practice 2

Write as a single power.

1 $6^{2} \times 6 \times 6 \times 6$

2 $6^{2} \times 6^{2} \times 6$

3 $5^{3} \times 5^{3}$

4 $(5^{3})^{2}$

5 $(5^{3})^{4}$

6 $(5^{3})^{2} \times 5$

7 $5^{5} \div 5^{2}$

8 $\dfrac{5^{7}}{5^{3}}$

9 $\dfrac{5^{7} \times 5^{3}}{5^{3}}$

10 $\left(\dfrac{5^{7} \times 5^{3}}{5^{3}}\right)^{2}$

11 $\dfrac{(5^{7} \times 5^{3})^{2}}{5^{3}}$

12 $\dfrac{5^{7} \times 5^{3}}{(5^{3})^{2}}$

Reflect and reason

Why do you 'add the indices' when multiplying powers of the same number? Use your answers to Purposeful practice 1 and 2 to explain.

△ Purposeful practice 3

1 Write as a power of 10

    a 100   **b** 1000   **c** 10 000   **d** 10

    e 1   **f** 0.1   **g** 100×1000 **h** 0.01

2 Write with powers of 10

    a 3×100 **b** 5×100 **c** 5.3×1000 **d** 3×0.01 **e** 3.8×0.001

Reflect and reason

Convert the decimals in **Q1f** and **Q1h** to fractions.
What do you notice about the denominator and the power of 10?

1 Write $2 \times \sqrt{4}$ as a single power of 2.

2 Write $\frac{9 \times 3^2}{\sqrt{81}}$ as a single power of 3.

3 Find the missing value.

$3^3 - \square = 3^2$

4 $\dfrac{3 \times 3 \times 5 \times 15}{3}$

Can this be written as a single power? Explain.

5 Change one number so that this calculation can be written as a single power of 10.

$$\frac{\left(10^2\right)^3 \times 4 \times 3}{40 \times 2}$$

6 Given that $3^k = 3^8 \div 3^5$, evaluate 5^k

7 $p^3\left(p^8 \div p^5\right) = p^g$

Find the value of g.

8 Amelia says that $4^3 + 5^3 = 9^3$.

Is Amelia correct? Explain.

9 Clark multiplied a number by 3. He then multiplied the answer by 3 again.

Clark says that this is the same as multiplying the original number by 6.

Allison says he is wrong and that this is the same as multiplying the original number by 3^2.

Who is correct? Explain.

1 **a** $3^2 \times 3^x = 3^{12}$

Find the value of x. **(1 mark)**

b $\left(4^3\right)^y = 4^6$

Find the value of y. **(1 mark)**

c $1000^a = 10^6$

Find the value of a. **(2 marks)**

Adapted from 1MA1/2F, November 2017, Q21

Exam feedback

Q1c: In a similar question, most students missed the connection to powers of 10 to work out the correct algebraic power.

Key point

- All numbers can be written as a product of prime factors. This is called prime factor decomposition.

△ Purposeful practice 1

Express these numbers as products of their prime factors.

| **1** 20 | **2** 40 | **3** 120 | **4** 60 | **5** 15 |
| **6** 45 | **7** 180 | **8** 360 | **9** 300 | **10** 200 |

Reflect and reason

How can you use the prime factors of 20 to help you find the prime factors of 40 and 60?

△ Purposeful practice 2

Express these numbers as products of their prime factors.

| **1** 16 | **2** 36 | **3** 81 | **4** 100 |
| **5** 64 | **6** 216 | **7** 1728 | **8** 7056 |

Reflect and reason

The numbers in **Q1–5** are all square numbers. The numbers in **Q5–7** are all cube numbers.
What do you notice about their prime factor decomposition?
Predict whether 7056 is a square number or a cube number.

△ Purposeful practice 3

Use prime factors to find the HCF of

| **1** 40 and 45 | **2** 80 and 45 | **3** 80 and 90 | **4** 120 and 300 |
| **5** 20 and 200 | **6** 200 and 300 | **7** 180 and 190 | **8** 180 and 19 |

Reflect and reason

What happens to the HCF between **Q1** and **Q2**? Why?

△ Purposeful practice 4

Use prime factors to find the LCM of

| **1** 40 and 45 | **2** 120 and 300 | **3** 120 and 200 | **4** 200 and 300 |
| **5** 80 and 45 | **6** 80 and 90 | **7** 180 and 190 | **8** 180 and 19 |

Reflect and reason

Do your answers follow the same rules as **Q1** and **Q5** in Purposeful practice 3?

⊠ Problem-solving practice

1 A cat needs to be taken to the vet every 180 days.
   A dog needs to be taken to the vet every 135 days.
   Both animals were taken to the vet on 3 February.
   Will they be taken to the vet together again this year? Explain.

2 A pack of 12 cartons of juice costs £3.
   A tub of ice cream containing 16 servings costs £6.
   Is it possible to buy equal amounts of juice and ice cream for £35 without any left over?

3 Given that $A = 2 \times 3 \times 5^2$ and $B = 3 \times 5 \times 7$, what is the LCM of A and B?

4 Given that the HCF of two numbers is 96, is it possible for one of the numbers to be 144? Explain.

5 The LCM of two numbers is 81.
   Thomas says that both the numbers have to be in the 3 times table.
   Is Thomas correct? Explain.

6 Ms Case teaches six classes of 30 students.
   A box of 25 pencils costs £2.50.
   A box of 20 erasers costs £2.
   Ms Case wants to buy each student a pencil and an eraser.
   How much will it cost?
   Will there be any pencils or erasers left over?

7 Jaden bakes cakes for a party.
   The cakes are baked in trays of 8.
   Jaden puts a marshmallow on each cake.
   Marshmallows come in packs of 3.

   a What is the least number of cakes Jaden can make without any marshmallows left over?

   b Each tray of cakes takes 25 minutes to bake. Jaden's party is at 6 pm.
      What is the latest time he could start baking?

✵ Exam practice

1 Express 160 as the product of its prime factors.   **(2 marks)**

Adapted from 1MA1/1F, June 2017, Q22

 2 Find the lowest common multiple (LCM) of 32 and 46.   **(2 marks)**

Adapted from 1MA1/2F, June 2018, Q21a

Exam feedback   ResultsPlus

Q1: Most students who achieved a **Grade 5** answered a similar question well.
Q2: Most students who achieved a **Grade 5** answered a similar question well.

2 Algebra

2.1 Algebraic expressions

Key points

- A term is a number, a letter, or a number and a letter multiplied together.
- Like terms contain the same letter to the same power (or do not contain a letter). You can simplify an expression by collecting like terms.
- When multiplying or dividing terms, you can simplify even if they are not like terms.

△ Purposeful practice 1

Copy and complete.

1 $5x + 4x = \square$

2 $6x + \square = 9x$

3 $8x + \square = 9x$

4 $6x - 2x = \square$

5 $6x - \square = 5x$

6 $6x - 5x = \square$

7 $6b - 3b - b = \square$

8 $6b - b\boxed{} = 2b$

9 $-3b\boxed{} + 6b = 2b$

10 $-3b\boxed{} - b = 2b$

11 $-b - 3b\boxed{} = 2b$

12 $-b + 6b\boxed{} = 2b$

Reflect and reason

Sam writes '4n − n = 4'. Explain why Sam is wrong.

When the terms in an expression are reordered, what happens to the signs? Give an example.

△ Purposeful practice 2

Simplify by collecting like terms.

1 $4y + 3 + 6y$

2 $4y + 3 + 6$

3 $4 + 3y + 6 + 2y$

4 $5t - 7 + 2t$

5 $5t - 7t + 2$

6 $5 - 7t + 2t + 3$

Simplify

7 $r \times s$

8 $5 \times r \times s$

9 $5 \times r \times s \times 2$

10 $5r \times 2s$

11 $5r \times 2t$

12 $3r \times 2t$

13 $3r \times 4 \times t$

14 $3r \times s \times t$

15 $3r \times 4t \times s$

16 $a \div b$

17 $b \div a$

18 $a \div 2$

19 $b \div 2$

20 $2 \div a$

21 $2 \div b$

Reflect and reason

Is the simplest form of an expression always only one term? Use your answers to questions on this page to explain.

⊠ Problem-solving practice

1 Write and simplify an expression for the perimeter of this triangle.

5 cm

2 Simplify these expressions. Which one is different to the others?

$2 \times 3x$ $4x - 7 + 2x + 7$ $2x + 4x$

$2x - 1 - 4x + 1$ $3x - 1 + 3x + 1$ $3x \times 2$

3 Copy and complete with operations + or −.
$7x \square 8 \square 2x \square 5 \square 3x = 8x + 3$

4 Write an expression for the area of this rectangle in its simplest form.

2 cm

5q

5 The area of this rectangle is $12b$.
What is the length of the rectangle?

3

6 Write three algebraic expressions that simplify to $12x$.

7 Each row and column in this magic square adds to the same total. Find the missing terms.

x		x
$-y$	$2x - y$	
$4y + x$		

✦ Exam practice

1 a Simplify $5 \times 3p$

   b Simplify $b - 4b + 5b$ **(2 marks)**

Adapted from 1MA1/1F, June 2018, Q6

Key points

- To multiply powers of the same letter, add the indices.
- To divide powers of the same letter, subtract the indices.

△ Purposeful practice 1

Simplify

1 $x \times x$ **2** $x \times x^2$ **3** $x \times x^3$ **4** $x^2 \times x^3$

5 $x^4 \times x^3$ **6** $x^4 \times x^3 \times x$ **7** $x^4 \times x^3 \times x^2$ **8** $x \times x^3 \times x^2$

9 $\dfrac{n^5}{n^2}$ **10** $\dfrac{n^6}{n^2}$ **11** $\dfrac{n^9}{n^3}$ **12** $\dfrac{n^9}{n}$

13 $\dfrac{n^4}{n}$ **14** $\dfrac{n^4}{n^3}$ **15** $\dfrac{n \times n^5}{n^2}$ **16** $\dfrac{n^2 \times n^4}{n^3}$

Reflect and reason

Kit writes $\dfrac{n^{10}}{n^2} = n^8$

Lee writes $\dfrac{n^{10}}{n^2} = n^5$

Who is correct? What has the other person done wrong?

△ Purposeful practice 2

Simplify

1 $2u \times 3$ **2** $-2u \times 3$ **3** $-2u \times -3$ **4** $-2u \times 3v$

5 $2u \times -3v$ **6** $-3u \times 2v$ **7** $2v \times -3v$ **8** $5y \times -x$

9 $5y \times x$ **10** $5y \times 2x$ **11** $-5y \times 2x$ **12** $-5y \times -2x$

13 $\dfrac{2p}{12}$ **14** $\dfrac{12p}{2}$ **15** $\dfrac{12p}{4}$ **16** $\dfrac{12p^2}{4}$

17 $\dfrac{4p^2}{12}$ **18** $\dfrac{4p^2}{12p}$ **19** $\dfrac{-2t^3}{6}$ **20** $\dfrac{-6t^3}{2}$

21 $\dfrac{-6t^3}{-2}$ **22** $\dfrac{6t^3}{2t}$ **23** $\dfrac{-6t^3}{2t}$ **24** $\dfrac{-6t^3}{-2t^2}$

Reflect and reason

Is each statement true or false?

Multiplying terms should always lead to a positive answer.

You should write letters in a term in alphabetical order.

Dividing terms should always lead to a whole number answer.

1   In this triangle, the terms in circles at the
    corners multiply to give the term in
    the rectangle in the middle of each side.
    Find the missing terms.

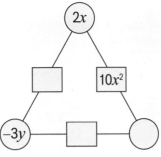

2   Write two different multiplications that simplify to $-15cd$.

3   Copy and complete by writing in the missing indices.

    a $t^2 \times t^\square = t^5$

    b $\dfrac{x^5}{x^\square} = x^2$

    c $\dfrac{n^\square}{n^2} = n^4$

    d $\dfrac{r^3 \times r^\square}{r^4} = r^2$

4   Write and simplify an expression for
    a the perimeter of this shape
    b the area of this shape

5   Write two different divisions that simplify to $4x^3$.

6   Copy and complete this multiplication wall.
    Each term is multiplied by the one beside it, to give the term above.

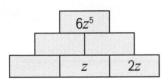

7   Simplify $\dfrac{5n + 3n}{2}$

1   **a**   Simplify $n^4 \times n^2$ **(1 mark)**

    b   Simplify $x^2 + x^2$ **(1 mark)**

    c   Simplify $2a \times 7c$ **(1 mark)**

    Adapted from 1MA1/2F, June 2018, Q20a, 1MA1/2F, June 2017, Q1b and 1MA1/2F,
    November 2017, Q3a

Exam feedback   Results**Plus**

Q1a: Most students who achieved a **Grade 3** or above answered a similar question well.

Q1b: In a similar question, many students gave an answer of x^4, adding the indices rather than the coefficients.

Q1c: In a similar question, only a minority of students failed to simplify and left a '×' sign in.

2.3 Substitution

Key point

- In algebra, 'substitute' means 'replace a letter with a number'.

⚠ Purposeful practice 1

Work out the value of these expressions when $m = 5$, $n = 4$ and $t = -2$

1 $m + n$	**2** $m - n$	**3** $n - m$	**4** $m + t$
5 $n + t$	**6** $n - t$	**7** $t - n$	**8** $m - t$

Reflect and reason

Substitute $a = -5$ into the expression $10 - a$.
How do you use the 'rules' for subtracting negative numbers?

⚠ Purposeful practice 2

Work out the value of these expressions when $a = -1$, $h = 6$ and $k = \frac{1}{2}$

1 $3h$	**2** $3a$	**3** $-2h$	**4** $-2a$
5 $2k$	**6** $-2k$	**7** $4k$	**8** $3k$
9 ah	**10** hk	**11** ak	**12** $-ak$
13 $-2hk$	**14** $-3ah$	**15** ahk	**16** $-2ahk$

Reflect and reason

What is the 'missing sign' between a and h in ah?

⚠ Purposeful practice 3

Work out the value of these expressions when $b = 2$, $c = -4$ and $f = 10$

1 $b + 2f$	**2** $b + 2c$	**3** $b - 2c$	**4** $f - 2c$
5 $bf - 1$	**6** $bc + 8$	**7** $bf - c$	**8** $\dfrac{b}{2}$
9 $\dfrac{c}{2}$	**10** $\dfrac{f}{b}$	**11** $\dfrac{3c}{2}$	**12** $\dfrac{-3c}{2}$
13 b^2	**14** c^2	**15** $-c^2$	**16** $b^2 + c^2$
17 $b^2 + f$	**18** $c^2 + 2f$	**19** $3b - c^2$	**20** $\dfrac{c^2}{4}$
21 $\dfrac{c^2}{c}$	**22** $\dfrac{f^2}{b^2}$	**23** $\dfrac{b^2}{f}$	**24** $\dfrac{c^2}{f}$

Reflect and reason

After substituting, in what order did you complete each calculation?

1   **a**   Find two positive values for m and n so that $m + n = 7$

     b   Find one positive and one negative value for m and n so that $m + n = 7$

2   Alex substitutes $s = 8$ and $t = \frac{1}{2}$ into the expression st.

  Alex says the answer is $8\frac{1}{2}$

  What mistake has Alex made?

3   Kim says, 'mhg, ghm and hmg always have the same value, for any values of m, h and g'.
  Choose some numbers to show that Kim is correct.
  Explain why.

4   Find the value of $2n - 1$ when $n = 1$, $n = 2$, $n = 3$, $n = 4$ and $n = 5$.
  Write your answers in order as a number sequence.
  What is this sequence of numbers usually called?

5   **a**   Work out the value of $4q - 3$ when $q = 6$.

     b $M = 3t - 2s$
        $t = 4$ and $s = -5$
        Work out the value of M.

6   Dilip says that $x^2 \geqslant 0$ for every possible value of x.
  Is Dilip correct? Explain.

7   Find a value of x so that $x^2 = 2x$.

8   Find a pair of values for p and q so that
  $6 + 2p = q - 2$

✦ Exam practice

1   $a = 4$
  $b = 3$

  Work out the value of $5a - 2b$ **(2 marks)**

Adapted from 1MA1/1F, Specimen papers, Set 2, Q10

2   $C = 5a + 3b$
  $a = 6$
  $b = -1$

  Work out the value of C.   **(2 marks)**

Adapted from 1MA1/1F, May 2018, Q16a

Exam feedback   Results**Plus**

Q2: Most students who achieved a **Grade 3** or above answered a similar question well.

Key point

- A formula is a general rule that shows a relationship between variables.

⚠ Purposeful practice 1

Find the missing numbers and terms.

1 1 bag costs 10 pence

2 bags cost ___ pence

3 bags cost ___ pence

n bags cost ___ pence

Formula for cost of n bags is $C =$ ___ pence

2 1 pen costs b pence

2 pens cost ___ pence

3 pens cost ___ pence

m pens cost ___ pence

Formula for cost of m pens is $C =$ ___ pence

Reflect and reason

How does using numbers to create a pattern help you to find a formula?

⚠ Purposeful practice 2

1 Write a formula beginning $C =$ ___ for the total cost of

a p items at £5 each

b n items at £5 each

c 4 items at £t each

d m items at £t each

e m items at £t each plus £4 postage and packing

f m items at £t each plus £r postage and packing

2 There are y nuts in a box.

Write a formula beginning $N =$ ___ for the total number of nuts in

a 1 box

b 1 box when 20 nuts are taken out

c x boxes

d x boxes and 30 extra nuts

e x boxes with 5 nuts taken out of each box

Reflect and reason

Which words in a problem tell you the formula will include these signs?

$+$ $\qquad$ $-$ $\qquad$ $\times$ $\qquad$ $\div$

◻ Problem-solving practice

1   Match each formula to a description.

$C = 3n$ the cost of n items at £10 each

$C = 10n$ the cost of n items at £10 each plus £3 delivery charge

$C = 3n + 10$ the cost of n items at £3 each

$C = 10n + 3$ the cost of n items at £3 each plus £10 delivery charge

2   The formulae for the lengths of 3 pieces of rope, in terms of g, are

length of rope A = $7 + g$
length of rope B = $g - 2$
length of rope C = $g + 5$

   a   Which rope is the longest?

   b   Which rope is the shortest?

3   The formula $P = 4x + y$ is used to work out the cost of 4 cakes and 1 box.

   a   Which letter represents the price of a cake?

   b   Which letter represents the price of a box?

   c   The formula for the cost of Parmit's cakes is $P = 9x + 2y$.
       How many cakes did Parmit buy?

4   The formula $C = 150n + 400$ is used to work out a cost in pence.
    Rewrite the formula to work out a cost in pounds (£).

✦ Exam practice

1   Here are four sections of toy train track.
    All measurements are in cm.
    The total length of the four sections is L cm.
    Find a formula for L in terms of x.
    Write your formula as simply as possible.

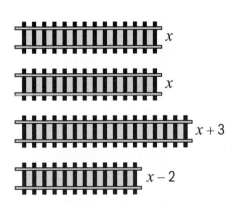

x

x

$x + 3$

$x - 2$

(3 marks)

Adapted from 1MA1/1F, November 2017, Q6

Exam feedback   ResultsPlus

In a similar question, many students identified the correct methods to form an expression or write an equation for L. Many understood the need to add all terms to form an expression but were unable to gain full marks due to poor algebraic manipulation skills.

2.5 Expanding brackets

Key point

- 'Expanding' single brackets means 'multiply each term inside the brackets by the term outside'.

$$5(x - 6) = 5x - 30$$

⚠ Purposeful practice 1

Expand

1 $3(x + 1)$ 2 $3(x + 2)$ 3 $3(x + 10)$

4 $3(x - 1)$ 5 $3(x - 2)$ 6 $3(x - 5)$

Reflect and reason

Kamal expands $5(x + 2)$ to give $5x + 2$

Explain what Kamal has done wrong.

⚠ Purposeful practice 2

Expand

1 $2(m + 1)$ 2 $2(m - 1)$ 3 $-2(m + 1)$

4 $-2(m - 1)$ 5 $-1(m + 7)$ 6 $-1(m - 7)$

7 $-(m + 7)$ 8 $-(m - 7)$ 9 $-(-m + 7)$

Reflect and reason

Are the signs always the same in the expanded and factorised expression? Why?

⚠ Purposeful practice 3

Expand

1 $4(n + 3)$ 2 $4(3 + n)$ 3 $-5(3 + n)$

4 $-5(n + 3)$ 5 $-5(n - 3)$ 6 $3(r - 6)$

7 $3(r + 6)$ 8 $3(2r + 6)$ 9 $3(4r + 6)$

10 $-3(2r + 6)$ 11 $-3(2r - 6)$ 12 $-3(6 + 2r)$

13 $t(t + 3)$ 14 $t(2t + 3)$ 15 $t(2t - 3)$

16 $k(k + 1)$ 17 $2k(k + 1)$ 18 $2k(k - 1)$

19 $2k(k + 4)$ 20 $2k(k - 4)$ 21 $-2k(k - 4)$

Reflect and reason

Is $2(5y + 3)$ equivalent to $2(3 + 5y)$? Show working to explain.

Is $2(4x - 1)$ equivalent to $2(1 - 4x)$? Show working to explain.

⊠ Problem-solving practice

1 Copy and complete.

   a $2(a + \boxed{}) = 2a + 8$

   b $\boxed{}(y - 7) = \boxed{} - 14$

   c $\boxed{}(n + \boxed{}) = n^2 + 5n$

   d $-3(\boxed{} + c) = -9 - \boxed{}$

   e $\boxed{}(6t \boxed{}) = 6t^2 - 2t$

   f $5p(\boxed{} - 3) = 5p^2 - \boxed{}$

2 Here is Simon's homework.

$$4(3d - 2) = 12d - 8$$
$$= 4d$$

What mistake has Simon made?

3 Erin says, 'When you expand brackets with two terms inside, you get two terms in your answer.'
Write two examples to show that Erin is correct.

4 In this rhombus, the two expressions in circles at the corners multiply to give
the expression in a rectangle in the middle of each side.
Find the missing expressions.

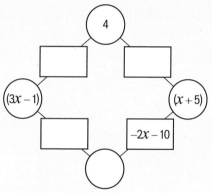

5 Expand and simplify

   a $5(x + 3) + 2$

   b $4(5 + n) - n$

✧ Exam practice

1 **a** Expand $2c(c + 5)$ **(2 marks)**

    b Expand $4d(2 - d)$ **(2 marks)**

    c Expand and simplify $2(x - 3) + 3(4x + 1)$ **(2 marks)**

Adapted from 1MA1/1F, May 2018, Q16b and 1MA1/3F, June 2018, Q20

Key points

- The factors of a term are all the numbers and letters that divide exactly into it.
- A common factor is a factor of two or more terms.

Factorise

$$3m + 12 = 3(m + 4)$$

Expand — highest common factor of 3 and 12

⚠ Purposeful practice 1

Copy and complete.

1 $2x + 6 = 2(\Box + \Box)$ **2** $2x + 4 = 2(\Box + \Box)$ **3** $2x + 2 = 2(\Box + \Box)$

Factorise. Check your answers by expanding the brackets.

4 $2x - 10$ **5** $2x - 8$ **6** $2x - 2$

7 $3y + 3$ **8** $3y + 6$ **9** $3y - 6$

Reflect and reason

Shay factorises $2x - 4$ to give $2(x - 4)$

Explain the mistake Shay has made.

⚠ Purposeful practice 2

Factorise

1 $4a + 8$ **2** $4a - 12$ **3** $6a + 12$ **4** $6a - 24$

5 $12t - 18$ **6** $12t + 20$ **7** $12t + 6$ **8** $12t - 9$

9 $21t - 9$ **10** $21t + 35$ **11** $20m + 35$ **12** $20m - 40$

13 $m^2 + m$ **14** $m^2 + 2m$ **15** $m^2 - 3m$ **16** $5m + m^2$

17 $4m - m^2$ **18** $2m^2 - m$ **19** $m^2 - 2m$ **20** $3m^2 + m$

21 $m^2 + 3m$ **22** $2b^2 + 2b$ **23** $2b^2 + 4b$ **24** $2b^2 - 6b$

25 $b^2 + bg$ **26** $b^2 - bg$ **27** $3b^2 - bg$ **28** $3b^2 - 6bg$

29 $3b^2 + 9bg$ **30** $3b^2 - 3bg$ **31** $6b^2 + 9bg$ **32** $6b^2 + 12bg$

Reflect and reason

Can a factor be

a letter

a number

a number and a letter?

Find examples from this page to explain.

1 Match each expanded expression with its factorised form.

$n^2 - n$	$n(n-2)$
$2n - n^2$	$n(2n-1)$
$n - 2n^2$	$n(n-1)$
$n^2 - 2n$	$2n(n-1)$
$-n^2 + 2n$	$n(1-2n)$
$2n^2 - n$	$n(2-n)$
$2n^2 - 2n$	$n(-n+2)$

2 Copy and complete.

a $\square - 24 = 3(x - \square)$

b $20x + \square = 5(\square + 3)$

c $x^2 - 2x = \square(x - \square)$

d $4x^2 + \square = 2x(\square + 3)$

e $3x^2 - \square = x(\square - a)$

3 Here is Mo's answer to a test question

Question	Mo's answer
Factorise $3y + 15$	$18y$

a Explain what Mo has done wrong.

b Factorise $3y + 15$

4 Tia says, 'When you factorise an expression with two terms, you get two terms inside the brackets in your answer.'
Write two examples to show that Tia is correct.

5 a Expand $6(x - 3)$

b Factorise $6x - 3$

c Simplify $6x - 3 + x + 2$

6 Factorise completely

a $4x + 36$

b $12n^2 + 3n$

1 a Factorise $4n - 12$ **(1 mark)**

b Factorise $x^2 + x$ **(1 mark)**

Adapted from 1MA1/2F, June 2017, Q14a and 1MA1/1F, Specimen Papers, Set 2, Q19a

Exam feedback **ResultsPlus**

Q1a: Most students who achieved a **Grade 5** answered a similar question well.

2.7 Using expressions and formulae

△ Purposeful practice 1

Substitute the values $x = 2$ and $y = 6$ in to each formula.

1 $T = x + y$

2 $R = x - y$

3 $S = -x + y$

4 $V = -x - y$

5 $L = 5x$

6 $B = 4y$

7 $C = \dfrac{1}{2}y$

8 $M = xy$

9 $K = -xy$

10 $P = \dfrac{x}{y}$

11 $N = \dfrac{y}{x}$

12 $Z = \dfrac{-y}{x}$

13 $D = \dfrac{-y}{-x}$

14 $F = \dfrac{-x}{-y}$

15 $H = \dfrac{x}{-y}$

Reflect and reason

$F = ma$ is a formula used in science.

Which of these is the correct way to calculate F when $m = 7$ and $a = 2$?

A $F = ma$
   $F = 72$

B $F = ma$
   $F = 7 \times 2$
   $F = 14$

C $F = ma$
   $F = 7^2$
   $F = 49$

△ Purposeful practice 2

Substitute the values $t = 8$, $v = -3$ and $n = 4$ in to each formula.

1 $A = t + 3$

2 $B = t + v$

3 $C = v + 3$

4 $D = 2t + v$

5 $D = t^2 + v$

6 $E = 2t - 3v$

7 $F = nt - 1$

8 $G = nt + v$

9 $H = nt + 2v$

10 $J = 2n$

11 $J = n^2$

12 $K = n^2 - 5$

13 $L = n^2 + t$

14 $M = n^2 + 2t$

15 $P = v + n^2$

16 $Q = tv + n^2$

17 $R = \dfrac{t}{n} + 7$

18 $S = \dfrac{t}{n} + v$

19 $W = \dfrac{n}{t} + v$

20 $X = \dfrac{n}{t} - v$

Reflect and reason

The same letters and numbers are used in **Q4** and **Q5**, and then in **Q10** and **Q11**.

Why don't you get the same answers when you substitute?

⊠ Problem-solving practice

1 Here are Ash's and Charlie's answers to a test question.

Question	Ash's answer	Charlie's answer
$d = st$ Work out the value of d when $s = 20 \quad t = \frac{1}{2}$	$d = 20 \times \frac{1}{2}$ $d = 10$	$d = 20\frac{1}{2}$

Whose answer is wrong?
Explain why it is wrong.

2 Write a formula starting $k = \underline{\quad}$
Use the letters a and/or n and any operations or numbers, so that $k = 8$ when $a = 6$ and $n = 3$.

3 Which formula does not give the same value of T when $x = -3$, $y = 2$ and $z = 6$?

   A $T = xy - z$ **B** $T = \frac{z}{y} + 5x$ **C** $T = x^2 - \frac{z}{y}$ **D** $T = zx + 3y$

4 The formula for speed is $s = \frac{d}{t}$

where s is speed, d is distance and t is time.
Calculate the speed in metres per second when a car travels a distance of 400 m in 25 seconds.

5 Use the formula $v = u + at$ to work out

   a v when $u = 0$, $a = 9.8$ and $t = 6$

   b v when $u = 4$, $a = -5$ and $t = 0.2$

✸ Exam practice

1 **a** $X = 3y + 1$

    Work out the value of X when $y = 5$ **(2 marks)**

  b $m = n + ch$

    Work out the value of m when

    $n = 7 \quad c = -4 \quad h = \frac{1}{2}$ **(2 marks)**

Adapted from 1MA1/3F, June 2017, Q11a and 1MA1/1F, May 2017, Q16

2 $p = s + \frac{r}{2}$

Work out the value of p when
$s = -7 \quad r = -10$

Exam feedback   Results**Plus**

Q1a: Most students who achieved a `Grade 3` or above answered a simliar question well.
Q1b: In a similar question, many students missed out the '$\times$' when substituting into ch.

3 Graphs, tables and charts

3.1 Frequency tables

⚠ Purposeful practice 1

1   a   Give two examples of discrete data.

    b   Give two examples of continuous data.

2   a   Design a frequency table to collect all possible results when rolling 1 dice.

    b   Design a frequency table to collect all possible totals when rolling 2 dice.

    c   Design a frequency table to collect all possible totals when rolling 10 dice.

Reflect and reason

How does your frequency table in **Q2a** differ from your frequency table in **Q2c**? Explain.

⚠ Purposeful practice 2

1   Here are the test marks for 30 students.

2, 6, 4, 2, 4, 4, 5, 4, 3, 1, 4, 5, 4, 2, 2,

1, 5, 5, 4, 5, 3, 1, 5, 4, 3, 1, 5, 4, 2, 5

    a   Design and complete a frequency table for these test results.

    b   What is the most common mark?

2   The frequency tables show the number of books on shelves and the length of books.

Number of books on shelves	Tally	Frequency
0–5		
6–10		
11–15		
16–20		

Length of books, L (cm)	Tally	Frequency
$0 < L \leqslant 5$		
$5 < L \leqslant 10$		
$10 < L \leqslant 15$		
$15 < L \leqslant 20$		

How are the groups represented differently in these frequency tables?

Explain why the data is presented in this way.

Reflect and reason

What differences do you notice between frequency tables for discrete and continuous data?

State the errors in these tables.

1

Number of matches in a box	Tally	Frequency
50–52		
53–54		
54–56		

2

Number of pens in a case	Tally	Frequency
$3 < p \leq 4$		
$4 < p \leq 5$		
$5 < p \leq 6$		

3

Road width (m)	Tally	Frequency
3–4		
4–5		
5–6		

4

Road width (m)	Tally	Frequency
$3 < p < 4$		
$4 < p < 5$		
$5 < p < 6$		

✵ Exam practice

1 Ben sells books in a shop.
The frequency table shows the number of books Ben sold on three days.

Day of week	Tally	Frequency
Thursday	卌 卌 |||	13
Friday	卌 卌 卌 ||||	20
Saturday	卌 卌 卌 卌		21

Write down one thing that is wrong with the frequency table. **(1 mark)**

Adapted from 1MA1/2F, June 2017, Q5a

Exam feedback   Results**Plus**

Most students who achieved a **Grade 1** or above answered a similar question well.

Key points

- A two-way table divides data into rows across the table and columns down the table.
- Calculate the totals across and down.

△ Purposeful practice 1

1 The distance chart shows distances (in km) between the houses of five sisters.

Nayna				
213	Mohini			
24	237	Janvi		
105	318	81	Heena	
3532	3745	3508	3427	Dina

How far is it from

a Nayna's house to Mohini's house?

b Nayna's house to Janvi's house?

c Nayna's house to Heena's house?

d Dina's house to Nayna's house?

e Dina's house to Mohini's house?

Reflect and reason

For each answer, what did you look at first in the table? What did you do next?

Did you use a different method for **Q1a–c** and for **Q1d** and **Q1e**? Explain.

△ Purposeful practice 2

1 The two-way table shows the number of students who study languages by year.
Copy and complete the table.

	Year 7	Year 8	Year 9	Total
French	20	15	35	
German	15	25		50
Spanish	10			
Total		50		170

Reflect and reason

How did you decide which value to work out first? Could you have completed the year 9 column first? Explain.

⊠ Problem-solving practice

1 The diagram shows the distances between the houses of three friends.
Draw a distance chart to represent this information.

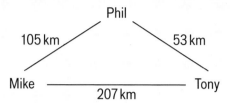

2 At a meeting, there are 50 teachers who travel by car or train only.
32 teach geography, the rest teach history.
14 history teachers travel by car
8 geography teachers travel by train

    a Identify row and column headings for a two-way table to represent this data.

    b Draw a two-way table to represent the data.

    c How many teachers teach history?

    d How many history teachers travel by train?

3 The two-way table does not include enough information to complete it.
How many more cells can you fill in without any further information?

	Child	Adult	Total
Sport	2		
Film	3	4	7
Music		2	6
Total			

◈ Exam practice

1 Jo asks 40 people if they prefer going to the cinema or the theatre.
22 of the people asked are children.
8 adults prefer going to the cinema.
12 of the people who preferred going to the theatre were children.
Use the information to complete the two-way table.

	Children	Adults	Total
Theatre			
Cinema			
Total			

(3 marks)

Adapted from 1MA1/1F, November 2017, Q12a

Exam feedback   Results**Plus**

Most students answered a similar question well. A number of students reversed the entries, so careful reading of the headings is required.

3.3 Representing data

Key points

- A comparative bar chart has bars side-by-side for each category.
- A multiple or composite bar chart compares features within a single bar.
- A line graph is useful for identifying trends in data. A trend is the general direction of change.
- A histogram is used for grouped continuous data. There are no gaps between the bars in a histogram.

△ Purposeful practice 1

1 The table shows the number of people who pass their driving test at two centres over four days.

	Mon	Tue	Wed	Thu
Centre A	7	8	5	9
Centre B	4	10	6	4

   a Draw a comparative bar chart for the data.

   b Draw a composite bar chart for the data.

   c On the same axes, draw line graphs for centre A, then centre B.

Reflect and reason

Which graph is best for comparing total passes across both centres? Explain.

Which graph is best for comparing the trends in passes at the two centres? Explain.

Which graph is best for comparing the number of passes at centre A and centre B? Explain.

△ Purposeful practice 2

1 The table shows the time each member of a class of 32 students takes to get to school.
  Calculate the frequency for the last row and draw a histogram for the data.

Time taken, t (minutes)	Frequency
$0 < t \leqslant 15$	5
$15 < t \leqslant 30$	14
$30 < t \leqslant 45$	9
$45 < t \leqslant 60$	

2 The histogram shows the speed of cars (mph) measured during one hour at a school junction. Complete the table.

Speed of cars at a junction (mph)

Car speed, s (mph)	Frequency
$5 < s \leqslant 10$	3
$10 < s \leqslant 15$	6
$15 < s \leqslant 20$	9
	15
	20

Reflect and reason

State one difference between a histogram and a bar chart. Give a reason for the difference.

1 The table shows the number of hours two students spent on homework over four days.

	Fri	Sat	Sun	Mon
Aum	1	4	3	2
Shreeya	2	5	4	8

a Give two reasons why you would not draw a histogram of this data.

b There is an error in the table. Where is the error likely to be?

c Aum spent a total of 10 hours and Shreeya spent a total of 14 hours. Draw the correct table.

d Draw a comparative bar chart for the data.

e How many hours would Aum have to study on Sunday to equal Shreeya's hours over the four days?

⚝ Exam practice

1 Jasmine and Fred work in a music shop.
The comparative bar chart shows their guitar sales over a five-day period.

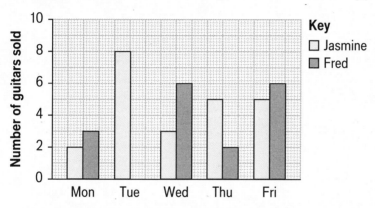

Key
☐ Jasmine
▦ Fred

a On which day did Jasmine sell the most guitars? **(1 mark)**

b Fred sold 4 guitars on Tuesday.
Show this information on the comparative bar chart. **(1 mark)**

c Fewer guitars were sold on Thursday than on Wednesday.
How many fewer? **(1 mark)**

d Jasmine and Fred sold half as many saxophones as they did guitars over
the five-day period.
What is the total number of guitars and saxophones sold? **(2 marks)**

Adapted from 1MA1/2F, June 2017, Q3

Exam feedback   Results**Plus**

Most students who achieved a **Grade 1** or above answered a similar question well.

3.4 Time series

◬ Purposeful practice 1

1 The table shows the temperature in a town during one day.

Time	2 am	4 am	6 am	8 am	10 am
Temperature (°C)	−4	4	11	17	22

   a Draw a time series graph to represent the data.

   b Look at your graph. Is the temperature likely to be higher or lower at midday than at 10 am?

   c Use your graph to predict the temperature at 3 am.

   d Use your graph to predict the temperature at 7.40 am.

Reflect and reason

How did you predict the temperatures at 3 am and 7.40 am? Which was easier to predict and why?

◬ Purposeful practice 2

1 The table shows the temperature of two towns during one day.

Time	2 am	4 am	6 am	8 am	10 am
Town A (°C)	−4	4	11	17	22
Town B (°C)	3	6	8	10	12

   a Draw a time series graph for each town on the same axes.

   b Estimate the time when the towns have the same temperature.

   c Predict the temperature of town B at midday.

Reflect and reason

Robin predicts town B's temperature at midday will be 14 °C. Why is this a good prediction?

◬ Purposeful practice 3

1 The graph shows the height of a ball in the seconds after it is thrown.

   a What was the highest height of the ball from the ground?

   b How many seconds did the ball take to get there?

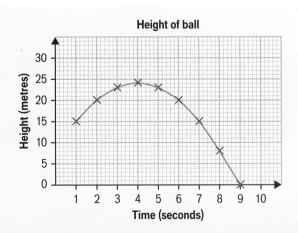

Height of ball

Reflect and reason

When did the ball hit the ground? Explain how you know.

1 Sam is a nurse. He works at three hospitals.
He records how much money he earns at hospitals A, B and C.

Oct: £1450 from A, £750 from B
Nov: £1050 from B, £1500 from C
Dec: £1700 from A, £550 from B, £430 from C

a Copy and complete the table for Sam.

	Oct	Nov	Dec
Total earned (£)		2550	

b Draw a time series graph to represent the data.

c Describe how Sam's earnings change from October to December.
Is it possible to predict Sam's earnings in January? Explain.

⊠ Exam practice

1 Bob draws this graph to show the percentage of trains that arrived late for six months.

Month	Jul	Aug	Sept	Oct	Nov	Dec
Percentage	25	23	15	13	8	7

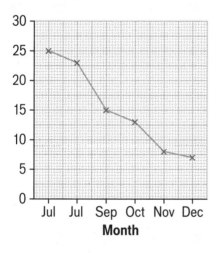

Write down **three** things that are wrong with the graph. **(1 mark)**

Adapted from 1MA1/2F, November 2017, Q8a

Exam feedback ResultsPlus

In a similar question, many students incorrectly referred to the graph as though it were a scatter graph.

3.5 Stem and leaf diagrams

Key points

- A stem and leaf diagram shows numerical data split into a 'stem' and 'leaves'.
- In a stem and leaf diagram, the numbers are placed in order.
- A back-to-back stem and leaf diagram compares two sets of data.

△ Purposeful practice 1

1   Here are the points scored by 10 players in a game.

19, 22, 25, 25, 31, 37, 40, 44, 47, 48

Draw a stem and leaf diagram to display this data.

2   These are marks for 20 girls in a physics test.

55, 42, 62, 47, 25, 43, 56, 62, 31, 27

30, 43, 55, 46, 26, 32, 50, 73, 51, 45

a   Draw a stem and leaf diagram to display this data.

b   What is the highest mark?

c   What is the lowest mark?

d   What is the difference between the highest and lowest marks?

Reflect and reason

When you drew the two stem and leaf diagrams, what did you do in the same way?

What did you do differently?

Rotate your diagram 90 degrees anticlockwise. What type of graph does the rotated shape remind you of?

△ Purposeful practice 2

1   These are marks for 20 boys in a physics test.

34, 55, 64, 74, 20, 35, 49, 67, 20, 38

50, 64, 56, 48, 45, 67, 43, 59, 74, 56

a   Draw a back-to-back stem and leaf diagram for this boys' data and the girls' data from Purposeful practice 1 **Q2**.

b   What is the difference between the highest and lowest boys' marks?

c   How many more boys than girls achieved a mark higher than 70?

Reflect and reason

Did you remember to draw a key with your stem and leaf diagrams?

Why is a key important?

1 Vikram and Penny grow eight bean plants each. The table shows the heights of their plants (in cm).

Vikram	20	16	21	21	19	14	20	15
Phoebe	44	44	42	37	45	34	28	27

  a Display the data in a back-to-back stem and leaf diagram.

  b Who has the shortest plant?

  c Who has the tallest plant?

  d What is the difference between the tallest and shortest plants for Vikram and Penny?

  e Who grew the taller plants?

2 The stem and leaf diagram shows percentage marks gained in an English exam by 20 students. Complete the frequency table for the data.

```
4 | 5 6 7 8 9
5 | 3 5 6 7 8 9
6 | 0 1 5 6 7 9
7 | 2 4 5
```

Percentage mark, m	Frequency
$40 < m \leq 50$	
$50 < m \leq 60$	
	5

3 Here are the number of missed appointments each month at a doctors' surgery.

321, 307, 288, 283, 309, 311, 295, 309, 312, 286, 285, 304

Draw a stem and leaf diagram to display this data.

✦ Exam practice

1 Here are the ages of 20 chess players.

15, 23, 30, 44, 18, 25, 31, 42, 18, 26,

18, 27, 36, 19, 27, 38, 29, 39, 45, 36

Show this information in a stem and leaf diagram. **(3 marks)**

Adapted from 1MA1/3F, June 2018, Q14a

Exam feedback   **ResultsPlus**

Most students who achieved a **Grade 4** or above answered a similar question well.

3.6 Pie charts

Key point

- A pie chart is a circle divided into sectors. Each sector represents a set of data.

△ Purposeful practice 1

1 a Draw a circle of radius 3 cm.

b Draw a pie chart with these sectors

Drink	Angle
Milk	45°
Tea	60°
Hot chocolate	100°

c The last sector is for Coffee. Measure this angle.

Reflect and reason

What property of a circle can you use to calculate the answer to **Q1c** without measuring?
The data in this pie chart was collected in a survey. What question do you think people were asked?

△ Purposeful practice 2

1 The pie chart shows the proportions of sports players in a city. The proportions are the same each year.

The total number of players was 400 in the year 2000, 1000 in the year 2005, 2800 in the year 2010, and 3500 in the year 2015.

Use the pie chart to copy and complete the table.

Proportion of players of different sports

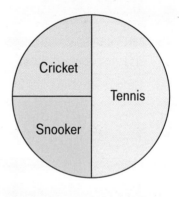

	2000	2005	2010	2015
Tennis				
Snooker				
Cricket				
Total				

2 The table shows the number of students in each year group who like different types of film.
Draw a pie chart for each year group to show this information.

	Year 8	Year 9	Year 10
Drama	20	20	10
Comedy	10	20	10
Action	10	20	40

Reflect and reason

In **Q2**, 20 students like drama in years 8 and 9. Explain why the drama sector is not the same size in both pie charts.

⊠ Problem-solving practice

1   The pie chart shows the proportions of fruit sold in a market.
    Each week, different amounts of fruit are sold but the proportions
    remain the same.

    a   In the first week, 200 kg of apples were sold.
        How many kg of peaches were sold?

    b   In the second week, 510 kg of pears were sold.
        How many kg of apples were sold?

    c   In the third week, 135 kg of peaches were sold.
        How many kg of pears were sold?

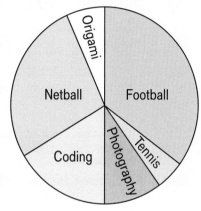

2   The pie chart shows the proportions of members of lunchtime clubs at a school.
    The Coding club has 20 members.
    Copy and complete the frequency table for the numbers of
    members of each club.

Club	Frequency
Football	
Tennis	
Photography	
Coding	
Netball	
Origami	

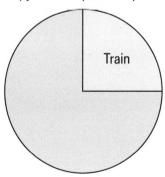

✦ Exam practice

1   60 teachers were asked how they get to work.
    Copy and complete the pie chart for the information in the table.

	Train	Car	Bike	Walk
Number of teachers	15	12	27	6

(4 marks)

Adapted from 1MA1/2F, November 2017, Q5b

3.7 Scatter graphs

Key point

- A scatter graph shows the relationship between two sets of data. Points are plotted with crosses and are not joined.

△ Purposeful practice 1

1 Sketch a scatter graph to show

   a positive correlation

   b no correlation

   c negative correlation.

2 These graphs show three different types of correlation.

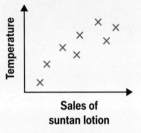 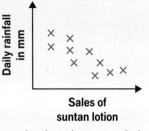 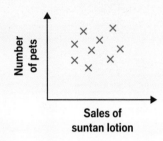

   Complete these sentences for the graphs that show correlation.

   As _____ increases, sales of suntan lotion _____

   As _____ increases, sales of suntan lotion _____

3 10 students recorded the amount of time they spent online and exercising at the weekend.

   a One of the points is an outlier. Identify this outlier.

   b Describe the correlation between time spent online and time spent exercising.

Time spent online and exercising

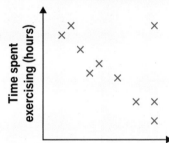

4 The table shows the number of pieces of homework completed by 11 students and their test scores.

Number of homeworks	8	4	10	9	6	9	8	6	7	2	5
Test score	40	15	48	45	22	12	31	28	22	7	25

   a Plot the information on a scatter graph.

   b One of the points is an outlier. Use your scatter graph to identify this outlier.

   c Describe the correlation between the number of pieces of homework and the test scores.

Reflect and reason

Which of these statements describes positive correlation?

As one quantity increases, the other quantity increases.

As one quantity increases, the other quantity decreases.

1 For each relationship, describe the correlation you would expect. Explain your reasoning.

   a Number of cars on the road and accident rate

   b Daily temperature and sales of soft drinks

   c Value of car and its age

   d Outside temperature and cost of heating a house

   e Amount spent on perfume advertising and sales of perfume

   f House price and distance from train station

   g Price of bread and number of people arriving late for work

   h Number of children in a family and height of parents

2 A chemistry exam has two papers. The table shows the marks of 7 students.

Paper 1	21	31	41	59	72	79	92
Paper 2	16	24	41	49	65	74	85

   a Plot the data on a scatter graph.

   b Describe the correlation between the marks for paper 1 and paper 2.

✧ Exam practice

1 The scatter graph shows the marks of 8 students in an English test and a Maths test.

English	22	30	42	58	68	73	78	93
Maths	39	37	31	23	45	17	15	14

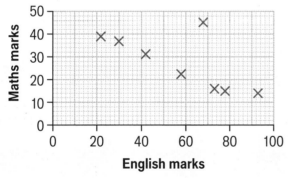

Marks of 8 students in an English test and a Maths test

   a One of the points is an outlier.
   Write down the coordinates of this point. **(1 mark)**

   b For all the other points write down the type of correlation. **(1 mark)**

   Adapted from 1MA1/1F, May 2017, Q21a and b

Exam feedback   Results**Plus**

Q1a: Most students who achieved a **Grade 1** or above answered a similar question well.

Q1b: Most students who achieved a **Grade 3** or above answered a similar question well.

Key point

• A line of best fit is a straight line drawn through the middle of the points on a scatter graph. It should pass as near to as many points as possible and represent the trend of the points.

△ Purposeful practice 1

1 The table shows the heights and widths in centimetres of various boxes.

Height (cm)	4	12	21	1	10	14	11	16
Width (cm)	7	12	21	5	13	15	13	16

   a Draw a scatter graph to display this data.

   b On the scatter graph, draw a line of best fit.

   c Estimate the width of a box with a height of 9 cm.

   d Estimate the height of a container with a width of 9 cm.

2 The table shows the heights and widths in centimetres of various boxes.

Height (cm)	12	2	17	8	3	20	9	5	14	19
Width (cm)	6	13	8	15	18	2	12	9	12	6

   a Draw a scatter graph to display this data.

   b On the scatter graph, draw a line of best fit.

   c Estimate the height of a box that is 14 cm wide.

3 The table shows the engine sizes of seven cars and the distance they travelled on 1 litre of diesel.

Engine size (litres)	Distance travelled (km)
0.8	14.0
1.6	9.2
2.6	6.4
1.0	11.0
2.1	8.8
1.3	10.2
1.8	9.5

   a Draw a scatter graph to display this data.

   b On the scatter graph, draw a line of best fit.

   c Estimate the distance travelled by a car with an engine size of 2.3 litres.

Reflect and reason

What did you do differently to work out your answers to **Q1c** and **Q1d**?

What did you do to ensure that your line was the line of best fit?

⊠ Problem-solving practice

1 The table shows the latitude of six cities and their average temperature in °C.

City G has a latitude of 36 degrees north.

Draw a scatter graph and estimate the average temperature in city G.

City	Latitude (degrees north)	Temperature (°C)
A	19	31
B	53	13
C	22	25
D	60	8
E	15	32
F	60	10
G	36	

2 The table shows the heights and wingspans of birds from the same family.

Height (cm)	90	98	88	97	90	95	85	101	91
Wingspan (cm)	175	195	170	193	174	182	166	198	178

   a Draw a scatter graph and line of best fit.

   b What is the type of correlation between height and wingspan?

   c A bird has a height of 93 cm and a wingspan of 196 cm. Is this bird likely to be from this family? Explain your answer.

⚛ Exam practice

1 The scatter graph shows the average temperature and the number of cartons of soup sold by a café over ten months.

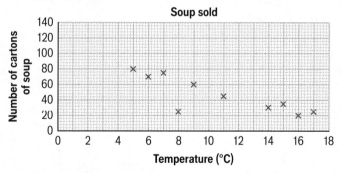

One of the points is an outlier.

   a Write down the coordinates of this point.   **(1 mark)**

   b For all the other points, write down the type of correlation.   **(1 mark)**

In the same year, the average temperature during one month was 3 °C.

   c Estimate the number of cartons of soup sold during that month.   **(2 marks)**

   d The café owner says, 'More soup is sold when it is colder.'
   Does the scatter graph support what the café owner says?
   Give a reason for your answer.   **(1 mark)**

   Adapted from 1MA1/1F, May 2017, Q21

4 Fractions and percentages

4.1 Working with fractions

Key points

- To compare fractions, write them with a common denominator.
- To add or subtract fractions, write them with a common denominator.
- A unit fraction has the numerator 1.

△ Purposeful practice 1

Which fraction is larger?

1 $\frac{1}{4}$ or $\frac{2}{4}$ 2 $\frac{1}{4}$ or $\frac{1}{2}$ 3 $\frac{1}{8}$ or $\frac{1}{2}$ 4 $\frac{3}{8}$ or $\frac{1}{2}$

5 $\frac{5}{8}$ or $\frac{1}{2}$ 6 $\frac{5}{8}$ or $\frac{2}{3}$ 7 $\frac{3}{5}$ or $\frac{2}{3}$ 8 $\frac{4}{5}$ or $\frac{7}{8}$

Reflect and reason

Two fractions have the same numerator. The second fraction has a larger denominator.
Is the first or the second fraction the largest?

△ Purposeful practice 2

Work out

1 $\frac{1}{4} + \frac{2}{4}$ 2 $\frac{1}{4} + \frac{1}{2}$ 3 $\frac{1}{8} + \frac{1}{2}$ 4 $\frac{3}{8} + \frac{1}{2}$

5 $\frac{5}{8} + \frac{1}{2}$ 6 $\frac{5}{8} + \frac{2}{3}$ 7 $\frac{3}{5} + \frac{2}{3}$ 8 $\frac{4}{5} + \frac{7}{8}$

Reflect and reason

Did you use equivalent fractions in Purposeful practice 1? Did these help you answer the questions in
Purposeful practice 2?

△ Purposeful practice 3

Work out

1 $\frac{1}{2} - \frac{3}{8}$ 2 $\frac{2}{3} - \frac{3}{8}$ 3 $\frac{4}{5} - \frac{3}{8}$ 4 $\frac{5}{5} - \frac{3}{8}$ 5 $\frac{8}{8} - \frac{3}{8}$

6 $1 - \frac{3}{8}$ 7 $1 - \frac{3}{5}$ 8 $2 - \frac{3}{5}$ 9 $\frac{2}{5} - \frac{3}{5}$

Reflect and reason

Look at your answers to **Q4**, **Q5** and **Q6**. What can you say that $\frac{5}{5}$ and $\frac{8}{8}$ are equivalent to?
Explain your answer.

1 Place the numbers 1, 2, 3, 4 into the boxes so that $\dfrac{\square}{\square} < \dfrac{1}{2} < \dfrac{\square}{\square}$

2 Write $\dfrac{3}{10}$ as the sum of two unit fractions.

3 Is it possible to write a fraction that is less than $\dfrac{1}{2}$ using any pair of the integers from 3 to 8? Explain your answer.

4 The sum of three fractions is $\dfrac{11}{15}$.
   a What could the three fractions be?
   b If none of the fractions have the same denominator, what could the fractions be?
   c If all of fractions have the same numerator, what could the fractions be?

5 The difference between two fractions is $\dfrac{1}{5}$.
   a What could the two fractions be?
   b If both fractions have different denominators, what could the fractions be?
   c If both fractions have the same numerators, what could the fractions be?

6 The difference between two fractions is $\dfrac{1}{9}$. The sum of the two fractions is $\dfrac{5}{9}$.
   a What could the two fractions be?
   b Write three more pairs of fractions that they could be.

7 Nisha gives $\dfrac{1}{3}$ of her stamp collection to her brother. She sells $\dfrac{3}{8}$ of the collection. What fraction of the collection is left?

✧ Exam practice

1 Michael works out

$$\frac{1}{4} + \frac{2}{3} = \frac{1}{12} + \frac{2}{12} = \frac{3}{12}$$

The answer of $\dfrac{3}{12}$ is wrong.

Describe one mistake that Michael has made.   **(1 mark)**

Adapted from 1MA1/2F, Specimen papers, Set 1, Q19a

2 Here is a list of four fractions.

$\dfrac{4}{12}$ $\dfrac{12}{36}$ $\dfrac{15}{48}$ $\dfrac{7}{21}$

One of these fractions is **not** equivalent to $\dfrac{1}{3}$.

Write down this fraction.   **(1 mark)**

Adapted from 1MA1/1F, May 2018, Q4

Exam feedback   ResultsPlus

Q2: Most students who achieved a Grade 2 or above answered a similar question well.

4.2 Operations with fractions

Key point

- To add or subtract mixed numbers, convert them to improper fractions first.

△ Purposeful practice 1

Work out

1 $\frac{1}{5}$ of 20

2 $\frac{1}{4}$ of 20

3 $\frac{2}{4}$ of 20

4 $\frac{1}{2}$ of 20

5 $\frac{1}{2}$ of 30

6 $\frac{1}{4}$ of 30

7 $\frac{1}{5}$ of 30

8 $\frac{2}{5}$ of 30

9 $\frac{4}{5}$ of 30

10 $\frac{4}{5}$ of 60

11 $\frac{5}{6}$ of 60

12 $\frac{5}{12}$ of 60

13 $\frac{5}{12}$ of 36

14 $\frac{5}{6}$ of 6

15 $\frac{3}{5}$ of 45

16 $\frac{4}{7}$ of 21

Reflect and reason

What do you notice about your answers to **Q8–10**? Explain your answer.

△ Purposeful practice 2

Work these out. Give your answers as mixed numbers.

1 $1 + \frac{3}{7}$

2 $2 + \frac{3}{7}$

3 $2\frac{3}{7} + \frac{2}{7}$

4 $1\frac{3}{7} + 1\frac{2}{7}$

5 $1\frac{3}{7} + 1\frac{4}{14}$

6 $1\frac{9}{21} + 1\frac{4}{14}$

7 $1\frac{8}{21} + 1\frac{5}{14}$

8 $1\frac{8}{21} + 5\frac{1}{14}$

9 $1\frac{3}{7} + 1\frac{8}{14}$

10 $1\frac{3}{7} + 1\frac{9}{14}$

11 $2\frac{3}{7} + 1\frac{9}{14}$

12 $2\frac{4}{7} + 1\frac{9}{14}$

Reflect and reason

What changes between **Q6** and **Q7** and how does it affect the answer?

△ Purposeful practice 3

Work out

1 $1 - \frac{1}{7}$

2 $2 - \frac{1}{7}$

3 $2\frac{2}{7} - \frac{1}{7}$

4 $2\frac{1}{7} - \frac{2}{7}$

5 $2\frac{3}{7} - \frac{4}{7}$

6 $2\frac{2}{3} - 1\frac{3}{7}$

7 $2\frac{2}{3} - 1\frac{3}{4}$

8 $3\frac{2}{3} - 2\frac{3}{4}$

Reflect and reason

Why do you get the same answer for **Q4** and **Q5**?
Can you write another calculation that will give the same answer?

1. Killian earns £1300 a month.

   He is offered either an extra $\frac{3}{4}$ of his monthly pay or $\frac{1}{15}$ of his yearly pay as a one-off bonus.

   Which is the better option? Show your working.

2. Tessa is working out $5\frac{1}{5} - 3\frac{3}{5}$

   She says the answer is $2\frac{2}{5}$

   Tessa is wrong. What has Tessa done wrong?

3. There are 800 students at a school.

   $\frac{3}{5}$ of the students walk to school.

   $\frac{1}{4}$ of the students travel to school by car.

   The rest of the students travel to school by bus.
   Work out how many students travel to school by bus.

4. A carpenter makes a table that is 77 cm tall.
   A ceiling light hangs down 40 cm above the table.

   The carpenter decreases the height of the table by $\frac{1}{11}$ of the current height.

   What is the distance between the ceiling light and the table now?

5. Katherine and Naomi drive from Bristol to Penzance.

   Katherine takes $4\frac{1}{4}$ hours.

   Naomi takes $2\frac{1}{2}$ hours.

   What is the difference in their journey times?

6. What is the missing number?

   $57\frac{3}{7} + \square = 60$

7. How many minutes are there in $3\frac{1}{4}$ hours?

8. Work out $2\frac{1}{4} + 3\frac{3}{8} - \frac{5}{12}$

9. Write three pairs of mixed numbers that add to 10.

✦ Exam practice

1. Work out

   $3\frac{1}{5} + 1\frac{1}{3}$

   (2 marks)

   Adapted from 1MA1/1F, June 2018, Q19a

Exam feedback

ResultsPlus

Most students who achieved a **Grade 5** answered a similar question well.

4.3 Multiplying fractions

Key points

- To multiply fractions together, multiply the numerators together and the denominators together.
- Numerators can be cancelled with denominators if they are divisible by the same number.

△ Purposeful practice 1

Work out

1 $\dfrac{3}{5} \times 30$

2 $30 \times \dfrac{3}{5}$

3 $\dfrac{60}{2} \times \dfrac{3}{5}$

4 $\dfrac{90}{3} \times \dfrac{3}{5}$

Reflect and reason

How do these questions relate to finding $\dfrac{3}{5}$ of 30?

△ Purposeful practice 2

State which of these calculations can be simplified. If they can be simplified, show how and then work out the answer.

1 $\dfrac{1}{5} \times \dfrac{2}{4}$

2 $\dfrac{2}{5} \times \dfrac{1}{4}$

3 $\dfrac{2}{5} \times \dfrac{1}{5}$

4 $\dfrac{2}{5} \times \dfrac{4}{5}$

5 $\dfrac{1}{10} \times \dfrac{3}{5}$

6 $\dfrac{2}{5} \times \dfrac{5}{3}$

Reflect and reason

When you work out the simplified calculations, do you need to simplify your answer?

△ Purposeful practice 3

Work these out, giving your answers in their simplest form.

1 $\dfrac{1}{5} \times \dfrac{3}{6}$

2 $\dfrac{3}{5} \times \dfrac{1}{6}$

3 $\dfrac{1}{5} \times \dfrac{3}{12}$

4 $\dfrac{3}{5} \times \dfrac{1}{12}$

5 $\dfrac{2}{5} \times \dfrac{3}{4}$

6 $\dfrac{3}{5} \times \dfrac{2}{4}$

7 $\dfrac{3}{5} \times \dfrac{3}{1}$

8 $\dfrac{3}{5} \times 3$

9 $\dfrac{3}{8} \times 2$

10 $\dfrac{2}{5} \times 2$

11 $2 \times \dfrac{2}{5}$

12 $5 \times \dfrac{2}{3}$

13 $\dfrac{3}{2} \times 5$

14 $1\dfrac{1}{2} \times 5$

15 $1\dfrac{1}{2} \times 3$

16 $1\dfrac{1}{3} \times 2$

17 $1\dfrac{1}{3} \times 3$

18 $1\dfrac{3}{4} \times 2$

19 $3 \times 2\dfrac{3}{4}$

20 $2 \times 3\dfrac{4}{5}$

Reflect and reason

How does **Q1** relate to **Q2**?

How does **Q7** relate to **Q8**?

How does **Q13** relate to **Q14**?

⊠ Problem-solving practice

1 A pet shop has 80 animals for sale.

   $\frac{2}{5}$ of the animals have four legs.

   How many of the animals do not have four legs?

2 What is the difference between $\frac{3}{4}$ of $\frac{1}{8}$ and $\frac{1}{4}$ of $\frac{3}{8}$?

3 Place integers into the boxes so that the multiplication is correct.

   $$\frac{\square}{22} \times \frac{3}{\square} = \frac{3}{88}$$

4 $\frac{3}{5}$ of a multi-coloured rectangle is coloured blue.

   $\frac{4}{7}$ of the blue is metallic blue.

   What fraction of the rectangle is metallic blue?

5 In a fun run, $\frac{1}{5}$ of the competitors are male.

   $\frac{2}{3}$ of the males are over 25.

   What fraction of the competitors are male and over 25?

6 In a Maths test, $\frac{1}{12}$ of the questions involve decimals.

   $\frac{2}{5}$ of the questions involving decimals also involve percentages.

   Work out the fraction of questions that involve both decimals and percentages.

7 Layla works in a bakery.

   She bakes 12 cakes per hour.

   She bakes cakes for $5\frac{3}{4}$ hours each day.

   Work out how many cakes Layla bakes each day.

8 Tim spends $1\frac{1}{2}$ hours on his homework.

   Sam spends half as long as Tim on her homework.

   Jo spends three times as long on his homework as Sam.

   Who spends the longest on their homework? Showing your working.

✸ Exam practice

1 Work out

   $$\frac{3}{5} \times \frac{7}{8}$$

   (1 mark)

   Adapted from 1MA1/1F May 2017, Q8a

Exam feedback

ResultsPlus

Most students who achieved a **Grade 4** or above answered a similar question well.

4.4 Dividing fractions

△ Purposeful practice 1

Work these out. Where necessary, write your answer as a mixed number.

1 $2 \div \frac{1}{2}$

2 $2 \times \frac{2}{1}$

3 $2 \div \frac{1}{3}$

4 $2 \times \frac{3}{1}$

5 $2 \div \frac{1}{4}$

6 $2 \div \frac{1}{5}$

7 $3 \div \frac{1}{5}$

8 $3 \div \frac{2}{5}$

9 $3 \times \frac{5}{2}$

10 $3 \div \frac{3}{5}$

11 $4 \div \frac{3}{5}$

12 $2 \div \frac{3}{4}$

13 $2 \div \frac{4}{3}$

14 $2 \div 1\frac{1}{3}$

15 $3 \div 1\frac{1}{3}$

16 $3 \div 2\frac{1}{2}$

Reflect and reason

Which calculations had the same answers? Explain why.

△ Purposeful practice 2

Work these out. Where necessary, write your answer as a mixed number.

1 $\frac{1}{2} \div 2$

2 $\frac{1}{2} \times \frac{1}{2}$

3 $\frac{1}{2} \div 3$

4 $\frac{1}{3} \div 3$

5 $\frac{2}{3} \div 4$

6 $\frac{5}{3} \div 4$

7 $1\frac{2}{3} \div 4$

8 $1\frac{2}{3} \div 3$

Reflect and reason

How does **Q1** relate to **Q2**?

△ Purposeful practice 3

Work these out.

1 $\frac{1}{2} \div \frac{1}{2}$

2 $\frac{1}{2} \times 2$

3 $\frac{1}{2} \div \frac{1}{5}$

4 $\frac{1}{3} \div \frac{1}{5}$

5 $\frac{1}{3} \div \frac{1}{4}$

6 $\frac{2}{3} \div \frac{1}{4}$

7 $\frac{2}{5} \div \frac{1}{4}$

8 $\frac{2}{5} \div \frac{1}{3}$

Reflect and reason

How does **Q1** relate to **Q2**?

⊠ Problem-solving practice

1 A length of wood that is 8 m long is cut into strips measuring $\frac{2}{3}$ of a metre. How many strips of wood are there?

2 Place integers into the boxes so that the division is correct.

$$4 \div \frac{\square}{\square} = 5$$

3 What fraction should 7 be divided by to give an answer equal to $\frac{3}{4}$ of 14?

4 Alesha spends $1\frac{3}{4}$ hours on her homework.

She spends half of that time on her Science homework.
What fraction of an hour does Alesha spend on her Science homework?

5 Bill is a machinist.

He makes 5 dresses in $4\frac{1}{2}$ hours.

a What fraction of an hour does it take Bill to make one dress?

b How many minutes does it take Bill to make a dress?

6 Neil is taking a test.

It takes him $\frac{5}{8}$ of a minute to answer each question.

The test is 60 minutes long.

a How many questions will Neil answer?

Neil fails the test and so practises for a retest.

It now takes him $\frac{3}{8}$ of a minute to answer each question.

b Can Neil answer all 150 questions on the test now?
You must show your working.

✾ Exam practice

1 Work out $\frac{3}{5} \div \frac{7}{10}$

Give your answer in its simplest form. **(2 marks)**

Adapted from 1MA1/1F/S2, Specimen papers, Set 2, Q9c

2 $\frac{5}{7}$ of a number is 45.

Find the number. **(2 marks)**

Adapted from 1MA1/3F, June 2017, Q4

Exam feedback

ResultsPlus

Q2: Most students who achieved a **Grade 4** or above answered a similar question well.

4.5 Fractions and decimals

Key point

- You can use short or long division to convert fractions to decimals. For example, $\frac{3}{5}$ means $3 \div 5$

△ Purposeful practice 1

Write these decimals as fractions in their simplest form.

1 0.1	**2** 0.4	**3** 0.01	**4** 0.04	**5** 0.14
6 0.001	**7** 0.014	**8** 0.140	**9** 0.144	**10** 0.104

Reflect and reason

Which other decimal is equivalent to 0.14? Explain.

△ Purposeful practice 2

Write each fraction as a decimal.

1 $\frac{1}{2}$	**2** $\frac{1}{4}$	**3** $\frac{1}{8}$	**4** $\frac{1}{10}$	**5** $\frac{3}{10}$
6 $\frac{9}{10}$	**7** $\frac{1}{100}$	**8** $\frac{27}{100}$	**9** $\frac{61}{100}$	**10** $\frac{61}{1000}$
11 $\frac{1}{5}$	**12** $\frac{3}{5}$	**13** $\frac{1}{20}$	**14** $\frac{17}{20}$	**15** $\frac{1}{25}$
16 $\frac{9}{25}$	**17** $\frac{3}{2}$	**18** $\frac{5}{2}$	**19** $\frac{7}{4}$	**20** $\frac{9}{4}$
21 $\frac{1}{3}$	**22** $\frac{2}{3}$	**23** $\frac{1}{6}$	**24** $\frac{5}{6}$	**25** $\frac{1}{12}$

Reflect and reason

Some of the fractions gave decimals that stopped and some did not. Using the fraction, how do you know if a decimal will terminate or not?

△ Purposeful practice 3

Write in ascending order

1 $\frac{4}{5}, 0.3, 0.03, \frac{2}{25}$ **2** $\frac{2}{5}, 0.3, 0.03, \frac{2}{25}$ **3** $\frac{4}{5}, 0.3, 0.23, \frac{2}{25}$ **4** $\frac{2}{3}, 0.3, 0.23, \frac{2}{25}$

5 $\frac{1}{3}, 0.3, 0.23, \frac{2}{25}$ **6** $\frac{1}{3}, 0.3, 0.33, \frac{2}{25}$ **7** $\frac{1}{3}, 0.34, 0.33, \frac{2}{25}$ **8** $\frac{1}{3}, 0.34, 0.33, \frac{1}{4}$

9 $\frac{7}{2}, 3.4, 3.38, \frac{17}{4}$ **10** $-\frac{7}{2}, 3.4, 3.38, \frac{17}{4}$ **11** $-0.27, -1, 0, -\frac{4}{5}$ **12** $0.27, -1, 0, -\frac{4}{5}$

Reflect and reason

How did you decide which is the smallest amount in **Q11**?

⊠ Problem-solving practice

1 Write a decimal that is greater than $\frac{2}{5}$ and less than $\frac{1}{2}$.

2 Craig is buying melons.
A melon weighing $1\frac{3}{5}$ kg costs £4.

Craig buys two melons that weigh a total of 3.2 kg.
How much will they cost?

3 Larry says that multiplying by 0.16 is the same as multiplying by $\frac{1}{6}$.
Explain why Larry is incorrect.

4 Naz is asked to write $\frac{8}{125}$ as a decimal.
Naz writes

$$8\overline{)1^12^45\cdot{}^50^20^40} \quad \frac{01\ 5\cdot6\ 2\ 5}{} \quad \text{So } \frac{8}{125} = 15.625$$

Naz is incorrect. Explain what Naz has done wrong.

5 Harry is asked to write 0.45, $\frac{3}{2}$, 2.3, $\frac{1}{5}$ in order, starting with the smallest.
Harry writes,

$\frac{3}{2} = 3.2$ and $\frac{1}{5} = 0.5$ so the correct order is 0.45, $\frac{1}{5}$, 2.3, $\frac{3}{2}$

Harry is incorrect.

  a Explain what Harry has done wrong when converting $\frac{3}{2}$ to a decimal.

  b Explain what Harry has done wrong when converting $\frac{1}{5}$ to a decimal.

  c Write 0.45, $\frac{3}{2}$, 2.3, $\frac{1}{5}$ in the correct order, starting with the smallest.

6 Which of these fractions is closest to 0.5?

$$\frac{3}{5}, \frac{7}{12}, \frac{9}{20}, \frac{21}{50}$$

7 Write a decimal that is greater than $\frac{13}{20}$ and less than $\frac{18}{25}$.

8 An engineer uses 18 screws that are $\frac{3}{4}$ of an inch long.

The engineer knows that screws measuring 1 inch weigh 3.2 g.
How much will 18 screws weigh?

✦ Exam practice

1 Write $\frac{3}{100}$ as a decimal.   **(1 mark)**

Adapted from 1MA1/2F, November 2018, Q1

2 Write $\frac{4}{10}$ as a decimal.   **(1 mark)**

Adapted from 1MA1/3F, June 2018, Q1

Exam feedback   Results**Plus**

Q1: The only common error was a misplaced decimal point. Most students answered a similar question well.

Q2: Most students who achieved a **Grade 1** or above answered a similar question well.

4.6 Fractions and percentages

Key point

- To convert a fraction to a percentage, you can convert the fraction to one with the denominator 100 or you can multiply by 100%.

⚠ Purposeful practice 1

Write these percentages as fractions in their simplest form.

1	1%	**2**	10%	**3**	20%	**4**	25%	**5**	50%
6	5%	**7**	15%	**8**	35%	**9**	4%	**10**	32%

Reflect and reason

How can you use your answer to **Q6** to help you work out the answer to **Q7**?

⚠ Purposeful practice 2

Write each fraction as a percentage.

1 $\dfrac{5}{100}$ **2** $\dfrac{50}{100}$ **3** $\dfrac{50}{1000}$ **4** $\dfrac{5}{1000}$

Reflect and reason

What was the difference in your method for **Q1** and **Q2** compared to **Q3** and **Q4**?

⚠ Purposeful practice 3

Write each fraction as a percentage, giving your answer to 1 decimal place where necessary.

1 $\dfrac{1}{2}$ **2** $\dfrac{1}{4}$ **3** $\dfrac{3}{4}$ **4** $\dfrac{3}{5}$ **5** $\dfrac{30}{50}$

6 $\dfrac{19}{50}$ **7** $\dfrac{1}{10}$ **8** $\dfrac{1}{20}$ **9** $\dfrac{1}{25}$ **10** $\dfrac{1}{3}$

Reflect and reason

Which would you find easier to work with in a calculation for **Q10**, the percentage or the fraction? Why?

⚠ Purposeful practice 4

Write these as percentages, giving your answer to 1 decimal place.

1	5 out of 100	**2**	5 out of 10	**3**	5 out of 1000	**4**	5 out of 20
5	5 out of 40	**6**	7 out of 40	**7**	7 out of 25	**8**	19 out of 25

Reflect and reason

How can you use your answer to **Q1** to work out the answers to **Q2** and **Q3**?

1 Chesterton has a population of 6700.

In 2012, the population was $\frac{3}{4}$ of the current population.

The mayor says that the population was 70% of what it is now. Is the mayor right?

2 30% of a row of houses have red doors.

$\frac{2}{5}$ of the houses have blue doors.

The rest have yellow doors.

What is the most popular colour door?

3 To pass a test, Zainab needs at least 60% of the marks.

Zainab answered $\frac{16}{25}$ of the questions correctly.

Does Zainab pass the test?

4 Cats need 16 hours of sleep a day.

Bianka says that means they are awake for less than 30% of the day.

Is Bianka right?

5 Shop A is offering a discount of 15%.

Shop B is offering a discount of $\frac{1}{5}$.

Which shop is offering the biggest discount?

6 Jazmin, Kate and Laura sat a test.

The total for the test was 80 marks.

Jazmin got 64 out of 80.

Kate got $\frac{5}{8}$ of 80.

Laura got 75% of 80.

Who got the highest mark?

You must show all your working.

✦ Exam practice

1 a Write 40% as a fraction. **(1 mark)**

b Write 65% as a fraction. **(1 mark)**

Adapted from, 1MA1/1F, May 2018, Q3

2 a Write $\frac{3}{25}$ as a percentage. **(1 mark)**

b Write $\frac{7}{20}$ as a percentage. **(1 mark)**

Adapted from 1MA1/2F, June 2018, Q1

Exam feedback

Q1a: Most students who achieved a **Grade 2** or above answered a similar question well.

Q2a: Most students who achieved a **Grade 3** or above answered a similar question well.

Key point

- Simple interest is interest paid out each year by banks and building societies.

⚠ Purposeful practice 1

Work out

1 1% of 300	**2** 10% of 300	**3** 20% of 300	**4** 5% of 300
5 25% of 300	**6** 15% of 300	**7** 11% of 300	**8** 0.5% of 300
9 1% of 150	**10** 10% of 150	**11** 20% of 150	**12** 5% of 150

Reflect and reason

How could you use values you have already found to find the answer for **Q6**? Would this also work if you wanted to work out 15% of 50?

⚠ Purposeful practice 2

Convert these percentages to decimals.

1 100%	**2** 10%	**3** 1%	**4** 0.1%
5 5%	**6** 15%	**7** 20%	**8** 0.5%

Reflect and reason

What is the relationship between your answers for **Q2**, **Q5** and **Q6**?

⚠ Purposeful practice 3

Work out

1 30% of 500	**2** 15% of 200	**3** 60% of 250	**4** 0.15×200
5 0.3×500	**6** 3×500	**7** 0.30×500	**8** 0.6×250

Reflect and reason

Which of the calculations in **Q1–8** give the same answers? Why?

⚠ Purposeful practice 4

£1900 is put into a bank account with simple interest. Calculate the simple interest.

1 After 5 years with 2% annual simple interest.   **2** After 2 years with 5% annual simple interest.

3 After 4 years with 5% annual simple interest.   **4** After 2.5 years with 2% annual simple interest.

Reflect and reason

Why do **Q1** and **Q2** have the same answer?

1   Which is more,
    8% of £120 or 12% of £75?

2   To find 20% of 180 g, Katie writes
    $\dfrac{180}{20} \times 100$
    Explain what Katie has done wrong. Work out the correct answer.

3   A cat food company's advert says, '80% of cats prefer our food'.
    Out of 274 cats, how many would you expect to prefer that company's food?

4   Write these percentages and decimals in order, starting with the smallest.
    40%   0.04   0.4%   0.44

5   Anabelle has an annual salary of £16 380.

    She is offered either 10% of her annual salary or 15% of her salary over $\frac{3}{4}$ of a year as a bonus.

    Which is the better option? You must show your workings.

6   Two schools hold elections for the school council.
    There are currently 1200 students in school A.
    65% of students in school A vote in the elections.
    There are currently 960 students in school B.
    75% of the students in school B vote in the elections.
    In which school do the most students vote in the elections? You must show your workings.

7   Isadora wants to invest £3000.
    A savings bond for 10 years pays 2.5% simple interest.
    A £3000 piece of art will be worth 20% more in 10 years' time.
    Which is the better option? Explain your answer.

8   A student in Year 11 receives their attendance report.
    They find out that they have achieved 95% attendance.
    There have been 80 school days so far this year.
    How many days of school has the student missed?

9   Carl sells a first edition book through a website.
    The book sells for £180
    The website charges 5% and Carl spends £5.60 on postage.
    How much does Carl have to pay altogether to sell the book?

Exam practice

1   Work out 40% of 90   **(2 marks)**

Adapted from 1MA1/1F, May 2017, Q5

Exam feedback

ResultsPlus

Most students who achieved a **Grade 3** or above answered a similar question well.

Key points

- To increase a number by a percentage, work out the increase and add this to the original number.
- To decrease a number by a percentage, work out the decrease and subtract this from the original number.

△ Purposeful practice 1

Increase

1 100 by 20%   **2** 80 by 20%   **3** 80 by 10%

4 80 by 1%   **5** 80 by 100%   **6** 80 by 120%

Reflect and reason

Having increased 80 by 100%, what percentage of 80 do you now have? Explain your answer.

△ Purposeful practice 2

Decrease

1 100 by 20%   **2** 80 by 20%   **3** 80 by 10%

4 80 by 1%   **5** 80 by 100%   **6** 80 by 6%

Reflect and reason

Why does increasing your answer to **Q1** by 20% not give you 100?

△ Purposeful practice 3

1 Fran has £300. Work out the percentage Fran has after
   a an increase of 10%
   b an increase of 100%
   c a decrease of 10%

2 Write each percentage from **Q1** as a decimal.

3 Multiply £300 by the decimals in **Q2** to find the new amounts after each change.

4 Increase
   a 180 by 13%
   b 180 by 10%
   c 90 by 10%
   d 90 by 13%

5 Decrease
   a 90 by 13%
   b 90 by 1.5%

Reflect and reason

What is the relationship between the answers for **Q4a** and **Q4d**? Explain.

1 Finn is paid £2500 per month.
   He is going to get a 3% pay increase.
   Work out how much money Finn will be paid per month after the increase.

2 Ashley buys 3 t-shirts.
   The original price of each t-shirt is £15.
   The shop assistant says each item has 20% off. She takes 60% off the total amount.
   Explain why the shop assistant is wrong.

3 Mandeep is an author. He earns £5.20 for each book that sells.
   In 2017, Mandeep's book sold 3000 copies. 15% fewer copies were sold in 2018.
   Work out how many of Mandeep's books were sold in 2018.
   How much did Mandeep earn in 2018 from sales of his book?

4 Archer says that he works 10% more hours than Thanika over the course of a year.
   Thanika works 42 hours a week for 45 weeks a year.
   Archer works from 9 am to 3 pm.
   How many days would Archer need to work in a year for Archer's statement to be true?

5 Jan has been saving to buy a house for 2 years.
   It was valued at £256 000 last year and has increased in price by 3% this year.

   a How much is the house worth this year?
   Jan earned £40 000 in the first year and £42 800 in the second year.
   Jan puts 30% of her earnings each year into a savings account for the house.

   b How much does Jan have in her savings account?
      Jan needs 20% of the house price to pay a deposit.

   c How much more money does she need?

✸ Exam practice

1 Jenny uses petrol to fuel her car.
   On Monday there were 20 litres of petrol in her car's tank.
   Jenny bought enough petrol to fill the tank completely.
   She paid £1.20 per litre for this petrol.
   She paid a total amount of £30.
   On Friday Jenny had 15 litres of petrol in the tank.
   She bought enough petrol to fill the tank completely.
   The cost of petrol had increased by 5%.
   Work out the total amount Jenny paid for the petrol she bought on Friday.   **(5 marks)**

   Adapted from 1MA1/2F, November 2017, Q15

Exam feedback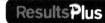

In a similar question, many students used a multiplier of 1.5 to calculate the increased price of petrol, rather than 1.05.

Mixed exercises A

1 Jordan has £10 to spend on chocolate bars.
Each chocolate bar costs 64p.
Jordan buys as many chocolate bars as possible.
Work out how much money Jordan has left.

2 Insert the missing term to complete the equation.
$2x \times \boxed{} = 10x^2$

3 **a** Work out the value of x when $a^2 \times a^x = a^{10}$
   b Work out the value of y when $\left(5^4\right)^y = 5^8$

4 Tia substitutes $u = 10$, $a = 4$ and $t = 5$ into the formula $v = u + at$
She writes

$v = 10 + 45$
$v = 55$

Explain what Tia has done wrong.

5 Kamil wants to buy 55 key rings.
Each key ring costs £3.80
Kamil does the calculation $60 \times 4 = 240$ to estimate the cost of 55 key rings.

   a Explain how Kamil's calculation shows the actual cost will be less than £240

   There is a special offer.
   'Buy 50 or more key rings, get 20% off'

   b Work out the actual cost of buying 55 key rings using the special offer.

6 James is asked to fully factorise $8x^2 + 4x$
He writes
$2x(4x + 2)$
Explain why James has not fully factorised $8x^2 + 4x$

7 The table shows the maths and science test results of 14 students.

Maths	8	10	12	15	15	20	21	21	23	25	28	30	34	28
Science	12	8	16	13	20	24	22	28	30	28	40	33	40	47

   a Draw a scatter graph for the data.

   b Write the type of correlation.

   Sophie scored 28 on the maths test but was absent for the science test.

   c Estimate a science mark for Sophie.

   A teacher says,
   'Students who score higher marks in science tests are those who score higher marks in maths tests.'

   d Does the scatter graph support what the teacher says?
   Give a reason for your answer.

8 Taylor's age is a square number.
Callum's age is a cube number.
Callum is 1 year younger than Taylor.
How old are Taylor and Callum?

9 Use the formula $A = bh$ to work out A when $b = 5.5$ and $h = 6$

10 Sarah takes $\frac{3}{5}$ of a cake to work.

Ali eats $\frac{1}{6}$ of the cake Sarah takes.

What fraction of the whole cake did Ali eat?

11 The table shows information about the average daily hours of sunshine in two Australian cities over five months.

	January	February	March	April	May
Darwin	7	7	8	9	9
Sydney	9	8	8	8	7

Ava wants to compare this information.

a Show this information in a suitable diagram.

b Compare the number of hours of sunshine in Darwin and Sydney.
Write down two comparisons.

12 Complete
$$\boxed{}(\boxed{} - 5) = 3y - 15$$

13 Emily, Finn and Tomas sat a science test.
The total score for the test was 80 marks.
Emily got 38 out of 80.
Finn got 45% of the 80 marks.
Tomas got $\frac{3}{10}$ of the 80 marks.

Who achieved the highest score? Show your working to explain your answer.

14 Sonu buys some boxes containing bags of crisps and some boxes containing cartons of juice.
There are 40 bags of crisps in a box.
There are 12 cartons of juice in a box.
Sonu buys exactly the same number of bags of crisps and cartons of juice.
What is the smallest number of boxes of crisps and boxes of juice she could have bought?

15 The pie chart shows information about the type of transport students use to get to college.

a What fraction of the students walk to college?

b 450 students travel by car. What is the total number of students at the college?

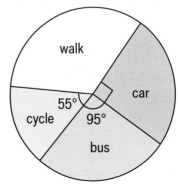

Mixed problem-solving practice A

16 Write down the first even multiple of 9 **(1 mark)**

Adapted from 1MA1/1F, May 2018, Q5

Exam feedback ResultsPlus

Most students who achieved a **Grade 5** answered a similar question well.

17 Here are four straight lines.

$$\leftarrow x-1 \rightarrow \quad \leftarrow x \rightarrow \quad \leftarrow x+2 \rightarrow \quad \leftarrow\quad x+3 \quad\rightarrow$$

All measurements are in centimetres.
The total length of the four lines is L cm.
Write a formula for L in terms of x.
Write your formula as simply as possible. **(3 marks)**

Adapted from 1MA1/1F, November 2017, Q6

Exam feedback ResultsPlus

In a similar question, some student's solutions showed incomplete simplification or gave an incorrect simplification when beginning to write an expression.

18 There are 90 students in Jack's year group.
50 of the students are 14 years old.
6 of the 15-year-old students wear glasses.
7 of the students who wear glasses are
14 years old.
Use the information to complete the two-way table. **(3 marks)**

	14 years old	15 years old	Total
Glasses			
No glasses			
Total			

Adapted from 1MA1/1F, November 2017, Q12

Exam feedback ResultsPlus

In a similar question, most students were comfortable with two-way tables but a small minority did reverse the entries so careful reading of the headings is required.

19 Here are two fractions

$$\frac{5}{9} \qquad \frac{9}{5}$$

Work out which of the fractions is closer to 1
You must show all your working. **(3 marks)**

Adapted from 1MA1/1F, November 2017, Q14

20 A car manufacturer sells diesel, petrol and electric cars.
The composite bar chart shows information about sales over three years.

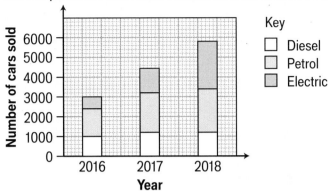

a Write down the number of diesel cars sold in 2016 **(1 mark)**

b Work out the total number of petrol cars sold in the 3 years. **(3 marks)**

c State the type of car that had the greatest increase in sales over the three years.

Give a reason for your answer. **(2 marks)**

Mark says, 'In 2018, more electric cars were sold than diesel cars. This means the manufacturer makes more profit from the sale of electric cars than from the sale of diesel cars.'

d Is Mark correct? You must justify your answer. **(1 mark)**

Adapted from 1MA1/1F, May 2018, Q12

21 Helen is paid £1800 per month. She is going to get a 2% pay increase.
Work out how much money Helen will be paid per month after the increase. **(2 marks)**

Adapted from 1MA1/1F, May 2017, Q20

22 A force of 90 newtons acts on an area of $30\,cm^2$.
The force is increased by 20 newtons, N.
The area is increased by $20\,cm^2$.
Claire says, 'The pressure decreases by less than 25%'.
Is Claire correct? You must show how you get your answer. **(3 marks)**

$$\text{pressure} = \frac{\text{force}}{\text{area}}$$

Adapted from 1MA1/2F, June 2018, Q25

5 Equations, inequalities and sequences

5.1 Solving equations 1

Key points

- An equation contains an unknown number (a letter) and an '=' sign.
- When you solve an equation you work out the value of the unknown number.
- In an equation, the expressions on both sides of the = sign have the same value.
- The expressions stay equal if you use the same operation on both sides.

△ Purposeful practice 1

1 Match each equation with the next steps in its solution.

$$a + 3 = 12 \qquad a - 3 = 12 \qquad 3a = 12 \qquad \frac{a}{3} = 12$$

$$a = \frac{12}{3} \qquad a = 3 \times 12 \qquad a = 12 - 3 \qquad a = 12 + 3$$

$$a = 4 \qquad a = 36 \qquad a = 9 \qquad a = 15$$

2 Solve these equations.

    a $b + 8 = 24$ **b** $8b = 24$ **c** $\dfrac{b}{8} = 24$

    d $8 + b = 24$ **e** $b - 8 = 24$ **f** $8 - b = 24$

Reflect and reason

How can you use inverse operations to write the next step to solve an equation?

△ Purposeful practice 2

1 7 is added to a number. The result is 18.
An equation for this statement is $x + 7 = 18$
Solve the equation $x + 7 = 18$

2 14 is added to a number. The result is 36.

    a Write an equation for the statement.

    b Solve your equation.

3 9 is subtracted from a number. The result is 15.

    a Write an equation for the statement.

    b Solve your equation.

4 A number is multiplied by 7. The result is 42.
Form and solve an equation to work out the number.

Reflect and reason

Explain how you know what goes on each side of the equals sign when forming an equation.

⊠ Problem-solving practice

1 Jane thinks of a number.
She adds 27 to this number.
The result is 62.
What number did Jane think of?

2 Abi has x cards.
Bashar has three times as many cards as Abi.
Chan has twice as many cards as Abi.
They have a total of 54 cards.
Work out the number of cards they each have.

3 Calculate the size of the larger angle.

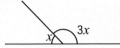

4 A square has sides x cm and a perimeter of 36 cm. Work out the area of the square.

5 The rectangle has a perimeter of 26 cm.

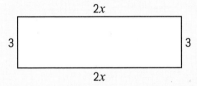

Draw the rectangle accurately and label the sides.

6 The perimeter of this rectangle is 48 cm.
Calculate the area of the rectangle.

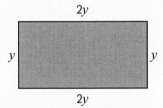

✦ Exam practice

1 Find the value of x.

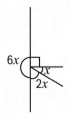

(3 marks)

Adapted from 1MA1/2F, June 2017, Q9

Key point

- To solve an equation, identify the operations in the equation and then use inverse operations in the reverse order.

  Solve the equation $3a + 7 = 13$

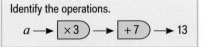

Identify the operations.

  $3a + 7 - 7 = 13 - 7$

  $3a = 6$

  $\dfrac{3a}{3} = \dfrac{6}{3}$

  $a = 2$

Subtract 7 from both sides.

Divide both sides by 3.

  Check: $3a + 7 = 3 \times 2 + 7 = 13$ ✓

Purposeful practice 1

1 Solve

  a $4x = 12$ **b** $5x = 30$ **c** $6x = 12$ **d** $7x = 28$

2 Solve

  a $4x + 18 = 30$ **b** $5x - 18 = 12$ **c** $6x + 14 = 26$ **d** $7x - 12 = 16$

  e $18 + 4x = 30$ **f** $-18 + 5x = 12$ **g** $14 + 6x = 26$ **h** $-12 + 7x = 16$

Reflect and reason

How do your solutions to the equations in **Q1** help you to solve the equations in **Q2**?

Purposeful practice 2

Solve

  1 $-4x - 18 = 30$ **2** $-5x - 18 = 12$ **3** $14 - 6x = 28$ **4** $-12 - 7x = 16$

Reflect and reason

In what way are these equations different from those in **Q2** of Purposeful practice 1? How did that change the way you approached the questions?

Purposeful practice 3

Solve

  1 $3y + 2 = 6$ **2** $6y + 4 = 12$ **3** $3y + 4 = 12$ **4** $3y + 4 = 6$

  5 $3y + 2 = 12$ **6** $6y + 2 = 12$ **7** $\dfrac{y}{3} + 2 = 6$ **8** $\dfrac{y}{6} + 4 = 12$

  9 $\dfrac{y}{6} + 2 = 12$ **10** $\dfrac{y}{6} + 2 = 6$ **11** $\dfrac{y}{3} + 2 = 12$ **12** $\dfrac{y}{3} + 2 = 24$

Solve these equations. Use a calculator to write the solutions as decimals.

  13 $5y + 14 = 20$ **14** $4y + 17 = 38$ **15** $8y + 21 = 34$

Reflect and reason

Is there any type of number that cannot be the solution to an equation?

⊠ Problem-solving practice

1 Theo thinks of a number.
He multiplies the number by 5 and then subtracts 7.
The result is 53.
What number did Theo think of?

2 Dec is x years old.
Emma is twice as old as Dec.
George is 7 years younger than Emma.
The sum of all their ages is 58 years.

   a Show that $5x - 7 = 58$

   b Work out how old Dec, Emma and George are.

3 Work out the size of each angle in the triangle.

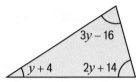

4 Calculate the length of the shorter side of this rectangle.
All measurements are in centimetres.

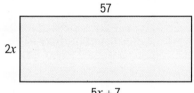

5 Here is a triangle.

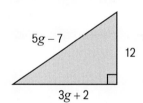

The perimeter of the triangle is 97 cm. Find the value of g.

⍟ Exam practice

1 Solve $3f + 2 = 14$ **(1 mark)**

Adapted from 1MA1/2F, June 2018, Q11c

Exam feedback   ResultsPlus

Most students who achieved a **Grade 3** or above answered a similar question well.

5.3 Solving equations with brackets

⚠ Purposeful practice 1

1 Solve

    a $4x + 12 = 24$ **b** $6x + 15 = 24$ **c** $8x - 8 = 24$ **d** $8x - 12 = 24$

2 Solve

    a $4(x + 3) = 24$ **b** $3(2x + 5) = 24$ **c** $8(x - 1) = 24$ **d** $4(2x - 3) = 24$

> **Reflect and reason**
>
> How do the equations in **Q2** relate to the equations in **Q1**?

⚠ Purposeful practice 2

Solve

1 $3(3x + 3) = 99$ **2** $3(3x + 3) = 33$ **3** $99 = 9(3x + 3)$

4 $99 = 9(3x + 9)$ **5** $9(3x + 9) = 0$ **6** $0 = 10(3x + 3)$

7 $30 = 10(3x + 3)$ **8** $10(3x - 3) = 30$ **9** $8(3x - 5) = 56$

> **Reflect and reason**
>
> Does it matter which side of the equals sign the brackets appear on? Does this change the way you solve the equation?

⚠ Purposeful practice 3

Solve

1 $6x + 12 = 24 + 2x$ **2** $4x + 15 = 24 - 2x$ **3** $10x - 8 = 24 + 2x$

4 $6x - 12 = 24 - 2x$ **5** $4x + 1 = x + 7$ **6** $5x - 1 = x + 11$

7 $5x + 3 = 11 + x$ **8** $x + 3 = 11 + 5x$ **9** $x + 11 = 3 + 5x$

10 $6x + 11 = 3 + 5x$ **11** $6x + 11 = 3 + 4x$ **12** $6x + 1 = 13 + 4x$

13 $2(x + 3) = 3x + 1$ **14** $3(x + 4) = 7x + 4$ **15** $3(x - 2) = 7(x - 6)$

16 $6(x - 1) = 3(x + 5)$ **17** $4(2x + 1) = 5(x - 1)$ **18** $3(3x + 5) = 6(x + 2)$

> **Reflect and reason**
>
> How is the equation in **Q7** different from the equation in **Q6**? How does this affect the solution?
> Compare the solutions to **Q12** and **Q13**. Explain what you notice.

⊠ Problem-solving practice

1   Charlie thinks of a number.
    He adds 8 to the number and then multiplies by 6.
    The result is 18.
    What number did Charlie think of?

2   Prisha thinks of a number.
    She adds 2 to the number and then multiplies by 4.
    The result is the same as when she multiplies her number by 3, subtracts 1 and then multiplies by 2.
    Work out the number Prisha thought of.

3   Find the value of h in this isosceles triangle.

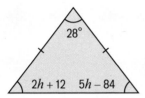

4   Rectangles A and B have equal perimeters.
    Which rectangle has the smallest area?

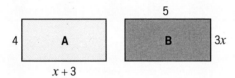

5   Here is a rectangle.
    All measurements are in centimetres.

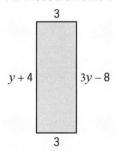

    Show that $y = 6$.

✵ Exam practice

1   Solve $5(p - 2) = 25$ **(2 marks)**

Adapted from 1MA1/1F, May 2018, Q16c

Exam feedback   ResultsPlus

Most students who achieved a **Grade 4** or above answered a similar question well.

Key points

- You can show solutions to inequalities on a number line.
- An empty circle ◯ shows the value is **not** included. A filled circle ⬤ shows the value is included.
- An arrow ◯⟶ shows that the solution continues in that direction towards infinity.
- An integer is a positive or negative whole number or zero.

△ Purposeful practice 1

Draw a number line from −4 to 5 to show each of these inequalities.

1 $x \leqslant 3$ **2** $x < 3$ **3** $x > 3$

4 $x \geqslant 3$ **5** $3 \geqslant x$ **6** $-3 \leqslant x \leqslant 3$

7 $-3 < x \leqslant 3$ **8** $-3 < x < 3$ **9** $-3 \leqslant x < 3$

Reflect and reason

Two of the inequalities describe the same interval on the number line. Explain why.

△ Purposeful practice 2

Write down three integer values that satisfy each inequality.

1 $x \leqslant 3$ **2** $x < 3$ **3** $x > 3$

4 $x \geqslant 3$ **5** $3 \geqslant x$ **6** $-3 \leqslant x \leqslant 3$

7 $-3 < x \leqslant 3$ **8** $-3 < x < 3$ **9** $-3 \leqslant x < 3$

Reflect and reason

Why is it not possible to list all possible integer solutions for **Q1** to **Q5**?
Is it possible to list all possible integer solutions for **Q6** to **Q9**?

△ Purposeful practice 3

Solve

1 $2x \leqslant 6$ **2** $2x < 6$ **3** $2x > 6$

4 $2x + 4 > 6$ **5** $x + 4 > 6$ **6** $x + 6 > 6$

7 $x - 6 > 6$ **8** $x - 6 \leqslant 6$ **9** $2(x - 6) \leqslant 6$

10 $\dfrac{x}{2} \leqslant 6$ **11** $\dfrac{x}{2} \geqslant 6$ **12** $6 \leqslant \dfrac{x}{2}$

13 $3 - x \leqslant 2x - 6$ **14** $3 - x < 2x - 6$ **15** $3 + x < 2x - 6$

16 $2x - 6 < 3 + x$ **17** $6x - 2 < 3 + x$ **18** $5x - 1 \geqslant 2x + 11$

Reflect and reason

Look at the method you used to answer these questions. What are the similarities and differences between solving equations and solving inequalities?

1 Rectangle A has a larger perimeter than rectangle B. What is the smallest integer value x could take for this still to be true?

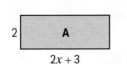

2 Jay doubled a number and then added 3.
   The result was less than 20.
   Write an inequality showing the numbers Jay could have used.

3 Abbie is 19.
   Abbie knows that even if David tripled his age, he would still be younger than her.
   Write an inequality to show this.
   What is the oldest David could be?

4 Tumay thought of a number.
   She multiplied it by 5 and then added 6.
   The result was greater than 46.
   Write an inequality to show this.
   What was the smallest number Tumay could have started with?

5 Alexei scored 40 on his first maths test.
   He wants to get at least 90 marks in total after taking the second test.
   Construct an inequality to show how many marks he needs for his second test.

6 Harbinder is buying books.
   Each book costs £6.
   Harbinder has a total of £34 to spend.
   Construct an inequality to show how many books she can buy.

7 Chris read that if he halves his body weight in pounds, it tells him the minimum number of ounces of water he should drink per day to be healthy.
   Chris weighs 240 pounds.
   Chris's cups each hold 16 ounces of water.
   Construct an inequality showing how many cups of water Chris needs to drink.

⟡ Exam practice

1 $-7 < h \leqslant -3$
   h is an integer.
   Write down all the possible values of h.   **(2 marks)**

   Adapted from 1MA1/1F, June 2017, Q19b

 2 Solve the inequality
   $3x + 6 > 10$ **(2 marks)**

   Adapted from 1MA1/3F, Specimen Papers, Set 2, Q20b

| Exam feedback | Results**Plus** |

Q1: Most students who achieved a **Grade 4** or above answered a similar question well.

5.5 More inequalities

Key points

- You can solve two-sided inequalities using a balancing method.
- When you multiply or divide both sides of an inequality by a negative number, you reverse the inequality signs.

Purposeful practice 1

Solve these inequalities and state all integer solutions.

1 $4 \leqslant 2x \leqslant 6$ **2** $4 \leqslant 2x < 6$ **3** $3 \leqslant 2x \leqslant 7$ **4** $3 \leqslant 2x \leqslant 5$

Reflect and reason

Compare your answers to **Q1** and **Q2**. Explain why they are different.

Purposeful practice 2

Solve

1 $4 < 2x < 6$ **2** $5 < 2x + 1 < 7$ **3** $3 < 2x - 1 < 5$

4 $6 < 4x - 2 < 10$ **5** $-6 < 4x - 2 < 10$ **6** $-10 < 4x - 2 < 6$

7 $-10 < 4x - 6 < 6$ **8** $-10 < 2(2x - 3) < 6$ **9** $0 < 2(2x - 3) < 6$

Reflect and reason

The inequality in **Q4** is the same as the inequality in **Q3** but with all numbers doubled. What impact does this have on the solution? Why?

Purposeful practice 3

Solve and find all possible integers that satisfy

1 $4 < -2x \leqslant 6$ **2** $4 \leqslant -2x \leqslant 6$ **3** $4 < -2x + 1 \leqslant 6$

4 $4 < -2x - 1 \leqslant 6$ **5** $-4 < -2x - 1 \leqslant 6$ **6** $-4 < 2x + 1 \leqslant 6$

Reflect and reason

Give an example to show that, when you multiply or divide an inequality by a negative number, the direction of the sign needs to be changed.

Purposeful practice 4

Find an integer solution that satisfies both inequalities.

1 $x > 3$ and $x \leqslant 4$ **2** $x < 3$ and $x \leqslant 4$ **3** $2x \leqslant 4$ and $x > 1.5$

4 $2x > 3$ and $x \leqslant 4$ **5** $x + 1 > 3$ and $x - 1 \leqslant 3$ **6** $2x + 1 > 3$ and $2x - 1 \leqslant 3$

Reflect and reason

Which of these inequality pairs can you express as a single, double-sided inequality?

⊠ Problem-solving practice

1 Hazel thought of a number between 7 and 13.
She added 4 to it and then multiplied the answer by 20.
Write an inequality to show what her final number could be.

2 Joe's pet has to have its medicine every 3 to 4 hours.
It last had its medicine at 9 am. It is now 10.30 am.
Construct an inequality showing how many minutes it might have to wait for its medicine.

3

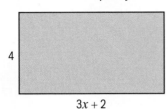 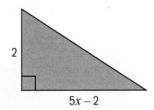

a The area of the rectangle is greater than 44 cm².
Is it possible for the area of the triangle to be less than or equal to 38 cm²?
Use inequalities to show this.

b The perimeter of the rectangle is less than or equal to its area.
Construct an inequality showing the possible values of x.

4 Toby is asked to solve the inequality $-8 < -2x \leqslant 10$
Toby writes
$$4 < x \leq -5$$
What error has Toby made?

5 A bag contains 300 g of rice.
The packaging says it could contain up to 50 g more or less rice.
A portion of rice is 100 g.
Construct an inequality showing the number of portions of rice that the bag could hold.

6 Every day, Stephen writes at least 1000 words.
The most he has ever written in one day is 4400 words.
Construct an inequality showing how many days it would take Stephen to write 55 000 words.

7 A chemistry teacher is planning a lesson where students are put into groups to do an experiment using 200 ml of a chemical.
There are 30 students in the class and the maximum group size is 6 students.
There is 3100 ml of the chemical available to be used.
Write an inequality showing the possible group sizes.

✦ Exam practice

1 Solve the inequality $9 \leqslant 4x - 7 < 21$ **(3 marks)**

Key points

- A formula shows the relationship between two or more variables (letters).
- The subject of a formula is the letter on its own, on one side of the equals sign.
- You can substitute one value into a formula and solve the resulting equation to work out the other value.

△ Purposeful practice 1

$y = 2x - 3$

Work out the value of y when

1 $x = 3$ **2** $x = 2$ **3** $x = 1$ **4** $x = 0$ **5** $x = -3$

Reflect and reason

How could you predict the point at which y would be less than 0?

△ Purposeful practice 2

$y = 2x - 3$

Work out the value of x when

1 $y = 3$ **2** $y = 2$ **3** $y = 1$ **4** $y = 0$ **5** $y = -3$

Reflect and reason

How was your method different from the one you used for Purposeful practice 1?

△ Purposeful practice 3

1 Rearrange $y = 2x - 3$ to make x the subject.

2 Use your rearranged equation to find the value of x when $y = 3$.

Reflect and reason

Purposeful Practice 3 involves the same problem as Purposeful Practice 2 **Q1**. Compare the methods you used in each case.

△ Purposeful practice 4

Rearrange each formula to make the letter in the square brackets the subject.

1 $y = 4x$ $[x]$ **2** $V = IR$ $[I]$ **3** $u = \frac{s}{t}$ $[s]$

4 $y = x + 3$ $[x]$ **5** $f = d + c$ $[c]$ **6** $f = ma$ $[a]$

Reflect and reason

How did you decide which operation to use when changing the subject of each formula?

⊠ Problem-solving practice

1 A seedling is given plant food daily using this formula.

$$F = 0.1h + 30$$

F is the amount of plant food in millilitres (ml).
h is the height of the seedling in centimetres (cm).
One day the plant is fed 31.4 ml of plant food. How tall was the plant on this day?

2 An exam question gives the equation $y = 3x - 4$ and asks for the value of x when $y = 48$

Student A writes
$y = 3 \times 48 - 4$
$y = 140$

a What mistake has student A made?

Student B writes
$3x = 48 - 4 = 44$
$x = 44 \div 3$

b What mistake has student B made?

3 The relationship between pressure (P), force (F) and area (A) is given by this equation.

$$P = \frac{F}{A}$$

a Adam wants to know how much force he needs to apply to an area of $3\,m^2$ to produce a pressure of $48\,N/m^2$.
Rearrange the formula so that he can calculate this easily.

b Work out how much force Adam needs to apply to an area of $3\,m^2$ to produce a pressure of $48\,N/m^2$.

4 The formula to work out how long a journey takes is $t = \frac{d}{s}$, where d = distance, s = speed and t = time taken.

a Work out how far a car travels when it is being driven at an average speed of 45 kilometres per hour for 4 hours.

b Work out the average speed of a car journey that is 120 miles and takes $2\frac{1}{2}$ hours.

5 In the formula $F = ma$, F is force, m is mass and a is acceleration.
A rocket has a mass of 1.5 kg and can go with a force of 18 N.
Work out the acceleration of the rocket.

✧ Exam practice

1 $G = 5T + 2$
    a Work out the value of G when $T = 3$ **(2 marks)**
    b Make T the subject of the formula $G = 5T + 2$ **(2 marks)**

Adapted from 1MA1/3F, June 2017, Q11

Exam feedback   ResultsPlus

Q1a: Most students who achieved a **Grade 3** or above answered a similar question well.
Q1b: Most students who achieved a **Grade 5** answered a similar question well.

Key points

- A sequence is a pattern of numbers or shapes that follow a rule.
- The numbers in a sequence are called terms.
- The term-to-term rule describes how to get from one term to the next.

△ Purposeful practice 1

Find the term-to-term rule for each sequence.

1 2, 4, 6, 8, 10, ...

2 2, 4, 6, 10, 16, ...

3 2, 4, 8, 16, 32, ...

4 3, 6, 9, 12, 15, ...

5 3, 6, 9, 15, 24, ...

6 3, 6, 12, 24, 48, ...

Reflect and reason

Could you have described the term-to-term rule accurately using only the first two terms?

△ Purposeful practice 2

Write down the next two terms in each sequence.

1 1, 3, 5, 7, ☐, ☐

2 −1, 1, 3, 5, ☐, ☐

3 −9, −7, −5, −3, ☐, ☐

4 9, 7, 5, 3, ☐, ☐

5 −2, −4, −6, −8, ☐, ☐

6 $\frac{1}{2}, \frac{3}{2}, \frac{5}{2}, \frac{7}{2}$, ☐, ☐

7 $\frac{1}{2}, 0, -\frac{1}{2}, -\frac{2}{2}$, ☐, ☐

8 $1, \frac{1}{2}, 0, -\frac{1}{2}, -1$, ☐, ☐

9 1, 1.5, 2, 2.5, ☐, ☐

Reflect and reason

Compare **Q1** and **Q6**. What is different about the term-to-term rule?

△ Purposeful practice 3

Generate the first five terms of each sequence.

1 start at 5 and add 5

2 start at 6 and add 5

3 start at 7 and add 5

4 start at 8 and add 5

5 start at 4 and add 5

6 start at 3 and add 5

7 start at −1 and add 2

8 start at −1 and add 1

9 start at −1 and add 0

10 start at −1 and add −1

11 start at −1 and subtract 1

12 start at −1 and subtract 2

Reflect and reason

Compare your answers to **Q1–6** with the **5** times table. What is the same?
What is the relationship between **Q10** and **Q11**?

1 Mr Uduehi would like to arrange his classroom as shown.
He has 30 students. How many more chairs and tables will he need?

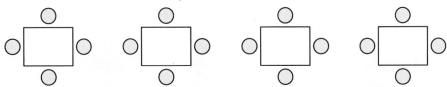

2 Sharon is colouring in thank you cards for her friends.
She uses red, orange and purple for the first card.
She uses orange, purple and green for the second card.
She uses purple, green and red for the third card.
She then goes back to red, orange and purple for the fourth card.
She continues this pattern until she has made 15 cards.
How many of each colour card will she make?

3 Daniel makes a sequence by squaring the last term and subtracting 3.
   a He starts at 2. Will the sequence ever have a positive term? Give reasons for your answer.
   b What is the smallest integer he can start with that will always give positive terms?

4 A sequence starts at 6. The term-to-term rule for the sequence is 'double then add 1'.
   a Explain whether 26 would appear in the sequence.
   b Is it possible to change the starting number so that the sequence produces only even numbers? Give reasons for your answers.

5 Ali uses 15 matchsticks to start this sequence.
Ali has 25 more matchsticks.
How many more terms in this sequence can be made?

  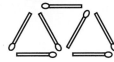

1   2   3

1 Here are the first five terms of a number sequence.

                2   5   8   11   14

   a i Write down the next term in the sequence.   (1 mark)
     ii Explain how you got your answer.   (1 mark)
   b Work out the 8th term of the sequence.   (1 mark)

Adapted from 1MA1/3F, June 2018, Q4

Exam feedback   Results**Plus**

Q1a: Most students who achieved a **Grade 1** or above answered a similar question well.
Q1b: Most students who achieved a **Grade 2** or above answered a similar question well.

Key point

- The nth term of a sequence tells you how to work out the term at position n (any position). It is also called the general term of the sequence.

⚠ Purposeful practice 1

Write down the first five terms of the sequences with these nth terms.

1 $4n$ **2** $4n + 1$ **3** $4n + 2$

4 $2n + 4$ **5** $2n - 4$ **6** $-2n + 4$

> ### Reflect and reason
>
> Compare **Q3** and **Q4**. What similarities and differences do the sequences have?

⚠ Purposeful practice 2

Find the nth term for each sequence.

1 2, 4, 6, 8, ...   **2** 1, 3, 5, 7, ...   **3** 1, 2, 3, 4, ...

4 2, 3, 4, 5, ...   **5** 4, 6, 8, 10, ...   **6** 4, 8, 12, 16, ...

7 15, 13, 11, 9, ...   **8** 20, 18, 16, 14, ...   **9** 9, 8, 7, 6, ...

10 36, 31, 26, 21, ...   **11** 20, 17, 14, 11, ...   **12** 19, 15, 11, 7, ...

> ### Reflect and reason
>
> Why did **Q5** not give the same nth term as **Q6**?
>
> What are the similarities and differences between the sequences and nth terms for **Q1–6** compared with **Q7–12**?

⚠ Purposeful practice 3

1 Calculate the 50th term of each sequence.

     a n **b** $2n$ **c** $2n + 1$ **d** $3n$

     e $3n - 1$ **f** $\frac{1}{2}n - 1$ **g** $-3n - 1$ **h** $-2n - 1$

2 For the sequences with these nth terms, decide if 50 is a term in the sequence.

     a n **b** $2n$ **c** $2n + 1$ **d** $3n$

     e $3n - 1$ **f** $\frac{1}{2}n - 1$ **g** $-3n - 1$ **h** $-2n - 1$

> ### Reflect and reason
>
> How does your method for **Q2** change from the method you used for **Q1**?

1   The nth term for sequence A is $5n - 7$.
    The nth term for sequence B is $2n + 5$.
    Will any of their terms be the same?

2   Tiles come in packs of 10, which cost £3.50. Jensen has £20.

    a   The number of tiles in a pattern can be expressed as $4n + 5$.
        Jensen needs enough tiles for the first four terms in the pattern.
        Can he afford to use this tile pattern?

    b   Write the nth term of a pattern that Jensen can afford to use for four terms.

3   A teacher is putting her class into groups.
    She starts counting at the third person in the line and makes a new group every four students.
    There are no students left over.
    There are at least 20 students in the class and no more than 32 students.
    How many students could there be?

4   A sequence has a difference of 4 between each term.

    a   The 8th term in the sequence is 40. What is the nth term of the sequence?

    b   Is 986 a term in the sequence?

5   A sequence starts at 5.
    It has a constant difference between terms.
    The third term is 17.
    What is the nth term?

6   The sum of the first and second terms of a linear sequence is 7.
    The sum of the second and third terms is 13.
    What is the nth term?

7   Makoto says that the sum of any four consecutive terms of $8n - 3$ will be greater than the
    sum of the equivalent four consecutive terms of $5n + 3$.
    Show that Makoto is correct.

8   Which of these sequences will include 82 first?

    a   3, 8, 13, 18

    b   5, 8, 11, 14, 17

    c   60, 60.1, 60.2, 60.3

    d   100, 98, 96

9   Write the nth term of a sequence that starts at 4 and becomes negative after three terms.

1   The nth term of a sequence is $4n^2 - 3$
    Work out the 6th term of the sequence.   **(2 marks)**

Adapted from 1MA1/1F, Specimen Papers, Set 2, Q24b

6 Angles

6.1 Properties of shapes

⚠ Purposeful practice 1

1. Copy and complete the table. On each shape, draw in any lines of symmetry.
   Colour equal angles the same colour and mark equal sides.
   The kite has been completed for you.

Shape							
Equal sides					2 pairs, adjacent		
Pairs of equal opposite sides					0		
Pairs of parallel sides					0		
Angles					1 pair equal, opposite		

Reflect and reason

Compare the properties of a square and a rectangle. Is a square a type of rectangle? Explain.

⚠ Purposeful practice 2

1. Trace each shape. Find the lengths of the sides labelled with letters.
   Find the sizes of the angles labelled with letters.

   a square

   5 cm
   x

   b rectangle
   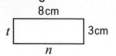
   8 cm
   t   3 cm
   n

   c rhombus
   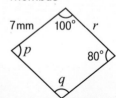
   7 mm 100° r
   p
   80°
   q

   d parallelogram
   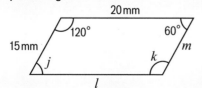
   20 mm
   120°   60°
   15 mm   m
   j   k
   l

   e isosceles trapezium
   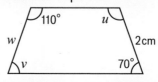
   110°   u
   w   2 cm
   v   70°

Reflect and reason

How can you use symmetry to solve missing side and angle problems?

1 **a** Draw an isosceles trapezium on squared paper.

   b Draw a rhombus on squared paper.

2 A description of a shape begins, 'This shape has four equal sides.'

   a Write two possible shapes it could be.

   b For each shape you wrote in **Q2a**, write one more property to identify the shape.

3 Is a rhombus a parallelogram? Explain your answer.

4 Here is a grid showing the points A, B and C.
   Write down the coordinates of a point D so that the quadrilateral ABCD is a rhombus.

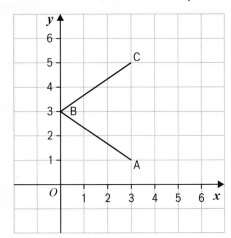

✪ Exam practice

1 Write down the mathematical name of the quadrilateral.   **(1 mark)**

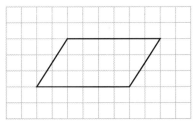

Adapted from 1MA1/2F, November 2017, Q10b

Exam feedback   Results**Plus**

In a similar question, many students had difficulty in naming the shape, giving almost any quadrilateral other than the correct one.

Key points

- Parallel lines are shown with arrows.
- Alternate angles are equal.
- Corresponding angles are equal.

△ Purposeful practice 1

1 Find the sizes of the missing angles in these diagrams.
State one of these reasons for each angle you find:

| Corresponding angles are equal. | Alternate angles are equal. | Vertically opposite angles are equal. | Angles on a straight line add to 180°. |

a

b

c

d

e

f

Reflect and reason

Here is Kai's attempt to find angle h in **Q1e**. Explain why he did not get the mark for writing the reason.

$h = 130°$ alternate

△ Purposeful practice 2

1 Find the sizes of the angles labelled with letters. Clearly state a reason for each angle you find, using the reasons from Purposeful practice 1, **Q1**, and | Angles in a triangle add to 180°. |

a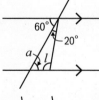

b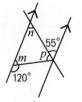

c

d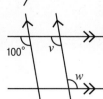

e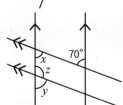

f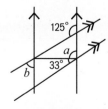

Reflect and reason

In part **c**, angle u looks like a right angle. Is it? In part **f**, angle a looks like a right angle. Is it?
In angle problems, can you assume that an angle is 90°, if it isn't labelled ⌐ ?

⊠ Problem-solving practice

1 Find the sizes of angles x and y.
Give a reason for each stage of your working.

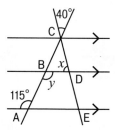

2 Here are some true statements about the angles in this diagram.
Write reasons to explain why they are true.

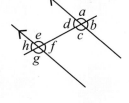

a $a = 180° - b$

b $d = h$

c $e = g$

3 Show that angles p and q add to 180°.

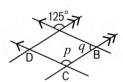

4 Show that lines ABC and DEF are not parallel.

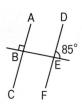

◈ Exam practice

1 Jamal needs to work out the size of angle x in this diagram.
He writes

Working	Reason
angle DEB = 119°	because corresponding angles are equal
$x = 180° - 119°$	
$x = 61°$	because angles on a straight line add up to 180°

One of Jamal's reasons is wrong.
Write down the correct reason.

(1 mark)

Adapted from 1MA1/2F, June 2018, Q15b

Exam feedback   **ResultsPlus**

In a similar question, students used incorrect language for alternate angles.

Key point

- An isosceles triangle has two equal sides and two equal angles.

△ Purposeful practice 1

1 For each isosceles triangle, write down the two equal angles.

a

b

c

d

e

f

Reflect and reason

For this triangle, Kim says, '$x = y$ because base angles of an isosceles triangle are equal.'

What mistake has Kim made?

△ Purposeful practice 2

1 For each triangle, write down whether it is

| equilateral | isosceles | scalene | right-angled |

a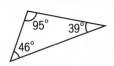

b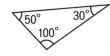

c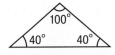

d

e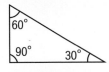

f

2 Find the missing angles in each triangle.
Which of these triangles are isosceles?

a

b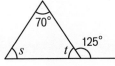

c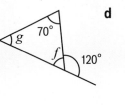

d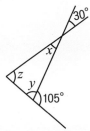

Reflect and reason

Do you need to know the side lengths to identify the type of triangle?

1   Jay draws a triangle. He says,
    'Only one of the angles of my triangle is acute.'
    Jay cannot be correct. Explain why.

2   In the diagram, ACE and BCD are straight lines.
    Show that triangle ABC is an isosceles triangle.
    Give a reason for each stage of your working.

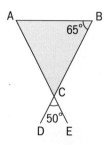

3   Triangle XYZ is isosceles.
    XY = XZ
    Find angle XZY.
    Give a reason for each stage of your working.

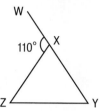

4   Here is triangle PQR with each of its sides extended.
    Show that triangle PQR is isosceles.
    Give a reason for each stage of your working.

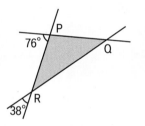

5   RST is an isosceles triangle where RS = ST.
    U lies on RT.
    RSU is an isosceles triangle where RS = RU.
    Angle SRU = 36°
    Show that triangle STU is isosceles.
    You must give a reason for each stage of your working.

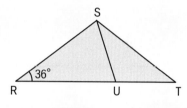

1   ABC is a straight line.
    BCD is a triangle.
    Show that triangle BCD is an isosceles triangle.
    Give a reason for each stage of your working.   **(4 marks)**

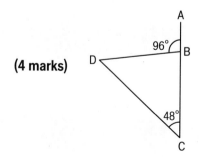

Adapted from 1MA1/3F, November 2017, Q7

Exam feedback   Results**Plus**

In a similar question, many students failed to complete the solution with a statement explaining why the
triangle is isosceles.

6.4 Exterior and interior angles

Key points

- You can draw an exterior angle of a shape by extending one of its sides.
- Alternate angles are equal.
- The sum of the exterior angles of a polygon is always 360°.

△ Purposeful practice 1

1 Copy these polygons.
   Draw all their exterior angles.

   a   **b**   **c**   **d**

Reflect and reason

Pip draws a shape and says, 'angle x is an exterior angle.'
Explain why Pip is wrong.

△ Purposeful practice 2

1 Work out the size of the angles marked with letters.

   a 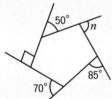 **b** 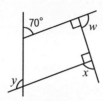 **c**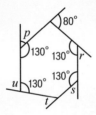

Reflect and reason

Which type of angle cannot be an exterior angle?
Explain your answer.

| acute angle | obtuse angle | reflex angle |

△ Purposeful practice 3

1 Work out the interior and exterior angles of each regular polygon.

   a equilateral triangle   **b** square   **c** octagon   **d** nonagon

Reflect and reason

Jade writes *You can find the exterior angle of a regular polygon using the formula*

$$\text{exterior angle} = \frac{360°}{\text{number of sides}}.$$ Is Jade correct? Explain.

△ Purposeful practice 4

1 Work out the number of sides of a regular polygon with the given exterior angle.

   a 10°   **b** 15°   **c** 20°   **d** 30°   **e** 72°

Reflect and reason

Explain why, for a regular polygon, $\dfrac{360°}{\text{exterior angle}}$ must be a whole number.

⊠ Problem-solving practice

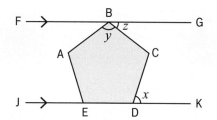

1 ABCDE is a regular pentagon.
FG and JK are parallel lines.
Find the size of each angle labelled with a letter.
You must give a reason for each answer.

2 The exterior angles of a regular polygon are equal to its interior angles.
What is the name of the polygon?

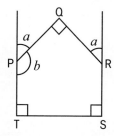

3 PQRST is an irregular pentagon.
The two angles labelled a are equal.
Work out the size of

  a angle a **b** angle b

4 Kelly measures the exterior angles of a regular polygon.
She says, 'Each exterior angle is 50°.'
Explain why Kelly is wrong.

5 Show that the exterior angle of a regular 9-sided polygon is double the exterior angle
of a regular 18-sided polygon.
Does this mean that the exterior angle of an equilateral triangle is three times the exterior angle
of a regular 9-sided polygon?
Show your working.

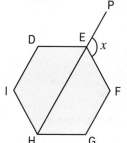

6 DEFGHI is a regular hexagon.
PEH is a straight line.
Find the size of angle x.
You must show your working.

✧ Exam practice

1 EAC, ABF and BCD are straight lines.

Work out the size of the angle marked x.
You must give reasons for your answer.

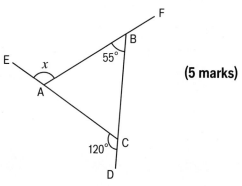

(5 marks)

Adapted from 1MA0/2F, June 2013, Q20

Exam feedback   Results**Plus**

In a similar question, few students were able to state the reasons for their calculations correctly, often
writing 'the triangle is 180°' and forgetting to state 'the angles in a triangle sum to 180°'.

6.5 More exterior and interior angles

Key point

- The angle sum of a polygon is the sum of its interior angles.

△ Purposeful practice 1

1 Copy and complete the table.

Polygon	△	▱	⬠	⬡	⬡	⬡
Number of sides	3					
Number of triangles	1	2				
Angle sum	180°	$2 \times 180° = 360°$				

Reflect and reason

Dee uses this method to calculate the angle sum of a polygon.

(number of sides − 2) × 180 = angle sum

Use your angle sums from **Q1** to explain why this works.

△ Purposeful practice 2

1 Work out the angle sum of

  a a 9-sided polygon   **b** a 10-sided polygon   **c** an 11-sided polygon

2 For each polygon

  i work out the angle sum

  ii calculate the size of the angle labelled with a letter.

a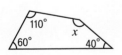

b

c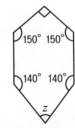

3 Work out the size of an interior angle in a

  a regular pentagon   **b** regular hexagon   **c** regular octagon

  d regular nonagon   **e** regular decagon   **f** regular 12-sided polygon

Reflect and reason

Use the words 'Interior' and 'Exterior' to complete these sentences.

_____ angles always add up to 360°.

_____ angles only add up to 360° in a quadrilateral.

1 The angle sum of a polygon is 1620°.
  How many sides does the polygon have?

2 A regular hexagon is divided into two trapeziums as shown.
  Find the size of angle n. You must show all your working.

3 The diagram shows a regular pentagon and a square.
  Find the size of the angle marked b. You must show all your working.

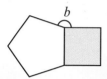

4 ABCDEFGHI is a regular nonagon.
  AC is a straight line.
  Show that angle BAC = 20°.

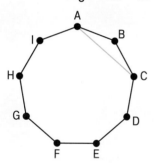

5 Find the size of angle x.

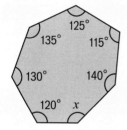

 ⟡ **Exam practice**

1 The diagram shows a regular hexagon and a regular pentagon.
  Find the size of the angle marked w
  You must show all your working.   **(3 marks)**

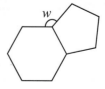

Adapted from 1MA1/2F, Specimen Papers, Set 2, Q25

Key point

- Use angle facts to write an equation. Solve the equation to find the value of the unknown.

△ Purposeful practice 1

1 **a** Find x **b** Find y **c** Find z **d** Find n

2 For each diagram

    i work out the value of the letter   **ii** write down the sizes of the angles

a   **b**   **c**   **d**

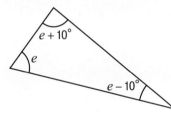 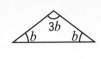 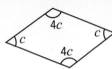 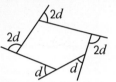

3 Work out the sizes of the angles in each diagram.

a   **b**

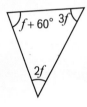 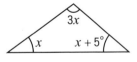

Reflect and reason

Here is Lee's working to find the angles in the triangle shown. What else does Lee need to do?

$$3x + x + x + 5° = 180°$$
$$5x + 5° = 180°$$
$$5x = 175°$$
$$x = 35°$$

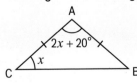

△ Purposeful practice 2

1 Find angle ACB and angle CAB.

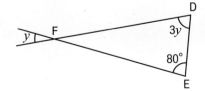

2 Find angle DFE and angle FDE.

Reflect and reason

Here is Min's working to find the value of x. What mistake has Min made?

$$3x + 2x = 180°$$
$$5x = 180°$$
$$x = 36°$$

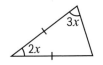

1 Work out the sizes of these angles.

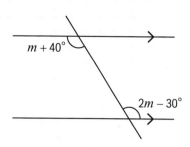

2 A and B are two identical regular hexagons.

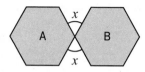

Find the size of the angles marked x.

3 Four identical regular octagons are joined to make a pattern.
Find the size of an acute angle in the shape between the octagons.

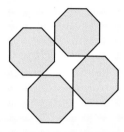

4 The size of the largest angle in a triangle is 3 times the size of the smallest angle.
The other angle is 16° less than the largest angle.
Work out, in degrees, the size of each angle in the triangle.
You must show your working.

5 ABCD is a kite with AD = AB.
Find the size of the smallest angle of the kite.

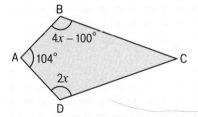

▦ ✫ Exam practice

1 ABC is a straight line.
ABE is a triangle.
EBCD is a quadrilateral.

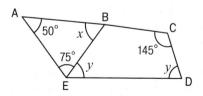

a **i** Work out the size of angle x. **(1 mark)**
  ii Give a reason for your answer. **(1 mark)**
b Work out the size of the angles marked y. **(2 marks)**

Adapted from 1MA1/3F, Specimen Papers, Set 2, Q13

7 Averages and range

7.1 Mean and range

Key points

- The mean of a set of values is the total of the set of values divided by the number of values.
- To compare two sets of data, compare an average (mode, median or mean) for each set of data and compare the range of each set of data.

△ Purposeful practice 1

Find the mean of each data set.

1 10, 10, 10, 10, 10   **2** 0, 10, 10, 10, 10   **3** 0, 0, 10, 10, 10   **4** 10, 0, 10, 10, 0

Reflect and reason

Why do the data sets in **Q3** and **Q4** have the same mean?

In **Q2**, you only need to add 4 values, because adding 0 has no effect. Why do you still need to divide by 5 to find the mean?

△ Purposeful practice 2

There are two bus routes to school. Here are the journey times on two routes, in minutes, for 5 days.

    Route 1:   4, 5, 9, 7, 20   Route 2:   10, 15, 17, 11, 12

1 Work out the range of the journey times for each route.

2 Work out the mean journey time for each route.

Reflect and reason

Adnan thinks it is most important for his journey time to school to be consistent.
Which bus route should he take? Explain.

Becki thinks it is more important to get there as quickly as possible on average.
Which route should she take? Explain.

△ Purposeful practice 3

1 Work out the mean of these numbers.
7, 7, 7, 8, 8, 9, 9, 9, 10, 10, 10, 10, 10, 10, 11, 11, 12, 13, 13, 13, 13, 14, 14, 14, 14

2 Copy and complete the table.
Work out the mean of the numbers.

Number, n	Frequency, f	$n \times f$
7	3	
8	2	
9	3	
10	6	
11	2	
12	1	
13	4	
14	4	
Total		

Reflect and reason

The data in **Q2** is the same as **Q1**. Which format helped you to calculate the mean more accurately?
Explain.

▦ ⊠ Problem-solving practice

1 Emir is finding the mean of 4 numbers.
  Here is his calculator display.

  $3+5+7+9÷4$

  17.25

  a Explain what he has done wrong.

  b Explain why he should have realised that an answer of 17.25 is wrong.

2 In a 100 m race, the mean time for 10 students was 18.75 seconds.
  Another student's time was 21 seconds.
  Work out the mean for all 11 students.
  Give your answer correct to 2 decimal places.

3 32 children are asked how many hours they spent watching TV last weekend.

Number of hours	Frequency
0	1
1	3
2	3
3	8
4	7
5	5
6	1
7	4

What is the mean amount of time spent watching TV?
Give your answer in hours and minutes.

✦ Exam practice

1 Raj and Ellen counted how many books they read each month, for six months.

	January	February	March	April	May	June
Raj	10	9	8	11	12	8
Ellen	2	10	7	14	4	10

Who read more consistently, Raj or Ellen?
Justify your answer.

(1 mark)

Adapted from 1MA1/1F, November 2017, Q10a

Exam feedback

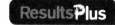

In a similar question, many students justified their answer by stating the person that had read the greater total number of books, rather than had the smaller range.

Key points

- The median is the middle value when the data is written in order.
- An outlier is an extreme data value that does not fit the overall pattern.

△ Purposeful practice 1

Find the median and the range of each set of data.

1 5, 11, 12, 17, 25　　　**2** 5, 11, 12, 14, 25　　　**3** 5, 11, 12, 14, 20

4 3, 11, 12, 14, 18　　　**5** 3, 11, 12, 14, 18, 26　　**6** 3, 11, 11, 15, 18, 26

7 3, 11, 12, 12, 18, 26　**8** −2, 11, 12, 14, 18, 26　**9** 11, 3, 18, 14, 12, 26

Reflect and reason

Are these statements always, sometimes or never true?

Changing the smallest and/or largest data values affects the median.

Changing the smallest and largest data values affects the range.

△ Purposeful practice 2

1 Here are the weights, in kilograms, of 10 newborn babies.

| 2.3 | 3.6 | 2.4 | 3.1 | 4.1 | 4.0 | 0.6 | 3.7 | 3.9 | 2.3 |

a Suggest which weight could be an outlier.

b Find the range, excluding the outlier.

c Find the median, excluding the outlier.

2 Here are two stem and leaf diagrams.
Find the median, mode and range of each data set.

a
```
21 | 4
22 | 1 2 3 3
23 | 0 0 2 3 4 5 8 9    Key
24 | 3 5 6 6 6          22|3 means 22.3
25 | 0
26 | 9
```

b
```
21 | 4
22 | 1 2 3 3
23 | 0 0 2 3 4 5 8 9    Key
24 | 3 5 6 6 6          22|3 means 223
25 | 0
26 | 9
```

Reflect and reason

In **Q2a**, the number 3 occurs most often in the stem and leaf diagram. Why is the mode not 3?

Identify an outlier in **Q2b**. Do you think it should be included when calculating the range?

1 A set of cards is numbered from 1 to 52. Five of these cards are shown, with one left blank.

    a Find a number for the blank card that would make the median 10.

    b Find a number for the blank card that would make the median 7.

    c Explain why there is only one extra value that will give a range of 16.

2 A bookshop records the number of books that they sell each day.

```
 9 | 3
10 | 0  2  5  6  7
11 | 2  2  2  4  5  6  9    Key
12 | 0  1                   9|3 means 93
13 | 6  9
```

    a Work out

       i the median

      ii the mode

     iii the range

    b The manager says the range of books sold was 6.
       Explain the error she has made.

3 Here are 5 data values.
54, 62, 68, 75, 75
Using integers, change

    a one data value so that the median changes, but the range and the mode stay the same

    b one data value so that the mean changes, but the range, mode and median stay the same

Exam practice

1 The stem and leaf diagram gives the heights, in centimetres, of 25 children.

```
12 | 0  3  5  8  9
13 | 0  2  3  3  3  5  6  7  8    Key
14 | 0  5  6  7  7  8  9          12|0 means 120 cm
15 | 0  1  3  8
```

Find the median height. **(1 mark)**

Adapted from 1MA1/3F, Specimen Papers, Set 2, Q10

Key points

- The modal class is the class with the highest frequency.
- In a frequency table, the median is in the class that contains the $\left(\frac{n+1}{2}\right)$th piece of data.

△ Purposeful practice 1

A vet weighs the cats she treats for four days, and rounds to the nearest whole kilogram.
For each day, find (in kg) the median and the mode weight.

Day 1		Day 2		Day 3		Day 4	
Weight (kg)	Frequency	Weight (kg)	Frequency	Weight (kg)	Frequency	Weight (kg)	Frequency
1	5	1	5	1	5	1	0
2	5	2	5	2	5	2	1
3	11	3	5	3	5	3	2
4	5	4	11	4	5	4	3
5	5	5	5	5	11	5	4

Reflect and reason

Elizabeth says the median for Day 1 is 11. Explain her error.

△ Purposeful practice 2

Dev records the number of cars that pass every minute on his street. Daisy records the number of cars that pass every minute on her street.

Dev's record			Daisy's record	
Number of cars	Frequency		Number of cars	Frequency
0–4	3		0–4	9
5–9	8		5–9	7
10–14	9		10–14	5
15–19	4		15–19	1
20–24	2		20–24	0

For each set of data, write down

1 The modal class.

2 How many pieces of data are recorded in the table.

3 The class interval that contains the median.

Reflect and reason

Dev says that the mode for his results is 9. Explain his error.

Explain why, for grouped data, it is called the modal class and not the mode.

⊠ Problem-solving practice

1 The table shows the heights of plants in an experiment.
   Show that the median height is between 35 cm and 40 cm.

Height, h (cm)	Frequency
$30 \leqslant h < 35$	3
$35 \leqslant h < 40$	7
$40 \leqslant h < 45$	8
$45 \leqslant h < 50$	0
$50 \leqslant h < 55$	1

2 Jo records how many minutes late the bus is for six days
   during two separate weeks.

   1st Week: 2, 2, 4, 6, 9, 10

   2nd Week: 3, 4, 4, 8, 9, 35

   a Calculate the mean and median for each week.

   b Which measure is least useful for comparing the two
      weeks? Explain why.

3 Here is a table of the favourite sports that 16 scouts play in their spare time.

Sport	Frequency
Football	5
Rugby	4
Hockey	4
Basketball	3

   a Which statistical measure is best for comparing this with data from another scout troop?

   b Which statistical measures cannot be calculated from this categorical data? Why not?

✦ Exam practice

1 Sam works as a sales assistant in a clothes shop and records the size of each item
   sold one morning.

   8

   10 10

   12 12 12

   14 14 14 14 14 14

   16 16 16 16 16

   18 18 18

   20 20

   22 22

   24

   The sizes are always even numbers. The mean size of the items sold that morning is 15.6.
   Sam says, 'The mean size of the items is **not** a very useful average.'

   a Explain why she is right.

   b Which is the more useful average for Sam to use, the median or the mode?
      Give a reason for your answer.   **(2 marks)**

   Adapted from 1MA1/2F, Specimen Papers, Set 1, Q10

Key point

- When the data is grouped, you cannot calculate an exact value for the mean, but you can calculate an estimate for the mean.

⚠ Purposeful practice 1

Work out an estimate of the mean for the data in each table. Give your answers rounded to 1 d.p.

1

Class	Frequency
$0 \leqslant x < 10$	4
$10 \leqslant x < 20$	4
$20 \leqslant x < 30$	4
$30 \leqslant x < 40$	4
$40 \leqslant x < 50$	4

2

Class	Frequency
$0 \leqslant x < 10$	0
$10 \leqslant x < 20$	4
$20 \leqslant x < 30$	4
$30 \leqslant x < 40$	4
$40 \leqslant x < 50$	4

3

Class	Frequency
$0 \leqslant x < 10$	0
$10 \leqslant x < 20$	4
$20 \leqslant x < 30$	4
$30 \leqslant x < 40$	4
$40 \leqslant x < 50$	0

4

Class	Frequency
$0 \leqslant x < 10$	4
$10 \leqslant x < 20$	4
$20 \leqslant x < 30$	0
$30 \leqslant x < 40$	4
$40 \leqslant x < 50$	4

5

Class	Frequency
$0 \leqslant x < 10$	1
$10 \leqslant x < 20$	2
$20 \leqslant x < 30$	3
$30 \leqslant x < 40$	4
$40 \leqslant x < 50$	5

6

Class	Frequency
$100 \leqslant x < 110$	1
$110 \leqslant x < 120$	2
$120 \leqslant x < 130$	3
$130 \leqslant x < 140$	4
$140 \leqslant x < 150$	5

Reflect and reason

Why can we ignore the row with frequency of 0 in **Q2**?
What is different about the values of x in **Q5** and **Q6**? How does this affect the mean?

⚠ Purposeful practice 2

Here is a data set: 1, 2, 3, 6, 7, 9, 10, 11, 11, 13, 14, 18, 19, 20, 22, 24

1 Find the mean of this data set.

2 The data set has been grouped into two frequency tables, using different class widths.
Work out an estimate of the mean in each case.

a

Class	Frequency
$0 \leqslant x < 10$	6
$10 \leqslant x < 20$	7
$20 \leqslant x < 30$	3

b

Class	Frequency
$0 \leqslant x < 5$	3
$5 \leqslant x < 10$	3
$10 \leqslant x < 15$	5
$15 \leqslant x < 20$	2
$20 \leqslant x < 25$	3
$25 \leqslant x < 30$	0

Reflect and reason

Is the answer to **Q2a** or **Q2b** closer to the mean from **Q1**?
Is the answer to **Q2a** less accurate than the answer to **Q2b**? Why?
How would you change the class widths to make the estimated mean more accurate?

▨ Problem-solving practice

1 A restaurant manager records the number of complaints that customers make per day.
Work out

a the estimated range

b the class that contains the median

c an estimate of the mean

Number of complaints	Frequency
0 to 4	4
5 to 9	5
10 to 14	4
15 to 19	7

2 The frequency in the class $60 \leqslant x < 70$ has been lost. An estimate of the mean is 80.
Find the missing frequency.

Class	Frequency
$50 \leqslant x < 60$	1
$60 \leqslant x < 70$	
$70 \leqslant x < 80$	2
$80 \leqslant x < 90$	4
$90 \leqslant x < 100$	4

✦ Exam practice

1 The table shows information about how much money 20 people spent on new televisions.

Amount spent (£x)	Frequency
$200 < x \leqslant 250$	3
$250 < x \leqslant 300$	8
$300 < x \leqslant 350$	7
$350 < x \leqslant 450$	0
$450 < x \leqslant 500$	2

a Work out an estimate for the mean amount spent.   **(3 marks)**

Terry says, 'The mean may **not** be the best average to use to represent this information.'

b Do you agree with Terry?
You must justify your answer.   **(1 mark)**

Adapted from 1MA1/1F, November 2017, Q27

Exam feedback   ResultsPlus

Q1b: In a similar question, many students suggested a different average to use, rather than justifying why the mean average was not appropriate to use.

Key points

- In a survey, a sample is taken to represent the population. A sample that is too small can bias the results.
- In a random sample, every member of the population has an equal chance of being included.

△ Purposeful practice 1

State what is meant by the **population** in each question.

Julie wants to find the average height of

1   12-year-olds in Year 7 in her school

2   a Year 7 class in her school

3   all Year 7 students in Cardiff schools

4   all Year 7 students who live in Cardiff

5   all Year 7 students in Lancashire schools

6   all Year 7 students in Scottish schools

Reflect and reason

Explain why a student in the population of **Q3** may not be in the population of **Q4**.

△ Purposeful practice 2

1   Chris wants to gather a random sample from students in his year group.
    Describe how he would select the data.

2   The Government carries out a national census in the UK to get accurate, detailed information about the UK population. This takes place every 10 years.
    Suggest why the Government does not carry out the census more frequently.

3   During a general election, the media carries out surveys to predict the election result.
    A newspaper plans to take a survey of 20 people outside a polling station at midday.

    a   Explain why the sample may be biased.

    b   Suggest a way they could improve the accuracy of the results.

4   Dan is carrying out a survey to find out how many calories people consume each day.
    He carries out the survey at the local gym. Explain why his sample may not be representative.

Reflect and reason

Complete the sentences using the words in the list.

quicker	census	expensive	bias
time-consuming	representative	more accurate	cheaper

If a sample is too small, it can _____ the results.

Data gathered that includes every element of the population is called a _____.

An unbiased sample will be _____ of the whole population.

Taking a sample can be _____ and _____ than carrying out a census.

Carrying out a census can be _____ and _____ but the results will be _____ than a sample.

1   There is a choice of 10 different sandwiches in a shop.
    The owner notes down the sandwiches chosen by 5 randomly selected customers to help him
    decide what to order the next day.

    a   Explain why the sample is not representative.

    b   How can the owner decrease the bias?

2   An engineering company makes steel beams.
    They want to find out the average length of the beams.
    They make 100 beams and find the average of the last 10 beams.
    Explain why this may not be a representative sample.

3   Josh is carrying out a survey to find the most popular rides at a theme park.
    He surveys 20 people at 10 am near the biggest roller coaster.

    a   Give reasons why his sample may be biased.

    b   Suggest how he could improve the survey.

4   Data in the sample is missing.
    The data has been used to predict that out of 800 cars:
    320 will be diesel
    10% will be electric.
    Find the missing data from the sample.

Engine type	Sample Frequency
Diesel	
Petrol	
Electric	5

✧ Exam practice

1   Joan predicts 1200 people will attend a music festival.
    Joan is organising the music playlist.
    She takes a sample of 60 people who will be there to see what music they like.
    She asks each person to tell her one type of music they want to hear.
    The table shows her results.

Choice	Number of people
Rock	20
Hip hop	15
Dance	8
Rap	17

Work out how many people will like rock music.
Write any assumptions you make and explain how this could affect your answer.   **(3 marks)**

8 Perimeter, area and volume 1

8.1 Rectangles, parallelograms and triangles

Key points

- The base of a parallelogram is b and its perpendicular height is h.
  Area of a parallelogram = base length × perpendicular height
  $$A = bh$$

- Area of a triangle $= \frac{1}{2} \times$ base length $(b) \times$ perpendicular height (h)
  $$A = \frac{1}{2}bh$$

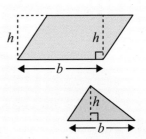

▲ Purposeful practice 1

Calculate the area of each parallelogram.

1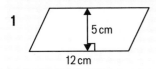

2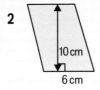

3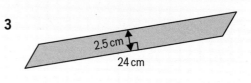

Reflect and reason

What do you notice about the area of the parallelograms in **Q1–3**? Explain why this happens.

▲ Purposeful practice 2

Calculate the area of each triangle.

1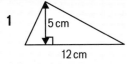

2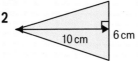

3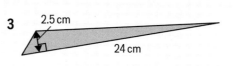

Reflect and reason

What do you notice about the relationship between the area of a parallelogram and the area of a triangle? Use your answers to Purposeful practice 1 and 2 to help you.

▲ Purposeful practice 3

Calculate the area of each shape.

1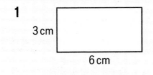

2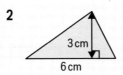

3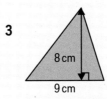

4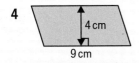

5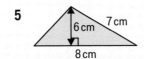

6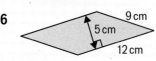

Reflect and reason

How did you know which lengths to use for the shapes in **Q5** and **Q6**?

⊠ Problem-solving practice

1 A parallelogram has an area of 40 cm² and a base of 8 cm.
  Work out the perpendicular height of the parallelogram.

2 The triangle has an area of 36 cm².
  Work out the missing length x.

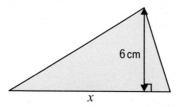

3 Sketch and label three triangles that have areas of 30 cm².

4 These isosceles and right-angled triangles have the same area.

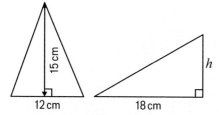

  Work out the height h of the right-angled triangle.

5 Kemi makes a kite from two triangular pieces of fabric.
  The height of the kite is 58 cm.
  Calculate the area of fabric that Kemi uses.

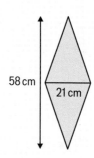

✦ Exam practice

1 Here are a triangle and a rectangle.
  The area of the rectangle is 4 times the area
  of the triangle.
  Work out the width w of the rectangle. **(4 marks)**

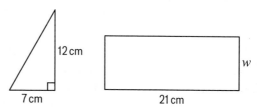

  Adapted from 1MA1/1F, May 2017, Q15

2 The base of a parallelogram is twice as long as the height of the parallelogram.
  The area of the parallelogram is 18 cm².
  Sketch an appropriate parallelogram, labelling its base and height measurements clearly.

  (2 marks)

  Adapted from 1MA1/1F, November 2017, Q8

Exam feedback   ResultsPlus

Q1: Most students who achieved a Grade 5 answered a similar question well.
Q2: In a similar question, many students gave measurements where the base and height were in the
  correct ratio, but that did not give a parallelogram with the correct area.

Key points

- This trapezium has parallel sides a and b and perpendicular height h. Two trapezia put together make a parallelogram, with base $(a + b)$ and perpendicular height h.
- Area of 2 trapezia = base × perpendicular height = $(a + b) \times h$
- Area of a trapezium = $\frac{1}{2}(a+b)h$

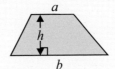
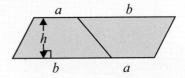

⚠ Purposeful practice

1   Here is a parallelogram made from two identical trapezia.

   a   What is the measurement of the base of the parallelogram?

   b   Work out the total area of the parallelogram.

   c   Calculate the area of one trapezium.

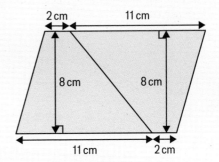

2   Here is a parallelogram made from two identical trapezia.

   a   Work out the total area of the parallelogram.

   b   Calculate the area of one trapezium.

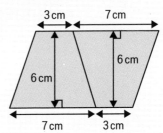

3   Here is a parallelogram made from two identical trapezia.

   Calculate the area of one trapezium.

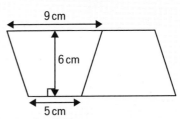

4   Calculate the area of each trapezium.

   a

   b

   c

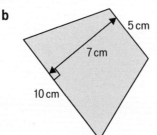
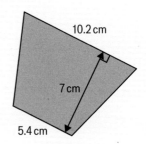

Reflect and reason

Compare your method for working out the area of each trapezium in **Q1–3** with your method for working out the area of each trapezium in **Q4**.

What was the same and what was different about your methods?

1 The area of the trapezium is 52.5 mm². Work out the height x of the trapezium.

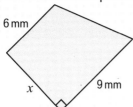

2 The diagram shows the cross-section of a boat.
   Calculate the area of the cross-section of the boat in m².

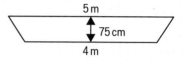

3 The rectangle and trapezium have the same area.
   Work out the height h of the rectangle.

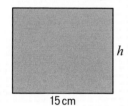 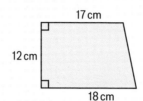

4 This shape is a regular hexagon made by joining two trapezia together.
   Calculate the area of the hexagon.

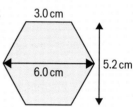

▦ ✦ **Exam practice**

1 Here is a trapezium drawn on a centimetre grid.

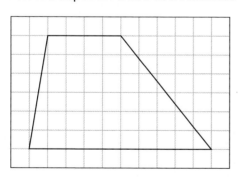

   The area of a triangle is half the area of the trapezium.
   Sketch an appropriate triangle, labelling its base and height measurements clearly.   **(2 marks)**

   Adapted from 1MA1/3F, June 2018, Q21

Exam feedback   Results **Plus**

In a similar question, many students gave the base and height measurements for a triangle with the same area as the trapezium.

8.3 Area of compound shapes

△ Purposeful practice

1 This compound shape is split into two rectangles, A and B.

   a The length of rectangle A is 12 cm. Write down the width of rectangle A.

   b Work out the area of rectangle A.

   c Write down the length and width of rectangle B.

   d Work out the area of rectangle B.

   e Work out the total area of the compound shape.

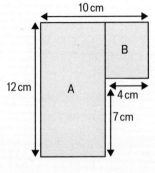

2 Here is a compound shape split into two rectangles, C and D.

   a Write down the lengths and widths of rectangles C and D.

   b Work out the areas of rectangles C and D.

   c Work out the total area of the compound shape.

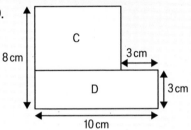

3 Here is a compound shape split into two rectangles, E and F.

   a Work out the areas of rectangles E and F.

   b Work out the total area of the compound shape.

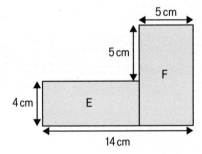

4 Work out the area of each compound shape.

   a

   b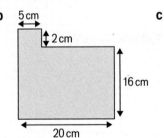

   c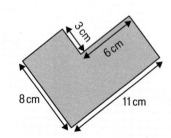

Reflect and reason

For **Q4a**, Joe writes

The total area is

12 × 2 + 11 × 2 = 24 + 22

       24 + 22 = 46'

Explain why Joe is incorrect.

⊠ Problem-solving practice

1 Here are two shapes made from rectangles and triangles.

Shape A   Shape B

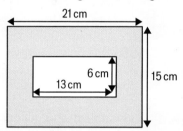

Which compound shape has the bigger area? By how much?

2 The shaded region in the diagram is formed by cutting out a smaller rectangle from a larger rectangle.

Work out the area of the shaded region in the diagram.

3 The diagram shows a plan of Caily's garden.
Caily is going to cover the garden with wooden decking.
The decking is sold in packs. One pack of decking will cover 1.75 m².
Work out how many packs of wooden decking Caily needs.
You must show all your working.

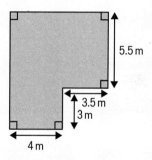

⬚ Exam practice

1 Here is a shape made from a rectangle and a triangle.

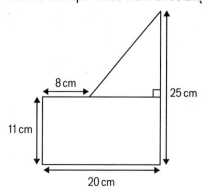

Work out the total area of the shape.   **(3 marks)**

Adapted from 1MA1/3F, Autumn 2017, Mock Set 3, Q13

Key points

- A prism is a 3D solid that has the same cross-section all through its length.
- The surface area of a 3D solid is the total area of all its faces.
- To find the surface area of a 3D solid, sketch the net and work out the areas of the faces.

⚠ Purposeful practice

1 The diagram shows a cuboid and its net.

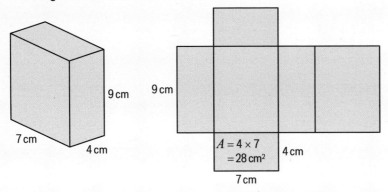

a Copy the net and complete the labels for the length and width of each rectangle.

b Work out the areas of all six rectangles on the net.

c Work out the total surface area of the cuboid.

2 For each cuboid, sketch its net and then use the net to work out the surface area.

a 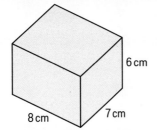   b 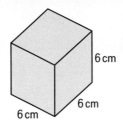   c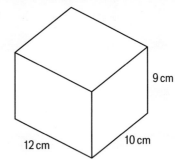

3 For each prism, sketch its net and then use the net to work out the surface area.

a 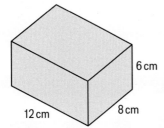   b 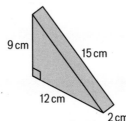   c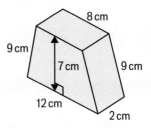

Reflect and reason

Explain how a sketch of a net helps you to work out the total surface area of a solid.

1 The diagram shows a cuboid.

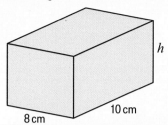

The cuboid has a width of 8 cm and a length of 10 cm.
The cuboid has a total surface area of 412 cm².
Work out the height h of the cuboid.

2 The cross-section of a swimming pool is in
the shape of a trapezium.
The inside four walls of the pool are to be tiled.
The tiles cost £8 per m².
Calculate the cost of tiling the four walls.

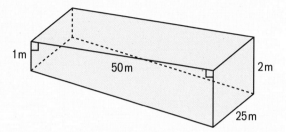

3 A cube has a surface area of 294 cm².
Work out the side length of the cube.

4 The cuboids A and B have the same surface area.

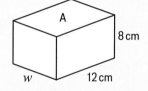 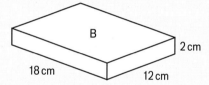

Work out the width w of cuboid A.

⊞ ⊠ **Exam practice**

1 Five identical wooden blocks are to be varnished.
Each block is a cuboid 10 cm by 180 cm by 185 cm.

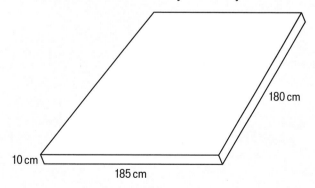

A can of varnish covers 6 m².
How many cans of varnish are required to cover all five blocks? **(5 marks)**

Adapted from 1MA1/3F, Spring 2017, Mock Set 2, Q19a

8.5 Volume of prisms

Key points

- The volume of a 3D solid is the amount of space inside it.
- Volume is measured in cubic units: millimetres cubed (mm^3), centimetres cubed (cm^3), metres cubed (m^3).
- Volume of a cuboid = length × width × height = lwh
- Volume of a prism = area of cross-section × length

△ Purposeful practice 1

1   These cuboids are made of centimetre cubes.
    Work out the number of centimetre cubes in each cuboid.

a   b   c

2   Work out the volume of each cuboid.

a 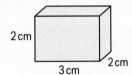   b 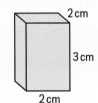   c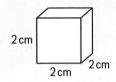

Reflect and reason

How is the number of cubes in each part of **Q1** related to the volumes in **Q2**?

△ Purposeful practice 2

1   Work out the volume of each prism.

a 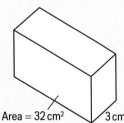   b 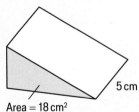   c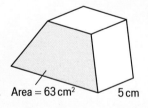

2   Work out the volume of each prism.

a 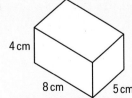   b 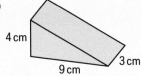   c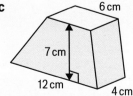

Reflect and reason

What is the same and what is different about finding the volume of the prisms in **Q1** and **Q2**?

1   The area of the cross-section of a prism is 9.5 cm².
    The prism is 10 cm long.
    Work out the volume of the prism.

2   A cube has a surface area of 54 cm².

    a   Work out the side length of the cube.

    b   Work out the volume of the cube.

3   The diagram shows a plan of the foundations of a house.
    The foundations are in the shape of a rectangle
    that measures 10 m by 15 m, and is 1 m wide.
    It is 1.5 m deep.

    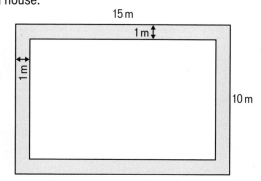

    a   Work out how many cubic metres of concrete
        are needed to fill the foundations.

    b   Concrete costs £72 per cubic metre.
        How much will the concrete cost?

✧ Exam practice

1   The total surface area of a cube is 384 cm².
    Work out the volume of the cube.   **(4 marks)**

Adapted from 1MA1/1F, November 2017, Q13

2   The diagram shows a cube of side length 5 cm.

    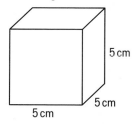

    Sian says, 'The volume of any solid made with 8 of these cubes is 1000 cm³.'

    a   Is Sian correct?
        You must show your working.   **(2 marks)**

    b   i   Draw a cuboid that can be made with 8 of these cubes.
            Write the dimensions of the cuboid on your diagram.   **(1 mark)**

        ii Work out the surface area of your cuboid.   **(2 marks)**

Adapted from 1MA1/3F, June 2017, Q12

Exam feedback

Q1: In a similar question, many students did not realise that they needed to start by working out the
         area of a single face of the cube from the total surface area.

Q2a: In a similar question, many students did all the correct calculations, but lost a mark because they
         forgot to state whether or not Sian was correct.

8.6 More volume and surface area

Key points

- Volume is measured in mm³, cm³ or m³. 1 cm³ = 1000 mm³. These two cubes have the same volume.

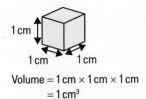

Volume = 1 cm × 1 cm × 1 cm
= 1 cm³

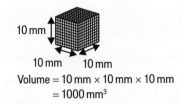

Volume = 10 mm × 10 mm × 10 mm
= 1000 mm³

Purposeful practice 1

1 Work out the volume of each 3D solid, giving your answers in the unit stated.

a in cm³

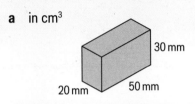

b in cm³

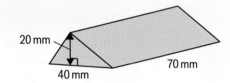

c in m³

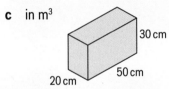

d in m³

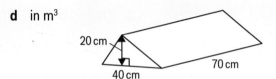

> **Reflect and reason**
>
> What is the same and what is different when finding the volumes of these 3D solids?

Purposeful practice 2

1 Work out the volume of each prism, giving your answers in the unit stated.

a in mm³

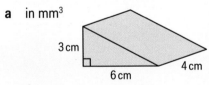

b in mm³

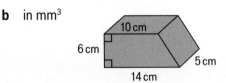

c in cm³

d in cm³

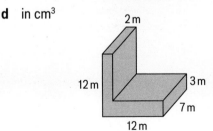

> **Reflect and reason**
>
> Did you divide or multiply to work out the correct volume dimensions? Why is this different from the questions in Purposeful practice 1?

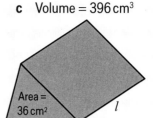

⊠ Problem-solving practice

1 Work out the length l of each triangular prism.

 a   Volume = $180\,cm^3$ **b**   Volume = $378\,cm^3$ **c**   Volume = $396\,cm^3$

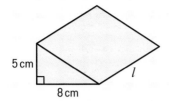

2 Lee has some soft clay in the shape of a cuboid, shown below.

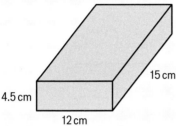

Lee reshapes his clay into another cuboid, shown below.
The cross-section of the new cuboid is a 60 mm by 60 mm.

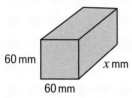

Work out the value of x.

3 A company makes dice that are all 2 cm cubes.
The dice are going to be packed into cuboid-shaped boxes.
The size of a box is 20 cm by 12 cm by 5 cm.
Will 150 dice fit in the box?
You must give reasons for your answer.

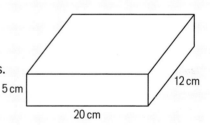

⊠ Exam practice

1 Kyle puts wooden blocks into boxes.
Each box is a cuboid, x cm by 12 cm by 20 cm.
Each block is a cuboid, 2 cm by 2 cm by 20 cm.
96 blocks completely fill a box.
Work out the value of x.   **(4 marks)**

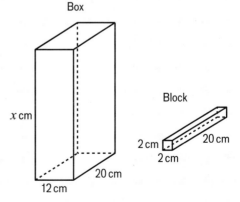

Adapted from 1MA0/1F, May 2017, Q18

Exam feedback   Results**Plus**

In a similar question, many students calculated the volume of the box but did not divide this by the cross-sectional area of the box to find the value of x.

Mixed exercises B

Mixed problem-solving practice B

1 The first four terms in an arithmetic sequence are

1   5   9   13

Esme thinks that the number 35 is in this sequence.
Is Esme correct? Show your working.

2 Here are a rectangle and a square.

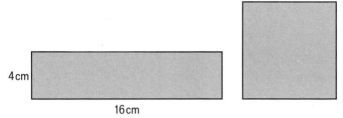

The area of the rectangle is the same as the area of the square.
Work out the length of one side of the square.

3 Amelia thinks of a number.
She subtracts 5 and then multiplies by 3. The answer is 21.
What number did Amelia think of?

4 Here are the first three terms of a sequence.

13   22   31

a   i Write down the next term in the sequence.

ii Explain how you got your answer.

b Work out the 12th term of the sequence.

5 Look at the angles. Work out the value of x.

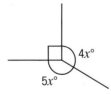

6 Here are a trapezium and a rectangle.

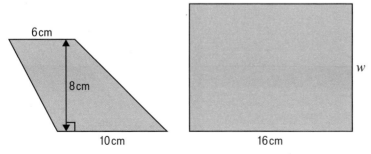

The area of the rectangle is three times the area of the trapezium.
Work out the width w of the rectangle.

7 Ethan puts wooden blocks into boxes.
Each box is a cuboid x cm by 12 cm by 10 cm.
Each block is a cuboid 2 cm by 4 cm by 5 cm.
36 blocks completely fill a box.
Work out the value of x.

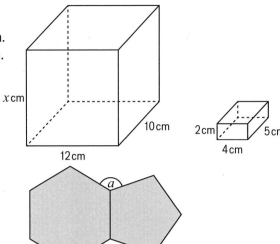

8 Here are two different regular shapes.
Work out the size of the angle marked a.

9 Here is a set of five cards.
There is a different whole number from 0 to 9 on each card.
The number on the last card is hidden.
The median of the numbers on the five cards is 5.

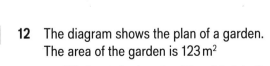

a Which whole number should be on the last card?
Three different cards each have a number on them.
The mode of the three numbers is 7.
The mean of the three numbers is 10.

b Work out the number on each of the three cards.

10 ABCD is a parallelogram.
CBE is a straight line.
F is the point on DE so that DFE is a straight line.
Angle ADE = 35°
Angle BCD = 105°
Work out angle BEF.
Give a reason for each stage of your working.

11 A 4-sided spinner labelled A, B, C and D is spun.
The pie chart shows the proportion of times the spinner lands on each letter.
The spinner is spun 720 times.
How many times does the spinner land on the letter D?

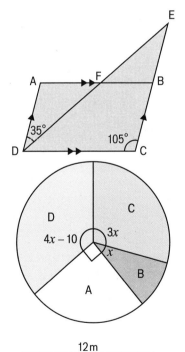

12 The diagram shows the plan of a garden.
The area of the garden is 123 m²

a Work out the length of the side labelled x.

70% of the garden is going to be a lawn.
Turf for a lawn is sold in square metres and costs £1.85 per square metre.

b Work out the cost of turf for the lawn.

13 Jakub and Kate have a spelling test each week.
The table shows their scores for each test during one half of a term.

Jakub	8	10	9	7	10	8
Kate	3	7	5	10	4	6

Who had the most consistent scores, Jakub or Kate?
Give a reason for your answer.

14 A triangle has an angle of 55°.
The triangle has a second angle, x, which is obtuse.
Write down an inequality that shows the possible integer sizes of x.

  ⊗ **Exam practice**

15 The total surface area of a cube is 486 cm².

Work out the volume of the cube. **(4 marks)**

Adapted from 1MA1/1F, November 2017, Q13

⊗ **Exam practice**

16 Here are the first six terms of an arithmetic sequence.

6   13   20   27   34   41

Find an expression, in terms of n, for the nth term of this sequence. **(2 marks)**

Adapted from 1MA1/2F, June 2017, Q25a

Exam feedback   Results**Plus**

Most students who achieved a **Grade 5** answered a similar question well.

⊗ **Exam practice**

17 ABCDEF is a hexagon.
The angle x is 5 times greater than
angle ABC.
Work out the size of the interior
angle DEF.
You must show all your working. **(5 marks)**

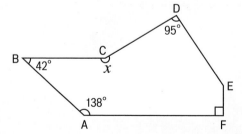

Adapted from 1MA1/3F, June 2018, Q26

Exam feedback   Results**Plus**

In a similar question, the majority of students did not know the sum of the interior angles of a hexagon
and some failed to spot that there was an angle of 90°.

18 The table shows information about the ages of 50 people who use a gym.

Age	Frequency
$15 < a \leqslant 25$	24
$25 < a \leqslant 35$	15
$35 < a \leqslant 45$	4
$45 < a \leqslant 55$	0
$55 < a \leqslant 65$	5
$65 < a \leqslant 75$	2

a Work out an estimate for the mean of the ages. **(3 marks)**

Zane says, 'The mean may not be the best average to use to represent this information.'

b Do you agree with Zane?
Justify your answer. **(1 mark)**

Adapted from 1MA1/1F, November 2017, Q27

Exam feedback **ResultsPlus**

In a similar question, students were encouraged to check their answer for **Q18a** was sensible, as a mean outside the data range is not. Most students commented on the accuracy of the answer in **Q18b** and not about the appropriateness of the mean average.

 Exam practice

19 The size of the largest angle in a triangle is 5 times the size of the smallest angle.
The other angle is 29° less than the largest angle.
Work out, in degrees, the size of each angle in the triangle.
You must show your working. **(5 marks)**

Adapted from 1MA1/3F, June 2017, Q13

Exam feedback **ResultsPlus**

Most students who achieved a **Grade 5** answered a similar question well.

 Exam practice

20 Here is a rectangle.
All measurements are in centimetres.
The area of the rectangle is $95\,cm^2$.
Show that $y = 5$

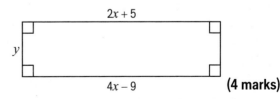

(4 marks)

Adapted from 1MA1/1F, November 2017, Q28

Exam feedback **ResultsPlus**

In a similar question, it was common for students to confuse area and perimeter. An equation for perimeter was incorrectly set equal to the area value.

9 Graphs

9.1 Coordinates

Key points

- On the line with equation $y = 1$, the y-coordinate is always 1. The line is parallel to the x-axis.
- On the line with equation $x = 3$, the x-coordinate is always 3. The line is parallel to the y-axis.
- The midpoint of a line segment is the point exactly in the middle of the line.

△ Purposeful practice 1

1   x can take values 1, 2 or 3.

   y can take values 3, 4 or 5.

   Form three different pairs of coordinates in the form (x, y).

2   Here is a set of incomplete coordinates.

   $(-4, \Box), (-3, \Box), (-2, \Box), (-1, \Box), (0, \Box), (1, \Box), (2, \Box), (3, \Box), (4, \Box)$

   Complete the set of coordinates for each of these lines.

   a $y = -3$ **b** $y = 0$ **c** $y = 3$

   d $y = x$ **e** $y = 2x$ **f** $y = -2x$

3   Here is a set of incomplete coordinates.

   $(\Box, -4), (\Box, -3), (\Box, -2), (\Box, -1), (\Box, 0), (\Box, 1), (\Box, 2) (\Box, 3) (\Box, 4)$

   Complete the set of coordinates for each of these lines.

   a $x = -3$ **b** $x = 0$ **c** $x = 3$

   d $y = x$ **e** $y = 2x$ **f** $y = -2x$

Reflect and reason

For which equations is the value of y constant? How could you describe these lines?

For the lines $y = x$, $y = 2x$ and $y = -2x$, how does the value of y depend on the value of x?

△ Purposeful practice 2

Draw a coordinate grid with both axes labelled from -8 to $+8$.

Using your answers from Purposeful practice 1, draw and label these graphs.

   1 $y = -3$ **2** $y = 0$ **3** $y = 3$

   4 $y = x$ **5** $y = 2x$ **6** $y = -2x$

Reflect and reason

How can you draw the line with the equation $y = -5$ without plotting coordinates first?

What about the line $x = 2$?

---

1 The points A, B and C are three vertices of a kite.
Find the coordinates of the fourth vertex of the kite.

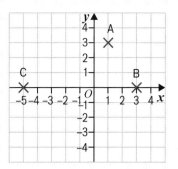

2 The graphs of $y = 3$, $y = 7$ and $x = 1$ are three sides of a square.
Find the equation of the fourth side of the square.

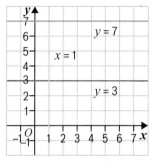

3 Name the shape enclosed by the lines $x = 5$, $y = 1$ and $y = x$.

4 a Show that the graphs of $y = x$ and $y = -x$ are perpendicular to each other.
  b Write down the coordinates where the graphs of $y = x$ and $y = -x$ cross each other.

5 a Draw a coordinate grid with x-axis and y-axis labelled between -3 and 8.
  b i Draw a line segment from $(-2, 0)$ to $(-2, 6)$.
    ii Find the midpoint of this line segment.
  c Find the midpoint of the line segment with end points $(-1, 0)$ and $(3, 4)$.
  d Draw a line segment with one end at $(0, 3)$ and midpoint at $(3, 3)$.

✦ Exam practice

1 a Write down the coordinates of point B.   **(1 mark)**

  b Copy the grid and draw the line with equation $y = -3$.   **(1 mark)**

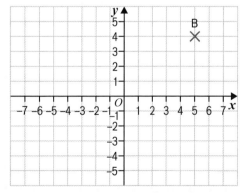

Adapted from 1MA1/1F, November 2017, Q7a and Q7c

Exam feedback   Results**Plus**

Q1b: In a similar question, many students drew a horizontal line through $(-3, 0)$. This is the line $x = -3$.
Some students just plotted the point $(0, -3)$ and drew no line.

Key point

- A table of values shows x and y values for the equation of a line.

△ Purposeful practice 1

Copy and complete the table of values for each line.
Write the coordinate pairs from each table.

1

x	−2	−1	0	1	2
$y = 2$					

$(-2, \Box)$ $(-1, \Box)$ $(0, \Box)$ $(1, \Box)$ $(2, \Box)$

2

x	−2	−1	0	1	2
$y = x$					

$(-2, \Box)$ $(-1, \Box)$ $(0, \Box)$ $(1, \Box)$ $(2, \Box)$

3

x	−2	−1	0	1	2
$y = 2x$					

$(\Box, \Box)$ $(\Box, \Box)$ $(\Box, \Box)$ $(\Box, \Box)$ $(\Box, \Box)$

4

x	−2	−1	0	1	2
$y = 2x + 1$					

$(\Box, \Box)$ $(\Box, \Box)$ $(\Box, \Box)$ $(\Box, \Box)$ $(\Box, \Box)$

5

x	−2	−1	0	1	2
$y = 2x - 1$					

$(\Box, \Box)$ $(\Box, \Box)$ $(\Box, \Box)$ $(\Box, \Box)$ $(\Box, \Box)$

Reflect and reason

Explain in words what you do to the value of x to calculate the value of y in **Q5**.

△ Purposeful practice 2

1 Draw a coordinate grid with both axes labelled from −5 to +5.
Plot the coordinates you found in Purposeful practice 1 to draw the graphs of

   a $y = 2x$ **b** $y = 2x + 1$ **c** $y = 2x - 1$

2 a Copy and complete a table of values like the ones in Purposeful practice 1 for

   i $y = -2x$ **ii** $y = -2x + 1$ **iii** $y = -2x - 1$

  b Draw these graphs on a coordinate grid with both axes labelled from −5 to +5.

   i $y = -2x$ **ii** $y = -2x + 1$ **iii** $y = -2x - 1$

Reflect and reason

Compare your graphs in **Q1** and **Q2**. What is the same and what is different?

1   For each line, work out the value of y when $x = 2$.
    Write your answers as coordinates.

    a $y = -4$ **b** $y = 2x - 4$ **c** $y = 3x + 2$ **d** $y = -3x - 2$

2   **a** Complete the table of values for $y = \frac{1}{2}x$

x	−2	−1	0	1	2
$y = \frac{1}{2}x$					

   b Draw a coordinate grid with both axes labelled from −2 to +2
         and plot the graph of $y = \frac{1}{2}x$.

3   For each line graph (A, B, C and D), find the value of y when $x = 2$.
    Write your answers as coordinates.

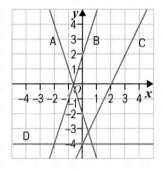

1   Here are six straight-line graphs.

Graph A

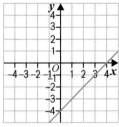

Graph B

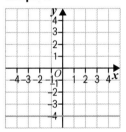

Graph C

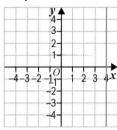

Graph D

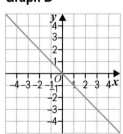

Graph E

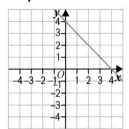

Graph F

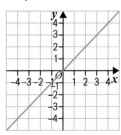

Match each equation with the correct graph.

a $x = 4$ **b** $y = x - 4$ **c** $y = -x$ **(2 marks)**

Adapted from 1MA1/3F, June 2018, Q13

Exam feedback   ResultsPlus

Most students who achieved a **Grade 5** answered a similar question well.

Key points

- The steepness of a graph is called the gradient.
- To find the gradient, work out how many units the graph goes up for each unit it goes across.
- Positive gradient ⟋   Negative gradient ⟍
- In the equation of a straight line the coefficient of x is the gradient of the line.

⚠ Purposeful practice 1

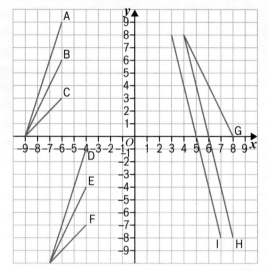

The diagram shows nine line segments labelled A to I.

1 Which line segments have positive gradients?

2 Which line segments have negative gradients?

3 Identify one pair of parallel line segments.

4 The gradient of line segment A is $\frac{9}{3} = 3$.
   Find the gradient of lines B to I.

Reflect and reason

What are the gradients of the two parallel line segments you found in **Q3**?

Compare the gradients of the other parallel lines. What do you notice about the gradients of parallel lines?

⚠ Purposeful practice 2

1 Work out the gradients of these line segments.

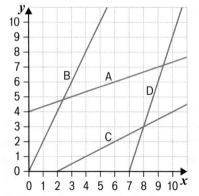

2 The equations of the lines in **Q1** are

$$y = 3x - 21$$

$$y = \frac{1}{3x} + 4$$

$$y = 2x$$

$$y = \frac{1}{2x} - 1$$

Match the equations with the lines.

Reflect and reason

What do you notice about the gradient of each line and its equation?

1 Line A has gradient 3.
  Line B has gradient 4.
  Which line is steeper? Explain how you know.

2 On a grid draw lines with these gradients.
  a Line C with gradient 2
  b Line D with gradient −3
  c Line E with gradient $-\frac{1}{2}$
  d Line F with gradient $\frac{1}{2}$
  e Line G with gradient 3

3 On a coordinate grid, draw the line with gradient 3 that passes through the point (0, 2).

4 For each of the line segments, find the missing value.

a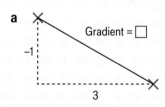

b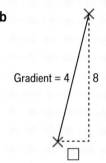

c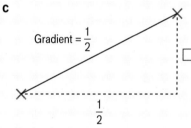

1 Here are the equations of five straight lines.
  Line A: $y = 3x + 7$

  Line B: $y = -3x + 7$

  Line C: $y = \frac{2}{3}x + 7$

  Line D: $y = \frac{1}{3}x + 7$

  Line E: $y = 7 - 3x$

  Two of these lines are parallel.
  Write down the two parallel lines.   **(1 mark)**

  Adapted from 1MA1/3F, Specimen Papers, Set 1, Q27

2 A is the point with coordinates (3, 12).
  B is the point with coordinates (6, d).
  The gradient of the line AB is 5.
  Work out the value of d.   **(3 marks)**

9.4 $y = mx + c$

⚠ Purposeful practice 1

1 On a graph, how can you find the y-intercept?

2 Write the coordinates of the y-intercept of each line.

    a $y = x + 5$ **b** $y = x - 2$ **c** $y - x = -2$

    d $y = 2x - 2$ **e** $y = -2x - 3$ **f** $y = x + 4$

    g $y = x - 4$ **h** $y = -x + 4$ **i** $y = -2x + 4$

    j $y = -2x - 4$ **k** $2x + y = -4$ **l** $y - 2x = 2$

> **Reflect and reason**
>
> For all straight lines, what is the value of the x-coordinate at the y-intercept?

⚠ Purposeful practice 2

1 For each line

    a work out the gradient

    b find the y-intercept

    c write the equation of the line

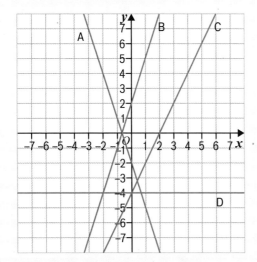

> **Reflect and reason**
>
> Line D is horizontal. What is its gradient?

⊠ Problem-solving practice

1 Draw these graphs from their equations.

   a $y = x$ **b** $y = x + 3$ **c** $y = -x$ **d** $y = -x - 1$

   e $y = -2$ **f** $y = 2x + 1$ **g** $y = -3x$ **h** $y = -3x + 2$

2 The table gives the coordinates of two points on lines A, B, C, D and E.
   Work out the equation of each line.

Line	Point 1	Point 2
A	(−9, 0)	(−6, 6)
B	(−9, 0)	(−6, 3)
C	(−7, −10)	(−4, −4)
D	(−7, −10)	(−4, −7)
E	(3, 8)	(7, −8)

3

$y = 3x + 1$		$y = x - 3$		$y = 5$
$y = -2x + 4$		$y = x - 4$		$y = -2x - 1$
$y = -4x + 1$		$y = 2x + 5$		$y = 3x$

   Which of these lines have

   a the same gradient?

   b the same y-intercept?

✸ Exam practice

1 The line L is shown on the grid.
   Find an equation for L.   **(3 marks)**

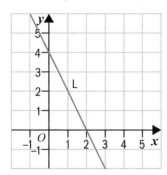

Adapted from 1MA1/2F, June 2018, Q22

Exam feedback   Results**Plus**

In a similar question, some students found the gradient of the line but few went on to use this value correctly in an equation.

Key point

• You can use graphs to show trends and relationships between two sets of data.

⚠ Purposeful practice 1

The graph shows the cost of three brands of coffee beans.
Brand A is the most expensive.
Brand C is the least expensive.

1 Match each line on the graph with the correct brand.

2 Find the cost per kg for each brand.

3 Scott decides to buy 5 kg of brand C, 3 kg of brand B and 1 kg of brand A.
How much will this cost?

4 There is a special offer on Brand A: Buy 1 kg, get 1 kg free.
Is Brand A still the most expensive brand?

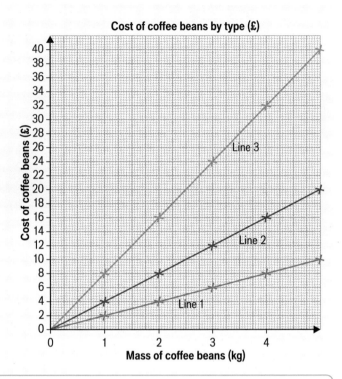

Reflect and reason

What feature of the line graph tells you which brand is cheapest?

⚠ Purposeful practice 2

1 Strawberries can be bought by the kilogram (kg).
A kilogram of strawberries costs £1.88.

a Copy and complete the table

Strawberries bought (kg)	1	2	3	4	5	6
Cost (£)	1.88					11.28

b Draw a graph of strawberries bought against cost.

c How much does 2.5 kg of strawberries cost?

d How many kilograms of strawberries cost £5.50?

Reflect and reason

The graph you plotted should pass through the point (0, 0). Why?

1 Brian pays 15p for every kilowatt hour (kWh) of electricity he uses.
Tom pays £15, plus 12p for every kilowatt hour (kWh) of electricity he uses.

   a Copy and complete the table.

Electricity used (kWh)	0	200	400	600	800	1000
Brian pays (£)	0.00					150.00
Tom pays (£)	15.00					135.00

   b Draw a graph of the data.

   c In summer, Brian and Tom both use 400 kWh.
   Who pays less?

   d In winter, Brian and Tom both use 700 kWh.
   Who pays less?

2 Ishver uses a motorcycle to travel to work.
A litre of fuel costs £1.30.

   a Copy and complete the table

Fuel bought (litres)	2	4	6	8	10	12
Cost (£)	2.60					15.60

   b Draw a graph of the data.

   c Last month, Ishver used a total of 45 litres of fuel.
   How much did this cost?

   d Ishver has 3 litres of fuel.
   He buys £12 worth of fuel and will use 9 litres next week.
   How many litres will he have remaining at the end of next week?

1 The graph shows the cost of hiring a bicycle for a number of hours.

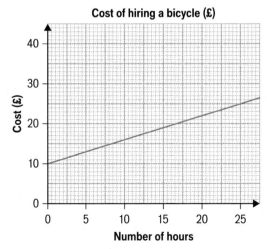

Cost of hiring a bicycle (£)

The cost includes a fixed rental charge and a charge for each additional hour the bicycle is hired.
Work out the charge for each hour the bicycle is hired. **(2 marks)**

Adapted from 1MA1/2F, Specimen Papers, Set 2, Q14

Key points

- A distance–time graph represents a journey.
  The vertical axis represents the distance from the starting point.
  The horizontal axis represents the time taken.

- Average speed $= \dfrac{\text{distance travelled}}{\text{time taken}}$

- On a distance–time graph, the gradient represents the speed of the journey.

△ Purposeful practice

Sarah and Kyle cycle on the same road from
Bedford to Cranfield and back to Bedford.
They both cycle through Aspley,
which is 15 km from Bedford.
Sarah starts her journey first, at 12 noon.

1 Which line represents Sarah's journey?

2 How far is Cranfield from Bedford?

3 Who stops for a rest 15 km from Bedford?
   How long for?

4 At what time does Sarah arrive at
   Cranfield? How long does she stay there?

5 At what time does Kyle leave Bedford?

6 At roughly what time do Sarah and Kyle
   pass each other? How far from Bedford
   are they when they pass each other?

7 Where is Sarah cycling to when she
   passes Kyle?

8 At what time does Sarah finish her journey?

9 Find these average speeds:

   a Sarah from Bedford to Cranfield

   b Kyle from Bedford to Cranfield

   c Kyle from Cranfield to Bedford

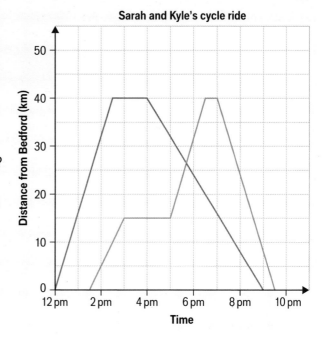

Sarah and Kyle's cycle ride

Reflect and reason

Look at the distance–time graph.

How do you know that Sarah was cycling more slowly on the way back to Bedford than on the way there?

1 Bill has an electric bicycle and starts from point A.
   100 seconds after he starts, he is 80 m from A.
   50 seconds later, he has travelled another 80 m.
   50 seconds later, he has travelled another 110 m.
   20 seconds later, he has travelled another 70 m.

   a Draw a distance–time graph to represent Bill's journey.

   b Is his speed increasing or decreasing? Explain your answer.

2 Sally drives 120 miles to visit a friend.
   She leaves home at 8 am.
   On the way, she stops at a service station for 30 minutes.
   Later on the journey, she gets stuck in roadworks without moving for 45 minutes.
   She later stops for 15 minutes to buy some flowers.
   She gets to her friend's house later than planned at 12 noon.
   Her friend comments that she must have been driving at an average speed of 30 mph
   because it took her 4 hours to get there.

   a Sally's friend is wrong. What mistake has she made?

   b Work out Sally's average speed for the journey.

✸ Exam practice

1 Dalva ran 100 m.
   The distance–time graph shows her journey.
   Seb also ran 100 m. His average speed was 22.3 km/h.
   Who ran faster? Show your working.   **(4 marks)**

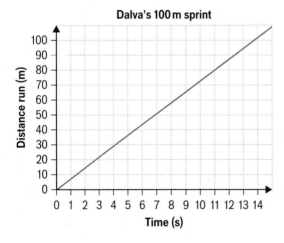

Dalva's 100 m sprint

Adapted from 1MA0/1H, June 2013, Q11

Exam feedback   ResultsPlus

In a similar question, students tried lots of different methods to compare speeds. The most common
was to work out Dalva's speed so that it could be compared with Seb's, but it was not always calculated
correctly.

Key point

* A rate of change graph shows how a quantity changes over time.

⚠ Purposeful practice 1

Look at these containers. Each container is filled with water at a constant rate.

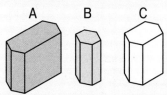

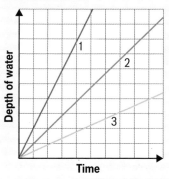

1 Which container will fill fastest?

2 Which container will fill slowest?

3 Match each container to a line on the graph.

Reflect and reason

What does the gradient of each line tell you?

⚠ Purposeful practice 2

1 Water flows into Tank A at a constant rate.

   a What is the depth of the water at 4.8 minutes?

   b At what time is the depth of the water 4.8 cm?

   c By how many centimetres does the depth increase each minute?

   d What is the gradient of the line?

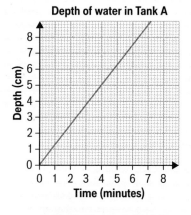

Depth of water in Tank A

2 Water flows into Tank B at a constant rate.

   a What is the depth of water at 4.8 minutes?

   b At what time is the depth of water 4.8 cm?

   c By how many centimetres does the depth increase each minute?

   d What is the gradient of the line?

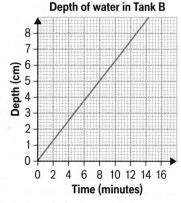

Depth of water in Tank B

Reflect and reason

The lines in **Q1** and **Q2** do not have the same gradient. Why?

⊠ Problem-solving practice

1   The graph shows how the price of a loaf of bread
has changed in a 40-year period from
1977 to 2017.

   a   In which 10-year period did the price increase
the most?
Show working to explain.

   b   Estimate the price of a loaf of bread in 2010.

   c   Dani says she cannot use the graph to make
a reliable prediction of the price of bread
in 2020.
Give one reason why Dani is correct.

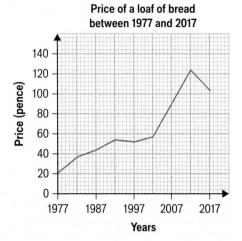

**Price of a loaf of bread
between 1977 and 2017**

2   The graph shows the test results in Maths and
History for some Year 8 students. Both tests were
marked out of 80.
The line of best fit has been marked on the graph.

   a   David scored 52 in the Maths test but was ill
on the day of the History test. Predict what he
might have scored in the History test.

   b   How reliable is your prediction? Explain
your answer.

   c   Sakina took the same Maths and History
tests. She scored 80 out of 80 in the History
test. From the results shown in the scatter graph,
what, if anything, can you predict about
Sakina's score in the Maths test?

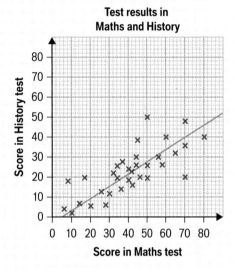

**Test results in
Maths and History**

✷ Exam practice

1   The graph shows the cost of hiring a plumber.

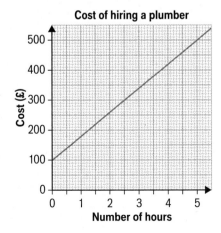

Cost of hiring a plumber

The cost includes a call-out charge of £100 and a charge for each hour of work.
Work out the plumber's hourly rate.   **(2 marks)**

Adapted from 1MA1/2F, Specimen Papers, Set 2, Q14

10 Transformations

10.1 Translation

⚠ Purposeful practice 1

Use the diagrams to answer these questions.

1   Start at A.
    Write down the shape that A maps to
    when translated by

    a $\binom{0}{6}$ b $\binom{0}{-6}$

    c $\binom{12}{0}$ d $\binom{-4}{0}$

    e $\binom{4}{2}$ f $\binom{4}{-4}$

    g $\binom{8}{2}$

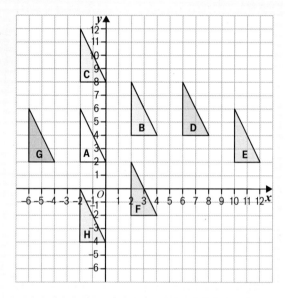

2   Write the column vector that translates

    a i   A to W   ii W to Y   iii A to Y
    b i   S to T   ii T to W   iii S to W
    c i   R to X   ii X to V   iii R to V

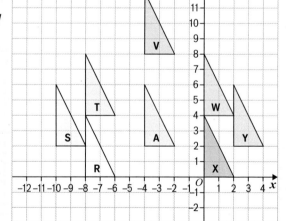

Reflect and reason

A shape is translated by $\binom{3}{5}$ and then by $\binom{-2}{4}$.

Write the single column vector for these combined translations. How did you work it out?

⊠ Problem-solving practice

1 Shape A is translated by $\begin{pmatrix} -3 \\ 0 \end{pmatrix}$ followed by a translation of $\begin{pmatrix} 0 \\ y \end{pmatrix}$.

The translation finishes at shape B.
What is the value of y?

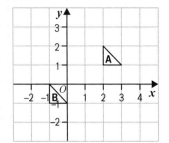

2 When translated by $\begin{pmatrix} -2 \\ 3 \end{pmatrix}$, which of these points will move to (4, 6)?

   A (3, 6)   B (0, 0)   C (6, 3)   D (2, −3)   E (−3, 2)

3 Translate (14, −3) by the column vector $\begin{pmatrix} 42 \\ 29 \end{pmatrix}$.

4 PQRS is a rectangle.
Write down the column vector translations that take
point P to points Q, R and S.

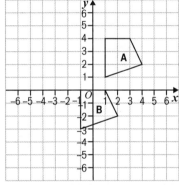

⬙ Exam practice

1 Describe in full the single transformation
that maps shape A onto shape B.

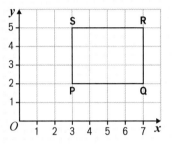

(2 marks)

Adapted from 1MA1/2F, Specimen Papers, Set 2, Q22

2 Translate trapezium A by the vector $\begin{pmatrix} 4 \\ -1 \end{pmatrix}$.
Label the new trapezium B.

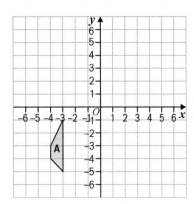

(1 mark)

Adapted from 1MA1/2F, November 2017, Q20b

Exam feedback

ResultsPlus

Q2: In a similar question, many students were not careful enough when counting squares, placing
shape B one square away from where it should have been.

Key point

- To describe a reflection on a coordinate grid, you need to give the equation of the mirror line.

△ Purposeful practice 1

1 From the diagram on the right, write down the equation of the mirror line for a reflection of

   a A to C   **b** A to E

   c A to G   **d** A to D

   e A to B   **f** A to F

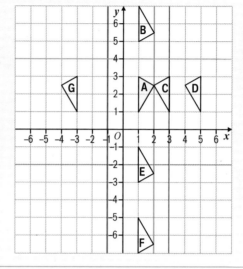

Reflect and reason

What can you say about the equations of vertical mirror lines and horizontal mirror lines?

△ Purposeful practice 2

1 For each shape on the diagram

   a draw its reflection in the line $y = x$

   b write down the original coordinates of the vertices of the shape

   c write down the coordinates of the vertices of the shape after the reflection

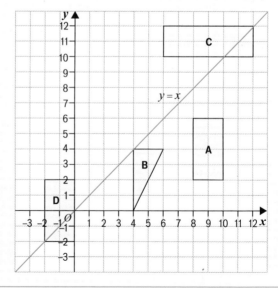

Reflect and reason

When you reflect a point in the line $y = x$, how do its coordinates change?

When you reflect a point in the line $y = -x$, how do its coordinates change?

⊠ Problem-solving practice

1 Look at this diagram.

Identify the mistakes in these students' answers.

a The reflection from shape A to shape B is in the line $x = 2$.

b The reflection from shape B to shape C is in the x-axis.

c The reflection from shape A to shape D is in the line $y = 4$.

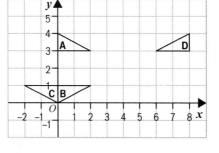

2 Look at this diagram.

Find the equation of the line which reflects A onto shape

a B   **b** C   **c** D   **d** E   **e** F

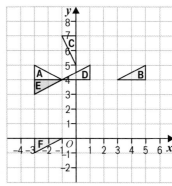

✦ Exam practice

1 Describe fully the single transformation that maps shape A onto shape B.

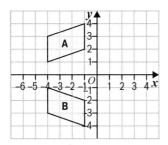

(2 marks)

Adapted from 1MA1/3F, November 2017, Q14

2 Describe fully the single transformation that maps shape A onto shape C.

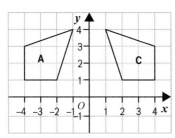

(2 marks)

Adapted from 1MA1/2F, June 2018, Q18

Exam feedback   **ResultsPlus**

Q1: In a similar question, many students did not use the correct language to describe the transformation; instead, they wrote 'flipped' or 'mirrored'.

Q2: Most students who achieved a **Grade 5** answered a similar question well.

Key point

• You rotate a shape by turning it around a point called the centre of rotation.

⚠ Purposeful practice 1

Copy this rectangle onto squared paper. Using a new copy for each question, rotate the rectangle 90° anticlockwise about

1 vertex A   **2** vertex B   **3** vertex C   **4** vertex D

Reflect and reason

What is the same and what is different in the four rotations you have drawn?

⚠ Purposeful practice 2

The blue shape is rotated to give the red shape.
Write down the angle used for each clockwise and anticlockwise rotation about the centre of rotation.

1 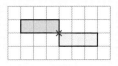   **2**   **3** 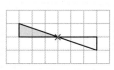   **4**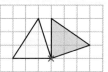

Reflect and reason

You do not need to state the direction for a 180° rotation. Explain why.

⚠ Purposeful practice 3

1 Which letter D, E, F, G or H is the centre of rotation used for each of these 180° rotations?

   a A to P   **b** A to Q   **c** A to R

   d A to S   **e** A to T

2 Which letter, P, Q, R or S is the centre of rotation for each of these 90° anticlockwise rotations?

   a A to B   **b** A to C

   c A to D   **d** A to E

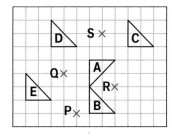

Reflect and reason

How do you find the centre of rotation?

⊠ Problem-solving practice

1 Alex answers this question.
'Draw a triangle and label its vertices A, B and C.
Rotate the triangle 90° clockwise about vertex B.
Label the vertices of the image so that A rotates onto D, B
rotates onto E, and C rotates on to F. '
Look at the diagram. What two errors has Alex made?

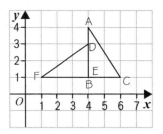

2 Describe these rotations fully.

   a A to C   **b** C to E   **c** E to A

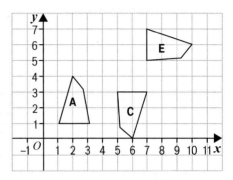

3 Describe fully the single transformation
that maps triangle R onto triangle T.

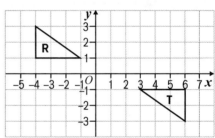

✵ Exam practice

1 Copy the diagram,
Rotate the shape 90° clockwise about centre *O*.

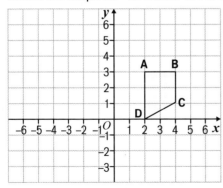

(2 marks)

Adapted from 1MA1/2F, June 2017, Q13a

Exam feedback   Results**Plus**

Most students who achieved a **Grade 3** and above answered a similar question well.

10.4 Enlargement

Key points

- To enlarge a shape, you multiply all the side lengths by the same number.
- The number that the side lengths are multiplied by is called the scale factor.
- When you enlarge a shape using a centre of enlargement, you multiply the distance from the centre to each vertex by the scale factor.

⚠ Purposeful practice 1

1 Which shape is an enlargement of A by scale factor 2?

2 Which shape is an enlargement of A by scale factor 3?

3 Which shape is an enlargement of A by scale factor $\frac{1}{2}$?

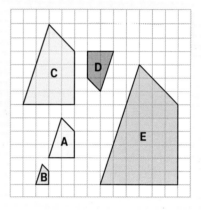

Reflect and reason

Which sides of shape A and shape C did you compare to find the scale factor?

Which sides did you use on the other shapes? Explain.

⚠ Purposeful practice 2

1 Copy the diagram.
   Enlarge the shape by scale factor 2,
   using each centre of enlargement P, Q, R and S.

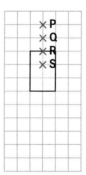

2 Copy the diagram.
   Enlarge the shape by scale factor $\frac{1}{2}$, using each

   centre of enlargement V, W, X and Y.

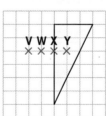

Reflect and reason

How does the position of the centre of enlargement affect the position of the enlargement by scale factor 2?

What is different when you use scale factor $\frac{1}{2}$?

1 Mary enlarges a photograph A to give photograph B.

   a What is the scale factor of this enlargement?

   b Mary enlarges photograph A by a scale factor $1\frac{1}{2}$.
   What are the dimensions of this photograph?

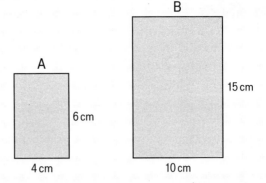

2 Write the instructions for an enlargement that gives

   a a larger version of shape A, in the same quadrant

   b a smaller version of shape B, in quadrant 1

   c a larger version of shape C, in quadrant 2

   d a smaller version of shape D, in quadrant 4

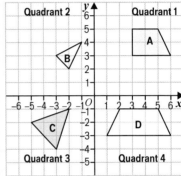

3 This triangle is enlarged by a scale factor 3.

   Anna says, 'The enlarged triangle has perimeter 24 cm.'

   Paul says, 'The difference between the longest and shortest side of the enlarged triangle is still 2 cm.'

   Charlie says, 'The original triangle has an area of 6 cm². The enlarged triangle is 3 times larger than the original so it will have an area of 18 cm².'

   Anna, Paul and Charlie have all made one mistake in their statement. Identify their mistakes.

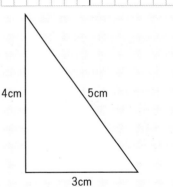

1 Copy the diagram.
   Enlarge the quadrilateral by scale factor 3.

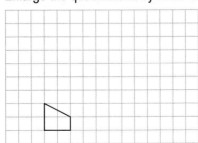

(2 marks)

Adapted from 1MA0/2F, June 2016, Q18

Exam feedback

In a similar question, students found producing the correct sloping side problematic.

10.5 Describing enlargements

Key point

- 'Describe fully' means write down the scale factor and the coordinates of the centre of enlargement.

⚠ Purposeful practice 1

1 Write the scale factor of enlargement that maps
   a shape A to shape B
   b shape A to shape C
   c shape A to shape D
   d shape C to shape B

2 Write the scale factor of enlargement that maps
   a shape C to shape A   b shape D to shape C
   c shape C to shape D   d shape B to shape C

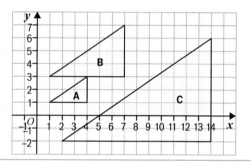

Reflect and reason

Describe the relationship between the scale factors of enlargement that map shape A to shape B and shape B to shape A.

⚠ Purposeful practice 2

Describe fully the enlargement that maps

1 shape A to shape B   2 shape B to shape A

3 shape B to shape C   4 shape C to shape B

Reflect and reason

What do you notice about the centre of enlargement needed to map shape A to shape B compared with the centre of enlargement needed to map shape B to shape A?

⚠ Purposeful practice 3

For each diagram, write the scale factor of enlargement that maps shape A to shape B.
An extra line has been added to the first diagram to help you.

1
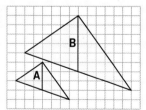

2
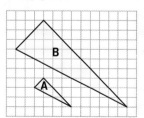

Reflect and reason

How can drawing an extra horizontal or vertical line to help you to find the scale factor?

1 Describe fully the transformation from shape A to shape B.

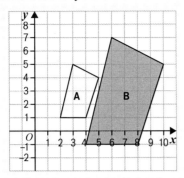

2 Describe fully the transformation from shape E to shape F.

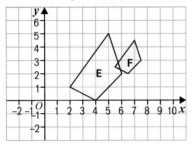

3 Describe fully the transformation that maps shape A onto shape B.

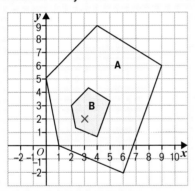

Exam practice

1 Describe fully the single transformation that maps trapezium A onto trapezium B.

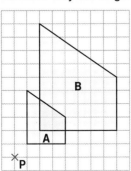

(2 marks)

Adapted from 1MA1/2F, Spring 2017, Mock Set 2, Q13b

Key point

• You can transform shapes using more than one transformation.

△ Purposeful practice 1

1 Which triangle do these combined transformations produce?

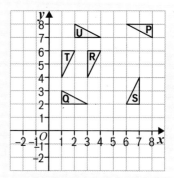

   a Rotate shape Q 180° around the point (3, 2) and then translate by $\begin{pmatrix} 3 \\ 6 \end{pmatrix}$.

   b Translate shape Q by $\begin{pmatrix} 3 \\ 6 \end{pmatrix}$ and then rotate by 180° around the point (6, 8).

   c Rotate shape Q 90° clockwise around the point (1, 3) and then translate by $\begin{pmatrix} 1 \\ 3 \end{pmatrix}$.

   d Translate shape Q by $\begin{pmatrix} 0 \\ 2 \end{pmatrix}$ and then rotate 90° clockwise around the point (3, 4).

   e Rotate shape U 90° anticlockwise around the point (2, 7) and then translate by $\begin{pmatrix} 5 \\ -5 \end{pmatrix}$.

   f Translate shape U by $\begin{pmatrix} 4 \\ -4 \end{pmatrix}$ and then rotate 90° anticlockwise around the point (7, 3).

2 Describe fully the single transformation which combines the two translations in each part. Use the diagram to help you.

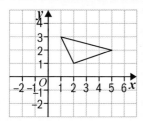

   a Reflection in the line $x = 2$, followed by reflection in the line $x = 4$

   b Reflection in the line $y = 3$, followed by reflection in the line $y = -1$

   c Reflection in the line $x = 2$, followed by reflection in the line $y = 3$

   d Reflection in the line $y = -1$, followed by reflection in the line $x = 4$

Reflect and reason

Use the words 'parallel' and 'perpendicular' to complete these sentences.

A translation is equivalent to reflection in two _____ lines.

A rotation is equivalent to reflection in two _____ lines.

1 A video game needs 8 rubies and 20 silver pieces to craft a necklace.
   Write the ratio for rubies and silver pieces in its simplest form.

2 There are 30 beads in a bag.
   12 of them are red, the rest are orange.
   Write the ratio of red beads to orange beads in its simplest form.

3 Tom and Peter buy a house.
   Tom pays £2500 of the deposit and Peter pays £20 000 of the deposit.
   In what ratio do they pay the deposit?
   Write your answer in its simplest form.

4 Harriet has some red and green marbles in the ratio 1 : 3.
   She says, 'I have twice as many green marbles as red marbles because green is 2 more than
   red in the ratio.'
   Explain why Harriet is wrong.

5 An animal feed is made of 200 g protein, 800 g carbohydrates and 50 g water.
   Write the ratio of protein, carbohydrates and water in its simplest form.

6 James and Karis are asked to write the ratio 16 : 20 in its simplest form.
   James writes 8 : 10
   Karis writes 5 : 4

   a Explain why James is wrong.

   b Explain why Karis is wrong.

7 A recipe for 10 scones needs 225 g flour, 50 g butter and 25 g caster sugar.
   Write the ratio of the ingredients in its simplest form.

8 To grow mushrooms, the soil needs to contain carbon and nitrogen in the ratio 5 : 2.
   A garden has 30 g of carbon for every 16 g of nitrogen.
   Is the garden suitable for growing mushrooms?
   You must show your workings.

9 A school trip needs a ratio of 1 : 12 adults to children.
   There are 5 adults and 62 children.
   Are there enough adults?

⬡ Exam practice

1 A conference room has 12 tables.
   Each table has 4 chairs.
   Write, as a ratio, the number of chairs around 3 of the tables to the total number of chairs.
   Give your answer in its simplest form.   **(2 marks)**

   Adapted from 1MA1/1F, May 2017, Q10

Exam feedback   ResultsＰlus

Most students who achieved a **Grade 5** answered a similar question well.

11.2 Using ratios 1

Key point

- Ratios in their simplest form only have integer parts.

△ Purposeful practice 1

All of these ratios are equivalent to 2 : 4.
Work out the missing part.

1 8 : ☐   **2** ☐ : 8   **3** 4 : ☐   **4** 1 : ☐

5 ☐ : 1   **6** ☐ : 2   **7** ☐ : 20   **8** 20 : ☐

> **Reflect and reason**
>
> Which question shows 2 : 4 in its simplest form? Why?

△ Purposeful practice 2

Write each ratio in its simplest form.

1 6 : 8   **2** 0.6 : 0.8   **3** 6 : 0.8   **4** 6 : 0.08

5 0.6 : 0.08   **6** 1.2 : 1.6   **7** 0.12 : 1.6   **8** 0.12 : 16

> **Reflect and reason**
>
> How do you decide whether to multiply by 10 or 100 to simplify the ratio?

△ Purposeful practice 3

1 Amara has red and black t-shirts in the ratio 3 : 6. She has 12 red t-shirts.
How many black t-shirts does Amara have?

2 Anthony has red and black t-shirts in the ratio 1 : 2. He has 12 red t-shirts.
How many black t-shirts does Anthony have?

3 Mary has red and black t-shirts in the ratio 1 : 2. She has 12 black t-shirts.
How many red t-shirts does Mary have?

4 Oliver has black and red t-shirts in the ratio 1 : 2. He has 12 black t-shirts.
How many red t-shirts does Oliver have?

5 Ebben has black and red t-shirts in the ratio 1 : 3. He has 12 black t-shirts.
How many red t-shirts does Ebben have?

6 Ruby has black and red t-shirts in the ratio 2 : 3. She has 12 black t-shirts.
How many red t-shirts does Ruby have?

> **Reflect and reason**
>
> How does the order of the words in the first sentence of each question relate to the ratio?

1 Georgina is making a drink. She needs water and orange squash in the ratio 10 : 3.
Georgina uses 90 ml of orange squash.
How much water should she use?

2 In an English text, the letter 'e' is used in the ratio to all other letters of 3 : 22.
Aaron counted 144 'e's in a chapter of a book.

   a Estimate the total number of other letters in the chapter.

   b Estimate the total number of letters in the chapter.

3 A map is drawn using the ratio 1 cm : 3 km.
Grigori measures a walking route that is 8 cm on the map.

   a How far is the actual walking route?

   Grigori takes 30 minutes to walk 2 km.

   b How long does it take Grigori to complete the walk?

4 A sculptor is making models of her statues.
She wants to make them so that the ratio of the real statue to its model is 9 : 2.

   a One statue is 2.7 m tall. How tall should she make the model?

   The sculptor has another statue that is 1.8 m tall and she makes the model 0.3 m tall.

   b Is the model the right height? Explain your answer.

5 Daniel is asked to write the ratio 0.5 : 2 in its simplest form.
Daniel writes 0.1 : 0.4.
Explain why Daniel is wrong.

6 A horse needs 2 acres of grass in which to run.
A farm has 12 horses and 18 acres of grass.
How many horses do they need to sell so that each horse has enough grass?

7 Kathy and Clara's ages are in the ratio 3 : 2.
Kathy is 9 years old.
How many years older than Clara is Kathy?

8 A mother gives her two children money in the ratio of their current ages, 7 years old and 3 years old.
Write the ratios of their ages for the next three years in their simplest forms.

✳ Exam practice

1 In a garden

      the number of vegetable plants and the number of shrubs are in the ratio 9 : 2

      the number of shrubs and the number of trees are in the ratio 4 : 3

   There are 9 trees in the garden.
How many vegetable plants are there in the garden? **(3 marks)**

Adapted from 1MA1/1F, May 2018, Q20

Exam feedback   Results**Plus**

Most students who achieved a **Grade 5** answered a similar question well.

Key point

- You can use ratios to convert between units.

⚠ Purposeful practice 1

1. 1 hour = 60 minutes. Convert these to minutes.

   a 2 hours   **b** 0.5 hours   **c** 2.5 hours

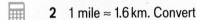

2. 1 mile ≈ 1.6 km. Convert

   a 3 miles to km   **b** 5 miles to km   **c** 3 km to miles   **d** 5 km to miles

3. 1 kg ≈ 2.2 pounds. Convert

   a 3 kg to pounds   **b** 5 kg to pounds   **c** 3 pounds to kg   **d** 5 pounds to kg

Reflect and reason

Explain how your method changed when working out miles in **Q2a–b** compared with working out km in **Q2c–d**. Do the same for kg and pounds in **Q3**.

⚠ Purposeful practice 2

1. Convert £200 into euros. The exchange rate is £1 : €1.12

2. Convert £200 into dollars. The exchange rate is £1 : $1.28

3. Convert €200 into pounds. The exchange rate is £1 : €1.12

4. Convert $200 into pounds. The exchange rate is £1 : $1.28

Reflect and reason

How are the ratios different in **Q1–2** and **Q3–4**? What effect does this have on your method?

⚠ Purposeful practice 3

Write these ratios in their simplest form.

1. Cube A has side length 2 cm. Cube B has side length 4 cm.

   a length of A : length of B   **b** area of a face of A : area of a face of B

   c volume of A : volume of B

2. Cube A has side length 2 cm. Cube B has side length 6 cm.

   a length of A : length of B   **b** area of a face of A : area of a face of B

   c volume of A : volume of B

3. Cube A has side length 2 cm. Cube B has side length 8 cm.

   a length of A : length of B   **b** area of a face of A : area of a face of B

   c volume of A : volume of B

Reflect and reason

Describe the connection between the ratios for length and the ratios for area and volume.

1   A newborn baby weighs 3.6 kg.
    Using 1 kg ≈ 2.2 pounds, what is the baby's weight in pounds?

2   The speed limit on a road is 30 mph.
    Using 1 mile ≈ 1.6 km, what is this speed limit in km/h?

3   Raj has 11 pounds of cherries.
    A recipe needs 8 kg of cherries.
    Raj knows that 1 kg ≈ 2.2 pounds.
    How many more pounds or kg of cherries does Raj need to buy?

4   1 mile ≈ 1.6 km
    Nana walks 2.5 miles to school.
    Charlie walks 3.5 km to school.
    Nana says she walks the furthest to school but Charlie says he does.
    Who is correct? Show your workings.

5   Adib wants to buy a designer coat.
    He can buy it in America for $400 and pay $25 to ship it to the UK.
    He can buy it in the UK for £350 and not have to pay shipping.
    Adib knows that the exchange rate is £1 : $1.28.
    Where should Adib buy this coat? Give reasons for your answer.

6   An airport is offering an exchange rate of £1 : €1.12.
    Callum wants to change €100 for pounds.
    He says, 'I should get £112 because 100 × 1.12 = 112.'
    Explain why Callum is incorrect.

7   Ollie plans to go to Japan on holiday.
    He converts £300 into Japanese yen with an exchange rate of £1 : ¥141.
    Ollie can no longer go on holiday.
    He converts his yen back to pounds, but the exchange rate has changed to £1 : ¥138.
    Does Ollie gain or lose money? Explain your answer.

8   A rectangle has area 10 cm².
    Each side of the rectangle is enlarged by scale factor 2.
    What is the area of the enlarged rectangle?

✸ Exam practice

1   A model train has a length of 68 cm.
    The scale of the model is 1 : 300.
    Work out the length of the real train.
    Give your answer in metres.

(2 marks)

Adapted from 1MA1/3F, Specimen Papers, Set 2, Q8

Key point

To share an amount in a given ratio
1. work out how many parts there are in total
2. work out the amount in 1 part
3. work out the amount for each part of the ratio
4. check that each amount adds up to give the total amount

△ Purposeful practice 1

Share these amounts in the ratios given.

1 £100 in the ratio 1 : 4   2 £100 in the ratio 2 : 8   3 £100 in the ratio 3 : 7

4 £200 in the ratio 3 : 7   5 £20 in the ratio 3 : 7   6 £20 in the ratio 9 : 21

7 £30 in the ratio 9 : 21   8 £30 in the ratio 10 : 20   9 £30 in the ratio 10 : 10

10 £20 in the ratio 10 : 9 : 1   11 £20 in the ratio 5 : 4 : 1   12 £30 in the ratio 5 : 4 : 1

13 £40 in the ratio 5 : 4 : 1   14 £50 in the ratio 5 : 4 : 1   15 £60 in the ratio 5 : 4 : 1

Reflect and reason

Look at questions that gave the same answers. Why did these questions give the same answers?

△ Purposeful practice 2

A drink is made from orange juice, pineapple juice and lemon juice in the ratio 3 : 5 : 2.
How much of each type of juice do you need to make the following quantities of the drink?

1 200 ml   2 2000 ml   3 2 litres   4 1 litre

5 500 ml   6 0.5 litres   7 5 litres   8 6 litres

Reflect and reason

How could you use your answers to **Q4** and **Q7** to help you answer **Q8**?

△ Purposeful practice 3

A dish is made from tuna and pasta in the ratio 2 : 3.
How much of each ingredient do you need to make the following quantities of the dish?

1 2 kg   2 20 g   3 200 g   4 2000 g

5 4 kg   6 1 kg   7 5 kg   8 6 kg

Reflect and reason

How could you use your answers to **Q1** and **Q5** to answer **Q8**?

1   Ross has 300 ml of orange paint.
    It was made using red and yellow paint in the ratio 1 : 2.
    How much of each colour paint does Ross need to use?

2   Mariela gives £30 000 to her two sons, Pavlo and Erik, in the ratio 2 : 3.

    a   How much do Pavlo and Erik each get?

    Erik gives half of his share to Pavlo and the rest to his two daughters.

    b   How much does Erik give to his two daughters?

    Erik's daughters, Marsha and Julia, share their money in the ratio 4 : 5.

    c   How much money does each daughter get?

3   Michelle makes jewellery.

    Each item is made of silver and gold in the ratio 7 : 3 and weighs 30 g.

    a   Work out how much silver and gold Michelle needs to make 12 pieces of jewellery.

    Michelle buys silver for £37 per 100 g and gold for £2995 per 100 g.

    b   How much does it cost Michelle to make the 12 pieces of jewellery?

4   Franci is asked to share £60 in the ratio 5 : 7 between her and her brother.
    Franci says, 'My share is £12 because my part of the ratio is 5 and £60 ÷ 5 = £12'.
    Franci is incorrect. Explain what Franci has done wrong.

5   Sia and Jago share some jelly beans in the ratio 8 : 11.
    Jago gets 18 more than Sia.
    How many jelly beans does Sia get?

6   In a field there are cows and sheep in the ratio 3 : 5.
    There are 12 fewer cows than there are sheep.
    How many cows and sheep are there in the field?

7   Joe is a librarian and needs to buy books for the library.
    The library must have recipe books, fiction and biographies in the ratio 2 : 5 : 3.
    Joe has £3500 to spend in total.
    Recipe books cost £10, fiction books cost £8 and biographies cost £9.
    What is the maximum number of books Joe can buy?

✴ Exam practice

1   288 chocolates are put into three boxes.
    The chocolates are put into a small box, a medium box and a large box in the ratio 1 : 3 : 8.
    Work out the number of chocolates in the medium box.   **(2 marks)**

Adapted from 1MA1/1F, November 2017, Q18

Exam feedback   Results**Plus**

In a similar question, many students divided the number of chocolates by 3, rather than dividing the number of chocolates by the total number of parts, and then multiplying by 3.

11.5 Comparing using ratios

Key points

- A proportion compares a part with the whole.
- You can compare ratios by writing them as unit ratios. In a unit ratio, one of the numbers is 1.

△ Purposeful practice 1

A bag contains red and blue counters.
These fractions show the proportion of counters that are red.
Write the ratio of red to blue counters.

1 $\dfrac{3}{4}$ **2** $\dfrac{1}{4}$ **3** $\dfrac{1}{3}$ **4** $\dfrac{2}{6}$

Reflect and reason

Two of the ratios are equivalent. Explain why they are equivalent.

△ Purposeful practice 2

These ratios show the ratio of blue to red counters.
Write the fraction of counters that are blue. Give your fractions in their simplest form.

1 $4:2$ **2** $8:4$ **3** $4:8$ **4** $3:7$ **5** $6:14$

Reflect and reason

How would your answers be different if you had been asked for the fraction of red counters?

△ Purposeful practice 3

Write each of these ratios in the form $1:n$ correct to a maximum of 2 decimal places.

1 $2:8$ **2** $2:4$ **3** $2:2$ **4** $2:1$ **5** $2:10$

6 $10:2$ **7** $10:3$ **8** $10:30$ **9** $5:30$ **10** $5:3$

Reflect and reason

What is similar and different about your answers to **Q5** and **Q6**?

△ Purposeful practice 4

1 Paint A has a blue to yellow ratio of $3:4$.
Paint B has a blue to yellow ratio of $4:3$.
Which is more yellow?

2 Paint A has a blue to yellow ratio of $3:4$.
Paint B has a blue to yellow ratio of $4:5$.
Which is more yellow?

Reflect and reason

How were unit ratios important when answering **Q1** and **Q2**?

1 $\frac{2}{3}$ of the cars in a car park are silver.

What is the ratio of silver cars to other cars?

2 The ratio of cranberries, apples and flour in a cake is 1 : 3 : 10.
What fraction of the ingredients is flour?
Write your fraction in its simplest form.

3 Louise is looking at the sugar content in a recipe.

The sugar is $\frac{3}{10}$ of the total ingredients.

Louise says, 'The ratio of sugar to other ingredients is 3 : 10.'
Is Louise correct? Explain your answer.

4 $\frac{2}{5}$ of the weight of a toy is plastic.

The rest of the toy is metal.
Write down the ratio of the weight of plastic to the weight of metal.
Give your answer in the form 1 : n.

5 $\frac{2}{7}$ of the music on a radio station is metal.

$\frac{3}{7}$ of the music on the station is rock music. The rest is pop.

Write the ratio of pop to the rest of the music in the form 1 : n.

6 Paul, Salim and Tom share some money.

Paul gets $\frac{3}{10}$ of the money.

Salim and Tom share the rest of the money in the ratio 4 : 1.
What is Salim's share of the money written as a fraction in its simplest form?

✦ Exam practice

1 a Arjune and Liam share some money in the ratio 5 : 6.
  What fraction of the money does Liam get? **(1 mark)**
 b Rebecca and Daisy share some biscuits.

  Daisy gets $\frac{1}{3}$ of the biscuits.

  Write down the ratio of the number of biscuits Rebecca gets to the number
  of biscuits Daisy gets. **(1 mark)**

Adapted from 1MA1/2F, November 2017, Q6

Exam feedback   Results**Plus**

Q1a: In a similar question, many students gave the fraction corresponding to a ratio of 6 : 5.
Q1b: In a similar question, many students gave their ratio back-to-front.

11.6 Using proportion

Key points

- In the unitary method, you find the value of one item before finding the value of more.
- You can use the unitary method to work out which product gives better value for money.

△ Purposeful practice 1

A recipe for 4 people needs 120 g of flour.
Work out how much flour is needed for

1 1 person   **2** 2 people   **3** 6 people   **4** 9 people

Reflect and reason

How could you use your answer to **Q1** to help you answer the rest of the questions?

△ Purposeful practice 2

Three dogs need 22.5 kg of food.
Work out how much food is needed for

1 1 dog   **2** 2 dogs   **3** 6 dogs   **4** 9 dogs

Reflect and reason

Did you need to use your answer to **Q1** to get the answer to **Q3**? Explain why.

△ Purposeful practice 3

Write each of these as the unit ratio £1 : ☐ ml.

1 875 ml costs £5.00   **2** 900 ml costs £5.00   **3** 900 ml costs £4.70

4 800 ml costs £4.00   **5** 850 ml costs £4.25   **6** 875 ml costs £4.60

Reflect and reason

Which offers the best value for money? How do you use the ratio to help you to decide?

△ Purposeful practice 4

Write each of these as the unit ratio £ ☐ : 1 ml.

1 875 ml costs £5.00   **2** 900 ml costs £5.00   **3** 900 ml costs £4.70

4 800 ml costs £4.00   **5** 850 ml costs £4.25   **6** 875 ml costs £4.60

Reflect and reason

Which offers the best value for money?
Are your answers to Purposeful practice 3 or Purposeful practice 4 more useful for deciding which is better value for money? Why are they more useful?

1   Cola is sold in a can and a bottle.
    A 330 ml can of cola costs 75p
    A 500 ml bottle of cola costs £1.25
    Which cola is the best value for money? Show all your working.

2   Bags of cement are sold by weight.
    An 11 kg bag costs £3.50
    A 25 kg bag costs £5.70
    Which bag of cement is the best value for money? Show all your working.

3   Tea bags are sold in three sizes of box.
    A small box of 80 tea bags costs £3
    A medium box of 160 tea bags costs £4.50
    A large box of 240 tea bags costs £5.75
    Which size of box is the best value for money? Show all your working.

4   Here are the costs of erasers in two shops.
    Shop A: 3 erasers for £1
    Shop B: 5 erasers for £1.50
    Mrs Ward wants to buy 30 erasers for her class for the cheapest possible cost.
    Which shop should she buy the erasers from? Show all your working.

✧ Exam practice

1   Here is a list of ingredients for making 20 biscuits.

350 g	flour
100 g	butter
175 g	brown sugar
60 g	syrup
1	egg

    Matt has

1 kg	flour
500 g	butter
600 g	brown sugar
100 g	syrup
2	eggs

    What is the greatest number of biscuits that Matt can make?
    You must show your working.   **(3 marks)**

    Adapted from 1MA1/2F, June 2018, Q17

Exam feedback

Most students who achieved a **Grade 3** or above answered a similar question well.

11.7 Proportion and graphs

Key points

- When two values are in direct proportion, if one value is zero, so is the other. When one value doubles, so does the other.
- When two quantities are in direct proportion, plotting them as a graph gives a straight line through the origin. The origin is the point (0, 0) on a graph.

⚠ Purposeful practice 1

1 Which of these graphs show direct proportion?

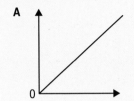 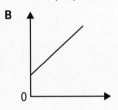 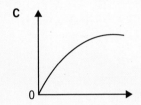 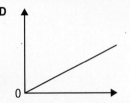

2 Plot a line graph for the values in the table.

a

x	0.5	1	4	10
y	2	4	16	40

b Are the values of x in direct proportion to the values of y? Explain your answer.

Reflect and reason

Explain why the graphs you chose in **Q1** show direct proportion and the other graphs do not.

⚠ Purposeful practice 2

The table shows how many grams of sugar are in a teaspoon.

Teaspoons	1	2	3	4	5
Grams of sugar	4	8	12	16	20

1 Plot the line graph with teaspoons on the x-axis from 0 to 5 and grams on the y-axis from 0 to 20.

2 How many teaspoons of sugar are needed for 10 g?

3 How many teaspoons of sugar are needed for 100 g?

4 How many grams of sugar are in 0 teaspoons?

5 How many grams of sugar are in 6 teaspoons?

6 How many grams of sugar are in 60 teaspoons?

Reflect and reason

How could you use the answer to **Q2** to help you answer **Q3** without extending your graph?

1   A plumber charges £20 for every hour she is at a job.

   a   Draw a graph to show this.

   b   Are the plumber's charges in direct proportion to the number of hours she works?
       Explain your answer.

2   A salesperson is paid £100 every day and then £50 for every sale they make.

   a   Draw a graph to show how much they make for their first 10 sales in a day.

   b   Explain, referring to the graph, why this graph does not show direct proportion.

   c   The salesperson is paid £70 for every sale and no longer gets £100 every day.
       Are they better or worse off if they make 8 sales a day?

3   A taxi driver charges £2.50 to start a journey and then £0.30 for every mile travelled.
   Is the total taxi fare in direct proportion to the distance travelled? Explain your answer.

✧ Exam practice

1   You can use this graph to change between km and miles.

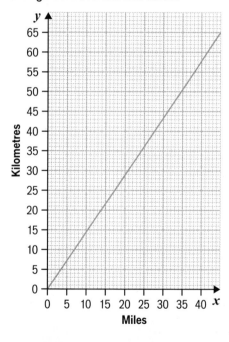

   Change 15 km to miles.   **(1 mark)**

   Adapted from 1MA1/2F, June 2017, Q11a

Exam feedback   Results**Plus**

Most students who achieved a **Grade 2** or above answered a similar question well.

Key point

• When two values are in inverse proportion, one increases at the same rate as the other decreases. For example, as one doubles ($\times 2$), the other halves ($\div 2$).

⚠ Purposeful practice 1

1 Nancy gets paid £5.90 an hour. She works for 4 hours.
   How much does she get paid?

2 5 people are making chairs. They make 8 chairs.
   How many chairs will 10 people make?

3 600 ml of washing up liquid costs £2.
   How much does 300 ml cost?

> **Reflect and reason**
>
> Why is **Q3** direct proportion, not inverse proportion?

⚠ Purposeful practice 2

1 Sophie has a fixed amount of money to spend on holiday.
   If she goes for 10 days, she has £5 a day.
   How much will she have per day if she only goes for 2 days?

2 5 people are painting a room. It takes 8 hours.
   How many hours will it take 10 people?

3 Some plant food is shared between 3 vases. Each vase gets 600 ml.
   How much would each vase get if it was shared between 6 vases?

> **Reflect and reason**
>
> What is different about the inverse proportion questions in Purposeful practice 2 compared to the direct proportion questions in Purposeful practice 1?

⚠ Purposeful practice 3

1 8 people are building a wall. It takes them 7 hours.
   How long would it take 2 people to build the same wall?

2 It takes 3 days for 7 monkeys to eat 20 bananas.
   a How many days would it take 14 monkeys to eat 20 bananas?
   b How many bananas are needed to feed 14 monkeys for 3 days?
   c How many monkeys would it take to eat 80 bananas in 3 days?

> **Reflect and reason**
>
> Which questions use inverse proportion? How do you know?

1 2 people take 7 hours to make a table.
  Each person is paid £8.25 an hour.

  a Would it be cheaper to hire 4 people to make the table? Explain your answer.

  b How long would it take 8 people to make the table?

2 A rectangle has an area of 20 cm².
  The side length is halved, but the area stays the same.
  What has happened to the other length?

3 Shahana is doing the laundry.
  It takes 1 washing machine 2 hours to wash 6 kg of clothes.
  Shahana needs to wash 60 kg of clothes.

  a How long will it take to wash the clothes using 1 washing machine?

  b Shahana can rent a second washing machine. How long will it take now?

4 At 30°C, 18 ice creams are sold.
  At 15°C, 10 ice creams are sold.
  Is the temperature inversely proportional to the number of ice creams sold?
  Explain your answer.

5 It takes 9 surgeons 2 hours to operate on 15 patients.

  a How many surgeons are working if it takes 6 hours to operate on 15 patients?

  b There are 18 surgeons and 45 patients.
    How long will it take to operate on all the patients?

  c 3 surgeons are operating for 12 hours.
    How many patients can they operate on?

6 It takes 2 people 6 hours to water 300 m² of garden.
  Each person is paid £9.25 an hour.

  a How much does it cost to hire 2 people to water 300 m² of garden?

  b How much does it cost to hire 4 people to water 300 m² of garden?

  c 600 m² needs to be watered in less than 12 hours.
    What is the smallest number of people that need to be hired to do this?

✸ Exam practice

1 It takes 5 decorators 3 days to paint a house.

  a Work out how many days it would take 2 decorators to paint the same house. **(2 marks)**

  b i State one assumption you made in working out the answer. **(1 mark)**

    ii How will your answer be affected if your assumption is not correct? **(1 mark)**

  Adapted from 1M1/1F, Spring 2017, Mock Set 2, Q22

12 Right-angled triangles

12.1 Pythagoras' theorem 1

Key points

- In a right-angled triangle, the longest side is called the hypotenuse.
- Pythagoras' theorem shows the relationship between the lengths of the three sides of a right-angled triangle: $c^2 = a^2 + b^2$

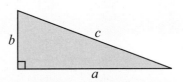

△ Purposeful practice 1

Write

a the letter of the hypotenuse

b the letters of the two perpendicular sides

1

2

3

4

Reflect and reason

How does the location of the right angle help you to identify the hypotenuse?

△ Purposeful practice 2

Calculate the length of the hypotenuse in each right-angled triangle.

1

3 cm
4 cm

2 8 cm 6 cm

3 16 cm
12 cm

4

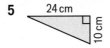

5 cm
12 cm

5 24 cm
10 cm

6

24 cm
7 cm

Reflect and reason

Compare your answers to **Q1–3**. When you double the length of both of the perpendicular sides, what happens to the hypotenuse?

▦ △ Purposeful practice 3

Calculate the length of the hypotenuse in each right-angled triangle.
Give your answers correct to 1 decimal place.

1

3 cm
8 cm

2 8 cm
12 cm

3

5 cm
24 cm

Reflect and reason

In these triangles, is the length of the hypotenuse an integer? Explain why or why not.

⊠ Problem-solving practice

1 Shape 1 is translated by vector $\begin{pmatrix} 2 \\ 1 \end{pmatrix}$.

It is then enlarged with centre of enlargement (1, 5) by scale factor 2 to create shape 2. Copy the diagram and draw shape 2.

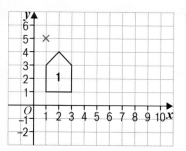

2 Show that these pairs of transformations applied to shape A give the same final result.

  a Reflection in the line $y = x$ followed by reflection in the x-axis.

  b Translation by $\begin{pmatrix} 2 \\ -2 \end{pmatrix}$ followed by rotation 90° clockwise about (2, 0).

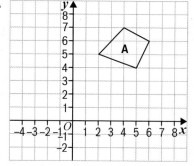

3 Rotate trapezium T 90° clockwise about the origin. Which shape does it map onto? Now reflect this trapezium in the y-axis. Which shape does it map onto?

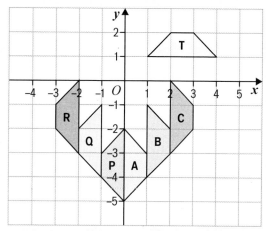

✦ Exam practice

1 Copy the diagram.

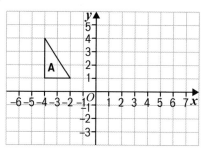

  a Translate shape A by the vector $\begin{pmatrix} 5 \\ -2 \end{pmatrix}$. Label the new shape B.   **(1 mark)**

  b Translate shape B by the vector $\begin{pmatrix} 4 \\ 3 \end{pmatrix}$. Label the new shape C.   **1 mark)**

  c Write the column vector for the single translation that maps shape A onto shape C.   **(1 mark)**

Adapted from 1MA1/1F, Autumn 2016, Mock Set 1, Q10

11 Ratio and proportion

11.1 Writing ratios

Key points

- A ratio is a way to compare two or more quantities.
- You can simplify a ratio by making the numbers as small as possible (keeping them as integers).
- To simplify a ratio, divide the numbers in the ratio by their highest common factor (HCF).
- Ratios are equivalent if they have the same simplest form.

△ Purposeful practice 1

Draw diagrams to show each ratio of squares to triangles. The first one is done for you.

1 1 : 2 □ : △△   2 3 : 2   3 2 : 3   4 4 : 5
5 4 : 6   6 4 : 4   7 4 : 2   8 2 : 1

Reflect and reason

Which two diagrams show equivalent ratios? Explain how you recognised them.

△ Purposeful practice 2

Which of these ratios are equivalent to 10 : 14?

1 5 : 7   2 14 : 10   3 6 : 8   4 14 : 18
5 3 : 5   6 20 : 28   7 25 : 49   8 30 : 42

Reflect and reason

Why was **Q2** not equivalent to 10 : 14?

△ Purposeful practice 3

Write each ratio in its simplest form.

1 4 : 6   2 10 : 15   3 15 : 10   4 30 : 20
5 40 : 30   6 40 : 15   7 20 : 15   8 15 : 15
9 4 : 6 : 8   10 4 : 8 : 6   11 8 : 16 : 12   12 6 : 12 : 9
13 3 : 12 : 9   14 3 : 24 : 9   15 15 : 9   16 3 : 21

Reflect and reason

Why is **Q3** equivalent to **Q4** but not to **Q7**?

📱 ⊠ Problem-solving practice

1   Ladders A and B are leaning against a wall.
    The foot of ladder A is 3 m from the wall.
    The foot of ladder B is 5 m from the wall.
    The top of each ladder is 4 m above the ground.
    How much longer is ladder B than ladder A, in metres?

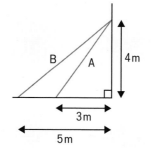

2   Footballer A is passing a ball to Footballer B.
    Footballer C is standing 10 m from Footballer A.
    Footballer B is standing 8 m from Footballer C.
    Footballer C has to turn through 90 degrees to move
    from facing Footballer A to facing Footballer B.
    How far does the ball travel between Footballer A and
    Footballer B, in metres?

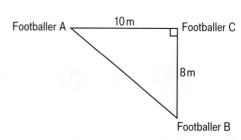

3   Two straight roads meet at right angles.
    They are 12 km and 13 km long.
    A new straight road is built from A to C.
    A car travels 1 km in 2 minutes.
    The car can travel from A to B to C, or directly from A to C.
    Which is quicker, and by how much?

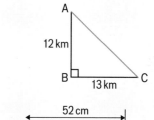

4   A shelf is 52 cm deep.
    It is attached to the wall by a diagonal piece of metal.
    The metal meets the wall 40 cm below the shelf.
    It is attached to the shelf 7 cm from the front edge.

    a   How long is the piece of metal, in centimetres?

    b   Write any assumptions you made to answer **Q4a**.

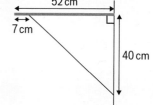

🖩 ⊠ Exam practice

1   ABCD is a trapezium.

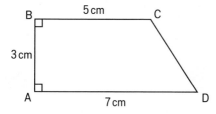

    A square has the same perimeter as this trapezium.
    Work out the area of the square.
    Give your answer correct to 3 significant figures.   **(5 marks)**

    Adapted from 1MA1/2F, Specimen Papers, Set 1, Q28

Key points

- You can use Pythagoras' theorem to work out the length of a shorter side in a right-angled triangle.
- A triangle with sides a, b and c, where c is the longest side, is right-angled only if $c^2 = a^2 + b^2$.

△ Purposeful practice 1

1   This table shows five pairs of coordinates.
Copy and complete the table.

Coordinates	x length	y length	Length of a line between the points
(0, 0), (3, 4)			
(0, 0), (4, 3)			
(1, 1), (5, 4)			
(1, 2), (5, 5)			
(−1, −2), (−5, −5)			

Reflect and reason

Why is it possible to use Pythagoras' theorem to calculate the length of a line between two points on a coordinate grid?

△ Purposeful practice 2

For each right-angled triangle

a   substitute the values into Pythagoras' theorem

b   find the value of x, in centimetres. Give your answers correct to 1 decimal place.

1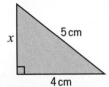

2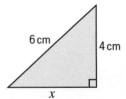

3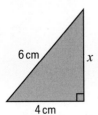

4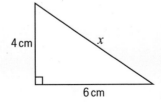

Reflect and reason

How did you identify whether you should add or subtract to find the unknown side?

1 Ladder A and ladder B are leaning against a wall.
   The foot of ladder A is 3 m from the wall.
   The foot of ladder B is 8 m from the wall.
   The top of each ladder is 11 m above the ground.

   Both ladders are now 5 m from the wall.
   a Which ladder reaches higher up the wall, A or B?
   b How much further up the wall does it reach?
       Show working to explain.

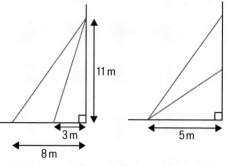
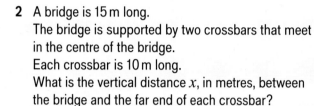

2 A bridge is 15 m long.
   The bridge is supported by two crossbars that meet
   in the centre of the bridge.
   Each crossbar is 10 m long.
   What is the vertical distance x, in metres, between
   the bridge and the far end of each crossbar?

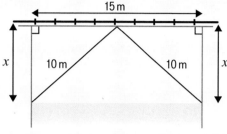

3 Calculate the vertical height of this triangle.

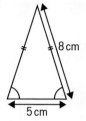

4 The sides of a triangle are 9 cm, 40 cm and 41 cm. Show that the triangle is right-angled.

5 A right-angled triangle with a height of 7 cm and a base of 3 cm will
   have a greater perimeter than an equilateral triangle with sides of 6 cm.
   Is this statement correct? Show how you know.

6 The hypotenuse of a right-angled isosceles triangle is 50 cm. What is its perimeter?

✵ Exam practice

1 Triangle ABC has a perimeter of 20 cm.
   AB = 7 cm   BC = 4 cm
   By calculation, deduce whether triangle ABC is a right-angled triangle.   **(4 marks)**

   Adapted from 1MA1/1F, Specimen Papers, Set 2, Q22

2 ABCDE is a pentagon.
   Work out the area of ABCDE.   **(5 marks)**

   A
   5 cm   5 cm
   B   E
   4 cm   4 cm
   C   D
       8 cm

   Adapted from 1MA1/2F, Spring 2017, Mock Set 2, Q26

Key points

- The side opposite the right angle is called the hypotenuse.
- The side opposite the angle θ is called the opposite.
- The side next to the angle θ is called the adjacent.
- In a right-angled triangle, the sine of an angle is the ratio of the opposite side to the hypotenuse.
- The sine of angle θ is written as sin θ.
- $\sin \theta = \dfrac{\text{opp}}{\text{hyp}}$

⚠ Purposeful practice 1

Write the sine ratio $\sin \theta = \dfrac{\square}{\square}$ for each right-angled triangle.

1   **2**   **3**   **4**

Reflect and reason

In **Q1** and **Q2**, what is the same and what is different in the sine ratio for θ? Explain why.

⚠ Purposeful practice 2

Find the value of x in each right-angled triangle. Give your answers to 1 decimal place.

1 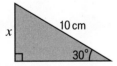   **2** 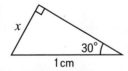   **3**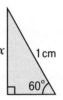

4 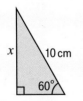   **5** 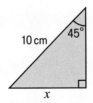   **6**

7 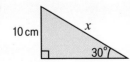   **8**   **9**

Reflect and reason

How did your method change for **Q7–9**, compared with the method used for **Q1–6**? Why?

1. A ladder is leaning against a wall.
   The angle between the top of the ladder and the wall is 50°.
   The ladder is 5 m long.
   How far away from the wall, in metres, is the foot of the ladder?

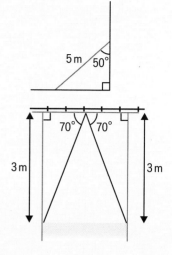

2. A bridge above a river is supported by two crossbars that meet in the centre.
   The crossbars are attached to the bridge at a 70° angle.
   The crossbars meet the riverbank 3 m below the bridge.
   How long is each crossbar, in metres?

3. Calculate the vertical height of this triangle.

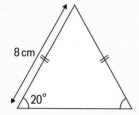

4. Triangle ABC has a right angle at BAC.
   Angle ACB is 64°.
   Side AB is 5.1 m long.
   Calculate the length of side BC in this triangle, giving your answer to 1 decimal place.

5. Calculate the vertical height of the parallelogram.

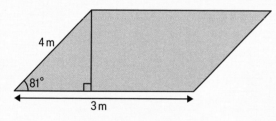

🧮 ✳️ **Exam practice**

1. Work out the value of x.   **(2 marks)**

Adapted from 1MA1/1F, Specimen Papers, Set 1, Q26b

Key point

- When you know the value of sin θ, you can use the inverse, $\sin^{-1}$, on a calculator to find θ.

⚠ Purposeful practice 1

Calculate the size of angle θ in each right-angled triangle.

1

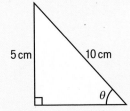

5 cm   10 cm θ

2

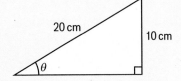

20 cm   10 cm θ

3

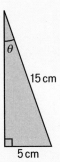

θ 15 cm   5 cm

Reflect and reason

Which two of **Q1–3** have the same value for sin θ? Explain why.

In **Q2** and **Q3** the hypotenuse is 10 cm longer than the opposite side. Does this mean they have the same value for sin θ?

⚠ Purposeful practice 2

Calculate the size of angle θ in each right-angled triangle. Give your answer correct to 1 decimal place.

1

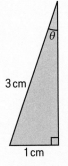

θ 3 cm   1 cm

2

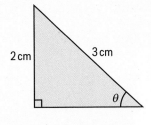

2 cm   3 cm θ

3

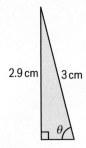

2.9 cm   3 cm θ

4

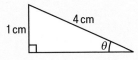

1 cm   4 cm θ

5

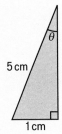

θ 5 cm   1 cm

6

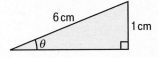

6 cm   1 cm θ

Reflect and reason

What happens to the size of angle θ as the length of the opposite side increases?

Does the same thing happen as the length of the hypotenuse increases? Explain.

1   Two footballers, A and B, are on a
    football pitch near the goal.
    Their positions are shown on the diagram.
    Find angle θ.

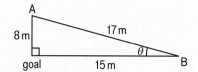

2   Calculate the size of angle θ.

3   Calculate the size of angle θ in each rectangle.

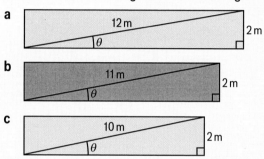

4   A shelf is supported by a diagonal beam.
    The shelf is 0.5 m wide.
    The diagonal beam meets the shelf 15 cm away
    from the edge of the shelf.
    The diagonal beam is 45 cm long.
    Calculate the angle the diagonal beam makes
    with the wall.

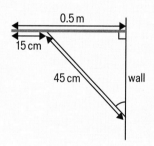

1   The diagram shows a quadrilateral ABCD.

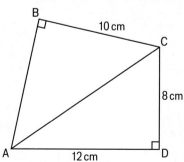

Work out the size of angle BAC.
Give your answer correct to 3 significant figures.   **(4 marks)**

Adapted from 1MA1/3F, Autumn 2017, Mock Set 3, Q24

Key points

- In a right-angled triangle, the cosine of an angle is the ratio of the adjacent side to the hypotenuse.
- The cosine of angle θ is written as $\cos \theta$.
- $\cos \theta = \dfrac{\text{adj}}{\text{hyp}}$
- When you know the value of $\cos \theta$, you can use $\cos^{-1}$ on a calculator to find θ.

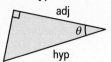

⚠ Purposeful practice 1

Write the cosine ratio $\cos \theta = \dfrac{\square}{\square}$ for each right-angled triangle.

1   **2** 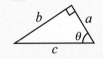 **3**   **4**

Reflect and reason

In **Q1** and **Q2**, what is the same and what is different in the cosine ratio for θ? Explain why.

⚠ Purposeful practice 2

Calculate the length of the side marked x in each right-angled triangle, in centimetres. Give your answers correct to 1 decimal place.

1   **2** 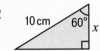 **3**   **4**

5 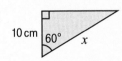 **6**   **7** 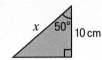 **8**

Reflect and reason

Compare **Q1–8** with **Q1–6** in 12.4, Purposeful practice 2. What is the same and what is different?

⚠ Purposeful practice 3

Find the value of θ in each right-angled triangle. Give your answers correct to 1 decimal place.

1  **2** 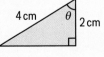 **3**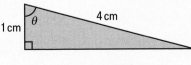

4 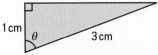 **5** 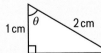 **6**

Reflect and reason

What happens to the size of the unknown angle as the adjacent side gets shorter?
What happens when the hypotenuse gets shorter?

1 A ladder is leaning against a wall.
The foot of the ladder is 3 m from the wall.
The angle between the ground and the foot of the ladder is 30°.
The angle between the top of the ladder and the wall is 60°.
Calculate the length of the ladder to the nearest centimetre.

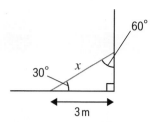

2 A shelf is supported by a beam.
The shelf is 65 cm deep.
The beam meets the shelf 10 cm away
from the edge of the shelf at an angle of 35°.
Calculate the length of the beam in metres, giving your
answer to two decimal places.

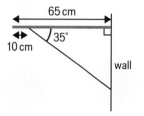

3 This square and this triangle have the same perimeter.

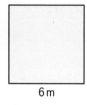 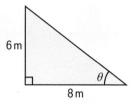

Calculate the unknown angle θ.
Give your answer correct to 1 decimal place.

4 Two paths, one red and one blue, are joined
by a new path as shown in the diagram.
Calculate the length of the blue path.
Give your answer to the nearest metre.

 📐 **Exam practice**

1 Work out the value of x.
Give your answer correct to 1 decimal place. **(2 marks)**

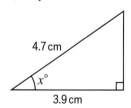

Adapted from 4I 1387, November 2006, Q21

Key points

- In a right-angled triangle, the tangent of an angle is the ratio of the opposite side to the adjacent side.
- The tangent of angle θ is written as $\tan \theta$.
- $\tan \theta = \frac{\text{opp}}{\text{adj}}$
- When you know the value of $\tan \theta$, you can use $\tan^{-1}$ on a calculator to find θ.

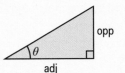

△ Purposeful practice 1

Write the tangent ratio $\tan \theta = \frac{\square}{\square}$ for each right-angled triangle.

1   **2**   **3**   **4**

Reflect and reason

What is the same and what is different in your answers to **Q1** and **Q2**? Explain.
How has your answer changed between **Q1** and **Q2**? Why do you think this is?

△ Purposeful practice 2

Calculate the length of side x in each right-angled triangle.

1 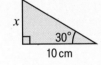 **2** 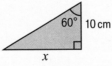 **3**   **4**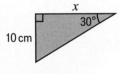

5   **6**   **7**   **8**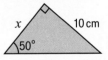

Reflect and reason

How did your method change for **Q4–6**, compared with the method used for **Q1–3**? Why?

△ Purposeful practice 3

Find the value of θ in each right-angled triangle.

1   **2**   **3**

4   **5**   **6**

Reflect and reason

What is the same and what is different about **Q5** and **Q6**? Explain why your answers to **Q5** and **Q6** have a sum of 90°.

1 In this right-angled triangle the side adjacent to the angle θ is double the length of the line opposite the angle θ.
Calculate the size of angle θ.

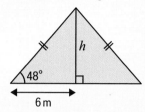

2 Calculate the height, h of this triangle.

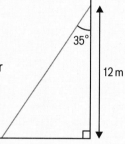

3 A ladder is leaning against a wall.
The angle between the top of the ladder and the wall is 35°.
The top of the ladder is 12 m above the ground.

   a Calculate the distance, in metres, between the foot of the ladder and the wall.

   b Work out the length, in metres, of the ladder.

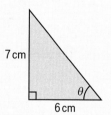

4 Which of these calculations would find the size of the missing angle in this triangle?

   A $\tan^{-1}\left(\dfrac{6}{7}\right)$ **B** $\tan^{-1}\left(\dfrac{7}{6}\right)$ **C** $6 \div \tan\theta$ **D** $\dfrac{6}{7}$

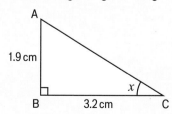

⊞ ✦ **Exam practice**

1 ABC is a right-angled triangle.

Work out the size of the angle marked x.
Give your answer correct to 1 decimal place.   **(2 marks)**

Adapted from 1MA1/3F, Specimen Papers, Set 1, Q27

12.7 Finding lengths and angles using trigonometry

Key point

- You need to know these ratios and be able to choose the one you need to solve a problem.

$$\sin \theta = \frac{\text{opp}}{\text{hyp}} \qquad \cos \theta = \frac{\text{adj}}{\text{hyp}} \qquad \tan \theta = \frac{\text{opp}}{\text{adj}}$$

 ### Purposeful practice 1

For each right-angled triangle

a write a trigonometric ratio

b calculate the missing value(s)

1

2

3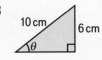

4

5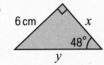

6

Reflect and reason

How did you identify which trigonometric ratio to use?

Purposeful practice 2

Use your knowledge of exact trigonometric values to state the missing value in each right-angled triangle.

1

2

3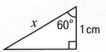

4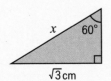

5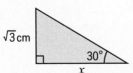

6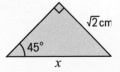

Values needed:

$$\tan 45° = 1 \qquad \sin 30° = \frac{1}{2} \qquad \sin 60° = \frac{\sqrt{3}}{2} \qquad \cos 60° = \frac{1}{2} \qquad \tan 30° = \frac{\sqrt{3}}{3} \qquad \sin 45° = \frac{\sqrt{2}}{2}$$

Reflect and reason

How did your knowledge of exact trigonometric values help you to answer these questions?

1 What is $\cos 60° + \sin 30° + \tan 45°$?

2 Write these ratios in ascending order of size.
  $\sin 30°$ $\cos 30°$ $\tan 30°$ $\sin 45°$ $\tan 45°$

3 What is the perimeter of this triangle?

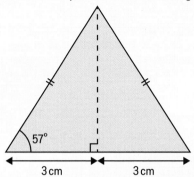

4 The angle BAD in this parallelogram is 43°.
  The perpendicular height of the parallelogram is 8 cm.
  What is the length of CD?

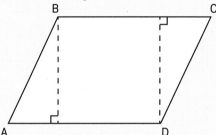

5 Ladders are not safe if the angle they make with the ground is less than 75°.
  A ladder that is 6.5 m long is placed so that it reaches 5 m up the wall.
  Is this ladder at a safe angle? Give reasons.

 ⊠ Exam practice

1 ABCD is a trapezium.

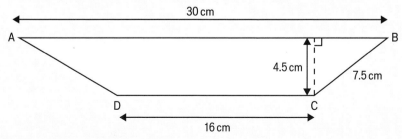

Work out the size of angle DAB.
Give your answer correct to 1 decimal place.   (5 marks)

Adapted from 1MA1/2F, November 2017, Q22

Exam feedback   ResultsPlus

In a similar question, many students did not realise that trigonometry was needed.

Mixed exercises C

Mixed problem-solving practice C

1   Copy the diagram.

    a Rotate shape A 90° clockwise about the origin.
       Label the new shape B.

    b Reflect shape B in the *y*-axis.
       Label the new shape C.

    c Describe fully the single transformation that
       maps shape A onto shape C.

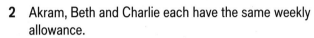

2   Akram, Beth and Charlie each have the same weekly
    allowance.

    Each week: Akram saves $\frac{3}{5}$ and spends the rest.

                Beth spends 42% and saves the rest.
                Charlie saves and spends in the ratio save : spend = 13 : 7
    Who saves the most? Show your working.

3   Aron and Mela share some money in the ratio 4 : 7
    Mela gets £60 more than Aron.
    How much money does Aron get?

4   Here are the ingredients needed to make 8 pancakes:

    100 g flour   2 eggs   300 ml milk

    Caitlin is going to make some pancakes.
    She has these ingredients.
    325 g flour   9 eggs   825 ml milk
    Work out the greatest number of pancakes that Caitlin can make with her ingredients.
    Show your working.

5   A shop has two special offers on burgers.

       4 frozen burgers: Special offer 15% off
      Individual burgers: Special offer 35p off for every 4 burgers you buy

    The normal price of a box of 4 frozen burgers is £2.45.
    The normal price of an individual burger is 62p.
    Shey is going to buy 3 boxes of the frozen burgers on special offer or 12 individual burgers
    on special offer.
    Which special offer is the better value for money?

6   The line L is shown on the grid.
    Write the equation for L.

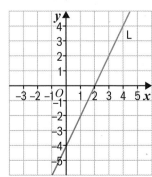

7 Each day, Alex cycles from his house to college.
The travel graph shows Alex's journey to college on Monday.

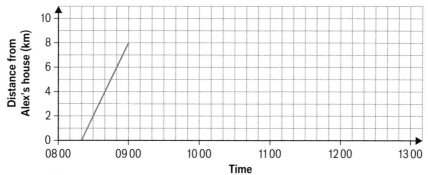

a What time does he leave home?

b How far is the college from Alex's house?

Alex stays at college for $2\frac{1}{2}$ hours.

He then cycles back to his house at 16 km/h.

c Copy and complete the travel graph.

8 This gate is made from 8 straight pieces of metal.
The weight of the metal is 1.2 kg per metre.
Work out the total weight of the metal in the gate.
Give your answer to 1 decimal place.

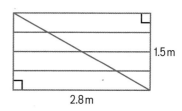

9 Trapezium ABCD is made of two triangles
ABF and CDE and a rectangle BCEF.
Work out the length of side AD.
Give your answer correct to 3 significant
figures.

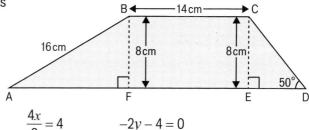

10 a Solve these four equations.

$$7x + 9 = 2 \qquad 8y - 5 = 3 \qquad \frac{4x}{3} = 4 \qquad -2y - 4 = 0$$

Draw a grid with axes from −5 to 5. Plot the solutions to the equations as lines on the grid.

b What is the area of the shape enclosed by the four lines?

✦ Exam practice

11 4 kg of fish costs £56
Dean buys 3 kg of the fish.
Work out how much Dean pays.   **(2 marks)**

Adapted from 1MA1/1F, May 2018, Q8

Exam feedback   Results**Plus**

Most students who achieved a **Grade 3** or above answered a similar question well.

✦ Exam practice

12 Draw the graph of $y = 2 - 3x$ for values from −3 to 3.   **(3 marks)**

Adapted from 1MA1/1F, May 2018, Q25

Mixed problem-solving practice C

13 Describe fully the single transformation that maps shape S onto shape T. **(2 marks)**

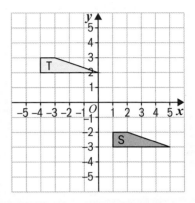

Adapted from 1MA1/2F, June 2018, Q18

Exam feedback

ResultsPlus

Most students who achieved a **Grade 5** answered a similar question well.

✦ Exam practice

14 You can use this graph to change between kilograms and pounds.

    a Change 7 kilograms to pounds. **(1 mark)**

    Abi's weight is 8 stone and 3 pounds.
    1 stone = 14 pounds

    b What is Abi's weight in kilograms?
       Give your answer to 1 decimal place. **(3 marks)**

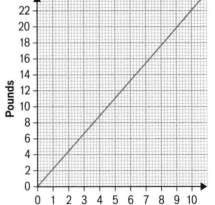

Adapted from 1MA1/2F, June 2017, Q11

Exam feedback

ResultsPlus

Most students who achieved a **Grade 4** or above answered a similar question well.

✦ Exam practice

15 At a school, the number of teachers and the number of support staff are in the ratio 7 : 6 and the number of support staff and the number of students are in the ratio 3 : 40
There are 800 students at the school.

How many teachers are there at the school? **(3 marks)**

Adapted from 1MA1/1F, May 2018, Q20

⬡ Exam practice

16 Alfie buys a motorbike for £10 500 plus VAT at 20%
Alfie pays a deposit for the motorbike.
He then pays the rest of the cost in 15 equal payments of £315 each month.

Find the ratio of the deposit Alfie pays to the total of the 15 equal payments.
Give your answer in its simplest form.　　　　　　　　　　**(5 marks)**

Adapted from 1MA1/2F, June 2018, Q23

Exam feedback　　　　　　　　　　　　　　　　**Results Plus**

Most students who achieved a **Grade 5** answered a similar question well.

⬡ Exam practice

17 Here is a triangular prism.
Work out the volume of the prism.
Give your answer correct to 3 significant figures.　　**(5 marks)**

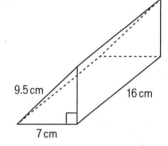

Adapted from 1MA1/2F, June 2018, Q26

Exam feedback　　　　　　　　　　　　　　　　**Results Plus**

In a similar question, students did not recognise this required the use of Pythagoras' theorem.

⬡ Exam practice

18 PQR is a right-angled triangle.
Work out the size of angle PRQ.
Give your answer correct to 1 decimal place.　　**(2 marks)**

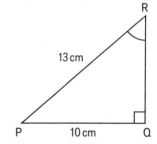

Adapted from 1MA1/3F, June 2018, Q23a

Exam feedback　　　　　　　　　　　　　　　　**Results Plus**

Most students who achieved a **Grade 5** answered a similar question well.

13 Probability

13.1 Calculating probability

Key points

- Probability = $\dfrac{\text{number of successful outcomes}}{\text{total number of possible outcomes}}$

- If the probability of an event happening is P, then the probability of it not happening is $1 - P$.

△ Purposeful practice 1

Write down the probabilities P(red) and P(white) for each set of spots.
In questions **5** and **6**, also write down the probability P(black).

1 ● ● ○   2 ● ● ○ ○   3 ● ● ○ ○ ○   4 ● ● ○ ○ ○ ○

5 ● ● ○ ○ ○ ○ ●   6 ● ● ○ ○ ○ ○ ● ●

Reflect and reason

What are the missing words from these sentences: **always** or **sometimes** or **never**?
Adding one more spot changes the probability by:
_____ increasing the numerator by 1.   _____ increasing the denominator by 1.
_____ decreasing the denominator by 1.

△ Purposeful practice 2

The blue (B) and yellow (Y) sections in the spinners are all of equal size.
Write down the probabilities P(B) and P(Y) for each spinner.

1   2   3   4   5   6

Reflect and reason

Jan says, 'When a spinner has only two colours, blue and yellow, then P(B) = P(Y) = $\frac{1}{2}$.'
Use your answers to **Q1–6** to explain why Jan is wrong.

△ Purposeful practice 3

Write down the probabilities for choosing one cube
out of this set of cubes.

1 P(P)	2 P(B)	3 P(Y)	4 P(W)
5 P(P or B)	6 P(P or Y)	7 P(P or W)	8 P(P or B or Y)
9 P(P or B or W)	10 P(B or Y or W)	11 P(W or Y or P)	12 P(not B)
13 P(not Y)	14 P(not W)	15 P(not B or Y)	16 P(not B or P)
17 P(not B or W)	18 P(not W or Y)		

Reflect and reason

Use your answers to **Q1–18** to explain why P(not W) = P(P or B or Y) = 1 – P(W).

1 Draw a set of black and white counters, where the probability of picking a black counter is 4 times the probability of picking a white counter.

2 There are only men and women on a train.
   The probability of picking a man at random is $\frac{5}{8}$
   What is the probability of picking a woman?

3 The probability of snow tomorrow is 95%.
   What is the probability that it does not snow tomorrow?

4 A tin contains chocolate biscuits and plain biscuits.
   There are twice as many chocolate biscuits as plain biscuits.
   A biscuit is picked at random.
   Work out the probability that it is a chocolate biscuit.

5 There are only £1, 50p and 20p coins in a bag.
   There are three times as many £1 coins as 20p coins.
   There are twice as many 50p coins as £1 coins.
   Sara takes a coin from the bag at random.
   What is the probability that she takes a £1 coin?

6 A spinner has scores from 1 to 4.
   The probability of landing on 1 is the same as the probability of landing on 4.
   The table shows the probabilities of landing on 2 and 3.
   Copy and complete the table.

Number on spinner	1	2	3	4
Probability		0.4	0.1	

✸ Exam practice

1 There are only 3 red sweets, 4 yellow sweets and 7 green sweets in a bag.
   One sweet is taken at random from the bag.
   Write down the probability that this sweet is red.   **(2 marks)**

   Adapted from 1MA1/1F, May 2017, Q12

Exam feedback   ResultsPlus

Most students who achieved a **Grade 2** or above answered a similar question well.

Key point

- A sample space diagram shows all the possible outcomes of an event. You can use it to find a theoretical probability.

△ Purposeful practice 1

Each column of the table shows two events.

	1	2	3	4
Event 1: Coin is flipped	(coin)	(coin)	(coin)	(coin)
Event 2: Spinner is spun	R Y B spinner	B Y G R spinner	3 2 4 1 spinner	R Y B R spinner

Answer these questions for the two events in each column.

a How many possible outcomes are there for Event 1?

b How many possible outcomes are there for Event 2?

c List all the possible outcomes when Event 1 **and** Event 2 happen together. The first one has been done for you. (Heads, Red)

d How many are possible outcomes are there when Event 1 **and** Event 2 happen together?

Reflect and reason

How can you use the number of possible outcomes from two separate events to work out the number of possible outcomes when both events happen together?

△ Purposeful practice 2

Luke spins each spinner once.
He adds the two numbers together to get his score.

1 Copy and complete this sample space diagram for each possible score.

2 Find the probability that Luke's score is

    a 4   **b** less than 4

    c more than 4   **d** 4 or more

    e 4 or less

		4-sided spinner			
		1	2	4	5
3-sided spinner	1	2			
	2				
	3			7	

Reflect and reason

Do you need to draw a sample space diagram to answer questions like **Q1–2**? Could you list the possible outcomes instead?

Write one advantage of a list, and one advantage of a sample space diagram.

1 Lea has three cards: Jack, Queen and King.
  She picks one card at random.
  She also throws a fair six-sided dice once.

  a How many possible outcomes include the Queen card?

  b Work out the probability of picking a Jack **and** throwing a 6.

2 Lin spins each spinner once.
  Each spinner lands on a number.
  She multiplies the two numbers together to get a score.
  Work out the probability that she scores zero.

3 A café menu has three different starters and four different main courses.
  How many different ways can you choose one starter and one main course?

4 Deepal spins the spinner and rolls a fair six-sided dice.
  He adds the two numbers together to get a score.
  Work out the probability that his score is an even number.

5 Bob and Cat play a game.
  They roll two fair six-sided dice and add the numbers to get a score.
  Cat wins if the score is more than 6.
  Bob wins if the score is 6 or less.
  Is this game fair? Explain.

1 There are 3 cards in Box A and 3 cards in Box B.
  There is a number on each card.

  Box A   Box B

  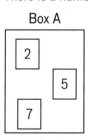 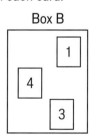

  Jim takes a card at random from Box A and a card from Box B.
  He adds together the numbers on the two cards to get a total score.
  Work out the probability that the total score is 6 or less.   **(2 marks)**

  Adapted from 1MA1/1F, November 2017, Q17

Exam feedback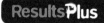

In a similar question, students who took an unsystematic approach to listing the possible outcomes often missed one or more possible outcome, and got the wrong probability as a result.

Key points

- You can estimate the probability of an event from the results of an experiment or survey.

    $$\text{estimated probability} = \frac{\text{frequency of event}}{\text{total frequency}}$$

- The estimated probability is also called the experimental probability.
- Predicted number of outcomes = probability × number of trials

△ Purposeful practice 1

Dice A and dice B are rolled 100 times each. The tables show the results.

Dice A

Score	1	2	3	4	5	6
Frequency	15	16	16	18	17	18

Dice B

Score	1	2	3	4	5	6
Frequency	18	16	15	15	19	17

For each dice

1 Use the results to estimate the probability of rolling a 6. Do you think the dice are fair?

2 Rounding to the nearest whole number, predict the number of times you would expect it to land on a six in   **a** 10 rolls   **b** 50 rolls   **c** 200 rolls

3 In a game at an arcade, you pay £1 to roll the dice. You win £3 if you get a 6. Otherwise you lose. Copy and complete this table to estimate the profit for 200 rolls with each dice.

	Number of rolls	Money paid to arcade	Estimated prize money paid	Estimated profit
Dice A	200			
Dice B	200			

Reflect and reason

Will says, 'The probability of rolling a 6 on a fair dice is $\frac{1}{6}$. So in 100 rolls you should get each score $100 \div 6$ times.' Explain why Will is wrong.

△ Purposeful practice 2

The table gives information about the parrots in a zoo.

	Male	Female	Totals
Red	12	7	19
Green	5	13	18
Totals	17	20	37

1 What is the total number of parrots?

2 What is the number of red parrots?

3 What is the probability of picking a red parrot at random from all the parrots?

4 What is the total number of female red parrots?

5 Write the probability of picking a female red parrot at random from all the parrots.

6 Write the probability of picking a female red parrot at random from the red parrots.

7 Write the probability of picking a green male parrot at random from the male parrots.

Reflect and reason

Using the table in Purposeful practice 2, find the probability that a parrot picked from the green parrots is male.

1   In a hoopla game, you throw a hoop over a cube to win.
    10 people throw four hoops each. The results are shown in the table.

Won a prize	Did not win
2	38

   a   Estimate the number of wins for 100 hoops.

   b   It costs £1 to throw a hoop. Each prize is £10.
       Estimate the expected profit when 60 people have one go each.

   a   Give a reason why the actual profit may be different from your answer to **b**.

2   The table shows numbers of people in the first 70 cars in a
    car park one morning.

Number of people	Frequency
1	21
2	15
3	17
4	11
5	6

   a   A car is picked at random. What is the most likely
       number of people in the car?

   b   The car park holds 400 cars.
       Estimate the number of cars in the car park that had
       more than one person.

3   Seb has 52 chocolates.
    20 of the chocolates are plain chocolate.
    14 of the milk chocolates are orange flavoured.
    7 of the mint-flavoured chocolates are plain chocolate.

   a   Use this information to copy and complete the
       two-way table.

   b   Seb picks a chocolate at random.
       Write down the probability that this chocolate is
       milk chocolate and mint flavoured.

	Milk	Plain	Total
Mint			
Orange			
Total			

1   A biased dice was rolled 50 times.
    The table shows the number of times it landed on 2, on 3, on 4, on 5 and on 6.

Number on dice	1	2	3	4	5	6
Frequency		7	4	9	12	8

    Peter rolls this dice 200 times.
    Work out an estimate for the number of times the dice will land on 1 or 2.   **(2 marks)**

Adapted from 1MA1/2F, June 2017, Q17

Exam feedback   Results**Plus**

Most students who achieved a **Grade 5** answered a similar question well.

Key points

- Curly brackets {} show a set of values.
- ξ means the universal set – all the elements being considered.
- A ∩ B means 'A intersection B'. This is all the elements that are in A *and* B.
- A ∪ B means 'A union B'. This is all the elements that are in A *or* B *or* both.
- A′ means the elements *not* in A.

△ Purposeful practice 1

1 ξ = {numbers from 1 to 20}

A = {1, 3, 8, 10, 15}   B = {1, 2, 5, 8, 10, 12, 14, 19}

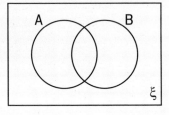

   a Which numbers are in A *and* B?

   b Copy and complete the Venn diagram for ξ, A and B.

   c Write down the numbers that are in set

   i A ∪ B   **ii** A ∩ B   **iii** B′   **iv** (A ∪ B)′

2 Repeat **Q1** for these sets.

   ξ = {even numbers from 10 to 30 (including 10 and 30)}.

   A = {multiples of 3}   B = {multiples of 4}

3 Repeat **Q1** for these sets.

   ξ = {numbers from 1 to 12}.

   A = {odd numbers}   B = {multiples of 5}

Reflect and reason

How many times should each number in ξ appear in the Venn diagram?

△ Purposeful practice 2

The numbers 1 to 11 are put into a Venn diagram.

1 How many numbers are there in the universal set ξ?

2 How many numbers are there in C ∩ D?

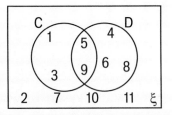

3 A number is chosen at random from the Venn diagram.

   a What is the probability that this number is in the set C ∩ D?

   b What is the probability that this number is in the set D?

   c What is the probability that this number is in the set C ∪ D?

   d What is the probability that this number is in the set (C ∪ D)′?

Reflect and reason

Why do all the answers to **Q3** have the same denominator?

1 Here is a Venn diagram.

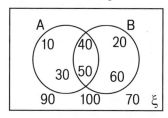

One of the numbers in the diagram is chosen at random.
Write down the probability that the number is in set A ∩ B.

2 The numbers 5 to 12 are put into a Venn diagram.
5, 6, 7, 10 and 12 have already been placed.
The number 8 is in set Q but not in set P.
The number 9 is in both set P and set Q.
The number 11 is not in set P or set Q.

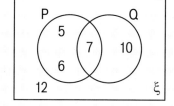

a Copy and complete the Venn diagram.

A number is chosen at random from the Venn diagram.

b Write down the probability that this number is not in set P.

3 Draw a Venn diagram to represent these sets.

ξ = {1, 2, 3, 4, 5, 6, 7, 8, 9, 10, 11, 12}
M = {multiples of 3}
M ∩ P = {3, 9}
M ∪ P = {2, 3, 6, 7, 9, 12}

1 ξ = {even numbers less than 20}   A = {6, 12, 18}   B = {4, 8, 12, 16}

a Copy and complete the Venn diagram to represent this information.   **(4 marks)**

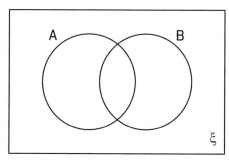

b A number is chosen at random from the universal set, ξ.
What is the probability that the number is in the set A ∪ B?   **(2 marks)**

Adapted from 1MA1/3F, June 2017, Q15

Exam feedback   Results**Plus**

Most students who achieved a **Grade 5** answered a similar question well.

Key points

- A frequency tree shows the number of options for different choices.
- A probability tree diagram shows the probabilities of different outcomes.

△ Purposeful practice 1

The frequency tree shows the different counters in a box.

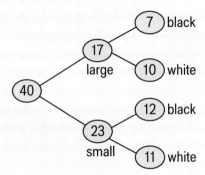

1 What is the total number of counters?

2 What is the total number of black counters?

3 What is the probability that a counter picked at random from the box is black?

4 How many small counters are there?

5 How many small white counters are there?

6 What is the probability that a counter picked at random from the small counters is white?

Reflect and reason

Using the frequency tree in Purposeful practice 1, match each probability to its description.

$\frac{21}{40}$	The probability that a counter picked from the large counters is white
$\frac{10}{17}$	The probability that a counter picked from all the counters is large and white
$\frac{10}{40}$	The probability that a counter picked from all the counters is white

△ Purposeful practice 2

1 This spinner is spun twice.
   Copy and complete the tree diagram.

```
  1st      2nd
         ┌─ R   P(R,R) =
   3/5 ─ R
         └─ Y   P(R,Y) =

         ┌─ R   P(Y,R) =
   2/5 ─ Y
         └─ Y   P(Y,Y) =
```

2 This spinner is spun twice.
   Draw a tree diagram like the one in **Q1** for this spinner.

Reflect and reason

What do the probabilities on each pair of branches add up to?

What do the probabilities of all the possible outcomes add up to? Explain.

1 100 students had a project.
53 of these students are girls the rest are boys.
9 of the 100 students did *not* do the project.
42 of the boys did do the project.

    a Use this information to copy and complete the frequency tree.

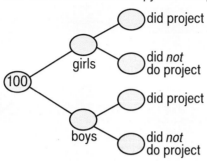

    b One of the girls is chosen at random.
       Work out the probability that this girl did *not* do the project.

2 70 people took an eye test.
31 of these people were children.
26 of the 70 people needed glasses.
15 adults needed glasses.
One of the adults is chosen at random.
Work out the probability that this adult needed glasses.

3 Nic has a biased dice. On this dice, the probability of rolling a 3 is 0.25.
Nic rolls the dice twice.
Work out the probability that she rolls exactly one 3. Draw a tree diagram to help you.

✦ Exam practice

1 Each person who works in an office either drives to work or uses public transport.

83 of the 200 employees use public transport.

46 of the 92 male employees drive to work.

Copy and complete the frequency tree for this information.

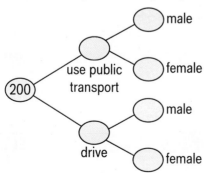

(3 marks)

Adapted from 1MA1/2F, June 2018, Q14

Exam feedback   ResultsⓅlus

Most students who achieved a **Grade 2** or above answered a similar question well.

Key point

- When the outcome of one event changes the possible outcomes of the next event, the two events are not independent.

⚠ Purposeful practice 1

1 Sam has three blue cubes and three red cubes.

He takes one at random and keeps it.
Then he takes another cube at random.

   a Copy and complete the probability
     tree diagram to show this.

   b Find the probability that Sam picks

     i two red cubes

     ii one red cube

     iii at least one red cube

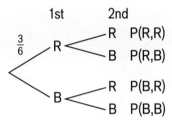

Reflect and reason

How can you use P(R, R) to work out the probability that at least one cube is blue?

⚠ Purposeful practice 2

1 Josip has 4 red and 7 black sweets.
He picks one sweet at random and eats it.
Then he picks another.

   a Draw a probability tree diagram like the one in Purposeful practice 1, **Q1** to show this.

   b Work out the probability that Josip picks at least 1 red sweet.

2 Luisa has 3 white and 5 black socks in a drawer.
She takes 1 sock at random, and then another.

   a Draw a probability tree diagram like the one in Purposeful practice 1, **Q1** to show this.

   b Work out the probability that Luisa picks 2 socks the same colour.

Reflect and reason

When a problem involves picking one thing, keeping it, and then picking another, what can you say about the probability of picking the second thing?

1   In a bag of sweets there are 5 toffees and 7 mints.
    Sze takes one sweet at random from the bag.
    Then she takes another sweet.
    Work out the probability that Sze takes two different types of sweet.

2   The letters of the word 'purposeful' are written on cards.
    Tina picks two of the letter cards at random.
    Work out the probability that she picks two vowels.

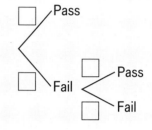

3   The probability that a student passes the driving test
    the first time is 0.7.
    The probability that a student passes the driving test
    the second time is 0.8.

    a   Copy and complete this probability tree diagram.

    b   Work out the probability that a student picked at
            random fails both driving tests.

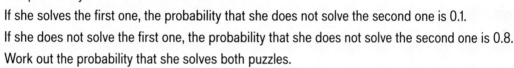

4   May has two puzzles to solve.

    The probability that she solves the first one is 0.6.

    If she solves the first one, the probability that she does not solve the second one is 0.1.

    If she does not solve the first one, the probability that she does not solve the second one is 0.8.

    Work out the probability that she solves both puzzles.

✧ **Exam practice**

1   The probability that Mark wins a game of tennis is 0.58
    He plays two games of tennis.

    Mark draws a probability tree diagram. The diagram is **not** correct.

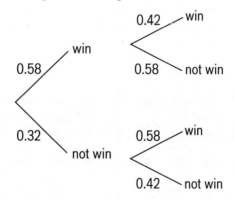

    Write down two things that are wrong with the probability tree diagram.   **(2 marks)**

    Adapted from 1MA1/3F, June 2018, Q22

Exam feedback   Results**Plus**

Most students who achieved a **Grade 5** answered a similar question well.

---

14 Multiplicative reasoning

14.1 Percentages

Key points

- The original amount is always represented as 100%. If the amount is **increased**, the new amount will be **more** than 100%. If the amount is **decreased**, the new amount will be **less** than 100%.
- You can calculate a percentage change using the formula:

$$\text{percentage change} = \frac{\text{actual change}}{\text{original amount}} \times 100$$

Purposeful practice 1

1 The original amount is £100. Calculate the new amount after an increase of
   a 25%   b 10%   c 5%   d 2.5%

2 The new amount is £100. Calculate the original amount before an increase of
   a 25%   b 10%   c 5%   d 2.5%

3 The original amount is £100. Calculate the new amount after a decrease of
   a 25%   b 10%   c 5%   d 2.5%

4 The new amount is £100. Calculate the original amount before a decrease of
   a 25%   b 10%   c 5%   d 2.5%

Reflect and reason

In **Q2**, why can't you find the correct answer by working out 25%, 10%, 5% and 2.5% of £100, and then subtracting the results from £100?

Purposeful practice 2

1 Calculate the percentage change.
   a £300 increased to £330   b £400 increased to £440
   c £440 decreased to £400   d £400 decreased to £360
   e £360 increased to £400   f £36 increased to £40
   g £3.60 increased to £4.00   h £4.00 decreased to £3.60
   i £400 decreased to £3.60

2 Calculate the percentage profit or loss.
   a cost price £3.60, selling price £4.00
   b cost price £4.00, selling price £3.60
   c cost price £36, selling price £40
   d cost price £40, selling price £36

Reflect and reason

Q1c–e all involved a £40 difference. Why was the percentage change not the same each time?

1 The income of the Soda Pop company increased by 35% over the last year.
Soda Pop's income is now £15 000 a year. What was Soda Pop's income last year?

2 A company sells two bottles of shampoo.
A large 750 ml bottle costs £2.50. A small 600 ml bottle costs £1.75.
During a special offer, the small bottle has 25% extra free.
Is it better to buy the small bottle with the offer or the large bottle without the offer? Give reasons.

3 Morena sold her guitar. She made a profit of 20% compared to the original price.
She sold the guitar for £360 but had to spend £40 on postage.
How much did the guitar originally cost?

4 Clary is writing an essay that must be between 5000 and 7500 words long.
Her second draft is 20% over the upper word limit and 30% longer than her first draft.

   a How long was her first draft?

   b By what percentage does she need to reduce her second draft to be within the word limit?

5 A takeaway restaurant offers a 15% discount for orders over £30.
Anita has spent £27.30 so far. She can also order a dessert for £4.60.
Will Anita's order be cheaper with the dessert or without?

6 Dogs sleep 25% less than cats and 50% more than humans. Dogs sleep for 12 hours a day.
By what percentage do cats sleep longer than humans?

7 A rectangle has a width of 3 cm and a height of 5 cm.
The width is increased by 20% and the height is decreased by 20%.

   a By what percentage does the area change?

   b By what percentage does the perimeter change?

Exam practice

1 Fayyaz bought a mobile phone for £180.
He sold it at a profit of 22%.
How much money did Fayyaz sell the mobile phone for?   **(2 marks)**

Adapted from 1MA1/1F, May 2017, Q20

2 Sam buys 3.5 kg of fudge to sell. He pays £72 for the fudge.
Sam puts all the fudge into boxes. He puts 175 g of fudge into each box.
He sells each box for £4. Sam sells all the boxes of fudge.
Work out his percentage profit.
Give your answer correct to 1 decimal place.   **(4 marks)**

Adapted from 1MA1/1F, May 2018, Q21

Exam feedback

ResultsPlus

Q1: Most students who achieved a **Grade 4** or above answered a similar question well.
Q2: Most students who achieved a **Grade 4** or above answered a similar question well.

Key point

- Banks and building societies pay compound interest. At the end of the first year, interest is paid on the money in the account. The interest is added to the amount in the account. At the end of the second year, interest is paid on the original amount in the account **and** on the interest earned in the first year, and so on.

Purposeful practice 1

£1000 is put into a bank account with 5% annual compound interest.
Calculate the total amount in the bank account after

1 1 year   **2** 2 years   **3** 3 years   **4** 6 years

Reflect and reason

Why is the amount of interest earned after 6 years not equal to double the amount of interest earned after 3 years?

Purposeful practice 2

A car is worth £1000 and decreases in price by 5% per year.
Calculate how much it is worth after

1 1 year   **2** 2 years   **3** 3 years   **4** 6 years

Reflect and reason

Will the car ever have a value of £0?
Try calculating the value after a large number of years to check.

Purposeful practice 3

Calculate the interest received on £350 after

1 5 years at 3% annual compound interest   **2** 3 years at 5% monthly compound interest

3 3 years at 5% annual compound interest   **4** 5 years at 3% monthly compound interest

Reflect and reason

Why do **Q1** and **Q3** give different answers?
Compare with simple interest at the same interest rate.

Purposeful practice 4

Using multipliers, find the overall percentage change after a

1 10% increase, then 10% increase   **2** 10% increase, then 5% decrease

3 10% increase, then 5% increase   **4** 10% increase, then 10% decrease

Reflect and reason

Explain why the answer to **Q4** is not 0%.

1 A chocolate bar cost 12p in 1995. It costs 20p in 2018.
   Prices are expected to increase by 2% every year from the previous year.
   Has the chocolate bar increased in price more or less than expected?
   You must show your working.

2 Chelsea wants to take out a loan to go on holiday.
   The holiday costs £1500.
   Chelsea can take out a loan that she pays back after 4 weeks at 0.2% compound interest
   per day. Or she can take out a loan that she pays back after 2 years at 2.5% compound interest
   per annum.
   Which loan is cheaper?

3 Tom bought a piece of art in 2012 for £16 700. It increases in value by 3% per year.
   Tom wants to sell the piece of art for more than £20 000.
   In what year can he sell the piece of art?

4 Dennis had a collection of toys that was worth £340 in 1997.
   For the first 2 years, the collection increased in value by 14% each year.
   After that, it decreased in value by 3% every year.
   In what year (other than 1997) will the value of the collection be closest to £340?

5 Adib buys shares in a company for £745.
   The share price increases by 30%, then again by 54%.
   The price of the shares then drops by 60%.
   Adib decides to sell his shares.
   Will he make a profit? Give reasons.

6 A radioactive material has a half-life of 10 days. 30 days go by.
   What percentage of radioactive material is left?

1 Jakc invests £670 in a savings account.
   He receives 1.7% per annum compound interest.
   How much money will Jake have in the account at the end of 7 years?   **(2 marks)**

   Adapted from 1MA1/2F, Specimen Papers, Set 1, Q25

2 Monica wants to invest £52 000 for 4 years in a bank.
   Friendly Bank gives 2.1% compound interest every year.
   Aspiration Bank gives 5% interest for the first year and 0.8% interest for every year after that.
   Which bank should Monica use? You must show all your working.   **(3 marks)**

   Adapted from 1MA1/2F, June 2017, Q22

Exam feedback   `ResultsPlus`

Q2: In a similar question, many students used the wrong multiplier for the 0.8% interest rate.

Key points

- Density is a compound measure. It is the mass of substance contained in a certain volume.

  $$\text{density} = \frac{\text{mass}}{\text{volume}} \text{ or } D = \frac{M}{V}$$

- Density is usually measured in g/cm³. To calculate density in g/cm³, you need to know the mass in grams (g) and the volume in cubic centimetres (cm³). It can also be measured in kg/m³.

- Pressure is a compound measure. It is the force applied over an area.

  $$\text{pressure} = \frac{\text{force}}{\text{area}} \text{ or } P = \frac{F}{A}$$

- Pressure is usually measured in N/m².

Purposeful practice 1

Calculate the density in kg/m³ when

1 mass = 3 kg, volume = 1 m³   2 mass = 6 kg, volume = 1 m³   3 mass = 6 kg, volume = 2 m³

4 mass = 3 kg, volume = 2 m³   5 mass = 2 kg, volume = 3 m³   6 mass = 1 kg, volume = 3 m³

Reflect and reason

What happens to the density when the volume doubles?

Purposeful practice 2

1 Calculate the pressure in N/m² when

   a force = 6 N, area = 2 m²   b force = 12 N, area = 2 m²

   c force = 12 N, area = 3 m²   d force = 12 N, area = 4 m²

2 Calculate the rate of flow in litres per minute, when

   a 12 litres of water flow in 4 minutes   b 6 litres of water flow in 4 minutes

   c 3 litres of water flow in 4 minutes   d 12 litres of water flow in 1 hour

   e 6 litres of water flow in 1 hour   f 12 litres of water flow in 1 second

Reflect and reason

In **Q2d** and **Q2f**, how did you decide whether to multiply or divide to convert litres per hour and litres per second into litres per minute?

Purposeful practice 3

Calculate

1 the mass when the density is 2 kg/m³ and the volume is 10 m³

2 the force when the pressure is 3 N/m² and the area is 6 m²

3 the volume when the density is 2 kg/m³ and the mass is 10 kg

4 the area when the pressure is 3 N/m² and force is 6 N

Reflect and reason

How was the method used for **Q3** and **Q4** different from the method used for **Q1** and **Q2**?

1 Samantha says, 'A person wearing a pair of shoes with a heel area of 25 cm² on Earth will exert more pressure than the same person wearing a pair of shoes with a heel area of 10 cm² on the Moon, because the person is exerting less force on the Moon.'
The force (in newtons) this person exerts on Earth is 9.8 multiplied by their weight of 65 kg.
The force (in newtons) this person exerts on the Moon is 1.6 multiplied by their weight of 65 kg.
Is Samantha right?

2 Two bowls each hold 5 litres of water.
The first bowl fills at a rate of 50 ml/minute. The second bowl fills at a rate of 120 ml/minute.

   a The first bowl has 2.5 litres of water and the second bowl has no water. Which bowl will finish filling first?

   b How much water should the first bowl contain before starting to fill the second bowl, for both bowls to be full at the same time?

3 Mischa is paid a fixed monthly wage of £1239, and he usually works 160 hours a month.

   a How much does Mischa earn in one hour?

   b Mischa starts to work an extra 10 hours per month. How much does he earn in one hour now?

   c Sandra is paid hourly. She gets £11.30 per hour. In one month, Sandra and Mischa both work 150 hours. Who is paid more that month?

4 An English teacher says that, for every three sentences in an essay, there should be one quote from the book.

   a An essay has 82 quotes. How many sentences should the essay contain?

   b A second essay was written that was half the length of the first essay.

   How many sentences and quotes should the second essay contain?

5 Material A has a density of 3 kg/m³.
A sample of material B has a volume of 5 m³ and a mass of 18 kg.
Material C is made from 40 m³ of material A and 60 m³ of material B.
What is the mass of material C?

6 The density of silver is 10.49 grams per cm³. The density of gold is 19.32 grams per cm³.

   a A jeweller has 2 cm³ of silver. What mass of silver is this?

   b A jeweller has 0.2 cm³ of gold. What mass of gold is this?

   c Work out the density of the silver and gold together.

✦ Exam practice

1 The density of pineapple juice is 1.06 grams per cm³. The density of sugar syrup is 1.3 grams per cm³. The density of lemonade is 0.98 grams per cm³.
48 cm³ of pineapple juice is mixed with 12 cm³ of sugar syrup and 200 cm³ of lemonade to make a drink with a volume of 260 cm³.
Work out the density of the drink. Give your answer correct to 2 decimal places. **(4 marks)**

Adapted from 1MA1//3F, June 2017, Q20

Exam feedback

ResultsPlus

In a similar question, many students gave the total mass of the drink as their answer, rather than its density.

14.4 Distance, speed and time

Key points

- You can calculate speed using the formula:

  $$\text{speed} = \frac{\text{distance}}{\text{time}} \text{ or } S = \frac{D}{T}$$

- Speed is often measured in metres per second (m/s), kilometres per hour (km/h) or miles per hour (mph).

- You can use the kinematics formulae for calculations with moving objects. a is a constant acceleration, u is the initial velocity, v is the final velocity, t is the time taken and s is the displacement from the position when $t = 0$.

  $$v = u + at \qquad s = ut + \frac{1}{2}at^2 \qquad v^2 = u^2 + 2as$$

△ Purposeful practice 1

1 Calculate speed in m/s when

   a distance = 6 m, time = 3 s

   b distance = 3 m, time = 6 s

2 Calculate distance in metres when

   a speed = 6 m/s, time = 3 s

   b speed = 3 m/s, time = 6 s

3 Calculate time in hours when

   a speed = 6 metres per hour, distance = 3 m

   b speed = 3 metres per hour, distance = 6 m

Reflect and reason

What objects might travel at these speeds?

△ Purposeful practice 2

Use the kinematics formulae to work out

1 v when

   a $u = 3\,\text{m/s}$, $a = 4\,\text{m/s}^2$, $t = 5\,\text{s}$

   b $u = 5\,\text{m/s}$, $a = 3\,\text{m/s}^2$, $t = 4\,\text{s}$

2 s when

   a $u = 3\,\text{m/s}$, $a = 4\,\text{m/s}^2$, $t = 5\,\text{s}$

   b $u = 5\,\text{m/s}$, $a = 3\,\text{m/s}^2$, $t = 4\,\text{s}$

3 v when

   a $u = 3\,\text{m/s}$, $a = 4\,\text{m/s}^2$, $s = 5\,\text{m}$

   b $u = 5\,\text{m/s}$, $a = 3\,\text{m/s}^2$, $s = 4\,\text{m}$

Reflect and reason

How did you recognise which kinematics formula to use for each question?

1   Jenny travels from Leicester to Manchester, then on to Southampton.
    The total distance is 331 miles.
    Jenny takes 2 hours and 55 minutes to travel from Leicester to Manchester
    It takes her 3 hours and 8 minutes to travel from Manchester to Southampton.
    What is Jenny's average speed?

2   A ball is thrown upwards into the air. Its initial velocity is 20 m/s.
    It loses speed at 9.8 m/s^2.

    a   For how long is the ball in the air before it starts to fall back down?

        (The ball stops moving forward before it begins to fall back.)

    b   What height does the ball reach?

3   The speed limit on a road in France is 90 km/h.
    Anjali drives at the speed limit for 81 km.
    She then drives through a town that is 4 km wide, at a speed of 40 km/hr.

    a   What is the total time Anjali spent driving?

    b   What is Anjali's average speed over the whole journey?

4   A cheetah is running at a speed of 10 m/s.
    It accelerates at a constant 0.05 m/s^2 for 1 minute.
    How far does the cheetah travel in this time?

5   A child is cycling down a road.
    They start at 5 m/s and accelerate at 0.2 m/s^2.
    What will their speed be when they have cycled 45 m?

6   A horse trots at 4.47 m/s.
    A car is travelling at 20 km/h.
    Can the horse beat the car in a race? Explain your answer.

🕸 Exam practice

1   Gary drove 77 km from Glasgow to Edinburgh.
    He then drove 166 km from Edinburgh to Newcastle.
    Gary's average speed from Glasgow to Edinburgh was 80 km/h.
    Gary took 150 minutes to drive from Edinburgh to Newcastle.
    Work out Gary's average speed for his total drive from Glasgow to Newcastle.   **(4 marks)**

    Adapted from 1MA1/2F, June 2017, Q20a

Exam feedback   Results**Plus**

In a similar question, many students calculated the average of the average speeds for the two parts of
the journey, rather than dividing the total distance by the total time.

Key points

- When two variables are in direct proportion, pairs of values are in the same ratio.
- $y \propto x$ means 'y is proportional to x'.
- When $y \propto x$, then $y = kx$, where k is the constant of proportionality.
- When two variables X and Y are in inverse proportion:

$$X \propto \frac{1}{Y} \qquad X = \frac{k}{Y} \qquad Y = \frac{k}{X} \qquad YX = k$$

△ Purposeful practice 1

For each ratio, write a formula connecting the variables.

1 $x : y$
  1 : 4

2 $x : y$
  4 : 1

3 $x : y$
  3 : 2

4 $x : y$
  2 : 3

5 $x : y$
  2 : 6

6 $x : y$
  1 : 3

Reflect and reason

Two ratios give the same formula. Which two?

△ Purposeful practice 2

1 g is directly proportional to h.
  a When $g = 5$, $h = 2$
    i Write an equation connecting g and h.
    ii When $g = 12$, what is h?   **iii** When $h = 9$, what is g?
  b When $g = 2$, $h = 5$
    i Write an equation connecting g and h.
    ii When $g = 12$, what is h?   **iii** When $h = 9$, what is g?

2 f is inversely proportional to w.
  a When $f = 5$, $w = 2$
    i Write an equation connecting f and w.
    ii When $f = 12$, what is w?   **iii** When $w = 9$, what is f?
  b When $f = 2$, $w = 5$
    i Write an equation connecting f and w.
    ii When $f = 12$, what is w?   **iii** When $w = 9$, what is f?

Reflect and reason

Fran says, 'a is inversely proportional to b' and writes this equation

$$\frac{a}{b} = 10$$

Is Fran correct? Explain your answer.

1 The number of cleaners is inversely proportional to the hours it takes to clean an office block.

a Which formula connects cleaners (c) and hours (h), where k is the constant of proportionality?

$$c = kh \qquad h = ck \qquad c = \frac{h}{k} \qquad h = \frac{c}{k} \qquad c = \frac{k}{h}$$

b It is estimated that it will take 2 cleaners 12 hours to clean the office block.

Write the formula connecting c and h.

c Estimate how long it will take to clean the office block when there are 4 cleaners.

2 The amount of water in a bath is directly proportional to how long the tap has been running.

a There are 24 litres of water in the bath after 4 minutes.

Write a formula connecting the amount of water in the bath and the amount of time.

b How much water will be in the bath after 10 minutes?

c The bath holds a maximum of 80 litres of water.

Will the bath overflow after 15 minutes?

3 The number of books Veronica reads is directly proportional to the amount of time she spends reading.
If Veronica reads for 15 hours, she will finish reading 5 books.
How many books will Veronica finish in 42 hours of reading?

4 For each situation, state whether variables are directly proportional, inversely proportional or neither.

a number of litres of fuel in the car (l) and the distance travelled (d)

b number of people in a choir (c) and the time it takes to sing a song (s)

c number of hours worked (h) and the number of pounds earned (p)

5 It takes 4 workers 10 hours to paint a room.
Each worker is paid £13.70 an hour.

a How long would it take 6 workers to paint the room?

b Alfred says that it will cost the same amount of money no matter how many workers are painting the room.

Is Alfred right? Explain.

✕ Exam practice

1 It takes 8 painters 3 days to paint a room.

a Work out how many days it would take 2 painters to complete the same job. **(2 marks)**

b i State one assumption you made in working out your answer. **(1 mark)**

ii How will your answer be affected if your assumption is not correct? **(1 mark)**

Adapted from 1MA1/1F, Spring 2017, Mock Set 2, Q22

15 Constructions, loci and bearings

15.1 3D solids

△ Purposeful practice 1

Here are some three-dimensional shapes. For each shape, write the number of

    a faces   **b** edges   **c** vertices

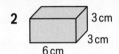

1 3 cm, 3 cm, 3 cm

2 3 cm, 3 cm, 6 cm

3 8 cm, 8 cm, 8 cm

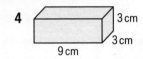

4 3 cm, 3 cm, 9 cm

> **Reflect and reason**
>
> Why do you think a cube is sometimes described as a special type of cuboid?

△ Purposeful practice 2

1 Name these three-dimensional solids.

    a   **b**   **c**

> **Reflect and reason**
>
> Sam says, 'All these 3D shapes have at least one circular face and one curved surface.'
>
> Is Sam correct? Explain.

△ Purposeful practice 3

1 Draw a sketch of a square-based pyramid.

    a What are the names of the shapes of the faces?

    b How many vertices does the pyramid have?

2 Here are some pyramids.

    i   **ii**   **iii**

    a How many edges does each pyramid have?

    b How many vertices does each pyramid have?

> **Reflect and reason**
>
> Write a rule connecting the number of edges on the base and the number of vertices on a pyramid.

1   A pyramid has 9 vertices.
    What 2D shape forms the base?

2   Helen is asked to count the edges on a cube.
    She says,
    'A cube is made from 6 squares.
    Each square has 4 edges.
    So the cube has 24 edges.'
    Explain why Helen's answer is incorrect.

3   Here is a prism.

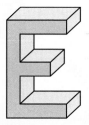

    Evan says,
    'It has 14 faces, 24 edges and 36 vertices.'
    Is he correct? Explain your answer.

✺ Exam practice

1   Here is a cuboid.

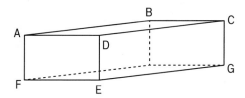

    a   Copy and shade the face ADEF.   **(1 mark)**
    b   How many faces does a cuboid have?   **(1 mark)**

    Adapted from 1MA1/3F, Specimen Papers, Set 1, Q14

2   Here is a hexagonal-based pyramid.

    a   How many faces does the pyramid have?   **(1 mark)**
    b   How many edges does the pyramid have?   **(1 mark)**

    Adapted from 1MA1/1F, Specimen Papers, Set 2, Q4

Key points

- A plane is a flat (2D) surface. A solid shape has a plane of symmetry when a plane cuts the shape in half so that the part of the shape on one side of the plane is an identical reflection of the part on the other side of the plane.
- The plan is the view from above an object.
- The front elevation is the view of the front of an object.
- The side elevation is the view of the side of an object.

△ Purposeful practice 1

1 Here are three planes of symmetry for a cube.
Sketch the other six planes of symmetry for a cube.

2 Write how many planes of symmetry each shape has.

a a pentagonal-based prism   **b** a pentagonal-based pyramid   **c** a hexagonal-based prism   **d** a hexagonal-based pyramid

Reflect and reason

Write a rule connecting the number of planes of symmetry in a prism and a pyramid with the same base shape.

Use your rule to predict how many planes of symmetry there are for an octagonal-based prism and an octagonal-based pyramid.

△ Purposeful practice 2

1 For each plan, write down two solids they could belong to.

a

b

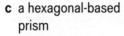

2 Draw the plan view, the front elevation and the side elevation of each cuboid on squared paper.

a 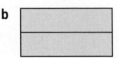 4 cm 2 cm 3 cm

b 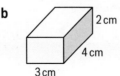 2 cm 4 cm 3 cm

c   4 cm 3 cm 2 cm

Reflect and reason

The images in **Q2** show rotations of the same cuboid.

What changes can you see in the three views of each cuboid?

⊠ Problem-solving practice

1   Here are the plan and front elevation view of a 3D shape, drawn on centimetre squared paper.

   a   Sketch two possible 3D shapes that could have these views. Write the dimensions on the shapes.

   b   Sketch the side elevation for each possible 3D shape. Write the dimensions on the shapes.

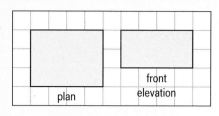

2   The diagram shows a tent.
    The front of the tent is pentagonal in shape.
    Draw the side elevation, marking the dimensions on your diagram.

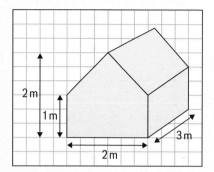

3   Here is a prism in the shape of three steps in a doll's house.
    Each step is 2 cm deep, 2 cm high and 5 cm wide.
    Draw an accurate diagram of

   a   the plan view

   b   the front elevation (shown by the arrow)

   c   the side elevation

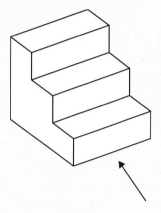

⬡ Exam practice

1   The diagram shows a prism made from two cuboids.
    On centimetre squared paper, draw the front elevation and the side elevation of the prism.
    Use a scale of 1 cm to 2 m.   **(4 marks)**

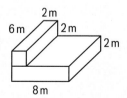

Adapted from 1MA1/2F, June 2017, Q19

2   The diagram represents a solid made from 11 centimetre cubes.
    On a centimetre squared paper, draw a plan of the solid. **(2 marks)**

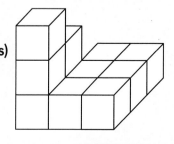

Exam feedback   Results**Plus**

Q1: Most students who achieved a Grade 5 answered a similar question well.

15.3 Accurate drawings 1

Key points

- You can draw an accurate diagram of a triangle with a ruler and protractor if you know three measurements.
- Two triangles are congruent if they have the same:
    - two angles and side length in between (ASA)
    - two side lengths and angle in between (SAS)
    - three side lengths (SSS)
    - right angle, hypotenuse and another side length (RHS)

⚠ Purposeful practice 1

1 Make an accurate drawing of each triangle.
  Mark the length of every side and the size of every angle.

a 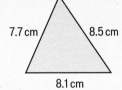   b 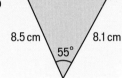   c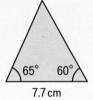

Reflect and reason

What do you notice about the three triangles?

⚠ Purposeful practice 2

1 Make accurate drawings of two triangles with sides of 4 cm and 5 cm and with a 60° angle.

2 Make an accurate drawing of a triangle with sides of 6 cm and 8 cm and an angle of 36° between the two sides.

Reflect and reason

Why are there two possible answers to **Q1** but only one possible answer to **Q2**?

⚠ Purposeful practice 3

1 Which pairs of triangles are congruent? Explain why.

A   B   C   D 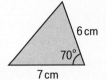 E

Reflect and reason

Which two rules for congruency are not used in **Q1**?

1   Jamie says, 'All of these triangles are congruent because their angles are the same.'

A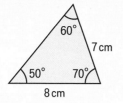

B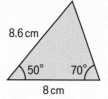

C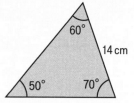

Is Jamie correct? Explain.

2   Abbie makes an accurate drawing of a triangle ABC.

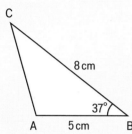

She measures the angle at A as 37°.
Make your own accurate drawing of the triangle and
measure angle A.
What is Abbie's error?

3   Triangles ABC and DEF are congruent.

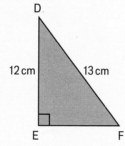

a   Which rule of congruency applies?

b   What is the length of BC?

c   What is the length of EF?

d   Angle C is 22.6°. What is the size of angle F?

1   Make an accurate drawing of this triangle.   **(3 marks)**

Adapted from 1MA0/2F, June 2015, Q7

15.4 Scale drawings and maps

Key point

- A scale is a ratio that shows the relationship between a length on a map or drawing and the actual length. Scale 1 : 25 000 means 1 cm on the map represents 25 000 cm in real life.

⚠ Purposeful practice 1

1 Here is a sketch of a village hall.
   On centimetre squared paper, draw a scale diagram of the village hall, using these scales.

   12 m
   18 m

   a 1 cm represents 1 m   **b** 1 cm represents 2 m   **c** 1 : 300

   d 1 : 400   **e** 1 : 600   **f** 1 : 500

Reflect and reason

1 : 1000 would be a less appropriate scale. Explain why.

⚠ Purposeful practice 2

1 A map has a scale of 1 : 25 000.

   a   **i** 1 cm on the map represents ☐ cm in real life.

   ii 1 cm on the map represents ☐ m in real life.

   iii 1 cm on the map represents ☐ km in real life.

   iv 1 km in real life is represented by ☐ cm on the map.

   b What distance in metres do these measurements on the map represent?

   i 10 cm   **ii** 5 cm   **iii** 2 cm   **iv** 8 cm

   c What distance in kilometres do these measurements on the map represent?

   i 10 cm   **ii** 5 cm   **iii** 2 cm   **iv** 8 cm

   d Here are the actual lengths of three roads. How long will each road be on the map?

   i 10 km   **ii** 6 km   **iii** 1750 m

Reflect and reason

Explain how you can use **Q1a** to help answer **Q1c**. Explain how you can use **Q1b** to help answer **Q1c**.

⚠ Purposeful practice 3

1 A plan for a new office has a scale of 1 : 50.
   What measurements on the plan represent these features of the room?

   a a small desk 50 cm × 100 cm   **b** a meeting table 100 cm × 300 cm

   c a large desk 75 cm × 150 cm   **d** a doorway 1 m × 1.25 m

   e a fridge 750 mm × 500 mm

Reflect and reason

The office manager asks for the plan using a scale of 1 : 25. Will the furniture appear larger or smaller on a plan that uses scale 1 : 25 than on a plan that uses scale 1 : 50? Explain.

⊠ Problem-solving practice

1 The sketch map of an island has a scale of 3 cm to represent 10 km.

   a What is the total distance if you travel in a straight line from A to B and then B to C?

   b James says, 'There is nowhere on the island more than 40 km (in a straight line) from town C.'
Is James correct? Explain why or why not.

2 Aberdeen and Fort William are 150 km apart. How many centimetres on a map represent this distance at each scale?
Comment on the suitability of each scale.

   a 1 : 25 000   **b** 1 : 100 000

   c 1 : 500 000   **d** 1 : 10 000 000

3 A new town is being built.
There is a railway station in the centre of the town.
The swimming pool is 5 km north of the railway station.
The school is 2 km west of the railway station.
The car park is 4 km south of the railway station.

   a Draw a diagram of the town, using a scale of 1 cm to 500 m.

   b Use your diagram to find the distance from

      i the school to the swimming pool   **ii** the school to the car park

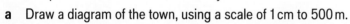

Town B

Town A

Town C

Scale 3 cm : 10 km

10 km

✸ Exam practice

1 The length of a car is 2.8 metres.
Karl makes a scale model of the car. He uses a scale of 1 cm to 40 cm.
Work out the length of the scale model of the car. Give your answer in centimetres.   **(2 marks)**

Adapted from 1MA1/2F, Specimen Papers, Set 1, Q12

2 Here is part of an accurately drawn map showing two towns, Rainham and Purfleet.

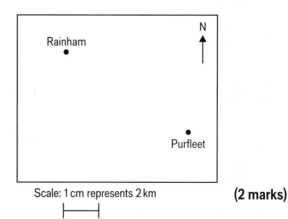

Rainham

N

Purfleet

Scale: 1 cm represents 2 km

   a How far apart are the two towns?   **(2 marks)**

   b A park is 10 km west of Purfleet.

     On a copy of the map, mark with a cross the position of the park.   **(2 marks)**

Adapted from 1MA1/1F, Mock Set 3, Q8

Key points

- Regular polygons can be constructed using compasses, a protractor and a ruler.
- A net is a 2D shape that folds to make a 3D solid.

Purposeful practice 1

1 **a** Which diagram(s) show the net of a cube?

A    B 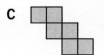   C   D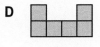

b Sketch two different nets for a cube.

2 Construct two different accurate nets for this cuboid.

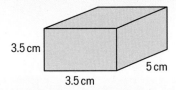

3 Construct two different accurate nets for this square-based pyramid.

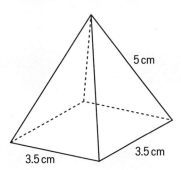

Reflect and reason

What mathematical equipment did you use to construct your accurate nets of the cuboid and square-based pyramid? Explain how you decided on the equipment to use.

Purposeful practice 2

1 Construct a regular pentagon inside a circle with radius 5 cm.

2 Construct a regular octagon inside a circle with radius 5 cm.

3 Construct a regular decagon inside a circle with radius 5 cm.

Reflect and reason

How did you use angles to help you with your constructions?

⊠ Problem-solving practice

1 Henry tries to draw a triangle ABC, with AB = 8.2 cm, BC = 7.2 cm and AC = 15.5 cm.
   Sketch the triangle and explain why Henry's task is impossible.

2 Mark is drawing a regular dodecagon (12 sides) in a circle.
   What size is angle x?

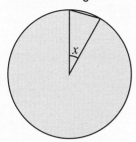

3 Here is a container used to transport
   goods on ships and lorries.
   Choose an appropriate scale and draw
   an accurate net of this container.
   Write your scale beside your net.

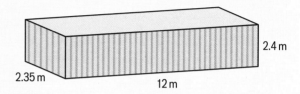

4 Here is a cuboid.

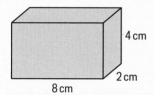

   Lydia sketches a net of the cuboid as shown.
   a   Describe the errors in Lydia's net.
   b   Draw an accurate net of the cuboid.

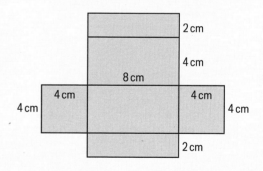

⬡ Exam practice

1 Draw an accurate net of this cuboid.   (3 marks)

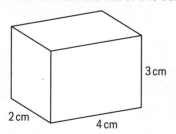

Key points

- Constructions are accurate drawings made using a ruler and pair of compasses. To bisect a line means to cut a line exactly in half. A perpendicular bisector cuts a line in half at right angles.
- You can also use a ruler and compasses to construct a perpendicular from a point to a line.
- An angle bisector cuts an angle exactly in half.

△ Purposeful practice 1

1 **a** Draw a straight line 12 cm long.

    b Construct its perpendicular bisector.

    c 3 cm above one half of your line, mark a point P.

    d Construct a perpendicular from point P to your line.

    e 3 cm below the other half of your line, mark a point Q.

    f Construct a perpendicular from point Q to your line.

Reflect and reason

Compare the construction marks (arcs) you have made for **b**, **d** and **f**.
How are they the same? How are they different?

△ Purposeful practice 2

1 **a** Draw a straight line AB.
Construct its perpendicular bisector.
Label the bisector XYZ, where Y crosses the line AB.

    b Bisect angle XYB. Label the line of the angle bisector CY.
Bisect angle ZYB. Label the line of the angle bisector DY.

Reflect and reason

Explain why angle CYD is a right angle.

△ Purposeful practice 3

1 **a** Draw a scalene triangle with three acute angles.

    b Construct the angle bisector of each angle.

2 **a** Draw a scalene triangle with one obtuse angle.

    b Construct the angle bisector of each angle.

3 **a** Draw a scalene triangle with three acute angles.

    b Construct the perpendicular bisector of each side.

4 **a** Draw a scalene triangle with one obtuse angle.

    b Construct the perpendicular bisector of each side.

Reflect and reason

What do you notice about the perpendicular bisectors in **Q3** and **Q4**?

Problem-solving practice

1 Draw a line 5 cm long.
  Construct a right angle on one end of the line.

2 Jenna is standing at point A in a triangular field.

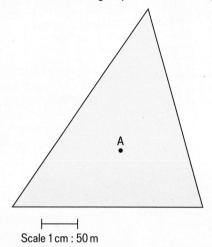

Scale 1 cm : 50 m

She needs to get to the edge of the field as quickly as possible.
Find the shortest distance to the edge of the field.

3 Construct a rhombus with side length 6 cm.

4 Construct a 30° angle.

5 Draw around a circular object and then find the centre of the circle.
  (Remember that a perpendicular bisector of a chord will pass
  through the centre of the circle.)

Exam practice

1 Copy or trace the line AB and then use a ruler and compasses to construct the perpendicular
  bisector of line AB.

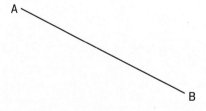

(3 marks)

Adapted from 1MA1/2F, Mock Set 2, Q24

2 Use a ruler and compasses to construct an equilateral triangle with sides of length 6 cm.
  You must show all your construction lines. **(2 marks)**

Adapted from 1MA1/3F, Mock Set 4, Q10

Key points

- A locus is a set of all points that obey a given rule. This produces a path followed by the points. The plural of locus is loci.
- A region is an area bounded by loci.

⚠ Purposeful practice 1

1 Draw point A.
    Construct the locus of all points 3 cm from A.

2 Draw two points B and C, 3 cm apart.
    Construct the locus equidistant from B and C.

3 Draw a line DE.
    Construct the locus of points exactly 3 cm from the line.

4 Draw a square.
    Construct the locus of points exactly 3 cm outside the square.

5 Construct an equilateral triangle.
    Construct the locus of points exactly 3 cm outside the triangle.

> **Reflect and reason**
>
> Consider your method for drawing a locus around a square in **Q4** and a triangle in **Q5**.
> Explain how you would draw a locus of points exactly 3 cm outside a regular pentagon.

⚠ Purposeful practice 2

1 Draw point A.
    Construct the region defined by the locus of points between 3 cm and 4 cm away from A.

2 Draw two points B and C, 3 cm apart.
    Shade the region of points nearer to B than C.

3 Draw a line DE.
    Construct the locus of points which are less than or equal to 3 cm away.

4 Draw a square of side length 5 cm.
    Construct the region of points that are inside the square but more than 3 cm away from the middle.

5 Construct an equilateral triangle of side length 4 cm.
    Shade the region of points that are within 3 cm of one corner and more than 2 cm away from the opposite side.

> **Reflect and reason**
>
> How do **Q1–3** in Purposeful practice 1 help you with **Q1–3** in Purposeful practice 2?

Problem-solving practice

1 A 4 m by 2 m shed has a security light on each corner.
   Each light has a range of 1 m.
   Make a scale drawing of the shed, using the scale 1 : 100.
   Add loci to your diagram to show the areas that the security lights can reach.

2 The diagram shows a 10 m by 6 m garden outside a house.

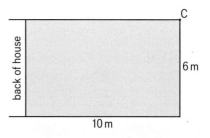

   a Make an accurate scale drawing of the garden.

   b A patio is laid at the back of the house.
      It runs the full width of the house and extends
      4 m into the garden.
      Add the patio to your drawing.

   c A tree is to be planted in the garden, so it is
      within 3 m of the patio and within 4 m of corner C.
      Shade the region where the tree may be planted.

3 James draws the locus of all points 2 cm from this rectangle.

   a What error has he made?

   b Draw the locus correctly.

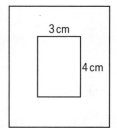

Exam practice

1 The diagram shows an accurate scale drawing of a
   school playground.
   Paula is going to put a seat in the playground.
   The seat has to be

       less than 10 m from C
       closer to DC than to BC
       more than 3 m from AB

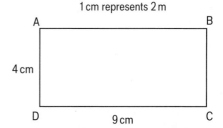

   Copy the diagram and shade the region where Paula can put the seat.   **(4 marks)**

   Adapted from 1MA1/3F, Mock Set 3, Q21

2 A, B and C are three points on a map.
   1 cm represents 100 metres.
   Point Y is less than 200 m from point C, and
   nearer to point A than point B.
   Copy the diagram and shade the region where
   point Y could be.

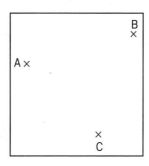

       (3 marks)

   Adapted from 1MA1/2F, June 2017, Q16

Key points

- A bearing is an angle measured in degrees clockwise from north.
- A bearing is always written using three digits.

⚠ Purposeful practice

1 Write the bearing of each point from A.

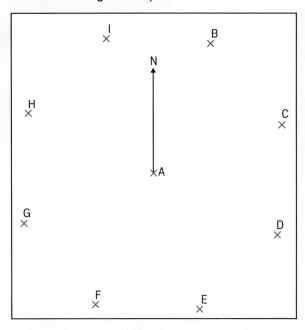

2 The bearing of B from A is shown on each diagram.
Write the bearing of A from B.

a

N

N

40°

A

B

b

N

N

105°

A

B

c

N

N

150°

A

B

d

N

N

15°

A

B

Reflect and reason

In each part of **Q2**, what is the connection between the bearing of B from A and the bearing of A from B?

1 A group of walkers are lost in a national park.
   They use their mobile phone to call for help.
   They are on a bearing of 141° from the mobile phone mast at X, and a bearing of 231° from the mobile phone mast at M.
   The mobile phone mast at X lies 10 km due west of the phone mast at M.

   a Draw an accurate scale diagram of the positions of the walkers and the mobile phone masts.

   b The walkers are told that there is a shelter 5 km away. The shelter is on a bearing of 043° from where the walkers make their call. Mark the shelter on your diagram.

2 Town R is 12 miles from town P, on a bearing of 065°.
   Town S is 18 miles from town P, on a bearing of 110°.

   a Draw an accurate scale diagram of the position of towns P, R and S.

   Use your diagram to find

   b the distance between town R and town S

   c the bearing of town R from town S

3 A plane flies for 200 km on a bearing of 105° from the airport.
   It turns to a bearing of 240° and flies for 350 km to its destination.

   a Use a scale of 1 cm represents 25 km and draw an accurate scale diagram of the journey.

   b Use your diagram to find the direct distance and bearing of the end of the journey from the airport.

✵ Exam practice

1 Here is a map of an island.
   Straight roads join C to D and D to E.
   The map is drawn to scale: 1 cm represents 0.2 km.
   Use the map to find

   a the real distance between C and D   **(2 marks)**

   b the bearing of D from C   **(1 mark)**

   c the bearing of E from D   **(1 mark)**

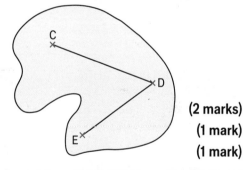

Adapted from 1MA1/2F, November 2017, Q9

2 The diagram shows the position of two castles, C and D.
   George says, 'The bearing of D from C is 60°.'
   George has made two mistakes.
   Explain what they are.

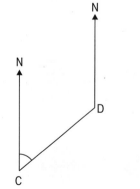

(1 mark)

Adapted from 1MA1/3F, Specimen Papers, Set 2, Q18

Exam feedback   ResultsPlus

Q1: In a similar question, students did not measure the angle correctly using a protractor.

16 Quadratic equations and graphs

16.1 Expanding double brackets

Key points

- To expand or multiply double brackets, multiply each term in one bracket by each term in the other bracket.
- A quadratic expression always has a squared term (with a power of 2). It cannot have a power higher than 2.

△ Purposeful practice 1

Expand and simplify

1 $(x + 1)(x + 7)$ 2 $(x + 7)(x + 1)$ 3 $(z - 2)(z - 3)$

4 $(z - 3)(z - 2)$ 5 $(y - 1)(y + 4)$ 6 $(y + 4)(y - 1)$

Reflect and reason

When you multiply two numbers, does the order of the two numbers matter? Write an example.

When you multiply two brackets, does the order of the two brackets matter? Write an example.

△ Purposeful practice 2

For each pair of double brackets

  a Find the product of the two number terms.

  b Expand the brackets.

The first one has been done for you.

1 $(x + 3)(x + 5)$
   a $3 \times 5 = 15$ b $x^2 + 8x + 15$

2 $(x + 3)(x + 6)$ 3 $(x + 2)(x + 6)$ 4 $(x + 2)(x + 1)$ 5 $(x + 2)(x + 10)$

6 $(x - 2)(x + 10)$ 7 $(x - 2)(x + 3)$ 8 $(x + 2)(x - 3)$ 9 $(x + 2)(x - 5)$

10 $(x + 2)(x + 2)$ 11 $(x + 3)^2$ 12 $(x - 3)^2$ 13 $(x - 4)(x - 4)$

Reflect and reason

What similarities do you notice between your answers to parts **a** and **b** for each question?

△ Purposeful practice 3

Expand and simplify

1 $(x + 1)(x - 1)$ 2 $(x + 2)(x - 2)$ 3 $(x + 3)(x - 3)$ 4 $(x - 4)(x + 4)$

Reflect and reason

Why are there only two terms in these expansions?

⊠ Problem-solving practice

1 A rectangle has a length of $x + 5$ and a width of $x - 5$.

    a Why must x be greater than 5?

    b Write a simplified expression for the area of the rectangle.

$$x + 5$$

$$x - 5 \;\boxed{}$$

2 Which expression is the correct expansion of $(x + 5)(x + 3)$?

    $\boxed{x^2 + 15x + 8}$ $\boxed{x^2 + 8x + 8}$ $\boxed{x^2 + 8x + 15}$ $\boxed{x^2 + 15}$

3 Find the missing numbers.

    a $(x + \square)(x + 3) = x^2 + 5x + 6$

    b $(x - \square)(x + 3) = x^2 + x - 6$

    c $(x + 2)(x - \square) = x^2 - 4x - 12$

    d $(x + \square)(x + 3) = x^2 + 4x + 3$

    e $(x - \square)(x - 3) = x^2 - 7x + 12$

4 Rowan says these two expressions expand to give the same quadratic expression.

    $(y - 1)(y + 4)$ $(y + 1)(y - 4)$

    Show that Rowan is wrong.

5 The area of this rectangle is $x^2 - x - 6$.

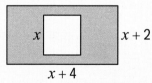

$$x + 2$$

    One side of the rectangle has length $x + 2$.

    Show that the shorter side of the rectangle has length $x - 3$.

6 A square of side x is cut out of this rectangle.

$$x \;\boxed{}\; x + 2$$

$$x + 4$$

    Write an expression for the shaded area.

7 The product of $(x - a)$ and $(x + a)$ is $x^2 - 289$.

    Find the value of a.

⬦ Exam practice

1 Expand and simplify $(n + 2)(n + 7)$ **(2 marks)**

Adapted from 1MA1/1F, Specimen Papers, Set 1, Q27

Key points

- A quadratic function has a symmetrical ∪-shaped curve called a parabola.
- A quadratic function with a $-x^2$ term has a symmetrical ∩-shaped curve.
- The curve always has a minimum or maximum turning point.

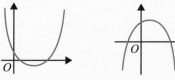

⚠ Purposeful practice 1

1 a Copy and complete the table of values.

  b Plot the graphs of $y = x^2$, $y = x^2 + 1$, $y = x^2 - 2$, $y = 2 + x^2$ on a single grid where the x-axis goes from -3 to 3, and the y-axis goes from -3 to 12. Join the points with a smooth curve. Label your graph.

x	-3	-2	-1	0	1	2	3
$y = x^2$							
$y = x^2 + 1$							
$y = x^2 - 2$							
$y = 2 + x^2$							

2 a Copy and complete the table of values.

  b Plot the graphs of $y = -x^2$, $y = -x^2 + 5$, $y = 4 - x^2$, $y = -x^2 - 1$ on a single grid where the x-axis goes from -3 to 3, and the y-axis goes from -11 to 6. Join the points with a smooth curve. Label your graph.

x	-3	-2	-1	0	1	2	3
$y = -x^2$							
$y = -x^2 + 5$							
$y = 4 - x^2$							
$y = -x^2 - 1$							

Reflect and reason

Taylor says all the graphs are the same shape, but in a different position on the grid. Is Taylor correct?

⚠ Purposeful practice 2

1 Copy and complete the table of values. Then plot a graph for each expression.

a $y = x^2 + x$

x	-3	-2	-1	0	1	2
x^2						
$x^2 + x$						

b $y = x^2 + 2x + 1$

x	-4	-3	-2	-1	0	1	2
x^2							
$2x$							
$x^2 + 2x + 1$							

c $y = x^2 - 2x - 1$

x	-2	-1	0	1	2	3	4
x^2	4						
$2x$	4						
$x^2 - 2x - 1$							

Reflect and reason

Does a quadratic graph always pass through $(0, 0)$? Find examples on this page to explain.

How does the equation of a quadratic graph tell you its value when $x = 0$?

⊠ Problem-solving practice

1 Which of these are graphs of quadratic functions?

A ![y-axis, curve decreasing from upper left toward x-axis]

B ![y-axis, upward parabola crossing x-axis]

C ![y-axis, downward parabola]

D ![y-axis, wave-like curve]

2 The monthly profits P, in £1000, for a fireworks company are modelled by the equation
$P = -x^2 + 5x - 2$, where x is the month number.

Here are the profits for the first 4 months.

Month	1	2	3	4
Profit (£)	2000	4000	4000	2000

    a Plot the graph of the profit against the month.

    b Estimate the maximum profit.

3 Pat makes this table of values for $y = x^2 - 3$ and plots this graph.

x	−3	−2	−1	0	1	2	3
x^2	−9	−4	−1	0	1	4	9
$y = x^2 - 3$	−12	−7	−4	−3	−2	1	6

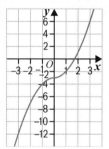

    a Explain why Pat's graph is not correct.

    b Draw the graph of $y = x^2 - 3$

    c Write down the coordinates of the turning point of this graph,
and state whether it is a maximum or minimum.

✷ Exam practice

1 Olivia draws the graph of $y = 16 - x^2$
Here is her graph.

Write down one thing that is
wrong with Olivia's graph.   **(1 mark)**

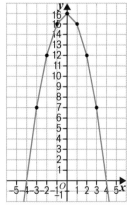

Adapted from 1MA1/1F, November 2017, Q29

Exam feedback   **Results Plus**

In a similar question, common wrong answers did not relate to the graph itself but to the lack of a title
or a table of values.

Key point

- To solve equations of the form $ax^2 + bx + c = 0$, read the x-coordinates where the graph crosses the x-axis. The values of x that satisfy the equation are called roots.

△ Purposeful practice 1

1 Use the graphs to find the solutions to the equations.

a $x^2 + 5x + 6 = 0$

b $x^2 - 2x + 1 = 0$

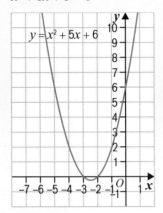

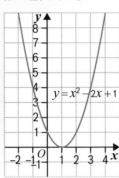

Reflect and reason

How can you tell from its graph whether a quadratic equation has one root or two roots?

△ Purposeful practice 2

1 Use this graph to estimate the solutions to the equations.

a $x^2 + 5x - 2 = 0$

b $x^2 + 5x - 2 = 4$

c $x^2 + 5x - 2 = -4$

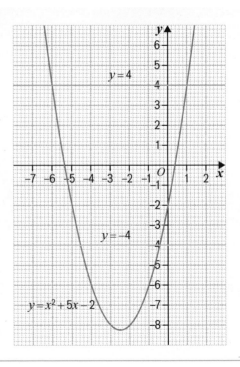

Reflect and reason

When can you find accurate solutions to quadratic equations using graphs and when can you only estimate solutions?

⊠ Problem-solving practice

1 a Use the table of values to plot the graph of $y = -x^2 + 6x + 5$

x	−1	0	1	2	3	4	5	6	7
y	−2	5	10	13	14	13	10	5	−2

   b Estimate the roots of the equation
$-x^2 + 6x + 5 = 0$

   c Explain why the equation $-x^2 + 6x + 5 = 14$ has only one solution.

   d Use the graph to solve the equation
$-x^2 + 6x + 5 = 5$

2 Here is the graph of $y = x^2 - 4x + 1$

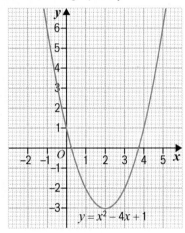

Estimate the solutions to

   a $x^2 - 4x + 1 = 0$

   b $x^2 - 4x + 1 = -3$

   c $x^2 - 4x + 1 = 1$

✦ Exam practice

1 a Complete the table of values for $y = x^2 + x - 1$.

x	−3	−2	−1	0	1	2	3
y	5				1		

                                                                       (2 marks)

   b On graph paper, draw the graph of $y = x^2 + x - 1$ from $x = -3$ to $x = 3$.　　**(2 marks)**

   c Use your graph to find estimates of the solution to the equation $x^2 + x - 1 = 3$　　**(2 marks)**

Adapted from 1MA1/2F, June 2018, Q24

Exam feedback　　　　　　　　　　　　　　　　　　　　Results**Plus**

Q1a: Most students who achieved a **Grade 5** answered a similar question well.

Key points

-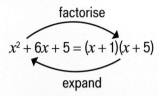

  $$x^2 + 6x + 5 = (x + 1)(x + 5)$$

  factorise / expand

- The difference of two squares is a quadratic expression with two squared terms, and one term is subtracted from the other.
  For example, $x^2 - 25$

  x^2 5^2

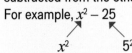

Purposeful practice 1

Factorise

1   $x^2 + 8x + 7$ 2 $x^2 + 6x - 7$ 3 $x^2 - 6x - 7$ 4 $x^2 - 8x + 7$

5   $x^2 - 4x - 5$ 6 $x^2 + 6x + 5$ 7 $x^2 + 4x - 5$ 8 $x^2 - 6x + 5$

Reflect and reason

What do the signs in the quadratic expression tell you about the signs in the two brackets?
Copy and complete the table.

Quadratic expression	Both signs +	Both signs −	− before x term, + before number term	+ before x term, − before number term
In the two brackets				

Purposeful practice 2

1   Factorise

   a $x^2 + 5x + 4$ b $x^2 - 5x + 4$ c $x^2 + 4x + 4$

   d $x^2 - 4x + 4$ e $x^2 + 3x - 4$ f $x^2 - 3x - 4$

2   Factorise

   a $x^2 - 5x - 6$ b $x^2 + 7x + 6$ c $x^2 + 5x + 6$ d $x^2 + x - 6$

   e $x^2 + 5x - 6$ f $x^2 - x - 6$ g $x^2 - 7x + 6$ h $x^2 - 5x + 6$

3   Factorise

   a $x^2 - 3x - 18$ b $x^2 + 7x - 18$ c $x^2 - 9x + 18$ d $x^2 + 19x + 18$

   e $x^2 + 11x + 18$ f $x^2 - 7x - 18$ g $x^2 + 17x - 18$ h $x^2 + 9x + 18$

   i $x^2 - 11x + 18$ j $x^2 - 17x - 18$ k $x^2 + 3x - 18$ l $x^2 - 19x + 18$

Reflect and reason

Alex says, '2 and 3 are factors of 6 that add to make 5. So a quadratic expression with 5 and 6 in it will have 2 and 3 in its factorisation.'

Use your answers from this page to that show Alex is wrong.

Problem-solving practice

1 Ben and Jill factorise $x^2 + 2x - 8$.

Ben's answer **Jill's answer**

$(x + 4)(x - 2)$ $(x - 2)(x + 4)$

Explain why they are both correct.

2 Desi factorises $x^2 + 2x - 15$.

Desi's answer is $x(x + 2) - 15$.

It is wrong.

a Work out the correct answer.

b Explain what Desi has done wrong.

3 The area of each rectangle is given by a quadratic expression.

Write expressions for the lengths of the sides of each rectangle.

a

$x^2 - 8x + 15$

b

$x^2 - 12x + 35$

c

$x^2 - 11x + 28$

4 Write a quadratic expression that

a does not include an x term

b is the difference of two squares.

5 Copy and complete

a $(x + \square)(x - 6) = x^2 - \square - 12$

b $(x - \square)(x + 7) = x^2 + \square - 21$

c $(x - \square)(x - \square) = x^2 - 6x + 5$

Exam practice

1 Factorise $x^2 - 6x + 9$ **(1 mark)**

Adapted from 1MA1/2F, November 2017, Q24c

2 Factorise $x^2 + 5x + 6$ **(2 marks)**

Adapted from 1MA1/3F, Specimen Papers, Set 1, Q26

Exam feedback   Results**Plus**

In similar questions, students tried to factorise into one bracket rather than two brackets.

16.5 Solving quadratic equations algebraically

Key point

- Solutions to quadratic equations can be found algebraically as well as from a graph.

△ Purposeful practice 1

Solve

1 $x^2 = 49$
2 $x^2 - 49 = 0$
3 $x^2 + 10 = 59$
4 $x^2 = 64$
5 $x^2 - 64 = 0$
6 $x^2 - 6 = 58$

Reflect and reason

How many solutions does a quadratic equation have?

Why do **Q1**, **Q2** and **Q3** have the same solutions? Explain.

△ Purposeful practice 2

1 Work out

  a 5×0
  b 0×8
  c 0×0
  d $x \times 0$
  e $0 \times x$
  f $(x + 1) \times 0$
  g $(x - 3) \times 0$
  h $0 \times (x + 5)$

2 Look at the expressions and answer the related questions.

  a $a \times b = 0$ What does this tell you about the values of a and b?
  b $a(x - 3) = 0$ What does this tell you about the values of a and $(x - 3)$?
  c $(x + 4)(x - 3) = 0$ What does this tell you about the values of $(x + 4)$ and $(x - 3)$?

3 Solve

  a $2x = 0$
  b $x - 5 = 0$
  c $2(x + 3) = 0$
  d $2(x - 5) = 0$
  e $x(x - 5) = 0$
  f $x(x + 3) = 0$
  g $(x + 3)(x - 5) = 0$
  h $(x + 3)(x - 3) = 0$

Reflect and reason

Bailey says the solutions to $(x + 2)(x - 5) = 0$ are $x = 2$ and $x = -5$. Explain why Bailey is wrong.

△ Purposeful practice 3

1 Solve by factorising

  a $x^2 + 7x + 12 = 0$
  b $x^2 - x - 12 = 0$
  c $x^2 - 7x + 12 = 0$
  d $x^2 + x + 12 = 0$
  e $x^2 - 2x - 24 = 0$
  f $x^2 + 2x - 24 = 0$
  g $x^2 - 10x + 24 = 0$
  h $x^2 + 10x + 24 = 0$
  i $x^2 - 8x + 15 = 0$
  j $x^2 + 2x - 15 = 0$
  k $x^2 + 8x + 15 = 0$
  l $x^2 - 2x - 15 = 0$

2 Solve by factorising

  a $x^2 + 4x + 4 = 0$
  b $x^2 - 4x + 4 = 0$
  c $x^2 - 6x + 9 = 0$
  d $x^2 + 6x + 9 = 0$
  e $x^2 + 2x + 1 = 0$
  f $x^2 - 10x + 25 = 0$
  g $x^2 + 14x + 49 = 0$
  h $x^2 - 20x + 100 = 0$

Reflect and reason

How many solutions should you write for each equation in **Q2**, so it has the same number of solutions as any other quadratic equation? How do you make sure you have this number of solutions?

1 $x^2 = 100$

   Why are there two solutions to this equation?

2 **a** Factorise $x^2 + 3x$

   b Solve $x^2 + 3x = 0$

   c Solve $x^2 + 3x + 2 = 0$

3 Write a quadratic equation for each pair of solutions.

   a $x = -4, x = 4$

   b $x = -8, x = -9$

   c $x = -5, x = -5$

   d $x = 0, x = -7$

4 $x^2 - 3x - 10 = 0$

   a Show that $x = -2$ is one solution to this quadratic equation.

   b Find the other solution to this quadratic equation.

5 Solve

   a $x^2 - 169 = 0$

   b $x^2 - 361 = 0$

   c $x^2 - 625 = 0$

6 Solve $x^2 + 30x + 225 = 0$

7 Find the positive solution of $x^2 - 2x - 8 = 0$

8 The area of a rectangle is $51\,\text{cm}^2$.
   An expression for the area of the same rectangle is $x^2 - 49$.
   Find the value of x.

9 Find the x-coordinates of the points where the graph of $x^2 + 2x - 3$ crosses the line $y = 5$.

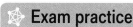
✩ Exam practice

1 Solve

   a $x^2 + 5x - 36 = 0$ **(3 marks)**

   b $x^2 - 12x + 32 = 0$ **(3 marks)**

Adapted from 1MA1/2F, June 2017, Q24

Exam feedback   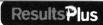

In a similar question, many students tried to solve by trial and improvement rather than by factorising.

Mixed exercises D

Mixed problem-solving practice D

1 The side elevation and the front elevation of a cuboid are drawn on the centimetre grid.

   a Draw an accurate plan of the cuboid.

   b Work out the volume of the cuboid.

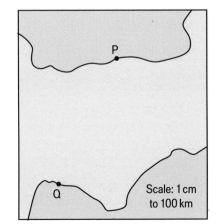

2 The diagram shows a keypad lock.
You have to enter the code **C2** to open the lock.
Karis does not know the code.
She enters one of the letters and then one of the numbers, both at random.
Work out the probability that Karis enters the correct code.

3 The table shows the probabilities that a spinner will land on B, on C, on D, on E and on F.

Letter on spinner	A	B	C	D	E	F
Probability		0.19	0.14	0.05	0.1	0.23

   a What is the probability for the spinner landing on A?

Liam spins the spinner 400 times.

   b Predict the number of times the spinner will land on A.

   c Predict the number of times the spinner will land on A or E.

4 There are 1200 homeowners in a town.
220 homeowners do not have a garage.
5% of the homeowners that have a garage do not own a car.
213 homeowners do not own a car.

   a Use this information to complete the frequency tree.

One of the homeowners who does not have a garage is chosen at random.

   b Write down the probability that this homeowner owns a car.
Give your answer as a fraction in its simplest form.

5 The map shows two ports, P and Q.
Scale: 1 cm to 100 km
A ship sails directly from P to Q.
The average speed of the ship is 40 km/h.
How long does the ship take to sail from P to Q?
Show your working.

6 Here is a triangular prism.

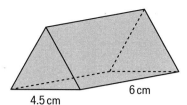

4.5 cm

6 cm

The cross-section of the triangular prism is an equilateral triangle with length 4.5 cm.
The length of the prism is 6 cm.
Using a pair of compasses and a ruler, make an accurate drawing of the net of the triangular prism.

7 Here is a scale drawing of an office.
The scale is 1 cm to 2 m.
A WiFi router is going to be put in the office.
The WiFi router has to be closer to C than it is to D.
The WiFi router also has to be less than 8 metres from B.
Show, by shading, the region where the WiFi router can be put.

8 The side length of a square tile is $x + 3$ cm.
Write a simplified expression for the area of the tile.

9 a Complete the table of values for $y = x^2 - 2x - 3$

x	−1	0	1	2	3	4
y	0			−3		

b Draw the graph of $y = x^2 - 2x - 3$ for values of x from −1 to 4

c Use your graph to find estimates of the solutions to the equation $x^2 - 2x - 3 = -1$

10 When a spinner is spun once, the probability that it will land on red is 0.55.
The spinner is spun twice.
Mohammed draws this tree diagram.

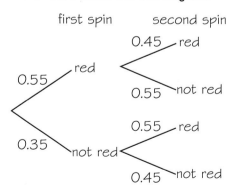

first spin   second spin

0.55 red   0.45 red
              0.55 not red

0.35 not red 0.55 red
               0.45 not red

The diagram is not correct.
Write down two things that are wrong with Mohammed's tree diagram.

11 p is directly proportional to q.
When $p = 7, q = 4$.
Work out p when $q = 10$.

Mixed problem-solving practice D

⬡ **Exam practice**

12 Jenny needs to draw the graph of $y = x^2 - 2$
Here is her graph.
Write down one thing that is wrong with Jenny's graph.   **(1 mark)**

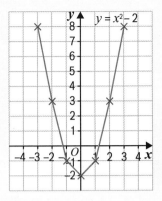

Adapted from 1MA1/1F, November 2017, Q29

⬡ **Exam practice**

13 The diagram shows a scale drawing of a football pitch.
The scale of the drawing is 1 : 2000
Work out the perimeter of the real football pitch.
Give your answer in metres.   **(5 marks)**

Adapted from 1MA1/3F, June 2018, Q12

Exam feedback   **ResultsPlus**

Most students who achieved a `Grade 5` answered a similar question well.

⬡ **Exam practice**

14 There are some sweets in a bag.
The sweets are red or green or brown or yellow.
Sasha is going to take a sweet from the bag at random.
The table shows the probabilities that the sweet will be brown or yellow.

Colour	Red	Green	Brown	Yellow
Probability			0.15	0.45

There are 24 brown sweets in the bag.
The probability that the sweet Sasha takes will be red is three times the probability that the sweet will be green.
Work out the number of red sweets in the bag.   **(4 marks)**

Adapted from 1MA1/3F, June 2018, Q24a

229

✦ Exam practice

15 In a sale, the normal price of a t-shirt is reduced by 40%.
The sale price of the t-shirt is £5.40
Work out the normal price of the t-shirt.   **(2 marks)**

Adapted from 1MA1/1F, November 2017, Q30

Exam feedback   **Results Plus**

In a similar question, the most common incorrect approach was to increase £5.40 by 40%.

✦ Exam practice

16 Sam wants to invest £42 000 for 3 years in a bank.

Bank A	**Bank B**
Compound Interest	Compound Interest
1.6% for each year	3.2% for the first year
	0.8% for each extra year

Which bank will give Sam the most interest at the end of 3 years?
Show your working.   **(3 marks)**

Adapted from 1MA1/2F, June 2017, Q22

Exam feedback   **Results Plus**

In a similar question, students often incorrectly used 1.08 as the multiplier for an increase of 0.8%.

✦ Exam practice

17 PQR is a right-angled triangle.

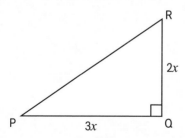

The area of the triangle is 27 cm².
Work out the value of x.   **(3 marks)**

Adapted from 1MA1/3F, June 2018, Q17

Exam feedback   **Results Plus**

In a similar question, many students did not use the correct formula for the area of a triangle, usually missing dividing by 2.

17 Perimeter, area and volume 2

17.1 Circumference of a circle 1

Key points

- The circumference is the perimeter of a circle.
- The Greek letter π (pi, pronounced 'pie') is the ratio of the circumference of a circle to the diameter. Its decimal value never ends, but starts as 3.1415926535897...
- The formula for the circumference of a circle is $C = \pi d$.
- If you know the radius you can use $C = 2\pi r$ to calculate the circumference.

△ Purposeful practice 1

1 Work out the circumference of each circle. Use $\pi = 3.14$.
   Round your answers to 2 decimal places (2 d.p.).

   a radius = 6 cm   **b** diameter = 12 m   **c** radius = 12 cm

   d diameter = 24 cm   **e** diameter = 5 m   **f** radius = 2.5 m

   g diameter = 0.5 m   **h** radius = $\frac{1}{4}$ m   **i** diameter = 50 cm

2 Work out the circumference of each circle from **Q1**.
   Use the π button on your calculator.
   Round your answers to 2 d.p.

Reflect and reason

Which of your answers to **Q1** are the same? Explain why.

Why are your answers to **Q2** more accurate than your answers to **Q1**?

△ Purposeful practice 2

Work out the circumference of each circle.
Use the π button on your calculator.
Round your answers to 2 d.p.

1
1 cm

2
2 cm

3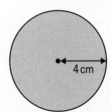
4 cm

4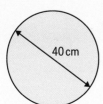
40 cm

5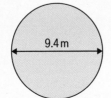
9.4 m

6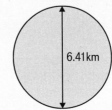
6.41 km

Reflect and reason

When the radius doubles, what happens to the circumference?

⊠ **Problem-solving practice**

1 The circumference of a circle is 25 cm. Work out the diameter.
Give your answer to 2 d.p.

2 Kasia is working with a circle with a 6 cm radius.
She enters '$2\pi6$' into her calculator and presses the $=$ button.
The calculator shows that there is a syntax error.

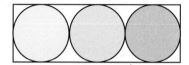

What mistake has Kasia made?

3 Three circles fit exactly inside a rectangle.

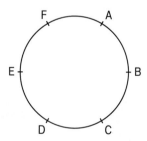

The area of the rectangle is 27 m^2.
Work out the circumference of one of the circles.
Give your answer to 3 significant figures.

4 The diameter of a bicycle wheel is 29 inches.
1 inch $= 2.54$ cm
How many complete revolutions will the wheel make to travel at least 1 km?

 ⬡ **Exam practice**

1 Adnan walks once round a circle with diameter 60 metres.

```
        F         A
          ×  ×  ×
      ×             ×
   E  +             +  B
      ×             ×
          ×  ×  ×
        D         C
```

There are 6 points equally spaced on the circumference of the circle.
Find the distance Adnan walks between one point and the next point. **(2 marks)**

Adapted from 1MA1/2F, November 2017, Q18a

Exam feedback — ResultsPlus

In a similar question, students did not work out the circumference of the circle.

17.2 Circumference of a circle 2

Key point

- Measurements given to the nearest whole unit may be inaccurate by up to one half of a unit below and one half of a unit above. For example, the range of possible values for a length given as 3 cm to the nearest cm is 2.5 cm ≤ length < 3.5 cm.

△ Purposeful practice 1

1. Write an inequality to show the possible values.
   - **a** 3500 (rounded to 3 s.f.)
   - **b** 3500 (rounded to 4 s.f.)
   - **c** 350 000 (rounded to 3 s.f.)
   - **d** 350 000 (rounded to 4 s.f.)
   - **e** 350 000 (rounded to 5 s.f.)
   - **f** 350 000 (rounded to 6 s.f.)

2. In a question, you are asked to find the circumference of a circle, using 3.14 to represent π. How many decimal places should you give your answer to? Explain why.

Reflect and reason

The inequality 3795 ≤ 3800 < 3805 shows the possible values of 3800 (rounded to 3 s.f.).

Explain why ≤ (not <) is used after 3795.

Explain why < (not ≤) is used before 3805.

△ Purposeful practice 2

1. Round each number to the given degree of accuracy.
   - **a** 2396.3463 to 1 s.f.
   - **b** 2396.3463 to 2 s.f.
   - **c** 2396.3463 to 3 s.f.
   - **d** 2396.3463 to 4 s.f.
   - **e** 2396.3463 to 5 s.f.
   - **f** 2396.3463 to 6 s.f.
   - **g** 2396.3463 to 1 d.p.
   - **h** 2396.3463 to 2 d.p.
   - **i** 2396.3463 to 3 d.p.

2. Write an inequality to show the possible values.
   - **a** 3000 (rounded to 1 s.f.)
   - **b** 3500 (rounded to 3 s.f.)
   - **c** 35 (rounded to 2 s.f.)
   - **d** 3.5 (rounded to 1 d.p.)
   - **e** 0.35 (rounded to 2 s.f.)

3. 35 000 rounded to 2 s.f. can also be described as 'rounded to the nearest 1000'. Write an equivalent statement for each part of **Q2**.

Reflect and reason

Riley uses his calculator to find the circumference of a circle with diameter 0.7798 m.

```
2.449813951
```

Riley writes the answer as 2.5 m (1 d.p.).

Explain Riley's rounding mistake. What is the correct answer, to 1 d.p.?

⊠ Problem-solving practice

1 The numbers in these questions are given to 2 s.f.
Work out the smallest possible answer to each question.

  a $350 + 470$

  b $4500 + 9600$

  c $8500 + 120$

  d 240×780

  e 6000×4100

  f 0.32×38

2 A circle has a radius of 12.63 m.
Using π as 3.14 to 3 s.f., work out the circumference.
Round your answer to an appropriate degree of accuracy.

3 Planet Earth has a radius of 6700 km, rounded to 2 s.f.

  a   Write an inequality to show the possible values of the radius.

  b   Work out the lowest possible value of the circumference.
      Give your answer to 2 s.f.

4 The equator of the planet Mars has a circumference of 21 000 km, rounded to 2 s.f.
What is the smallest possible diameter of the planet?
Give your answer to 2 s.f.

5 Planks of wood are 1 m long, to the nearest cm.
10 planks are laid end to end.
What is the shortest possible length that the 10 planks will cover?

6 A cubic box has sides of length 0.8 m, rounded to 1 s.f.

  a   Write an inequality to show the possible side lengths.

  b   What is the smallest possible volume of the box?

  c   What is the smallest possible surface area of the box?

⊠ Exam practice

1 Andrew's car has a value of £18 000 correct to 2 significant figures.

  a   Write down the smallest possible value of the car.

  b   Write down the greatest possible value of the car.   **(2 marks)**

Adapted from 1MA1/3F, June 2017, Q23

Exam feedback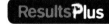

In a similar question, students were more successful in finding the smallest possible value than the greatest possible value.

Key point

- The formula for the area A of a circle with radius r is $A = \pi r^2$.

△ Purposeful practice

1 Work out the area of each circle.
   Give your answers to 2 d.p.

   a
   3 cm

   b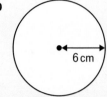
   6 cm

   c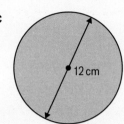
   12 cm

   d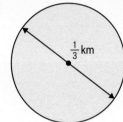
   $\frac{1}{3}$ km

   e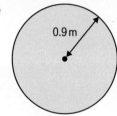
   0.9 m

   f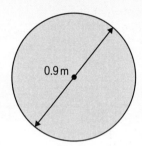
   0.9 m

2 Work out the area of each circle.
   Leave your answers in terms of π.

   a
   16 cm

   b
   1.6 m

   c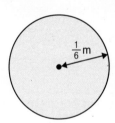
   $\frac{1}{6}$ m

   d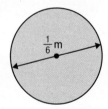
   $\frac{1}{6}$ m

3 Work out, to 2 d.p., the radius of a circle with area
   a 50 cm²   **b** 100 cm²   **c** 200 cm²   **d** 2.5 m²

4 Work out the radius of a circle with area
   a 9π cm²   **b** 81π cm²   **c** 6.25π m²   **d** $\frac{1}{16}\pi$ km²

Reflect and reason

Two students are asked to find the diameter of a circle, given the area.

Amber writes $D = \sqrt{\left(\dfrac{10}{\pi}\right)}$ Tommy writes $D = \left(\dfrac{10}{\pi}\right)^2 \times 2$

Each student has made a mistake. Explain the mistakes.
What is the correct answer?

1 A circle has an area of 50 cm².
Work out the circumference.
Give your answer rounded to 2 s.f.

2 Isabella is painting a circular design.
She has 18 litres of paint.
Each litre of paint can cover 2 m².
What is the radius of the largest circle Isabella can paint?
Round your answer to 3 s.f.

3 The diagram shows a small circle inside a larger circle.

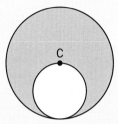

The larger circle, centre C, has a diameter of 10 cm.
Work out the shaded area.
Give your answer in terms of π.

4 Hoorain is working out the shaded area.

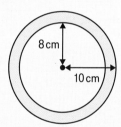

He subtracts 8 from 10 and uses that answer as the radius in $A = \pi r^2$.
His answer is incorrect.
Explain what he should have done.

 Exam practice

1 Jo has a garden in the shape of a circle with a diameter of 12 m.
Jo is going to cover the garden with grass seed to make a lawn.
Grass seed is sold in boxes.
Each box of grass seed will cover 23 m² of garden.
Jo wants to cover all the garden with grass seed.
Work out an estimate for the number of boxes of grass seed Jo needs.
You must show your working.

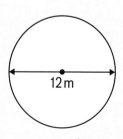

(4 marks)

Adapted from 1MA1/1F, June 2017, Q18a

Exam feedback　　　　　　　　Results**Plus**

Most students who achieved a **Grade 5** answered a similar question well.

Key points

- A chord is a line that touches the circumference at each end.
- An arc is a part of the circumference of a circle.
- A segment is a part of a circle between an arc and a chord.
- A sector is a slice of a circle between an arc and two radii.
- For a sector of a circle with an angle of $x°$ and radius r

$$\text{Arc length} = \frac{x}{360} \times 2\pi r \qquad \text{Area of sector} = \frac{x}{360} \times \pi r^2$$

△ Purposeful practice 1

Write the fraction of each circle that is shaded. Give each answer in its simplest form.

1

45°

2
135°

3

225°

4

40°

5

80°

6

200°

Reflect and reason

How could you use your answer to **Q2** to find the answer to **Q3**?

How could you use your answer to **Q4** to find the answer to **Q5**?

Explain how you can use the fractions in **Q1–6** to calculate the area of each shaded sector.

△ Purposeful practice 2

For each sector, work out

a the area

b the arc length

Give your answers to 3 s.f.

1
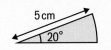
5 cm
20°

2
5 cm
40°

3
10 cm
40°

4
180°
12 m

5
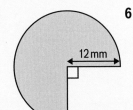
12 mm

6
1.3 m
60°

7
2.6 m
60°

8
60°
1.3 m

Reflect and reason

Complete these sentences.

When the angle of a sector doubles, the arc length _____ and the sector area _____.

When the radius of a sector doubles, the arc length _____ and the sector area _____.

1 Work out the perimeter of this shape.
Give your answer to 2 d.p.

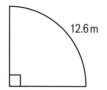
15 cm
25°

2 The arc length of this shape is 12.6 m.
Work out the radius.
Give your answer to 3 s.f.

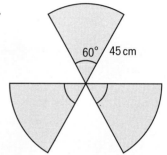
12.6 m

3 This shape is made from three sectors with the same dimensions.
Giving your answers to 3 s.f.

  a work out the area

  b work out the perimeter

Dan works out the area of one of the sectors and multiplies this by 3 to find the total area of the shape.

  c Explain a different way to work out the area.

60° 45 cm

4 The hour hand of a clock is 5 cm long.
The minute hand is 7 cm long.
A lecture starts at 4 pm and finishes at 6.30 pm.

  a Work out the distance travelled by the tip of the minute hand during the lecture.

  b Work out the distance travelled by the tip of the hour hand during the lecture.

Give your answers correct to 3 s.f.

5 A semicircular arch is being painted on a playground wall.
The radius from the centre to the outer edge is 1.2 m.
The arch is 0.2 m wide.
Work out the area that is being painted.
Give your answer correct to 3 s.f.

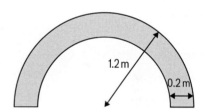
1.2 m
0.2 m

⊞ ✺ **Exam practice**

1 The arc ABC is a quarter of a circle with centre O and radius 5.3 cm.

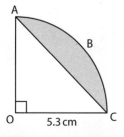
A
B
O
5.3 cm
C

AC is a chord of the circle.
Work out the area of the shaded segment.
Give your answer correct to 3 significant figures. **(3 marks)**

Adapted from 1MA1/2F, Specimen Papers, Set 2, Q28

17.5 Composite 2D shapes and cylinders

Key points

- The formula for the volume of a cylinder is $V = \pi r^2 h$.
- The surface area of a prism is the total area of all its faces.

△ Purposeful practice 1

Work out the volume of each cylinder. Give your answers to 3 s.f.

1

20 cm

6 cm

2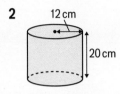
12 cm

20 cm

3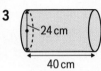
24 cm

40 cm

4
1.2 m

0.3 m

5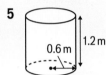
1.2 m

0.6 m

6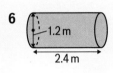
1.2 m

2.4 m

Reflect and reason

Jordan says, 'If I double the length of a cylinder, the volume doubles. So, if I double the radius, the volume doubles.'

Explain Jordan's error. Use the answers to **Q1–6** to help you.

△ Purposeful practice 2

Work out the curved surface area of each cylinder. Give your answers to 3 s.f.

1
1.3 m

1 m

2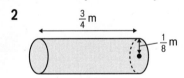
$\frac{3}{4}$ m

$\frac{1}{8}$ m

3
0.6 m

1.2 m

Reflect and reason

In **Q3**, how did you decide what value to use for h?

△ Purposeful practice 3

Work out the total surface area of each cylinder. Give your answers to 3 s.f.

1
10 cm

5 cm

2
15 cm

85 cm

3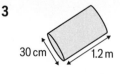
30 cm   1.2 m

4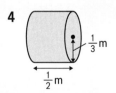
$\frac{1}{3}$ m

$\frac{1}{2}$ m

Reflect and reason

Explain the difference between the curved surface area and the total surface area of a cylinder.

1 A straight train tunnel is 800 m long.
The entrance is a semicircle 9 m across.
The tunnel is lined with bricks.
Work out the surface area that needs to be lined with bricks.
Give your answer to 3 s.f.

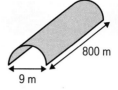

800 m

9 m

2 The semicircle fits perfectly inside the rectangle.
Work out the shaded area.
Give your answer to the nearest whole number of square centimetres.

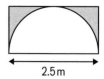

2.5 m

3 A label is wrapped around the curved surface of a can of soup.
The label has a 1 cm overlap.
Work out the area of the label.
Give your answer to 3 s.f.

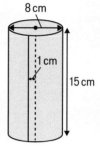

8 cm

1 cm

15 cm

4 The drum on the front of a road roller is 2.5 m wide and has a radius of 0.8 m.
The drum turns at a rate of 10 revolutions per minute.
Work out the area of road the drum can cover in 1 hour.
Round your answer to the nearest whole number of square metres.

5 The top, bottom and sides of the oil drum shown are painted.
Each tin of paint covers 0.4 m².
How many tins of paint are needed?

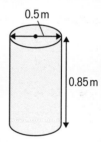

0.5 m

0.85 m

1 Here is a cylinder.

Work out the volume of the cylinder. **(2 marks)**

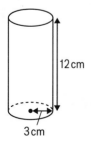

12 cm

3 cm

Key points

- The volume of a pyramid $= \frac{1}{3} \times$ area of base $\times$ vertical height.

- The volume of a cone $= \frac{1}{3} \times$ area of base $\times$ vertical height.

- The area of the curved surface of a cone $= \pi \times$ base radius $\times$ slant height $= \pi r l$.

△ Purposeful practice 1

Work out the volume of each pyramid. Give your answers to 3 s.f.

1   2   3   4

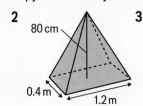
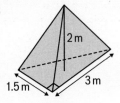

Reflect and reason

In **Q4**, how did you decide what value to use for h?

△ Purposeful practice 2

Work out the volume of each cone. Give your answers correct to 3 s.f.

1   2   3   4

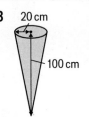
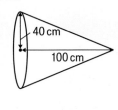

Reflect and reason

When the vertical height of a cone doubles, what happens to the volume?
When the radius of a cone doubles, what happens to the volume?

△ Purposeful practice 3

Work out the curved surface area of each cone. Give your answers in terms of π.

1   2   3

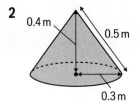
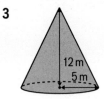

Reflect and reason

Compare the dimensions you need to work out the volume and the curved surface area of a cone.
Which dimension do you need for both? Which different dimension do you need for each?

⊠ Problem-solving practice

1 Work out the total surface area of the square-based pyramid.

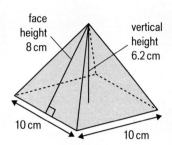

face height 8 cm
vertical height 6.2 cm
10 cm
10 cm

2 A conical party hat is made out of card.
Card costs £0.03/cm².

   a Work out the area of card needed to make the hat.
   Give your answer rounded to the nearest integer.

   b Work out the cost of making 50 hats.

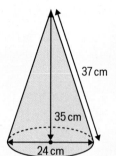

37 cm
35 cm
24 cm

3 A solid is made from two square-based pyramids.
Work out the total volume of the solid.
Give an exact answer.

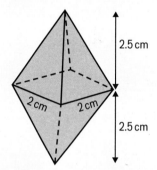

2.5 cm
2 cm   2 cm
2.5 cm

✦ Exam practice

1 Here are two pyramids, A and B.

A

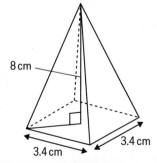

8 cm
3.4 cm
3.4 cm

B

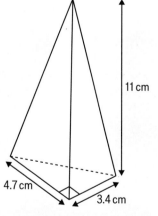

11 cm
4.7 cm
3.4 cm

Which pyramid has the greater volume?
You must show all your working.

(3 marks)

17.7 Spheres and composite solids

Key points

- A sphere is a solid where all points on the surface are the same distance from the centre.

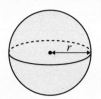

- The volume of a sphere $= \frac{4}{3}\pi r^3$
- The surface area of a sphere $= 4\pi r^2$.
- You can use Pythagoras' theorem to work out the slant height of a cone. This is useful when given the base radius (r) and vertical height (h) and asked for the area of the curved surface.

  Area of curved surface $= \pi r l$.

△ Purposeful practice 1

For each sphere, work out

  a the volume   **b** the surface area

Leave your answers in terms of π.

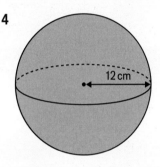

1 3 cm

2 6 cm

3 9 cm

4 12 cm

Reflect and reason

How would you find the surface area and volume of a sphere if given its diameter?

▦ △ Purposeful practice 2

For each shape, work out

  a the volume   **b** the total surface area

Give your answers to 2 d.p.

1 7 cm

2 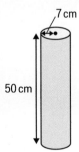 7 cm, 50 cm

3 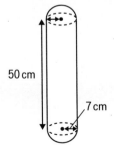 50 cm, 7 cm

4 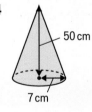 50 cm, 7 cm

Reflect and reason

The volumes in **Q1** and **Q2** add together to give the volume in **Q3**.

Explain why adding the surface areas in **Q1** and **Q2** will not give the surface area in **Q3**.

1   A cuboid has a hemispherical depression in the top.
    Work out
    a   the volume of the cuboid
    b   the total surface area of the cuboid
    Give your answers correct to 3 s.f.

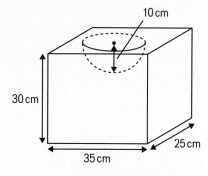

2   A glass sphere fits perfectly in a box with
    internal dimensions $20\,cm \times 20\,cm \times 20\,cm$.
    The volume of the box is $8000\,cm^3$.

    What is the volume of the space
    around the glass sphere?

    Give your answer to the nearest whole number.

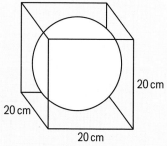

3   This solid is made from two cones.
    The maximum diameter of the shape is half the length.
    Work out the volume.
    Give your answer to the nearest whole number.

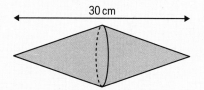

4   An ice cream can be represented by a hemisphere
    and a cone.
    Work out
    a   the total volume
    b   the total surface area
    Give your answers to 3 s.f.

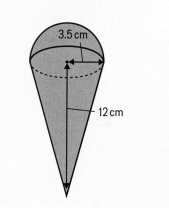

1   The diagram shows a solid sphere with radius of 8 cm.

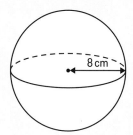

    Find the total surface area of the hemisphere made from cutting this sphere exactly in half.
    Give your answer to 1 d.p.   **(3 marks)**

18 Fractions, indices and standard form

18.1 Multiplying and dividing fractions

Key point

- To multiply or divide mixed numbers, change the mixed numbers to improper fractions first.

△ Purposeful practice 1

1 Change these mixed numbers to improper fractions.

   a $5\frac{1}{4}$ b $5\frac{1}{3}$ c $3\frac{1}{3}$ d $3\frac{2}{3}$

2 Copy and complete the multiplication grid. Change each final improper fraction to a mixed number. Show your working out. Simplify the fractional part where possible.

×	$3\frac{2}{3}$	$5\frac{1}{4}$
$3\frac{2}{3}$		
$5\frac{1}{4}$		

Reflect and reason

Look at the answers in the first row and the first column in **Q2**. What do you notice?

△ Purposeful practice 2

1 Simplify these fractions before multiplying them.

   a $\frac{3\times5\times2}{4\times10\times3}$ b $\frac{3\times10}{4\times30}$ c $\frac{40\times3}{15\times2}$ d $\frac{4\times30}{6\times5}$

2 Work out

   a $2\frac{2}{5}\times3\frac{3}{4}$ b $2\frac{2}{5}\times2\frac{1}{2}$ c $2\frac{2}{5}\times6\frac{2}{3}$ d $2\frac{2}{5}\times4\frac{1}{6}$

3 Work out these multiplications. Give your answers as mixed numbers.

   a $2\frac{8}{11}\times1\frac{2}{9}$ b $2\frac{8}{13}\times1\frac{4}{9}$ c $5\frac{1}{7}\times1\frac{4}{5}$ d $1\frac{4}{21}\times1\frac{9}{40}$

4 Copy and complete the division grid. Give your answers as mixed numbers where appropriate. One of the calculations has been done for you.

÷	$3\frac{2}{3}$	$5\frac{1}{4}$
$3\frac{2}{3}$		$\frac{44}{63}$
$5\frac{1}{4}$		

Reflect and reason

Why is the answer 1 to both the calculations on the diagonal of the table in **Q4**?

1 A rectangular postcard measures $5\frac{1}{3}$ inches by $3\frac{2}{5}$ inches.

What is the area of the postcard in square inches?

2 Work out the missing number in each calculation.

a $2\frac{\square}{4} \times 4\frac{3}{5} = 12\frac{13}{20}$

b $3\frac{1}{5} \div 3\frac{3}{\square} = \frac{8}{9}$

c $3\frac{3}{\square} \times 1\frac{5}{16} = 4\frac{1}{2}$

d $2\frac{2}{\square} \div \frac{6}{33} = 12$

3 A rectangle has an area of $6\frac{2}{15}$ cm² and a width of $1\frac{1}{3}$ cm.

Find the length of the rectangle.

4 Work out

a $\frac{2}{3} \times \frac{3}{4} \times \frac{4}{5}$

b $\frac{2}{3} \times \frac{3}{4} \times \frac{4}{5} \times \frac{5}{6} \times \frac{6}{7}$

c $\frac{2}{3} \times \frac{3}{4} \times \frac{4}{5} \times \frac{5}{6} \times \frac{6}{7} \times \frac{7}{8} \times \frac{8}{9} \times \frac{9}{10} \times \frac{10}{11} \times \frac{11}{12} \times \frac{12}{13}$

5 Sam pays $3\frac{1}{3}$ Egyptian pounds to buy $2\frac{1}{4}$ kg of apples.

a How many Egyptian pounds would 27 kg of apples cost?

b How many kg of apples could Sam buy with 10 Egyptian pounds?

1 Tim works out $2\frac{3}{7} \times 6\frac{1}{2}$

He writes

$2 \times 6 = 12$ and $\frac{3}{7} \times \frac{1}{2} = \frac{3}{14}$

So $2\frac{3}{7} \times 6\frac{1}{2} = 12\frac{3}{14}$

The answer of $12\frac{3}{14}$ is wrong.

Describe the mistake that Tim has made. **(1 mark)**

Adapted from 1MA1/2F, Specimen Papers, Set 1, Q19

Key points

- To raise a power of a number to another power, multiply the indices.
- Any number (or term) raised to the power 0 is equal to 1.
- Any number (or term) raised to the power −1 is the reciprocal of the number.

△ Purposeful practice 1

1 Write as a power of 2.

  a $(2^3)^2$ **b** $(2^2)^3$ **c** $(2^2)^0$ **d** $(2^5)^3$ **e** $(2^3)^5$ **f** $(2^0)^5$

  g $(2^0)^4$ **h** $(2^3)^4$ **i** $(2^4)^a$ **j** $(2^a)^0$ **k** $(2^{10})^a$ **l** $(2^a)^{10}$

2 Write as a power of 2. The first one has been done for you.

  a $4^5 = (2^2)^5 = 2^{10}$ **b** 4^2 **c** 4^3 **d** 4^4 **e** 4^0 **f** 8 **g** 8^2 **h** 8^3

Reflect and reason

Gil says that $(2^3)^4$ is equivalent to 2^7. Explain the mistake that Gil has made.

△ Purposeful practice 2

Work out the value of

1 3^{-1} **2** 5^{-1} **3** $\left(\dfrac{1}{3}\right)^{-1}$ **4** $\left(\dfrac{1}{5}\right)^{-1}$ **5** $\left(\dfrac{2}{5}\right)^{-1}$ **6** 3^{-2}

7 4^{-2} **8** 5^{-2} **9** $\left(\dfrac{1}{3}\right)^{-2}$ **10** $\left(\dfrac{1}{5}\right)^{-2}$ **11** $\left(\dfrac{2}{5}\right)^{-2}$ **12** $\left(\dfrac{2}{5}\right)^{-3}$

Reflect and reason

How are 4^{-1} and $\left(\dfrac{1}{4}\right)^{-1}$ related to each other?

△ Purposeful practice 3

Work out

1 **a** $(3^{-1})^0$ **b** $(3^0)^{-1}$ **2** **a** $(2^3)^{-1}$ **b** $(2^{-1})^3$ **3** **a** $(3^{-1})^2$ **b** $(3^2)^{-1}$

Reflect and reason

In each question, the answers to parts **a** and **b** are the same. Why is this?

△ Purposeful practice 4

Write as a single power.

1 $\dfrac{m^5}{m^2}$ **2** $\dfrac{m^5 \times m^3}{m^2}$ **3** $\dfrac{m^5 \times m^{-3}}{m^2}$ **4** $\dfrac{m^5 \times m^{-3}}{m^{-2}}$ **5** $\dfrac{m^5}{m^{-2} \times m^3}$

6 $\dfrac{m^5 \times m^2}{m^3}$ **7** $m^2 \times m^{-3} \times m^5$ **8** $\dfrac{m^2 \times m^5}{m^{-3}}$ **9** $\dfrac{m^{-2} \times m^{-5}}{m^{-3}}$

Reflect and reason

What can you say about multiplying by m^2 and dividing by m^{-2}?

1 Tina says the reciprocal of 4.5 is $2\frac{1}{4}$.

Here is her working.

$4.5 = 4\frac{1}{2}$

The reciprocal of 4 is $\frac{1}{4}$ and the reciprocal of $\frac{1}{2}$ is 2, so the answer is $2\frac{1}{4}$.

a Explain the mistake that she has made.

b Work out the correct reciprocal of 4.5.

2 Write these numbers as powers of 2.

a 8 **b** $\frac{1}{8}$

c 32 **d** $\frac{1}{32}$

e 32^3 **f** $\frac{1}{32^3}$

3 Write 9^4 as a power of 3.

4 Work out the missing numbers.

a $4^{\square} = \frac{1}{64}$ **b** $\left(3^{-2}\right)^{\square} = \frac{1}{81}$

c $\left(5^{\square}\right)^2 = 5^{18}$ **d** $\left(35^{12}\right)^{\square} = 1$

5 Find the value of y.

a $\dfrac{x^3 \times x^5}{x^y} = x^2$ **b** $\dfrac{x^y \times x^7}{x^4} = x^2$

c $\dfrac{x^{-4} \times x^{16}}{x^y} = x^2$ **d** $\dfrac{x^y \times x^y}{x^6} = x^2$

✦ Exam practice

1 a Write down the value of 3^{-2}. **(1 mark)**

b Write down the value of 17^0. **(1 mark)**

Adapted from 1MA1/1F, November 2017, Q22b

Exam feedback   Results**Plus**

Q1a: In a similar question, many students gave an answer of −9, having calculated -3^2 rather than $\frac{1}{3^2}$.

Key point

- Standard form is a way of writing very large or very small numbers.
  A number in standard form looks like this:

$$8.4 \times 10^5$$

This part is a number between 1 and 10

This part is a power of 10

⚠ Purposeful practice 1

1 Write each number in standard form.

   a 52   **b** 520   **c** 5200   **d** 52 000   **e** 52 000 000

2 Write each number in standard form.

   a 101   **b** 110   **c** 10 100   **d** 1100   **e** 100 100   **f** 1001

Reflect and reason

$520 \times 10 = 5200$

Compare 520 and 5200 in standard form.

When you multiply a number by 10, how does its standard form change?

⚠ Purposeful practice 2

1 Write each number as an ordinary number.

   a 3.01×10^3 **b** 3.01×10^6 **c** 3.01×10^2 **d** 3.01×10^4 **e** 3.01×10

2 Convert these from standard form to ordinary numbers:

   a 2.05×10^3 **b** 2.5×10 **c** 2.005×10^3

   d 5.21×10^6 **e** 5.0201×10^6 **f** 5.021×10^6

Reflect and reason

What is the power of 10 in 3.01×10 and 2.5×10?

⚠ Purposeful practice 3

1 Write these numbers in order from smallest to largest.

   570   5700   5070   5007   507

2 Write these numbers in standard form.
   Then write them in order from smallest to largest.

   570   5700   5070   5007   507

Reflect and reason

Describe how to order numbers in standard form.

⊠ Problem-solving practice

1 Write these populations in standard form.

Country	Population
Canada	36 286 400
India	1 339 000 000
Thailand	67 959 000
Monaco	38 400

2 Write each of these masses as an ordinary number.

    a 2.9×10^3 kg   **b** 3.4×10^3 kg   **c** 4.3×10^3 kg   **d** 8.2×10^4 kg   **e** 2.5×10^4 kg

3 In Science, energy is measured in joules (J).
KJ means 10^3 J, MJ means 10^6 J and GJ means 10^9 J.
Rewrite these energy measurements in joules in standard form.

    a 5 MJ   **b** 0.48 GJ   **c** 25 000 J   **d** 0.25 MJ   **e** 3.2 GJ

4 Use these prefixes to write the frequencies in hertz (Hz) in standard form.

Tera (T) = 10^{12}	Peta (P) = 10^{15}	Giga (G) = 10^9	Mega (M) = 10^6

    a 300 THz   **b** 30 PHz   **c** 40 GHz   **d** 65 MHz

5 Below are some vehicles used in space exploration.
Write their masses in kilograms in standard form.

    a The lunar module that first landed on the moon: 16 400 kg

    b The Saturn 1 space launcher: 510 000 kg

    c The Endeavour Space Shuttle: 74 800 kg

    d The first satellite in Space, Sputnik 1: 83.6 kg

    e Vostok 1, the capsule that housed the first human to go into space: 4725 kg

6 Write these numbers in order of size. Start with the largest number.

    2.5×10^4 250 2.5×10^7 2.5×10^3 250 000

✪ Exam practice

1 **a** Write 2.563×10^4 as an ordinary number.   **(1 mark)**

    b Write 8.093×10^3 as an ordinary number.   **(1 mark)**

Adapted from 1MA1/2F, June 2017, Q15a

2 **a** Write 43 000 000 in standard form.   **(1 mark)**

    b Write 40 506 in standard form.   **(1 mark)**

Adapted from 1MA1/3F, Autumn 2017, Mock Set 3, Q26b

Exam feedback   Results**Plus**

Q1: Most students who achieved a **Grade 3** or above answered a similar question well.

18.4 Writing small numbers in standard form

Key point

- To write a small number in standard form, place the decimal point after the first non-zero digit. How many places has this moved the digit? This is the negative power of 10.

◬ Purposeful practice 1

1 Write these numbers in standard form.

   a 0.52   **b** 0.052   **c** 0.00052   **d** 0.00000052

2 Write these numbers in standard form.

   a 0.001025   **b** 0.0001025   **c** 0.0952   **d** 0.952

3 Write these numbers in standard form.

   a 0.00404   **b** 0.00044   **c** 0.404   **d** 0.44

Reflect and reason

$0.52 \div 10 = 0.052$

Compare 0.52 and 0.052 in standard form.

When you divide a number by 10, how does its standard form change?

◬ Purposeful practice 2

1 Write each number as an ordinary number.

   a 3.5×10^{-3} **b** 3.5×10^{-1} **c** 3.5×10^{-7}

   d 3.5×10^{-2} **e** 1.09×10^{-2} **f** 1.09×10^{-1}

   g 2.508×10^{-7} **h** 2.508×10^{-2} **i** 1.03×10^{-2}

   j 1.3×10^{-1} **k** 1.003×10^{-7} **l** 1.003×10^{-2}

2 Write these numbers as ordinary numbers.
Then write them in order, smallest first.

   3.1×10^{-4} 0.31×10^{-2} 30.1×10^{-4} 0.32×10^{-2}

3 Write these numbers as ordinary numbers.
Then write them in order, largest first.

   65.1×10^{-2} 6.15×10^{-3} 6.51×10^{-2} 6.14×10^{-3}

4 Write these numbers in standard form.
Then write them in order, smallest first.

   0.000102   0.000012   0.0001002   0.00012

5 Write these numbers in standard form.
Then write them in order, largest first.

   0.0007008   0.000078   0.000708   0.00078

Reflect and reason

Joe writes,

1.25×10^{-4} is greater than 1.25×10^{-2}, because 4 is greater than 2.

Joe is wrong. Explain the mistake he has made.

⊠ Problem-solving practice

1 $1\,dl = 10^{-1}$ litres, $1\,cl = 10^{-2}$ litres and $1\,ml = 10^{-3}$ litres

Write these measurements in litres in standard form.

  a A jug has a capacity of 25 dl.

  b A bottle has a capacity of 50 cl.

  c A sink can hold a maximum of 120 cl of water.

  d A mug is filled with 350 ml of coffee.

  e A tablespoon can hold 15 ml of liquid.

2 Robyn scored 1 out of 5 on her homework.

Check her answers, and correct the ones that are wrong.

  a $0.05 = 5 \times 10^{2}$ **b** $0.002\,01 = 2.1 \times 10^{-3}$ **c** $0.05 = 2 \times 10^{-5}$

  d $0.402 = 4.02 \times 10^{-1}$ **e** $0.001\,024 = 1.2 \times 10^{-5}$

3 $1\,mm = 1 \times 10^{-3}\,m$, $1\,\mu m = 1 \times 10^{-6}\,m$ and $1\,nm = 1 \times 10^{-9}\,m$.

Write these measurements in metres in standard form.

  a The width of a thread of spider web is $4\,\mu m$.

  b A typical human hair is about $150\,\mu m$ in diameter.

  c Lightweight paper has a thickness of 0.065 mm.

  d Thick card has a thickness of 0.41 mm.

  e A credit card has a thickness of $760\,\mu m$.

  f DNA has a diameter of 2.3 nm.

4 Three students answered this question.

'Write 0.000 406 in standard form.'

Here are some incorrect answers.

James: 4.06×10^{4}

Hannah: 4.6×10^{-4}

Katy: 40.6×10^{-3}

  a Explain what each student has done wrong.

  b What is the correct answer?

✦ Exam practice

1 **a** Write 1.7×10^{-2} as an ordinary number.   **(1 mark)**

    b Write 7.34×10^{-3} as an ordinary number.   **(1 mark)**

Adapted from 1MA1/2F, June 2017, Q15a

2 **a** Write 0.025 in standard form.   **(1 mark)**

    b Write 0.5 in standard form.   **(1 mark)**

Adapted from 1MA1/3F, Autumn 2017, Mock Set 3, Q26b

Exam feedback

ResultsPlus

Q1: Most students who achieved a **Grade 3** or above answered a similar question well.

Key point

- To multiply and divide numbers in standard form, use the laws of indices to simplify the power of 10.

⚠ Purposeful practice 1

1 Giving your answer in standard form, work out
   a $3.5 \times 10^2 \times 2 \times 10^3$ b $3.5 \times 10^3 \times 2 \times 10^2$
   c $3.5 \times 10^6 \times 2 \times 10^{-3}$ d $3.5 \times 10^{-3} \times 2 \times 10^6$

2 Giving your answer in standard form, work out
   a $3.5 \times 10^2 \times 2.8 \times 10^3$ b $3.5 \times 10^3 \times 2.8 \times 10^2$
   c $3.5 \times 10^8 \times 2.8 \times 10^{-3}$ d $3.5 \times 10^{-3} \times 2.8 \times 10^8$

Reflect and reason

Lee says $4 \times 10^2 \times 6 \times 10^5$ written in standard form is 24×10^7. Explain his mistake.

⚠ Purposeful practice 2

Giving your answer in standard form, work out
1 $2.5 \times 10^5 \times 6.4 \times 10^6$ 2 $2.5 \times 10^5 \times 3.2 \times 10^2 \times 2 \times 10^4$
3 $1.25 \times 10^3 \times 4 \times 10^5 \times 3.2 \times 10^3$

Reflect and reason

Compare your answers for **Q1–3**. Look back at the numbers in the calculations to explain why this has happened.

⚠ Purposeful practice 3

1 Giving your answers in standard form, work out
   a $\dfrac{6 \times 10^2}{2 \times 10^4}$ b $\dfrac{6 \times 10^3}{2 \times 10^5}$ c $\dfrac{6 \times 10^8}{2 \times 10^6}$ d $\dfrac{6 \times 10^9}{2 \times 10^7}$ e $\dfrac{4.2 \times 10^5}{3.5 \times 10^2}$

2 Giving your answers in standard form, work out
   a $\dfrac{2 \times 10^4}{5 \times 10^2}$ b $\dfrac{2 \times 10^5}{5 \times 10^2}$ c $\dfrac{2.5 \times 10^5}{6.25 \times 10^6}$

   d $\dfrac{2.5 \times 10^{15}}{6.25 \times 10^{16}}$ e $\dfrac{2.5 \times 10^{-5}}{6.25 \times 10^{-4}}$ f $\dfrac{2.5 \times 10^{-11}}{6.25 \times 10^{-10}}$

3 Giving your answers as ordinary numbers, work out
   a $\dfrac{2.56 \times 10^{-5}}{1.6 \times 10^{-8}}$ b $\dfrac{2.56 \times 10^{12}}{1.6 \times 10^8}$ c $\dfrac{2.56 \times 10^{12}}{1.6 \times 10^{10}}$

Reflect and reason

You can input **Q2c** into your calculator like this:
   $(2.5 \times 10^5) \div (6.25 \times 10^6)$
Check this gives the correct answer. Explain why the brackets are needed.

1 Below are the distances of some stars from our solar system.
1 light year is 9×10^{12} km
Convert the distances to kilometres.

    a Alpha Centauri is 4.2 light years away.   **b** Procyon is 11.4 light years away.

2 **a** Cell A has mass 2.3×10^{-12} kg. Cell B's mass is 100 times larger.
    Work out the mass of Cell B.

    b Cell C's mass is 20 times smaller than Cell A's.
    Work out the mass of Cell C.

3 A bottle of water contains 800 g of water.
1 mole of water has a mass of 16 g. A mole contains 6.02×10^{23} molecules.
How many molecules are there in the bottle of water?

4 A cuboid block of wood is measured to be 0.3 m by 0.2 m by 0.5 m.

    a Work out the volume in m^3. Give your answer in standard form.

    b A small van can carry a load of 3 m by 2 m by 2 m.
    How many blocks of wood can it carry?
    Give your answer as an ordinary number and in standard form.

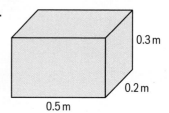

5 The distance from Earth to the Sun is 1.496×10^{11} metres.
The speed of light is 3×10^8 metres per second.

    a Show that light takes about 8 minutes to reach Earth from the Sun.

    The Moon is about 400 times nearer to Earth than the Sun is.

    b Work out how long it takes light reflected by the Moon to reach Earth.
    Give your answer in seconds.

1 Work out $\dfrac{0.002 \times 0.04}{0.001}$

Give your answer in standard form.   **(3 marks)**

Adapted from 1MA1/1F, November 2017, Q21

2 Work out $(1.38 \times 10^2) \times (5.4 \times 10^{-5})$
Give your answer in standard form.   **(2 marks)**

Adapted from 1MA1/2F, June 2017, Q15b

3 Work out the value of $\dfrac{8.288 \times 10^6}{2.24 \times 10^2}$

Give your answer in standard form.   **(2 marks)**

Adapted from 1MA1/3F, June 2018, Q18

Exam feedback   **Results Plus**

Q1: In a similar question, many students worked out the correct answer to the calculation but forgot to convert this to standard form, losing one mark.

Q2: Most students who achieved a **Grade 5** answered a similar question well.

Q3: Most students who achieved a **Grade 4** or above answered a similar question well.

19 Congruence, similarity and vectors

19.1 Similarity and enlargement

Key points

- When one shape is an enlargement of another, the shapes are similar.
- For similar shapes:
    corresponding sides are all in the same ratio
    corresponding angles are equal.

△ Purposeful practice 1

1 For each set of similar shapes, find the ratio of the sides and the scale factor of the enlargement of:

   a shape A : shape B   **b** shape A : shape C   **c** shape B : shape A   **d** shape C : shape A

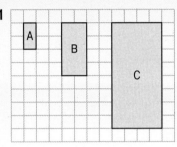

Reflect and reason

Is it enough to check just the ratio of one pair of sides to state that two shapes are similar?

△ Purposeful practice 2

For each pair of similar triangles, state the pairs of corresponding angles and corresponding sides.
The first one has been started for you.

1 Corresponding angles   Corresponding sides

   angle BAC and angle EFD   AB and FD

   angle ☐ and angle ☐   ☐ and ☐

   angle ☐ and angle ☐   ☐ and ☐

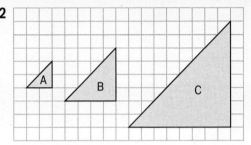

2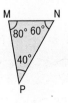

3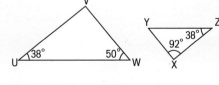

Reflect and reason

Do you need to check all sides and all angles of a pair of triangles to decide if they are similar?

255

⬚ Problem-solving practice

1 Identify the two similar rectangles and give a reason for your answer.

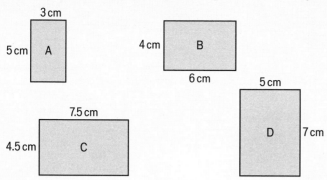

2 Identify two similar triangles and give reasons for your answer.

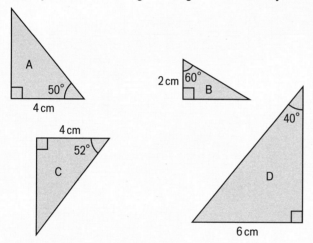

3 For the pairs of similar rectangles and triangles you found in **Q1** and **Q2**, state the ratio of the corresponding sides.

⬚ Exam practice

1 Show that these triangles are mathematically similar. **(2 marks)**

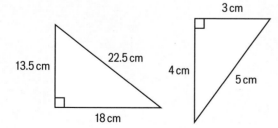

Adapted from 1MA1/3F, June 2017, Q21

Exam feedback

ResultsPlus

In a similar question, many students checked that two out of three pairs of corresponding sides were in the same ratio, but did not check for the third pair.

Key points

- Angle facts can be used to find missing angles.
- Corresponding sides can be used to work out the scale factor of an enlargement and calculate missing lengths.

△ Purposeful practice 1

Find the scale factor of enlargement and the missing side length for these pairs of similar shapes.

1   6 cm   12 cm
3 cm a

2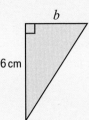
2 cm
3 cm
b
6 cm

3   5 cm c
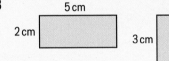
2 cm   3 cm
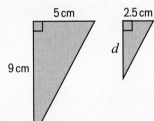

4   5 cm   2.5 cm
d
9 cm

5   4 cm
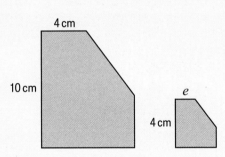
10 cm
e
4 cm

Reflect and reason

For **Q4**, Alfie says the missing length is 18 cm. What mistake has Alfie made?

△ Purposeful practice 2

The lines AB and DE are parallel.

1   State which angle is equal to angle CAB.
2   State which angle is equal to angle CBA.
3   State which angle is equal to angle ACB.
4   State which side corresponds to AC.
5   State which side corresponds to BC.
6   State which side corresponds to AB.
7   Fill in the missing values.
  a   DE = ☐ × AB   **b**   DC = ☐ × BC   **c**   CE = ☐ × AC
8   What is the scale factor of the enlargement?

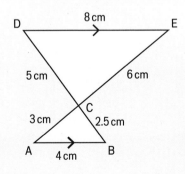

Reflect and reason

Why are the pairs of angles in **Q1–3** equal? Why does this mean the two triangles are similar?

⊠ Problem-solving practice

1 The lines AB and DE are parallel.
AB = 12 cm
AC = 8 cm
DE = 9 cm
Find the length of CE.

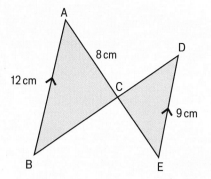

2 The lines BC and DE are parallel.
AD = 4 cm
DE = 6 cm
BC = 7.5 cm
Find the length of BD.

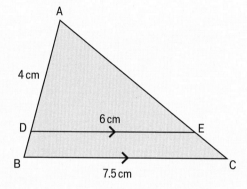

✦ Exam practice

1 PQR and RST are straight lines.
QS is parallel to PT.
PR = 8.5 cm
PT = 7.2 cm
QR = 3.4 cm

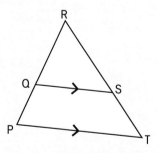

a Work out the length of QS.   **(2 marks)**
SR = 3.8 cm

b Work out the length of RT.   **(2 marks)**

Adapted from 1MA1/2F, June 2017, Q21

Exam feedback   Results**Plus**

In a similar question, many students tried to use Pythagoras' theorem, rather than using the ratios of corresponding sides.

Key point

- When a shape is enlarged, the perimeter of the shape is enlarged by the same scale factor.

△ Purposeful practice 1

Using the shapes to help you, say whether the groups of shapes will always be similar.
State your answer as either yes or no.

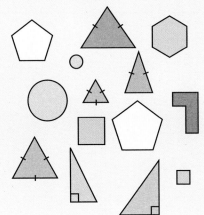

1 squares
2 right-angled triangles
3 isosceles triangles
4 equilateral triangles
5 hexagons
6 regular pentagons
7 circles

Reflect and reason

Not all rectangles are similar. Explain why.

△ Purposeful practice 2

Here are two similar shapes.

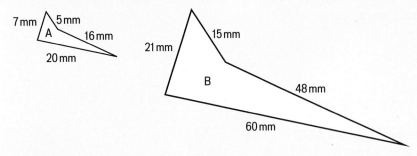

1 Write the ratio of the side length for shape A to shape B in its simplest form.
2 Work out the perimeter of shape A.
3 Work out the perimeter of shape B.
4 Write down the ratio of the perimeter of shape A to the perimeter of shape B, in its simplest form.

Reflect and reason

Write a statement about the ratio of the side lengths and the ratio of the perimeters for the two similar shapes.

Is your statement true for all pairs of similar shapes?

⊠ Problem-solving practice

1   These pairs of shapes are similar. Find the perimeter of shape B in each pair.

a
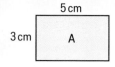
5 cm
3 cm   A

4.5 cm   B

b
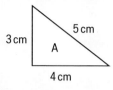
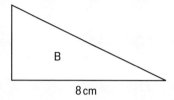
3 cm   5 cm
A
4 cm

B
8 cm

c   Perimeter of A = 27 cm

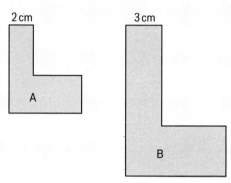
2 cm   3 cm

A

B

2   A circle has circumference 11 cm. It is enlarged by a scale factor of 3.
    Work out the circumference of the enlargement.

3   A regular octagon has side length 8 cm. It is enlarged by a scale factor of 0.75.
    Find the perimeter of the enlargement.

4   A square with an area of 25 cm² is enlarged by a scale factor of 4.
    Find the perimeter of the enlarged square.

▦ ⟐ Exam practice

1   Triangle ABC and triangle DEF are similar.

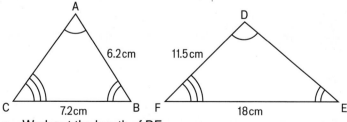
A
6.2 cm   11.5 cm
C   7.2 cm   B   F   18 cm   E
D

a   Work out the length of DE.   **(2 marks)**
b   Work out the length of AC.   **(2 marks)**

Adapted from 1MA1/3F, June 2018, Q27

Exam feedback   Results**Plus**

Most students who achieved a **Grade 5** answered a similar question well.

Key points

- Triangles are congruent if they have equivalent
    SSS (all three sides)
    SAS (two sides and the included angle)
    ASA (two angles and the included side)
    RHS (right angle, hypotenuse, side)
- When two shapes are congruent, one can be rotated or reflected to fit exactly over the other.

△ Purposeful practice

1   These pairs of triangles are congruent.
    State the condition for congruence for each pair.
    Choose from
        SSS (all three sides)
        SAS (two sides and the included angle)
        ASA (two angles and the included side)
        RHS (right angle, hypotenuse, side)

a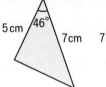

b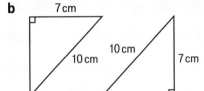

c

2   Are these triangles congruent?
    Use congruence condition SSS to check.
    State any pairs of corresponding sides.

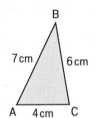 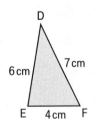

3   Which of these triangles are congruent?

A 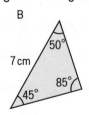   B 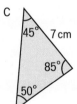   C 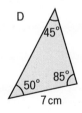   D

Reflect and reason

When two triangles have three sides equal, are they congruent?

When two triangles have three angles equal, are they congruent?

◻ Problem-solving practice

1   Triangle XYZ is isosceles and M is the midpoint of YZ.
Is triangle XYM congruent to triangle XZM?
Give your reasons.

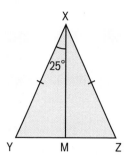

2   Triangle A and triangle B are congruent.
Find angles x and y.
Show your working.

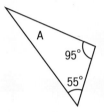 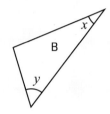

3   Find the missing angle, x.
Show your working.

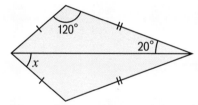

✦ Exam practice

1   Triangles P and Q are congruent.

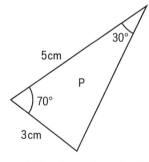 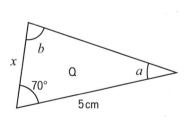

a   What is the length of side x?   (**1 mark**)

b   Find the size of angle

  i a

  ii b (**2 marks**)

Key point

- You can prove that two triangles are congruent by stating the corresponding sides or angles and the condition SSS, SAS, ASA or RHS.

△ Purposeful practice

1 For each pair of congruent triangles
  i find and label the size of all the angles
  ii state the pairs of corresponding sides

a
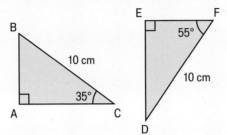

b
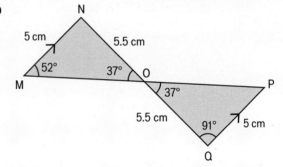

2 For each pair of congruent triangles, state the pairs of corresponding sides and angles, and the condition SSS, SAS, ASA or RHS.

a
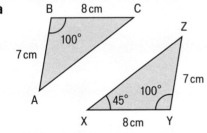

b
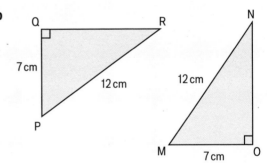

c
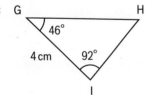

Reflect and reason

How can visualising rotations and reflections help you to identify congruence?

1 ABCD is a rectangle.
   Show that triangle ABD is congruent to triangle CDB.

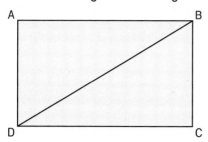

2 EFGH is a parallelogram.
   Show that triangle EFH is congruent to triangle GHF.

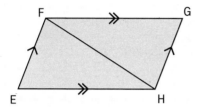

3 XW is parallel to ZY. V is the midpoint of XZ and WY.
   a Show that WVX is congruent to YVZ.
   b Find the length of WV.
   c Find the length of XV.

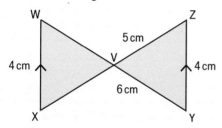

■ **Exam practice**

1 Triangles ABC and PQR are isosceles triangles.

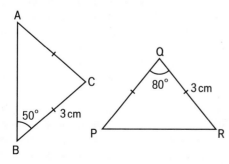

   Prove that triangles ABC and PQR are congruent.
   Give reasons.   **(3 marks)**

Key points

- To add two column vectors, add the top numbers and add the bottom numbers.
- Two translations can be combined into a single translation by adding the column vectors.
- You can show vectors using different notation: $\begin{pmatrix} 2 \\ -1 \end{pmatrix}$, $\overrightarrow{AB}$, **a** or <u>a</u>.
- The sum of two vectors is called the resultant.

△ Purposeful practice 1

Write each vector as a column vector.

1   **2**   **3**

4    **5**

Reflect and reason

How does a column vector change if the vector is in the opposite direction?

△ Purposeful practice 2

1 Add these column vectors. Write your answers as a single vector.

a $\begin{pmatrix} 1 \\ 3 \end{pmatrix}$ and $\begin{pmatrix} 2 \\ 5 \end{pmatrix}$ **b** $\begin{pmatrix} 1 \\ 3 \end{pmatrix}$ and $\begin{pmatrix} -2 \\ -5 \end{pmatrix}$ **c** $\begin{pmatrix} -1 \\ -3 \end{pmatrix}$ and $\begin{pmatrix} 2 \\ 5 \end{pmatrix}$

d $\begin{pmatrix} 1 \\ -3 \end{pmatrix}$ and $\begin{pmatrix} 2 \\ -5 \end{pmatrix}$ **e** $\begin{pmatrix} -1 \\ 3 \end{pmatrix}$ and $\begin{pmatrix} -2 \\ 5 \end{pmatrix}$ **f** $\begin{pmatrix} -1 \\ -3 \end{pmatrix}$ and $\begin{pmatrix} -2 \\ -5 \end{pmatrix}$

2 Give the resultant vector of these pairs of vectors.

a $\overrightarrow{AB}$ and $\overrightarrow{BC}$ **b** $\overrightarrow{AC}$ and $\overrightarrow{CB}$ **c** $\overrightarrow{BC}$ and $\overrightarrow{CD}$

d $\overrightarrow{OA}$ and $\overrightarrow{AE}$ **e** $\overrightarrow{XY}$ and $\overrightarrow{YZ}$ **f** $\overrightarrow{OX}$ and $\overrightarrow{XY}$

Reflect and reason

Look at **Q2a** and **Q2c**. How could you use the answers to those questions to state the resultant vector of $\overrightarrow{AB}$, $\overrightarrow{BC}$ and $\overrightarrow{CD}$?

Problem-solving practice

1 $\overrightarrow{AB} = \begin{pmatrix} 1 \\ 2 \end{pmatrix}$, $\overrightarrow{BC} = \begin{pmatrix} 3 \\ -1 \end{pmatrix}$, $\overrightarrow{BD} = \begin{pmatrix} -2 \\ 4 \end{pmatrix}$ and $\overrightarrow{DE} = \begin{pmatrix} 5 \\ -2 \end{pmatrix}$

Write as column vectors.

a $\overrightarrow{AC}$

b $\overrightarrow{AD}$

c $\overrightarrow{BE}$

d $\overrightarrow{AE}$

2 Find the missing values.

a $\begin{pmatrix} x \\ 4 \end{pmatrix} + \begin{pmatrix} 3 \\ 6 \end{pmatrix} = \begin{pmatrix} 8 \\ 10 \end{pmatrix}$

b $\begin{pmatrix} x \\ 2 \end{pmatrix} + \begin{pmatrix} 5 \\ y \end{pmatrix} = \begin{pmatrix} 7 \\ 9 \end{pmatrix}$

c $\begin{pmatrix} 2x \\ 4 \end{pmatrix} + \begin{pmatrix} 7 \\ y \end{pmatrix} = \begin{pmatrix} 15 \\ -5 \end{pmatrix}$

d $\begin{pmatrix} 3x \\ 9 \end{pmatrix} + \begin{pmatrix} -2 \\ x \end{pmatrix} = \begin{pmatrix} 13 \\ y \end{pmatrix}$

3 Find the resultant of $\begin{pmatrix} m+3 \\ n+7 \end{pmatrix}$ and $\begin{pmatrix} m-2 \\ 2n+1 \end{pmatrix}$ in terms of m and n.

4 The resultant of $\overrightarrow{AB}$ and $\overrightarrow{BC}$ is $\begin{pmatrix} 0 \\ -5 \end{pmatrix}$.

Find $\overrightarrow{AB}$ if $\overrightarrow{BC} = \begin{pmatrix} 7 \\ 4 \end{pmatrix}$.

5 $\mathbf{p} = \begin{pmatrix} 3x \\ y \end{pmatrix}$ $\mathbf{q} = \begin{pmatrix} x+2 \\ 2y-4 \end{pmatrix}$

Find x and y if $\mathbf{p} + \mathbf{q} = \begin{pmatrix} 18 \\ -7 \end{pmatrix}$

Exam practice

1 $\mathbf{s} = \begin{pmatrix} 4 \\ 2 \end{pmatrix}$ and $\mathbf{t} = \begin{pmatrix} 5 \\ 3 \end{pmatrix}$

Write down $\mathbf{s} + \mathbf{t}$ as a column vector. **(1 mark)**

Adapted from 1MA1/3F, Spring 2017, Mock Set 2, Q20ai

Key points

- $\mathbf{a} - \mathbf{b}$ is the same as $\mathbf{a} + (-\mathbf{b})$
- To subtract column vectors, subtract the top numbers and subtract the bottom numbers.
- You can multiply a vector by a constant number, for example, $3\mathbf{a}$, $-2\mathbf{b}$.

△ Purposeful practice 1

Subtract these column vectors.

1 $\begin{pmatrix} 4 \\ 7 \end{pmatrix} - \begin{pmatrix} 3 \\ 2 \end{pmatrix}$ 2 $\begin{pmatrix} 4 \\ 7 \end{pmatrix} - \begin{pmatrix} 2 \\ 3 \end{pmatrix}$ 3 $\begin{pmatrix} 3 \\ 2 \end{pmatrix} - \begin{pmatrix} 4 \\ 7 \end{pmatrix}$

4 $\begin{pmatrix} 2 \\ 3 \end{pmatrix} - \begin{pmatrix} 4 \\ 7 \end{pmatrix}$ 5 $\begin{pmatrix} 7 \\ 4 \end{pmatrix} - \begin{pmatrix} -3 \\ 2 \end{pmatrix}$ 6 $\begin{pmatrix} -7 \\ -4 \end{pmatrix} - \begin{pmatrix} -3 \\ -2 \end{pmatrix}$

7 $\begin{pmatrix} 2 \\ 1 \end{pmatrix} - \begin{pmatrix} 1 \\ 5 \end{pmatrix}$ 8 $\begin{pmatrix} 1 \\ 5 \end{pmatrix} - \begin{pmatrix} 2 \\ 1 \end{pmatrix}$ 9 $\begin{pmatrix} -2 \\ -1 \end{pmatrix} - \begin{pmatrix} -1 \\ -5 \end{pmatrix}$

Reflect and reason

Look at your answers to **Q1** and **Q3**, then to **Q2** and **Q4** and then to **Q7** and **Q8**.

How does changing the order of the vectors in the calculation change the answer?

△ Purposeful practice 2

1 $\mathbf{p} = \begin{pmatrix} -3 \\ 5 \end{pmatrix}$ and $\mathbf{q} = \begin{pmatrix} 4 \\ -1 \end{pmatrix}$

Write as column vectors.

   a $2\mathbf{p}$ b $3\mathbf{p}$ c $-\mathbf{p}$ d $-\mathbf{q}$ e $-2\mathbf{q}$ f $-4\mathbf{q}$

2 $\mathbf{d} = \begin{pmatrix} 3 \\ -2 \end{pmatrix}$ and $\mathbf{e} = \begin{pmatrix} -1 \\ 4 \end{pmatrix}$

Write as column vectors.

   a $-\mathbf{d}$ b $-\mathbf{e}$ c $2\mathbf{d}$ d $2\mathbf{e}$ e $2\mathbf{d} + \mathbf{e}$ f $3\mathbf{d} - 2\mathbf{e}$

3 $\mathbf{m} = \begin{pmatrix} 0 \\ -6 \end{pmatrix}$ and $\mathbf{n} = \begin{pmatrix} 4 \\ 0 \end{pmatrix}$

Write as column vectors.

   a $-2\mathbf{m} + 2\mathbf{n}$ b $-4\mathbf{m} + 4\mathbf{n}$ c $3\mathbf{m} - 3\mathbf{n}$ d $0.5\mathbf{m} + 0.5\mathbf{n}$

Reflect and reason

What can you say about the direction of a vector that is a positive multiple of another?

What word describes those two vectors?

1   $r = \begin{pmatrix} 3 \\ -4 \end{pmatrix}$ and $t = \begin{pmatrix} -1 \\ 2 \end{pmatrix}$

On squared paper, draw a vector

   a twice as long as **r**

   b twice as long as **t** but in the opposite direction

   c half as long as $r + t$

   d half as long as $2t - 2r$

   e parallel to $r + t$ but 3 times as long

2   $u = \begin{pmatrix} x \\ 2x \end{pmatrix}$ and $v = \begin{pmatrix} 2 \\ y \end{pmatrix}$

   a Find x and y so that $u + v = \begin{pmatrix} 5 \\ 8 \end{pmatrix}$

   b State the value of y so that **u** is parallel to **v**.

3   Find x and y.

$$\begin{pmatrix} 2x \\ y \end{pmatrix} - \begin{pmatrix} 7 \\ 8 \end{pmatrix} = \begin{pmatrix} 9 \\ -3 \end{pmatrix}$$

4   Find x and y.

$$\begin{pmatrix} 10 \\ -7 \end{pmatrix} - \begin{pmatrix} 3x \\ -2y \end{pmatrix} = \begin{pmatrix} 16 \\ -3 \end{pmatrix}$$

5   Find p and q.

$$a = \begin{pmatrix} 4 \\ -7 \end{pmatrix} \qquad b = \begin{pmatrix} p \\ 5 \end{pmatrix} \qquad c = \begin{pmatrix} -1 \\ q \end{pmatrix}$$

$$2a - 3b - c = \begin{pmatrix} -3 \\ -30 \end{pmatrix}$$

⬦ **Exam practice**

1   $s = \begin{pmatrix} 6 \\ 4 \end{pmatrix} \qquad t = \begin{pmatrix} 1 \\ -2 \end{pmatrix}$

Work out $s + 3t$ as a column vector.   **(2 marks)**

Adapted from 1MA1/1F, May 2018, Q26

Exam feedback   Results**Plus**

Most students who achieved a **Grade 4** or above answered a similar question well.

20 More algebra

20.1 Graphs of cubic and reciprocal functions

Key points

- A cubic function contains a term in x^3 but no higher powers of x.
- It can also have terms in x^2 and x and number terms.
- A reciprocal function contains a number divided by x.

△ Purposeful practice 1

1 For each of these cubic functions

    i Copy and complete the table of values.

    ii Draw a coordinate grid with the x-axis from -3 to $+3$ and the y-axis from -35 to $+35$.
       Then draw the graph.

x	-3	-2	-1	0	1	2	3
a $y = x^3 + 1$ $x^3 + 1$							
b $y = x^3 - x + 1$ $x^3 - x + 1$							
c $y = x^3 + x^2 - x + 1$ $x^3 + x^2 - x + 1$							
d $y = x^3 + x^2 - x - 1$ $x^3 + x^2 - x - 1$							
e $y = -x^3 + 1$ $-x^3 + 1$							
f $y = -x^3 + 2x + 1$ $-x^3 + 2x + 1$							
g $y = -x^3 - x^2 + 2x + 1$ $-x^3 - x^2 + 2x + 1$							
h $y = -x^3 - x^2 + 2x - 3$ $-x^3 - x^2 + 2x - 3$							

Reflect and reason

Explain how you can use a table of values for $y = x^3 + 1$ to complete a table of values for

a $y = x^3 + 3$ **b** $y = x^3 + x + 1$

△ Purposeful practice 2

1 For each reciprocal function

    i Copy and complete the table of values.

    ii On graph paper, draw a coordinate grid with the
       x-axis and y-axis from 0 to $+10$. Plot the graph.

a

x	0.25	0.5	1	2	4	5	10
$y = \dfrac{2}{x}$							

b

x	0.5	1	2	3	4	5	10
$y = \dfrac{3}{x}$							

c

x	0.5	1	2	4	5	8	10
$y = \dfrac{4}{x}$							

Reflect and reason

In the graph of a reciprocal function, $y = \dfrac{\text{a number}}{x}$. Find the missing words.

As the value of x increases, the value of y _____ but never reaches _____.

As the value of x decreases, the value of y _____.

1 Match each equation to the correct graph.

  a $y = \dfrac{5}{x}$ **b** $y = \dfrac{8}{x}$

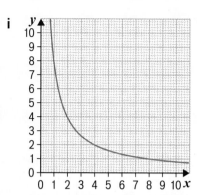
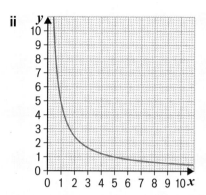

2 Match each equation to the correct graph.

  a $y = x^3 - x^2 - 2x - 1$ **b** $y = x$ **c** $y = \dfrac{1}{x}$ **d** $y = 1$

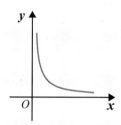

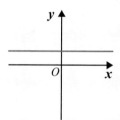

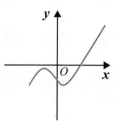
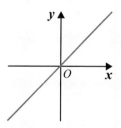

⊠ Exam practice

1 **a** Copy and complete the table of values for $y = \dfrac{3}{x}$ **(2 marks)**

x	0.5	1	1.5	2	3	4	5	6
y		3		1.5		0.75		

b On graph paper, draw a coordinate grid with the x-axis labelled from 0 to +6 and the y-axis labelled from 0 to +6. Draw the graph of $y = \dfrac{3}{x}$ for values of x from 0.5 to 6.   **(2 marks)**

Adapted from 1MA1/3F, June 2017, Q22

Exam feedback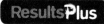

Most students who achieved a **Grade 4** or above answered a similar question well.

Key points

- A non-linear graph is any graph that is not a straight line. So a curved graph is a non-linear graph.
- You can estimate values from a non-linear graph.

⚠ Purposeful practice 1

1 The graph shows the number of ants in a nest.

    a How many ants were in the nest at the start?

    b Estimate the number of ants in the nest after 3 months.

    c When did the number of ants reach 500?

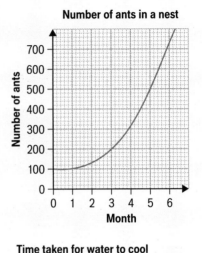

Number of ants in a nest

2 A pan of boiling water is left to cool.
The graph shows the temperature of the water at different times.
Estimate

    a the starting temperature of the water

    b the temperature of the water at time 6 minutes

    c the time taken for the water to cool to 35°C

    d how many degrees the water cools by in the first 3 minutes

Time taken for water to cool

3 Explain what the point (0, 40) means on each graph.

a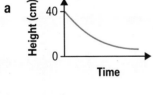

b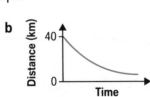

c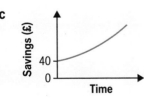

d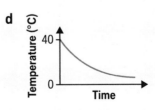

Reflect and reason

Why do you need the axis labels to help you to interpret the graphs?

1   The graph shows the number of hours
    it takes different numbers of bakers to
    ice 600 cupcakes.

    a   Estimate the time it would take 3 bakers
        to ice 600 cupcakes.

    b   How many cupcakes does one baker
        ice in one hour?

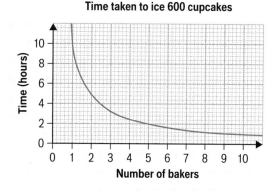

Time taken to ice 600 cupcakes

2   The graph shows the weight of a baby
    each week from birth.

    a   What was the baby's weight at birth?

    b   Between which two weeks did the baby
        gain the most weight?

Weight gain of baby

3   The table shows the distance of a car from its
    starting point, each second, as it accelerates.

Time (seconds)	0	1	2	3	4
Distance (m)	0	5	20	45	80

Draw an appropriate graph and use it to estimate the car's distance at 2.5 seconds.

✦ Exam practice

1   Joel was driving in a race.
    The graph shows his speed, in metres per second, t seconds after the start of the race.

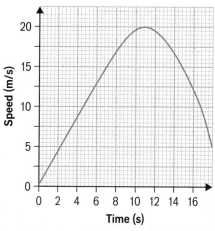

    a   Write down Joel's speed 6 seconds after the start of the race.   **(1 mark)**

    b   Write down Joel's greatest speed.   **(1 mark)**

    There were two times when Joel's speed was 15 m/s.

    c   Write down these two times.   **(1 mark)**

Adapted from 1MA1/2F, Specimen Papers, Set 2, Q10

Unit 20 Non-linear graphs   272

20.3 Solving simultaneous equations graphically

Key points

- Simultaneous equations are equations that are both true for a pair of variables (letters).
- To find the solution to linear simultaneous equations:
    1. Draw the lines on a coordinate grid.
    2. Find the points where the lines cross (the point of intersection).

△ Purposeful practice 1

1 Here is the graph of $2x + y = 7$.

a Use the graph to fill in this table of values for $2x + y = 7$.

x	-2	-1	0	2		4
y				0		

b Use the graph to write down two more pairs of x and y values that satisfy the equation $2x + y = 7$.

c Look at all your pairs of x and y values from **Q1a** and **Q1b**. Which pair of x and y values also satisfies the equation $x + y = 5$?

d Copy the graph and draw the line $x + y = 5$.

e Write down the x and y values where the two lines intersect. Is your answer the same as your answer to **Q1c**? Explain why you think this is.

f How many possible solutions (pairs of x and y values) did you find for $2x + y = 7$?

g How many of these possible solutions satisfied $2x + y = 7$ **and** $x + y = 5$?

Reflect and reason

When equations have two variables, how many equations do you think you need to solve simultaneously to find only one solution?

△ Purposeful practice 2

1 Draw graphs to solve these simultaneous equations.
Use a coordinate grid with the x-axis from -2 to $+9$ and the y-axis from -4 to $+5$ for each one.

a $x + 2y = 8$
$x + y = 6$

b $2x + 3y = 9$
$x - y = 2$

c $2x + y = 1$
$x + y = 3$

d $x - 2y = 8$
$x + y = -1$

e $2x - y = 4$
$y = 1$

f $2x + y = 6$
$4x - y = 3$

g $2x + 4y = 5$
$x + y = 2$

h $3x + y = -4$
$x - y = 2$

Reflect and reason

Are solutions to simultaneous equations always positive whole numbers? Use examples from the questions above to explain.

1 Draw a graph to show two simultaneous equations that have the solution $x = 4$, $y = 1$.

2 Solve the simultaneous equations.

$x + 3y = 9$

$x + y = 1$

3 The sum of two numbers is 9 and their difference is 10.
Work out the two numbers.

4 Here is the graph of $2x - 3y = -1$.

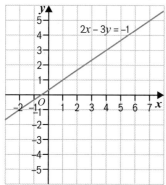

Find a solution that satisfies $2x - 3y = -1$ and $3x - 2y = 11$.

5 2 milkshakes and 1 cake cost £4.30
3 milkshakes and 5 cakes cost £9.25
Work out the cost of

  a 1 milkshake

  b 1 cake

Exam practice

1 Here is a graph of $y = 3 - 2x$

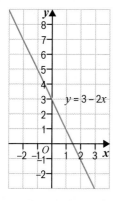

  a On a copy of the graph, plot the graph of $y = x - 3$. **(2 marks)**

  b Use your graph to solve the simultaneous equations $y = 3 - 2x$ and $y = x - 3$. **(1 mark)**

20.4 Solving simultaneous equations algebraically

Key point

- To solve simultaneous equations by the elimination method, add or subtract the equations to eliminate either the x or y terms.

⚠ Purposeful practice 1

1 Add together each pair of equations. The first one is done for you.

If adding the equations eliminates either x or y, solve to find the value of the remaining variable.

a $2x - y = 3$
$x + y = 3$
$3x = 6$ (y eliminated)
$x = 2$

b $4x + y = 11$
$x + y = 5$

c $2x + y = 8$
$-2x - 3y = -4$

2 For each pair of equations, subtract equation (2) from equation (1).

If subtracting the equations eliminates either x or y, solve to find the value of the remaining variable.

a $4x + y = 11$ (1)
$x + y = 5$ (2)

b $2x - y = -2$ (1)
$2x + 3y = 22$ (2)

c $2x - y = 3$ (1)
$x + y = 3$ (2)

Reflect and reason

How do you know when to add equations to eliminate a variable?

How do you know when to subtract equations to eliminate a variable?

⚠ Purposeful practice 2

1 In each pair, multiply one of the equations so that the x coefficients are the same.

a $x + 2y = 4$
$4x + y = 9$

b $3x + y = 8$
$x - 2y = -2$

c $2x - 3y = 7$
$x + y = 6$

2 For each pair of equations in **Q1**, multiply one of the equations so that you can add or subtract to eliminate y.

3 Multiply both equations so that the x coefficients are the same.

a $3x - y = 1$
$2x + y = 9$

b $2x + y = 5$
$5x + 2y = 14$

c $3x + y = 3$
$7x + 2y = 5$

4 Multiply both equations so that you can add or subtract to eliminate y.

a $x + 3y = 12$
$x - 2y = 2$

b $x + 2y = 11$
$4x + 5y = 35$

c $x - 4y = 11$
$4x + 5y = 10$

Reflect and reason

When you eliminate a variable by subtracting, do you get the same answer subtracting (1) from (2) as subtracting (2) from (1)? Does it matter which subtraction you do?

⊠ Problem-solving practice

1 Solve the simultaneous equations.

$2x + y = 11$

$5x - 2y = 14$

2 Danny solves a pair of simultaneous equations.

$2x + 3y = 20$ (1)

$3x + y = 23$ (2)

$9x + 3y = 23$ (3)   (2) × 3

$7x = 3$ (3) − (1)

   a What mistake has Danny made?

   b Correct the mistake and solve the equations to find x and y.

3 Write a pair of simultaneous equations with solution $x = 5$ and $y = 2$.

4 Here are the graphs of $2x + y = 3$ and $5x + 2y = 5$.
Solve this pair of simultaneous equations graphically and algebraically. Did you get the same solutions?

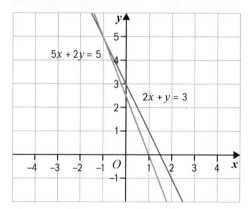

5 The sum of two numbers is 903 and their difference is 269.
Work out the two numbers.

6 At a cinema
2 adult tickets and 3 child tickets cost £42
1 adult ticket and 2 child tickets cost £24
Show that an adult ticket costs twice as much as a child's ticket.

⟡ Exam practice

1 Solve the simultaneous equations.

$2x + y = -4$

$2x - 3y = 8$ **(3 marks)**

Adapted from 1MA1/3F, June 2017, Q16

Exam feedback   ResultsPlus

In a similar question, students made errors when substituting the y value into one of the equations.

20.5 Rearranging formulae

Purposeful practice

1 Make t the subject of each formula.

  a $m = 3t$ **b** $p = 0.5t$ **c** $q = nt$

  d $r = 4nt$ **e** $v = tx$ **f** $w = 2tx$

  g $z = ntx$ **h** $y = \dfrac{1}{2}tx$ **i** $s = \dfrac{1}{2}nt$

2 Make h the subject of each formula.

  a $c = \dfrac{h}{3}$ **b** $d = \dfrac{h}{10}$ **c** $s = \dfrac{h}{a}$

  d $f = \dfrac{h}{ab}$ **e** $g = \dfrac{1}{h}$ **f** $m = \dfrac{2}{h}$

  g $n = \dfrac{r}{h}$ **h** $p = \dfrac{4s}{h}$ **i** $r = \dfrac{t}{4h}$

  j $s = \dfrac{ah}{v}$ **k** $u = \dfrac{ah}{w}$ **l** $v = \dfrac{ah}{wx}$

3 Make x the subject of each formula.

  a $y = x + 2$ **b** $a = x + b$ **c** $v = x - b$

  d $w = 2x + a$ **e** $c = 2x - a$ **f** $g = 3x + a$

  g $h = 3x - a$ **h** $k = bx + 3$ **i** $z = \dfrac{x}{2} + 3$

  j $f = \dfrac{x}{2} + c$ **k** $m = \dfrac{x}{a} + c$ **l** $m = \dfrac{x}{a} - d$

4 Make y the subject of each formula.

  a $t = 2xy$ **b** $n = ayz$ **c** $p = \dfrac{ay}{10}$

  d $q = \dfrac{yz}{10}$ **e** $r = \dfrac{yz}{2}$ **f** $s = \dfrac{ayz}{2}$

  g $t = y^2$ **h** $u = 3y^2$ **i** $v = 5y^2$

  j $x = by^2$ **k** $z = 4y^2$ **l** $b^2 = 9y^2$

Reflect and reason

For each formula, write down

a the operations on x in the formula

b the inverse operation(s) you use to make x the subject

$\boxed{y = nx}$ $\boxed{y = \dfrac{x}{t}}$ $\boxed{y = mx + c}$

⊠ Problem-solving practice

1 Rearrange the formula

$$\text{speed} = \frac{\text{distance}}{\text{time}}$$

   a to make distance the subject

   b to make time the subject

2 In the formula

$$v = u + at$$

   v is final velocity, u is initial velocity, a is acceleration and t is time.
   The initial velocity is $4\,\text{m/s}$ and the acceleration is $3\,\text{m/s}^2$.
   Find the time, in seconds, to reach a final speed of $31\,\text{m/s}$.

3 Kim rearranges the formula $x = 2y - 3$ to make y the subject.
   Here are the first two lines of her working.

$$x = 2y - 3$$

$$\frac{x}{2} = y - 3$$

   a Explain what Kim has done wrong.

   b Make y the subject of $x = 2y - 3$

4 Here are some equations of lines.

$5x + y = 3$	$y = 5x + 3$	$5x - y = 3$	$5y - x = -3$	$5x - y = -3$

   Which two equations represent the same line?

5 Here are two formulae for a circle of radius r.
   Circumference of circle, $C = 2\pi r$
   Area of circle, $A = \pi r^2$
   Write a formula for the radius of a circle when you know

   a the circumference

   b the area

✫ Exam practice

1 Make n the subject of this formula.
   $$D = 3n + 5$$
   (2 marks)

Adapted from 1MA1/3F, June 2017, Q11b

2 Make x the subject of this formula.
   $$y = \frac{x}{2} - 3z$$
   (2 marks)

Adapted from 1MA1/3F, Specimen Papers, Set 2, Q24

Exam feedback
ResultsPlus

Q1: Most students who achieved a **Grade 5** answered a similar question well.

Key point

- To show a statement is an identity, expand and simplify the expressions on one or both sides of the identity sign until the two expressions are the same.

⚠ Purposeful practice 1

1   Show that

a $(x+2)^2 \equiv x^2 + 4x + 4$

b $(x+2)^2 + 5 \equiv x^2 + 4x + 9$

c $(x+2)^2 + 3x \equiv x^2 + 7x + 4$

d $x^2 + 4x \equiv x(x+4)$

e $x^3 + 4x \equiv x(x^2 + 4)$

f $x^3 + 4x^2 \equiv x^2(x+4)$

g $x^2 + 8x + 4 \equiv (x+1)(x+4) + 3x$

h $x^2 + 5x + 7 \equiv (x+1)(x+4) + 3$

2   Each rectangle of card has a smaller rectangle cut out of the middle.

a

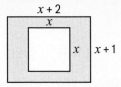

Show that the area of the remaining card is $3x + 2$

b

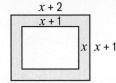

Show that the area of the remaining card is $2(x+1)$

Reflect and reason

To prove two statements are equal, do you always need to expand brackets?

Find two examples in **Q1** where you could factorise the left-hand expression to get the right-hand expression.

⚠ Purposeful practice 2

1   n is an integer. Match each general term to a description.

even number	$3n$
odd number	$2n$
multiple of 3	$n, n+1, n+2$
3 consecutive integers	$2n+1$

2   Show that

a   the sum of two consecutive numbers is an odd number.

b   the difference between two even numbers is even.

c   the difference between two odd numbers is even.

d   the difference between an odd and even number is odd.

Reflect and reason

Jen says, 'You can use $2n - 1$ as a general term for an odd number.' Explain why Jen is correct.

⊠ Problem-solving practice

1   a, b and c are consecutive numbers.

   a   Give an example to show that the value of $a + b + c$ is a multiple of 3.

   b   Show that, when a, b and c are consecutive numbers, the value of $a + b + c$ will always be a multiple of 3.

2   Here is a rectangle made out of card.

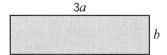

3a

b

Jon fits four of these rectangles together to make a frame.

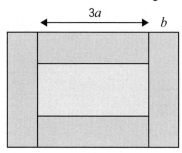

3a

b

The perimeter of the outside of the frame is P cm.

   a   Show that $P = 12a + 4b$

   b   Bella says, 'When a and b are whole numbers, P is always a multiple of 4.'
      Is Bella correct?
      You must give a reason for your answer.

3   **a**   Write an example to show that this statement is **not correct**.

   | The sum of an odd number and an even number is even. |

   b   Show that the sum of an odd number and an even number is **never** even.

⊠ Exam practice

1
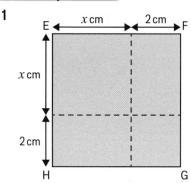

x cm   2 cm

E x cm   2 cm   F

x cm

2 cm

H   G

The area of square EFGH is $9\,cm^2$.
Show that $x^2 + 4x = 5$

(3 marks)

Adapted from 1MA1/1F, May 2017, Q24

Exam feedback

ResultsPlus

In a similar question, very few students simplified their expression and equated it to the area of the square.

Mixed exercises E

Mixed problem-solving practice E

1 Here are six graphs.

A
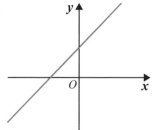

B
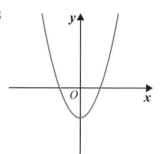

C
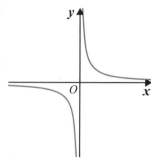

D
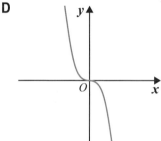

E
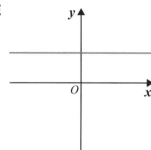

F
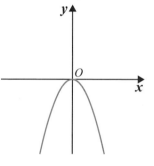

a Match each graph to its equation.

   i $x = 2$ ii $y = 2$ iii $y = x + 2$ iv $y = -x^2$

   v $y = x^2 - 2$ vi $y = x^3$ vii $y = -x^3$ viii $y = \dfrac{1}{x}$

b Sketch and label the graphs of the equations you have not matched to a graph.

2 Jane is asked to write the planets Earth, Jupiter, Mercury and Saturn in order of average distance from the Sun, starting with the shortest distance. She lists her results in the table.

Planet	Average distance from the Sun (km)
Saturn	1.427×10^9
Earth	1.496×10^8
Mercury	5.79×10^7
Jupiter	7.783×10^8

The values for each planet are correct but the planets are not in the correct order.
Explain what Jane has done wrong.

3 The circumference of a circle is 500 cm.
Work out the radius of the circle.
Give your answer to 3 significant figures.

4 Farrah is asked to work out the green shaded area of this shape.
Farrah says that exactly $\frac{1}{2}$ of the shape is shaded.
Is Farrah correct?
Show your working.

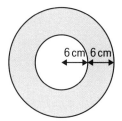

5 A rectangular fridge magnet measures $2\frac{3}{4}$ inches by $1\frac{5}{8}$ inches.
What is the area of the fridge magnet?

6 The minimum distance between Earth and Mars is approximately
54.6 million kilometres.
A probe is launched at a velocity of 4.8×10^4 km/h.
Assuming that the probe continues to travel at this velocity throughout its journey when
Earth and Mars are at their closest, estimate the time taken for the probe to reach Mars.
Give your answer in standard form in hours.

7 Show that the two triangles are congruent.

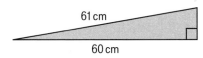 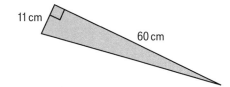

8 Solve the simultaneous equations.
$4x + y = -7$
$2x - 3y = 14$

9 m and n are both odd numbers.

a Give an example to show that the value of $3(m + n)$ is a multiple of 6.

b Show that, when m and n are both odd numbers, the value of $3(m + n)$ will always be a
multiple of 6.

10 M is the midpoint of AC.

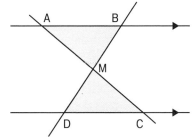

Show that triangles ABM and DCM are congruent.

11 Show that $A = \sqrt{x + y}$ can be written as $y = A^2 - x$

12 Show that $\left(\dfrac{p}{q}\right)^{-2}$ can be written as $\dfrac{q^2}{p^2}$

13 The diagram shows water in a water butt.
The water butt is in the shape of a cylinder of radius 27 cm.
The height of the water in the water butt is 95 cm.
135 litres of water are taken from the water butt.
1 litre = 1000 cm³
Work out the new height of the water in the water butt.
Give your answer correct to one decimal place.

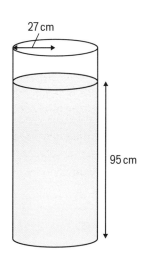

⚝ **Exam practice**

14 $\mathbf{a} = \begin{pmatrix} 5 \\ 1 \end{pmatrix}$ $\mathbf{b} = \begin{pmatrix} -3 \\ 2 \end{pmatrix}$

Work out $3\mathbf{a} + \mathbf{b}$ as a column vector.   **(2 marks)**

Adapted from 1MA1/1F, May 2018, Q26

Exam feedback

Most students who achieved a **Grade 4** and above answered a similar question well.

⚝ **Exam practice**

15   Work out

$$\frac{0.0004 \times 0.007}{0.02}$$

Give your answer in standard form.   **(3 marks)**

Adapted from 1MA1/1F, November 2017, Q21

Exam feedback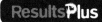

In a similar question, a common mistake when attempting to write a number in standard form was to write, for example, 2^{-2} rather than 2×10^{-2}.

⚝ **Exam practice**

16   A landscape gardener is building a stone wall around the edge of a flower garden.
The flower garden is in the shape of a semicircle with diameter 5 m.

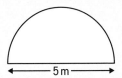

The landscape gardener uses this rule to work out his fee for building the wall.

Total cost = £103.38 per metre of wall plus £180 for each day's work

The landscape gardener takes 7 days to build the wall.
Work out the total cost.   **(5 marks)**

Adapted from 1MA1/2F, June 2018, Q19

Exam feedback   ResultsPlus

Most students who achieved a **Grade 5** answered a similar question well.

17 Triangle LMN and triangle PQR are similar.

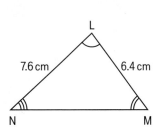

a Work out the length of PR. **(2 marks)**

b Work out the length of NM. **(2 marks)**

Adapted from 1MA1/3F, June 2018, Q27

Exam feedback ResultsPlus

Most students who achieved a **Grade 5** answered a similar question well.

⊠ Exam practice

18 The equation of the line L_1 is $y = 4x + 3$
The equation of the line L_2 is $3y - 12x - 7 = 0$
Show that these two lines are parallel. **(2 marks)**

Adapted from 1MA1/1F, May 2017, Q26

Exam feedback ResultsPlus

Most students who achieved a **Grade 4** and above answered a similar question well.

⊠ Exam practice

19

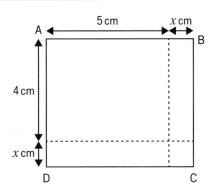

The area of rectangle ABCD is 30 cm².
Show that $x^2 + 9x = 10$ **(3 marks)**

Adapted from 1MA1/1F, May 2017, Q24

Exam feedback ResultsPlus

In a similar question, very few students simplified their expression and equated it to 10. It is essential to show all steps in a solution where the final answer is given in the question.

swers

1 Number

1.1 Calculations

Purposeful practice 1

1 16	**2** 16	**3** 40	**4** 24
5 0	**6** 0	**7** 16	**8** 16
9 16	**10** 8	**11** 4	**12** 2

Purposeful practice 2

1 5	**2** 8	**3** 5	**4** 12.5	**5** 5	**6** 5

Purposeful practice 3

1 $33 \div 3 = 11$ **2** $\sqrt[3]{1331} = 11$ **3** $\sqrt[3]{(1334 - 3)} = 11$

4 $\sqrt[3]{2744} - 3 = 11$ **5** $\sqrt[3]{\frac{3993}{3}} = 11$ **6** $\sqrt[3]{\frac{363 \times 11}{3}} = 11$

Problem-solving practice

1 Students' own answers, for example, $(1 + 2 + 3) \times 4 + 5$.

2 $7 + 5 \times (3 + 8) = 62$

3 Students' own answers, for example,

−3	2	1
4	0	−4
−1	−2	3

4 Pole C is 6 m long.

5 $\frac{2 \times (11 - 7)}{8} = 1$ or $\frac{2 \times (11 - 7)}{1} = 8$

6 Sarah is incorrect. To find the cost of 80 tins of paint, she needs to calculate $80 \times £4 = £320$.

7 Students' own answers, for example,
$(6 - 5) \times (4 - 3) = 1$ $(6 - 5) \div (4 - 3) = 1$
$(6 - 4) \div (5 - 3) = 1$

Exam practice

1 £316   **2** 38

1.2 Decimal numbers

Purposeful practice 1

1 300	**2** 30	**3** 3	**4** 0.3	**5** 0.03	**6** 0.03
7 3	**8** 30	**9** 300	**10** 30	**11** 3	**12** 0.3

Purposeful practice 2

1 2	**2** 5	**3** 2	**4** 5	**5** 4	**6** 10	**7** 4
8 10	**9** 1	**10** 1.6	**11** 1	**12** 10	**13** 100	**14** 100
15 25	**16** 25	**17** 2.5	**18** 2			

Purposeful practice 3

1 3.5	**2** 3.5	**3** 3.5	**4** 11.5	**5** 0.5
6 3.8	**7** 3.9	**8** 4.0	**9** 11.0	**10** 1.0
11 0.1	**12** 0.0	**13** 9.8	**14** 9.1	**15** 20.0

Problem-solving practice

1 a £4.67 **b** £0.47 (rounded)   **2 a** $3.84\dot{9}$ **b** 3.75

3 Calculations C and D

4 Students' own answers, for example, $10 \times 0.5 = 5$

5 £303.75   **6** No, he only has 15 kg of flour.

7 20 packs   **8** £6.40

Exam practice

1 4.2   **2** 212.5

1.3 Place value

Purposeful practice 1

1 100	**2** 200	**3** 1000	**4** 1000	**5** 1	**6** 0.1
7 0.001	**8** 0.002	**9** 0.0017	**10** 0.0011	**11** 0.0010	**12** 3.0

Purposeful practice 2

1 20 000	**2** 20	**3** 1	**4** 500	**5** 1200
6 500	**7** 4000	**8** 1200	**9** 300	

Purposeful practice 3

1 a 8640	**b** 270	**c** 86.4	**d** 2.7
e 270	**f** 27	**g** 27	**h** 2.7
2 a 295	**b** 354	**c** 236	**d** 300

Problem-solving practice

1 a £500 a month

b Yes, he will save £6000 which is greater than £5775.

2 a No, an estimate of five times their yearly earnings is £180 000.

b It is an underestimate, because Carrie and Arjun's earnings were rounded down.

3 a 12 ounces

b It is an underestimate, because both values were rounded down.

c The estimated weight will increase to 15 because 4.7 rounds up to 5.

4 Students' own answers, for example, 0.54×8.7

5 Sam should have found 400×60 and then divided by 0.5 or multiplied by 2.

6 Approximately 20 minutes

Exam practice

1 $\frac{200}{4^2 + 4} = \frac{200}{16 + 4} = \frac{200}{20} = 10$

Billy's answer is correct.

2 90

1.4 Factors and multiples

Purposeful practice 1

1 a 20, 22, 24, 26, 28, 30   **b** 21, 24, 27, 30
c 20, 25, 30   **d** 21, 28   **e** 22   **f** 23, 29

2 31, 37   **3** 41, 43, 47

Purposeful practice 2

1 a 1, 2, 3, 6   **b** 1, 5   **c** 1, 2, 3, 5, 6, 10, 15, 30
d 1, 2, 3, 4, 5, 6, 10, 12, 15, 20, 30, 60
e 1, 3, 5, 9, 15, 45

2 a 6, 12, 18, 24, 30   **b** 5, 10, 15, 20, 25
c 30, 60, 90, 120, 150   **d** 60, 120, 180, 240, 300
e 45, 90, 135, 180, 225

Purposeful practice 3

1 a 15	**b** 6	**c** 30	**d** 1	**e** 15
2 a 90	**b** 30	**c** 60	**d** 30	**e** 180

Problem-solving practice

1 Students' own answers, for example, 6 and 12.
There is more than one possible answer.

2 30 and 40, or 10 and 120.

3 Students' own answers, for example,
$45 \div 6 = 7.5$. This is not an integer, therefore 6 is not a factor of 45.

4 Tom is wrong because 2 is a prime number and $2^2 = 4$, which is not odd.

5 Students' own answers, for example,
$254 \div 8 = 31.75$. This is not an integer, therefore 8 is not a factor of 254.

6 $678 \div 3 = 226$. This is an integer, therefore 678 is a multiple of 3.

7 9.00 am   **8** £13   **9** Paul is 30; Luca is 45.   **10** 10 boxes

Exam practice

1 a 24   **b** 2, 17

2 Students' own answers, for example, 5 and 7.

1.5 Squares, cubes and roots

Purposeful practice 1

1 4	**2** 9	**3** 16	**4** 4	**5** 9	**6** −9	**7** 16
8 8	**9** 27	**10** 64	**11** −8	**12** −27	**13** −64	**14** −64

Purposeful practice 2

1 a 2   **b** 2, −2   **c** 3, −3   **d** 4, −4   **e** 3   **f** −3

2 a 1.26   **b** 0.4   **c** 1.39   **d** 0.646   **e** 0.3   **f** 0.03

   g 1.58   **h** 0.5   **i** 0.158   **j** 2   **k** 0.431   **l** 0.2

Purposeful practice 3

1 7   **2** 5   **3** 9   **4** 3   **5** $2\sqrt{3}$

6 $3\sqrt{3}$ **7** $\sqrt{3}$ **8** 6   **9** 2   **10** $2\sqrt{3}$

Problem-solving practice

1 1 or 0   **2** 21.16 cm^2 **3** 24 cm

4 4 cm   **5** 3 and 4 or −3 and −4   **6** 4 and 5 or −4 and −5

7 10 or −10   **8** 10 times longer

9 Students' own answers, for example, $(-3)^2 = 9$ but $(-3)^3 = -27$, so the square is larger.

10 Students' own answers, for example, $\sqrt{0.16} = 0.4$ and $0.4 > 0.16$.

Exam practice

1 27

2 $15 + 11 + 23 = 49$. $\sqrt{49} = 7$, so yes, Jordan is correct.

3 −125

1.6 Index notation

Purposeful practice 1

1 3^4 **2** $3^4 \times 5^2$ **3** $3^4 \times 5^2$

4 $3^4 \times 5^4$ (or 15^4)   **5** $3^4 \times 5^4$ (or 15^4)

Purposeful practice 2

1 6^5 **2** 6^5 **3** 5^6 **4** 5^6 **5** 5^{12} **6** 5^7

7 5^3 **8** 5^4 **9** 5^7 **10** 5^{14} **11** 5^{17} **12** 5^4

Purposeful practice 3

1 a 10^2 **b** 10^3 **c** 10^4 **d** 10^1

   e 10^0 **f** 10^{-1} **g** 10^5 **h** 10^{-2}

2 a 3×10^2 **b** 5×10^2 **c** 5.3×10^3 **d** 3×10^{-2} **e** 3.8×10^{-3}

Problem-solving practice

1 2^2 **2** 3^2 **3** 18

4 Yes − 15^2

Students' own reasoning, for example, simplifying the expression gives $3 \times 5 \times 15$ which can be written as 15×15 or 15 squared.

5 Change the 2 to a 3 or the 3 to a 2. The expression can then be written as 10^5.

6 125   **7** $g = 6$

8 Amal is wrong because $4^3 + 5^3 = 189$ and $9^3 = 729$.

9 Allison is correct because $\square \times 3 \times 3$ simplifies to $\square \times 3^2$.

Exam practice

1 a $x = 10$ **b** $y = 2$ **c** $a = 2$

1.7 Prime factors

Purposeful practice 1

1 $20 = 2^2 \times 5$ **2** $40 = 2^3 \times 5$

3 $120 = 2^3 \times 3 \times 5$ **4** $60 = 2^2 \times 3 \times 5$

5 $15 = 3 \times 5$ **6** $45 = 3^2 \times 5$

7 $180 = 2^2 \times 3^2 \times 5$ **8** $360 = 2^3 \times 3^2 \times 5$

9 $300 = 2^2 \times 3 \times 5^2$ **10** $200 = 2^3 \times 5^2$

Purposeful practice 2

1 $16 = 2^4$ **2** $36 = 2^2 \times 3^2$ **3** $81 = 3^4$

4 $100 = 2^2 \times 5^2$ **5** $64 = 2^6$ **6** $216 = 2^3 \times 3^3$

7 $1728 = 2^6 \times 3^3$ **8** $7056 = 2^4 \times 3^2 \times 7^2$

Purposeful practice 3

1 5   **2** 5   **3** 10   **4** 60

5 20   **6** 100   **7** 10   **8** 1

Purposeful practice 4

1 360   **2** 600   **3** 600   **4** 600

5 720   **6** 720   **7** 3420   **8** 3420

Problem-solving practice

1 No, it will be 540 days before they are taken to the vet together again and there are 365 days in a year.

2 Yes, 48 cans of orange juice and 3 tubs of ice cream (to serve 48 people) costs £30, so it is possible.

3 LCM = 1050

4 No, because 96 is not a factor of 144.

5 No, Thomas is not correct. The LCM of 1 and 81 is 81 but 1 is not in the 3 times table.

6 It will cost Ms Case £38. There will be no spare erasers but 20 spare pencils.

7 a 24 cakes   **b** 4:45 pm

Exam practice

1 $2^5 \times 5$ **2** 736

2 Algebra

2.1 Algebraic expressions

Purposeful practice 1

1 $9x$ **2** $3x$ **3** x **4** $4x$ **5** x **6** x

7 $2b$ **8** $-3b$ **9** $-b$ **10** $+6b$ **11** $+6b$ **12** $-3b$

Purposeful practice 2

1 $10y + 3$ **2** $4y + 9$ **3** $10 + 5y$ **4** $7t - 7$ **5** $-2t + 2$

6 $8 - 5t$ **7** rs **8** $5rs$ **9** $10rs$ **10** $10rs$

11 $10rt$ **12** $6rt$ **13** $12rt$ **14** $3rst$ **15** $12rst$

16 $\dfrac{a}{b}$ **17** $\dfrac{b}{a}$ **18** $\dfrac{a}{2}$ **19** $\dfrac{b}{2}$ **20** $\dfrac{2}{a}$

21 $\dfrac{2}{b}$

Problem-solving practice

1 $2x + 5$ cm

2 $2x - 1 - 4x + 1$ (all the rest simplify to $6x$)

3 $7x + 8 - 2x - 5 + 3x = 8x + 3$

4 $10q$ cm^2 **5** $4b$

6 Students' own answers, for example, $\dfrac{36x}{3}, 4x \times 3, 5x + 7x$

7 Every row and column adds to $2x + 3y$

x	$3y$	x
$-y$	$2x - y$	$5y$
$4y + x$	y	$x - 2y$

Exam practice

1 a $15p$ **b** $2b$

2.2 Simplifying expressions

Purposeful practice 1

1 x^2 **2** x^3 **3** x^4 **4** x^5 **5** x^7 **6** x^8

7 x^9 **8** x^6 **9** n^3 **10** n^4 **11** n^6 **12** n^8

13 n^3 **14** n **15** n^4 **16** n^3

Purposeful practice 2

1 $6u$ **2** $-6u$ **3** $6u$

4 $-6uv$ **5** $-6uv$ **6** $-6uv$

7 $-6v^2$ **8** $-5xy$ **9** $5xy$

10 $10xy$ **11** $-10xy$ **12** $10xy$

13 $\dfrac{1}{6}p$ or $\dfrac{p}{6}$ **14** $6p$ **15** $3p$

16 $3p^2$ **17** $\dfrac{1}{3}p^2$ or $\dfrac{p^2}{3}$ **18** $\dfrac{1}{3}p$ or $\dfrac{p}{3}$

19 $-\dfrac{1}{3}t^3$ or $-\dfrac{t^3}{3}$ **20** $-3t^3$ **21** $3t^3$

22 $3t^2$ **23** $-3t^2$ **24** $3t$

Problem-solving practice

1

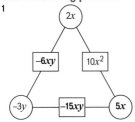

2 Students' own answers, for example, $15 \times -c \times d$ or $3c \times -5d$

3 a $t^2 \times t^3 = t^5$ **b** $\dfrac{x^5}{x^3} = x^2$ **c** $\dfrac{n^6}{n^2} = n^4$ **d** $\dfrac{r^3 \times r^3}{r^4} = r^2$

4 a $4x^3$ **b** x^6

5 Students' own answers, for example, $\dfrac{8x^3}{2}$ or $\dfrac{4x^4}{x}$

6

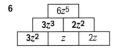

7 $4n$

Exam practice

1   **a** n^6 **b** $2x^2$ **c** $14ac$

2.3 Substitution

Purposeful practice 1

1 9   **2** 1   **3** −1   **4** 3
5 2   **6** 6   **7** −6   **8** 7

Purposeful practice 2

1 18   **2** −3   **3** −12   **4** 2
5 1   **6** −1   **7** 2   **8** $\dfrac{3}{2}$
9 −6   **10** 3   **11** −$\dfrac{1}{2}$ **12** $\dfrac{1}{2}$
13 −6   **14** 18   **15** −3   **16** 6

Purposeful practice 3

1 22   **2** −6   **3** 10   **4** 18   **5** 19
6 0   **7** 24   **8** 1   **9** −2   **10** 5
11 −6   **12** 6   **13** 4   **14** 16   **15** −16
16 20   **17** 14   **18** 36   **19** −10   **20** 4
21 −4   **22** 25   **23** $\dfrac{4}{10}$ or 0.4   **24** 1.6

Problem-solving practice

1 a Students' own answers, for example, $m = 1$ and $n = 6$
  b Students' own answers, for example, $m = 10$ and $n = -3$
2 Alex has forgotten that the expression st means $s \times t$.
  The answer should be $8 \times \dfrac{1}{2} = 4$
3 Students' own answers, for example,
  $2 \times 3 \times 4 = 3 \times 4 \times 2 = 4 \times 3 \times 2$.
  Three numbers multiplied together in any order give the same answer.
4 1, 3, 5, 7, 9. The odd numbers.
5 a 21   **b** 22
6 Yes, Dilip is correct. Any negative number squared is positive, zero squared is zero and any positive number squared is positive.
7 $x = 2$
8 Many possible answers, for example $p = 1, q = 10$

Exam practice

1 14   **2** $c = 27$

2.4 Formulae

Purposeful practice 1

1 20 pence, 30 pence $n \times 10$ or $10n$ pence. $C = 10n$ pence
2 $2b$ pence, $3b$ pence $m \times b$ or mb or bm pence. $C = bm$ pence

Purposeful practice 2

1 a $C = 5p$ **b** $C = 5n$ **c** $C = 4t$
  d $C = mt$ **e** $C = mt + 4$ **f** $C = mt + r$
2 a $N = y$ **b** $N = y - 20$ **c** $N = xy$
  d $N = xy + 30$ **e** $N = xy - 5x$

Problem-solving practice

1 $C = 3n$ the cost of n items at £3 each
  $C = 10n$ the cost of n items at £10 each
  $C = 3n + 10$ the cost of n items at £3 each plus £10 delivery charge
  $C = 10n + 3$ the cost of n items at £10 each plus £3 delivery charge
2 a Rope A   **b** Rope B
3 a x = price of a cake   **b** y = price of a box   **c** 9 cakes
4 $C = 1.5n + 4$

Exam practice

1 $L = 4x + 1$

2.5 Expanding brackets

Purposeful practice 1

1 $3x + 3$ **2** $3x + 6$ **3** $3x + 30$
4 $3x - 3$ **5** $3x - 6$ **6** $3x - 15$

Purposeful practice 2

1 $2m + 2$ **2** $2m - 2$ **3** $-2m - 2$
4 $-2m + 2$ **5** $-m - 7$ **6** $-m + 7$
7 $-m - 7$ **8** $-m + 7$ **9** $m - 7$

Purposeful practice 3

1 $4n + 12$ **2** $12 + 4n$ **3** $-15 - 5n$
4 $-5n - 15$ **5** $-5n + 15$ **6** $3r - 18$
7 $3r + 18$ **8** $6r + 18$ **9** $12r + 18$
10 $-6r - 18$ **11** $-6r + 18$ **12** $-18 - 6r$
13 $t^2 + 3t$ **14** $2t^2 + 3t$ **15** $2t^2 - 3t$
16 $k^2 + k$ **17** $2k^2 + 2k$ **18** $2k^2 - 2k$
19 $2k^2 + 8k$ **20** $2k^2 - 8k$ **21** $-2k^2 + 8k$

Problem-solving practice

1 a $2(a + 4) = 2a + 8$ **b** $2(y - 7) = 2y - 14$
  c $n(n + 5) = n^2 + 5n$ **d** $-3(3 + c) = -9 - 3c$
  e $t(6t - 2) = 6t^2 - 2t$ **f** $5p(p - 3) = 5p^2 - 15p$
2 The expansion is correct, but $12d - 8$ cannot be simplified as the two terms are not alike.
3 Students' own examples, for example, $3(5x + 2) = 15x + 6$ and $2x(x + 1) = 2x^2 + x$
4

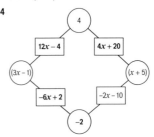

5 a $5x + 17$ **b** $20 + 3n$

Exam practice

1 a $2c^2 + 10c$ **b** $8d - 4d^2$ **c** $14x - 3$

2.6 Factorising

Purposeful practice 1

1 $2(x + 3)$ **2** $2(x + 2)$ **3** $2(x + 1)$
4 $2(x - 5)$ **5** $2(x - 4)$ **6** $2(x - 1)$
7 $3(y + 1)$ **8** $3(y + 2)$ **9** $3(y - 2)$

Purposeful practice 2

1 $4(a + 2)$ **2** $4(a - 3)$ **3** $6(a + 2)$ **4** $6(a - 4)$
5 $6(2t - 3)$ **6** $4(3t + 5)$ **7** $6(2t + 1)$ **8** $3(4t - 3)$
9 $3(7t - 3)$ **10** $7(3t + 5)$ **11** $5(4m + 7)$ **12** $20(m - 2)$
13 $m(m + 1)$ **14** $m(m + 2)$ **15** $m(m - 3)$ **16** $m(5 + m)$

17 $m(4 - m)$ **18** $m(2m - 1)$ **19** $m(m - 2)$ **20** $m(3m + 1)$
21 $m(m + 3)$ **22** $2b(b + 1)$ **23** $2b(b + 2)$ **24** $2b(b - 3)$
25 $b(b + g)$ **26** $b(b - g)$ **27** $b(3b - g)$ **28** $3b(b - 2g)$
29 $3b(b + 3g)$ **30** $3b(b - g)$ **31** $3b(2b + 3g)$ **32** $6b(b + 2g)$

Problem-solving practice

1 $n^2 - n \longrightarrow n(n - 1)$
  $2n - n^2 \longrightarrow n(2 - n)$
  $n - 2n^2 \longrightarrow n(1 - 2n)$
  $n^2 - 2n \longrightarrow n(n - 2)$
  $-n^2 + 2n \longrightarrow n(-n + 2)$
  $2n^2 - n \longrightarrow n(2n - 1)$
  $2n^2 - 2n \longrightarrow 2n(n - 1)$

2 a $3x - 24 = 3(x - 8)$ **b** $20x + 15 = 5(4x + 3)$
  c $x^2 - 2x = x(x - 2)$ **d** $4x^2 + 6x = 2x(2x + 3)$
  e $3x^2 - ax = x(3x - a)$

3 a Mo has tried to add the two terms (incorrectly, as they are not like terms) rather than factorise.
  b $3(v + 5)$

4 Students' own answers, for example, $15x + 6 = 3(5x + 2)$ and $2x^2 + x = 2x(x + 1)$

5 a $6x - 18$ **b** $3(2x - 1)$ **c** $7x - 1$

6 a $4(x + 9)$ **b** $3n(4n + 1)$

Exam practice

1 a $4(n - 3)$ **b** $x(x+1)$

2.7 Using expressions and formulae

Purposeful practice 1

1 $T = 8$ **2** $R = -4$ **3** $S = 4$
4 $V = -8$ **5** $L = 10$ **6** $B = 24$
7 $C = 3$ **8** $M = 12$ **9** $K = -12$
10 $P = \frac{2}{6}$ or $\frac{1}{3}$ **11** $N = 3$ **12** $Z = -3$
13 $D = 3$ **14** $F = \frac{2}{6}$ or $\frac{1}{3}$ **15** $H = -\frac{2}{6}$ or $-\frac{1}{3}$

Purposeful practice 2

1 $A = 11$ **2** $B = 5$ **3** $C = 0$
4 $D = 13$ **5** $D = 61$ **6** $E = 25$
7 $F = 31$ **8** $G = 29$ **9** $H = 26$
10 $J = 8$ **11** $J = 16$ **12** $K = 11$
13 $L = 24$ **14** $M = 32$ **15** $P = 13$
16 $Q = -8$ **17** $R - 9$ **18** $S = 1$
19 $W = -2\frac{1}{2}$ or $-2\frac{4}{8}$ **20** $X = 3\frac{1}{2}$ or $3\frac{4}{8}$

Problem-solving practice

1 Charlie's answer is wrong, because she has forgotten that st means $s \times t$.
2 Students' own answers, for example, $k = na - 10$
3 C. All the others give the value $T = -12$, whereas C gives the value $T = 6$.
4 16 m/s
5 a $v = 58.8$ **b** $v = 3$

Exam practice

1 a $X = 16$ **b** $m = 5$ **2** $p = -12$

3 Graphs, tables and charts

3.1 Frequency tables

Purposeful practice 1

1 Students' own answers, for example,
  a number of matches in a box, shoe size
  b heights or weights of people

2 a

Dice result	Tally	Frequency
1		
2		
3		
4		
5		
6		

b

Total dice score	Tally	Frequency
2		
3		
4		
5		
6		
7		
8		
9		
10		
11		
12		

c Example (students' own answers will vary)

Total dice score	Tally	Frequency
10–20		
21–30		
31–40		
41–50		
51–60		

Purposeful practice 2

1 a

Mark	Tally	Frequency
1	||||	4
2	ЖН	5
3	|||	3
4	ЖН ||||	9
5	ЖН |||	8
6	|	1
Total		30

b 4

2 The number of books on shelves is discrete, so it can only take whole number values. Therefore, each row has a simple range. The length of books is continuous, so it can take any number within the range. Therefore, each row has an inequality with no gaps.

Problem-solving practice

1 The ranges 53–54 and 54–56 overlap.
2 Items are discrete, not continuous, so the groups should not be defined using inequalities.
3 Items are continuous, not discrete, so groups should be defined using inequalities.
4 There is nowhere to record a road width of 4.0 m or 5.0 m.

Exam practice

1 Frequency and tally for Friday do not match.

3.2 Two-way tables

Purposeful practice 1

1 a 213 km   **b** 24 km   **c** 105 km   **d** 3532 km   **e** 3745 km

Purposeful practice 2

1

	Year 7	Year 8	Year 9	Total
French	20	15	35	**70**
German	15	25	**10**	50
Spanish	10	**10**	30	50
Total	**45**	50	**75**	170

Problem-solving practice

1

Phil		
105	Mike	
53	207	Tony

2 a Car, train and history, geography

b

	Car	Train	Total
History	14	4	18
Geography	24	8	32
Total	38	12	50

c 18   **d** 4

3 Male music and total number of males.

Exam practice

1

	Children	Adults	Total
Theatre	12	10	22
Cinema	10	8	18
Total	22	18	40

3.3 Representing data

Purposeful practice 1

1 Example answers (students' answers may vary).

a

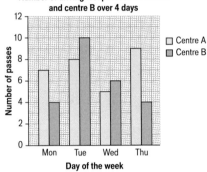

Number of driving test passes at centre A and centre B over 4 days

b

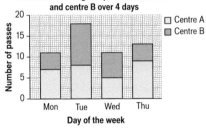

Number of driving test passes at centre A and centre B over 4 days

c

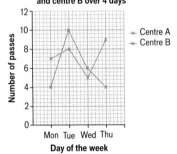

Number of driving test passes at centre A and centre B over 4 days

Purposeful practice 2

1

Time taken, t (minutes)	Frequency
$0 < t \le 15$	5
$15 < t \le 30$	14
$30 < t \le 45$	9
$45 < t \le 60$	4

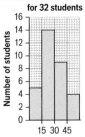

Time taken to travel to school for 32 students

2

Car speed, s (mph)	Frequency
$5 < s \le 10$	3
$10 < s \le 15$	6
$15 < s \le 20$	9
$20 < s \le 25$	15
$25 < s \le 30$	20

Problem-solving practice

1 a The data is not grouped.
  The data is not continuous.

b Shreeya's homework hours on Monday.

c

	Fri	Sat	Sun	Mon
Aum	1	4	3	2
Shreeya	2	5	4	3

d

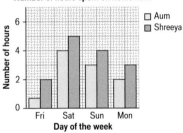

Number of hours spent on homework

e $3 + 4 = 7$ hours

Exam practice

1 a Tuesday

b

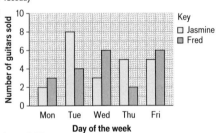

c 2   **d** 66

3.4 Time series

Purposeful practice 1

1 a

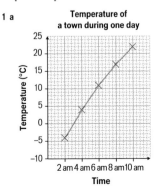

Temperature of a town during one day

b Higher

c Accept answers between −2 °C and 2 °C.

d Accept answers between 13 °C and 16 °C.

Purposeful practice 2

1 a

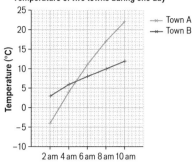

Temperature of two towns during one day

b 5 am

c Accept answers between 13°C and 15°C.

Purposeful practice 3

1 a 24 m   **b** 4 seconds

Problem-solving practice

1 a

	Oct	Nov	Dec
Earned (£)	2200	2550	2680

b

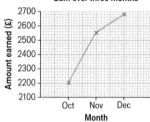

Amount earned by Sam over three months

c Example (students' answers will vary): Sam's earnings increase between October and December. The amount by which they increase, decreases each month. More data would be required to make a confident prediction of Sam's earnings in January. An estimate might be earnings of £2750 in January.

Exam practice

1 No vertical axis label, no title, July appears twice/no August

3.5 Stem and leaf diagrams

Purposeful practice 1

1
```
1 | 9
2 | 2  5  5
3 | 1  7
4 | 0  4  7  8
```
Key 2 | 5 = 25 points

2 a
```
2 | 5  6  7
3 | 0  1  2
4 | 2  3  3  5  6  7
5 | 0  1  5  5  6
6 | 2  2
7 | 3
```
Key 2 | 5 = 25 marks

b 73   **c** 25   **d** 48

Purposeful practice 2

1 a

Boys' marks							Girls' marks				
			0	0	2	5	6	7			
		8	5	4	3	0	1	2			
	9	8	5	3	4	2	3	3	5	6	7
9	6	6	5	0	5	0	1	5	5	6	
	7	7	4	4	6	2	2				
			4	4	7	3					

Key: boys' marks 0 | 2 = 20 marks

girls' marks 2 | 5 = 25 marks

b 54   **c** 2 − 1 = 1

Problem-solving practice

1 a

Vikram's plants					Penny's plants			
9	6	5	4	1				
1	1	0	0	2	7	8		
				3	4	7		
				4	2	4	4	5

Key: Vikram's plants 4 | 1 = 14 cm
Penny's plants 2 | 7 = 27 cm

b Vikram

c Penny

d Vikram = 7 cm, Penny = 18 cm

e Penny: all of Penny's plants are taller.

2

Percentage mark, m	Frequency
$40 < m \leq 50$	5
$50 < m \leq 60$	7
$60 < m \leq 70$	6
$70 < m \leq 80$	3

3
```
28 | 3  5  6  8
29 | 5
30 | 4  7  9  9
31 | 1  2
32 | 1
```
Key: 28 | 3 = 283 missed appointments

Exam practice

1
```
1 | 5  8  8  8  9
2 | 3  5  6  7  7  9
3 | 0  1  6  6  8  9
4 | 2  4  5
```
Key: 1 | 5 = 15 years old

3.6 Pie charts

Purposeful practice 1

1 a–b

c Final angle should measure 155°

Purposeful practice 2

1

	2000	2005	2010	2015
Tennis	200	500	1400	1750
Snooker	100	250	700	875
Cricket	100	250	700	875
Total	400	1000	2800	3500

2 Favourite film titles of students in Year 8

Favourite film types of students in Year 9

Favourite film types of students in Year 10

Problem-solving practice

1 a 150 kg peaches   **b** 120 kg apples
  c 765 kg pears

2

Club	Frequency
Football	42
Tennis	6
Photography	12
Coding	20
Netball	32
Origami	8

Exam practice

1 Transport used by teachers to get to work

3.7 Scatter graphs

Purposeful practice

1

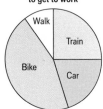

a Positive correlation   **b** No correlation

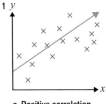

c Negative correlation

2 As **temperature** increases, sales of suntan lotion **increase**.
As **daily rainfall** increases, sales of suntan lotion **decrease**.

---

3 a The point shown in the top-right of the diagram.
  b (Moderate or strong) negative correlation.

4 a Homework and test scores

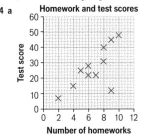

b (9, 12)   **c** Positive correlation

Problem-solving practice

1 a Positive correlation. More cars on the road will tend to lead to more accidents.
  b Positive correlation. People will tend to drink more when it is hotter.
  c Negative correlation. Car value will tend to decrease with age as people prefer to buy newer cars.
  d Negative correlation. As temperature increases, people will tend to spend less on heating.
  e Positive correlation. People will tend to buy more of an item that is advertised.
  f Negative correlation. Most people want a property that is close to public transport, so they will tend to pay more for it.
  g No correlation. Unlikely to be related.
  h No correlation. Unlikely to be related.

2 a Marks of 7 students in two Chemistry exams

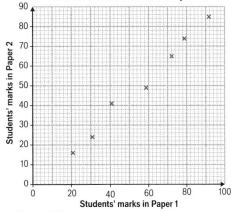

b Positive correlation

Exam practice

1 a (68, 45)   **b** Negative correlation

3.8 Line of best fit

Purposeful practice 1

1 Example answer (students' lines of best fit and estimations will vary).

a, b Heights and widths of boxes

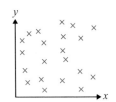

c Example answer (students' lines of best fit and estimations will vary):
Between 10 and 12 cm.

d Example answer (students' lines of best fit and estimations will vary):
Between 5 and 7 cm.

2 Example answer (students' lines of best fit and estimations will vary):

a, b

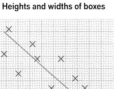

Heights and widths of boxes

c Example answer (students' lines of best fit and estimations will vary):
Between 4 and 6 cm.

3 **a, b** Example answer (students' lines of best fit and estimations will vary):

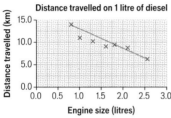

Distance travelled on 1 litre of diesel

c Example answer (students' lines of best fit and estimations will vary):
Between 6 and 8 km.

Problem-solving practice

1

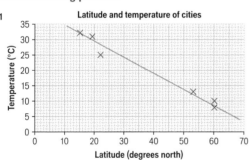

Latitude and temperature of cities

21 °C

2 a

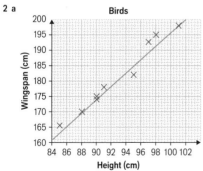

Birds

b Positive correlation

c No, the data point for the bird would lie a long way from the line of best fit so it is unlikely to be from the same family.

Exam practice

1 a (8, 25)   **b** Negative correlation

c Between 80 and 90

d Yes, as the temperature increases, fewer cartons of soup are sold.

4 Fractions and percentages

4.1 Working with fractions

Purposeful practice 1

1 $\frac{2}{4}$ **2** $\frac{1}{2}$ **3** $\frac{1}{2}$ **4** $\frac{1}{2}$

5 $\frac{5}{8}$ **6** $\frac{2}{3}$ **7** $\frac{2}{3}$ **8** $\frac{7}{8}$

Purposeful practice 2

1 $\frac{3}{4}$ **2** $\frac{3}{4}$ **3** $\frac{5}{8}$ **4** $\frac{7}{8}$

5 $\frac{9}{8}$ or $1\frac{1}{8}$ **6** $\frac{31}{24}$ or $1\frac{7}{24}$ **7** $\frac{19}{15}$ or $1\frac{4}{15}$ **8** $\frac{67}{40}$ or $1\frac{27}{40}$

Purposeful practice 3

1 $\frac{1}{8}$ **2** $\frac{7}{24}$ **3** $\frac{17}{40}$ **4** $\frac{5}{8}$ **5** $\frac{5}{8}$

6 $\frac{5}{8}$ **7** $\frac{2}{5}$ **8** $\frac{7}{5}$ or $1\frac{2}{5}$ **9** $-\frac{1}{5}$

Problem-solving practice

1 $\frac{1}{4}$ and $\frac{2}{3}$ **2** $\frac{3}{10} = \frac{1}{10} + \frac{1}{5}$

3 Yes, $\frac{3}{8} < \frac{1}{2}$ because $\frac{4}{8} = \frac{1}{2}$ and $\frac{3}{8} < \frac{4}{8}$

4 Students' answers will vary, for example

   a $\frac{1}{15} + \frac{2}{15} + \frac{8}{15}$ b $\frac{1}{15} + \frac{4}{30} + \frac{24}{45}$

   c $\frac{8}{120} + \frac{8}{60} + \frac{8}{15}$

5 Students' answers will vary, for example

   a $\frac{4}{5} - \frac{3}{5}$ b $\frac{4}{5} - \frac{6}{10}$ c $\frac{12}{15} - \frac{12}{20}$

6 Students' answers will vary, for example

   a $\frac{1}{3}$ and $\frac{2}{9}$

   b $\frac{2}{6}$ and $\frac{4}{18}$, $\frac{4}{12}$ and $\frac{6}{27}$, $\frac{5}{15}$ and $\frac{8}{36}$

7 $\frac{7}{24}$

Exam practice

1 Michael did not multiply the 1 by 3 or the 2 by 4.

2 $\frac{15}{48}$

4.2 Operations with fractions

Purposeful practice 1

1 4   **2** 5   **3** 10   **4** 10
5 15   **6** 7.5   **7** 6   **8** 12
9 24   **10** 48   **11** 50   **12** 25
13 15   **14** 5   **15** 27   **16** 12

Purposeful practice 2

1 $1\frac{3}{7}$ **2** $2\frac{3}{7}$ **3** $2\frac{5}{7}$ **4** $2\frac{5}{7}$

5 $2\frac{5}{7}$ **6** $2\frac{5}{7}$ **7** $2\frac{31}{42}$ **8** $6\frac{19}{42}$

9 3   **10** $3\frac{1}{14}$ **11** $4\frac{1}{14}$ **12** $4\frac{3}{14}$

Purposeful practice 3

1 $\frac{6}{7}$ **2** $1\frac{6}{7}$ **3** $2\frac{1}{7}$ **4** $1\frac{6}{7}$

5 $1\frac{6}{7}$ **6** $1\frac{5}{21}$ **7** $\frac{11}{12}$ **8** $\frac{11}{12}$

Problem-solving practice

1 $\frac{1}{15}$ of his yearly pay is the better option.

Students' reasoning may vary, for example, $\frac{3}{4}$ of £1300 is £975 whereas $\frac{1}{15}$ of (12 × £1300) is £1040.

2 Tessa has switched the $\frac{1}{5}$ and $\frac{3}{5}$ so worked out $\frac{3}{5} - \frac{1}{5}$ and not the other way around.

3 120   **4** 47 cm   **5** $1\frac{3}{4}$ hours

6 $2\frac{4}{7}$ **7** 195   **8** $5\frac{5}{24}$

9 Students' own answers, for example,

$2\frac{1}{2} + 7\frac{1}{2} = 10$, $5\frac{1}{4} + 4\frac{3}{4} = 10$, $3\frac{4}{11} + 6\frac{6}{11} = 10$

Exam practice

1 $4\frac{8}{15}$

4.3 Multiplying fractions

Purposeful practice 1

1 18   **2** 18   **3** 18   **4** 18

Purposeful practice 2

1 Yes, simplify to $\frac{1}{5} \times \frac{1}{2} = \frac{1}{10}$ **2** Yes, simplify to $\frac{1}{5} \times \frac{1}{2} = \frac{1}{10}$

3 No   **4** No   **5** No   **6** Yes, simplify to $2 \times \frac{1}{3} = \frac{2}{3}$

Purposeful practice 3

1 $\frac{1}{10}$ **2** $\frac{1}{10}$ **3** $\frac{1}{20}$ **4** $\frac{1}{20}$

5 $\frac{3}{10}$ **6** $\frac{3}{10}$ **7** $\frac{9}{5} = 1\frac{4}{5}$ **8** $\frac{9}{5} = 1\frac{4}{5}$

9 $\frac{3}{4}$ **10** $\frac{4}{5}$ **11** $\frac{4}{5}$ **12** $\frac{10}{3} = 3\frac{1}{3}$

13 $\frac{15}{2} = 7\frac{1}{2}$ **14** $\frac{15}{2} = 7\frac{1}{2}$ **15** $\frac{9}{2} = 4\frac{1}{2}$ **16** $\frac{8}{3} = 2\frac{2}{3}$

17 $\frac{12}{3} = 4$ **18** $\frac{14}{4} = 3\frac{1}{2}$ **19** $\frac{33}{4} = 8\frac{1}{4}$ **20** $\frac{38}{5} = 7\frac{3}{5}$

Problem-solving practice

1 48   **2** 0

3 Students' own answers, for example, 1 and 4 or 2 and 8

4 $\frac{12}{35}$ **5** $\frac{2}{15}$ **6** $\frac{1}{30}$ **7** 69

8 Jo spends longest. Tim spends $1\frac{1}{2}$ hours. Sam spends $\frac{1}{2} \times \frac{3}{2}$ hours = $\frac{3}{4}$ hours. Jo spends $3 \times \frac{3}{4} = \frac{9}{4} = 2\frac{1}{4}$ hours.

Exam practice

1 $\frac{21}{40}$

4.4 Dividing fractions

Purposeful practice 1

1 4   **2** 4   **3** 6   **4** 6

5 8   **6** 10   **7** 15   **8** $7\frac{1}{2}$

9 $7\frac{1}{2}$ **10** 5   **11** $6\frac{2}{3}$ **12** $2\frac{2}{3}$

13 $1\frac{1}{2}$ **14** $1\frac{1}{2}$ **15** $2\frac{1}{4}$ **16** $1\frac{1}{5}$

Purposeful practice 2

1 $\frac{1}{4}$ **2** $\frac{1}{4}$ **3** $\frac{1}{6}$ **4** $\frac{1}{9}$

5 $\frac{1}{6}$ **6** $\frac{5}{12}$ **7** $\frac{5}{12}$ **8** $\frac{5}{9}$

Purposeful practice 3

1 1   **2** 1   **3** $2\frac{1}{2}$ **4** $1\frac{2}{3}$

5 $1\frac{1}{3}$ **6** $2\frac{2}{3}$ **7** $1\frac{3}{5}$ **8** $1\frac{1}{5}$

Problem-solving practice

1 12

2 Several possible answers, for example, $\frac{4}{5}, \frac{8}{10}, \frac{12}{15}$

3 $\frac{2}{3}$ **4** $\frac{7}{8}$ **5 a** $\frac{9}{10}$ **b** 54 minutes

6 a 96

    b Yes, as he can now answer $60 \div \frac{3}{8} = 60 \times \frac{8}{3} = 160$ questions.

Exam practice

1 $\frac{6}{7}$ **2** 63

4.5 Fractions and decimals

Purposeful practice 1

1 $\frac{1}{10}$ **2** $\frac{2}{5}$ **3** $\frac{1}{100}$ **4** $\frac{1}{25}$ **5** $\frac{7}{50}$

6 $\frac{1}{1000}$ **7** $\frac{7}{500}$ **8** $\frac{7}{50}$ **9** $\frac{18}{125}$ **10** $\frac{13}{125}$

Purposeful practice 2

1 0.5   **2** 0.25   **3** 0.125   **4** 0.1   **5** 0.3
6 0.9   **7** 0.01   **8** 0.27   **9** 0.61   **10** 0.061
11 0.2   **12** 0.6   **13** 0.05   **14** 0.85   **15** 0.04
16 0.36   **17** 1.5   **18** 2.5   **19** 1.75   **20** 2.25
21 $0.\dot{3}$ **22** $0.\dot{6}$ **23** $0.1\dot{6}$ **24** $0.8\dot{3}$ **25** $0.08\dot{3}$

Purposeful practice 3

1 $0.03, \frac{2}{25}, 0.3, \frac{4}{5}$ **2** $0.03, \frac{2}{25}, 0.3, \frac{2}{5}$

3 $\frac{2}{25}, 0.23, 0.3, \frac{4}{5}$ **4** $\frac{2}{25}, 0.23, 0.3, \frac{2}{3}$

5 $\frac{2}{25}, 0.23, 0.3, \frac{1}{3}$ **6** $\frac{2}{25}, 0.3, 0.33, \frac{1}{3}$

7 $\frac{2}{25}, 0.33, \frac{1}{3}, 0.34$ **8** $\frac{1}{4}, 0.33, \frac{1}{3}, 0.34$

9 $3.38, 3.4, \frac{7}{2}, \frac{17}{4}$ **10** $-\frac{7}{2}, 3.38, 3.4, \frac{17}{4}$

11 $-1, -\frac{4}{5}, -0.27, 0$ **12** $-1, -\frac{4}{5}, 0, 0.27$

Problem-solving practice

1 Any decimal that is greater than 0.4 but less than 0.5, for example, 0.45

2 £8

3 Students' reasoning may vary, for example, $\frac{1}{6} = 0.1\dot{6}$. This is very close to 0.16 but is not exactly equal to it. Therefore, multiplying by 0.16 is not the same as multiplying by $\frac{1}{6}$

4 Naz worked out $125 \div 8$ instead of $8 \div 125$

5 a Harry has not divided 3 by 2 to give 1.5, he's just written the 3 and 2 around a decimal point.

    b Harry has not divided 1 by 5 to give 0.2, he's just written the 5 after a decimal point.

    c $\frac{1}{5}, 0.45, \frac{3}{2}, 2.3$

6 $\frac{9}{20}$ **7** Any decimal in between 0.65 and 0.72   **8** 43.2 g

Exam practice

1 0.03   **2** 0.4

4.6 Fractions and percentages

Purposeful practice 1

1 $\frac{1}{100}$ **2** $\frac{1}{10}$ **3** $\frac{1}{5}$ **4** $\frac{1}{4}$ **5** $\frac{1}{2}$

6 $\frac{1}{20}$ **7** $\frac{3}{20}$ **8** $\frac{7}{20}$ **9** $\frac{1}{25}$ **10** $\frac{8}{25}$

Purposeful practice 2

1 5%   **2** 50%   **3** 5%   **4** 0.5%

Purposeful practice 3

1 50%   **2** 25%   **3** 75%   **4** 60%   **5** 60%
6 38%   **7** 10%   **8** 5%   **9** 4%   **10** 33.3% (1 d.p.)

Purposeful practice 4

1 5%   **2** 50%   **3** 0.5%   **4** 25%
5 12.5%   **6** 17.5%   **7** 28%   **8** 76%

Problem-solving practice

1 No, it is 75%   **2** blue doors
3 Yes, Zainab's score is 64%
4 No, they are awake for 33.3% (1 d.p.).
5 Shop B as $\frac{1}{5}$ = 20%
6 Jazmin as $\frac{64}{80}$ = 80%, Laura got 75% and Kate got $\frac{5}{8}$ of the marks or 62.5%.

Exam practice

1 a $\frac{2}{5}$ **b** $\frac{65}{100} = \frac{13}{20}$ **2 a** 12%   **b** 35%

4.7 Calculating percentages 1

Purposeful practice 1

1 3   **2** 30   **3** 60   **4** 15
5 75   **6** 45   **7** 33   **8** 1.5
9 1.5   **10** 15   **11** 30   **12** 7.5

Purposeful practice 2

1 1   **2** 0.1   **3** 0.01   **4** 0.001
5 0.05   **6** 0.15   **7** 0.2   **8** 0.005

Purposeful practice 3

1 150   **2** 30   **3** 150   **4** 30
5 150   **6** 1500   **7** 150   **8** 150

Purposeful practice 4

1 £190   **2** £190   **3** £380   **4** £95

Problem-solving practice

1 8% of £120
2 Katie has divided by 20 and multiplied by 100. She should
have divided by 100 (to find 1%) and then multiplied by
20 (to find 20%). 20% of 180 g = 36 g
3 219   **4** 0.4%, 0.04, 40%, 0.44
5 £1638 is 10% of her annual salary. £1842.75 is 15% of her salary over $\frac{3}{4}$
of a year. She should take the second offer.
6 65% of 1200 = 780 students in school A voted.
45% of 960 = 720 students in school B voted.
So, more students voted in school A.
7 The bond gives £750 interest. The art would increase in value by £600.
Isadora should put all of her money into the savings bond.
8 4 days   **9** £14.60

Exam practice

1 36

4.8 Calculating percentages 2

Purposeful practice 1

1 120   **2** 96   **3** 88   **4** 80.8   **5** 160   **6** 176

Purposeful practice 2

1 80   **2** 64   **3** 72   **4** 79.2   **5** 0   **6** 75.2

Purposeful practice 3

1 a 110%   **b** 200%   **c** 90%
2 a 1.1   **b** 2   **c** 0.9
3 a £330   **b** £600   **c** £270
4 a 203.4   **b** 198   **c** 99   **d** 101.7
5 a 78.3   **b** 88.65

Problem-solving practice

1 £2575
2 20% off each item is a saving of £9.
60% off the total would be a saving of £27.
3 a 2550 copies   **b** £13 260
4 346.5 days
5 a £263 680   **b** £24 840   **c** £27 896

Exam practice

1 £37.80

Mixed exercises A

Mixed problem-solving practice A

1 40p   **2** $5x$
3 a $x = 8$ **b** $y = 2$
4 Tia has just replaced a with 4 and t with 5, but at means a multiplied
by t. Tia has not multiplied 4 by 5 to give 20.
5 a Both the values Kamil has used are larger than the actual values,
so the actual cost will be lower than his estimate.
   b £167.20
6 The HCF of $8x^2 + 4x$ is $4x$, not $2x$

7 a

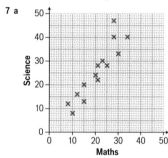

b Positive correlation   **c** 34 (students' answers may vary – found
by line of best fit)
d Yes, as the majority of the points for high science scores appear when
there are high marks for maths tests (positive correlation).
8 Taylor is 9 and Callum is 8.
9 $A = 33$ **10** $\frac{1}{10}$

11 a

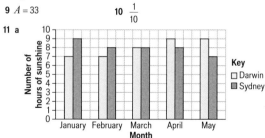

b Students' own answers, for example,
Overall, the number of hours of sunshine, increases over the five
months for Darwin but decreases for Sydney. In March, both Darwin
and Sydney have the same number of hours of sunshine.
12 $3(y - 5) = 3y - 15$
13 Emily because she scored 38 marks. Finn scored 36 marks.
Toby scored 24 marks.
14 3 boxes of crisps and 10 boxes of juice
15 a $\frac{1}{3}$ **b** 1800

Exam practice

16 18
17 $L = 4x + 4$

18

	14 years old	15 years old	Total
Glasses	7	6	13
No glasses	43	34	77
Total	50	40	90

19 $\frac{5}{9}$, $\frac{5}{9}$ is $\frac{4}{9}$ smaller than 1, $\frac{9}{5}$ is $\frac{4}{5}$ greater than 1. $\frac{4}{9}$ is smaller than

$\frac{4}{5}$ so $\frac{5}{9}$ is closer to 1 than $\frac{9}{5}$.

20 a 1000   **b** 5600

    c Electric, because the bars get proportionally longer over time.

    d No, because we do not know the cost, prices or profit of the different cars.

21 £1836

22 No, Claire is wrong, a 25% decrease would give a force of 2.25 N/cm^2 but the force is 2.2 N/cm^2 which is lower, and therefore is a larger percentage decrease.

5 Equations, inequalities and sequences

5.1 Solving equations 1

Purposeful practice 1

1 $a + 3 = 12, a = 12 - 3, a = 9$

$a - 3 = 12, a = 12 + 3, a = 15$

$3a = 12, a = \frac{12}{3}, a = 4$

$\frac{a}{3} = 12, a = 3 \times 12, a = 36$

2 a $b = 24 - 8 = 16$ **b** $b = 24 \div 8 = 3$ **c** $b = 24 \times 8 = 192$

   d $b = 24 - 8 = 16$ **e** $b = 24 + 8 = 32$ **f** $b = 8 - 24 = -16$

Purposeful practice 2

1 $x = 11$ **2 a** $x + 14 = 36$ **b** $x = 22$

3 a $x - 9 = 15$ **b** $x = 24$ **4** $7x = 42, x = 6$

Problem-solving practice

1 35

2 Abi has 9 cards, Bashar has 27 and Chan has 18.

3 135°   **4** 81 cm^2

5 A rectangle with height 3 cm and width 10 cm.

6 128 cm^2

Exam practice

1 $x = 30°$

5.2 Solving equations 2

Purposeful practice 1

1 a $x = 3$ **b** $x = 6$ **c** $x = 2$ **d** $x = 4$

2 a $x = 3$ **b** $x = 6$ **c** $x = 2$ **d** $x = 4$

  e $x = 3$ **f** $x = 6$ **g** $x = 2$ **h** $x = 4$

Purposeful practice 2

1 $x = -12$ **2** $x = -6$ **3** $x = -2$ **4** $x = -4$

Purposeful practice 3

1 $y = \frac{4}{3}$ **2** $y = \frac{4}{3}$ **3** $y = \frac{8}{3}$ **4** $y = \frac{2}{3}$

5 $y = \frac{10}{3}$ **6** $y = \frac{5}{3}$ **7** $y = 12$ **8** $y = 48$

9 $y = 60$ **10** $y = 24$ **11** $y = 30$ **12** $y = 66$

13 $y = 1.2$ **14** $y = 5.25$ **15** $y = 1.625$

Problem-solving practice

1 12

2 a $x + 2x + 2x - 7 = 58, 5x - 7 = 58$

  b Dec is 13, Emma is 26 and George is 19.

3 73°, 33.7°, 73.3°   **4** 20 cm   **5** $g = 11.25$

Exam practice

1 $f = 4$

5.3 Solving equations with brackets

Purposeful practice 1

1 a $x = 3$ **b** $x = 1.5$ **c** $x = 4$ **d** $x = 4.5$

2 a $x = 3$ **b** $x = 1.5$ **c** $x = 4$ **d** $x = 4.5$

Purposeful practice 2

1 $x = 10$ **2** $x = \frac{8}{3}$ **3** $x = \frac{8}{3}$ **4** $x = \frac{2}{3}$ **5** $x = -3$

6 $x = -1$ **7** $x = 0$ **8** $x = 2$ **9** $x = 4$

Purposeful practice 3

1 $x = 3$ **2** $x = 1.5$ **3** $x = 4$ **4** $x = 4.5$

5 $x = 2$ **6** $x = 3$ **7** $x = 2$ **8** $x = -2$

9 $x = 2$ **10** $x = -8$ **11** $x = -4$ **12** $x = 6$

13 $x = 5$ **14** $x = 2$ **15** $x = 9$ **16** $x = 7$

17 $x = -3$ **18** $x = -1$

Problem-solving practice

1 −5   **2** 5   **3** $h = 32°$

4 Rectangle B   **5** $y + 4 = 3y - 8$

                  $12 = 2y$

                  $y = 6$

Exam practice

1 $p = 7$

5.4 Introducing inequalities

Purposeful practice 1

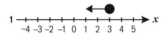

Purposeful practice 2

Students' own answers, for example,

1 3, 2, 1   **2** 2, 1, 0   **3** 4, 5, 6

4 3, 4, 5   **5** 3, 2, 1   **6** −3, −2, −1

7 −2, −1, 0   **8** −2, −1, 0   **9** −3, −2, −1

Purposeful practice 3

1 $x \leqslant 3$ **2** $x < 3$ **3** $x > 3$ **4** $x > 1$

5 $x > 2$ **6** $x > 0$ **7** $x > 12$ **8** $x \leqslant 12$

9 $x \leqslant 9$ **10** $x \leqslant 12$ **11** $x \geqslant 12$ **12** $x \geqslant 12$

13 $x \geqslant 3$ **14** $x > 3$ **15** $x > 9$ **16** $x < 9$

17 $x < 1$ **18** $x \geqslant 4$

Problem-solving practice

1 $x < 3$, so the smallest integer value x can take is 2.
2 $2y + 3 < 20$
3 $3d < 19$, so the oldest David can be is 6.
4 $5t + 6 > 46$
  $t > 8$
  Therefore the smallest number Tumay could have started with is 9.
5 $m + 40 \geqslant 90$ 6 $6b \leqslant 34$ 7 $c \geqslant 7.5$

Exam practice

1 $-6, -5, -4, -3$ 2 $x > \dfrac{4}{3}$

5.5 More inequalities

Purposeful practice 1

1 $x = 2$ or 3   2 $x = 2$ 3 $x = 2$ or 3   4 $x = 2$

Purposeful practice 2

1 $2 < x < 3$ 2 $2 < x < 3$ 3 $2 < x < 3$
4 $2 < x < 3$ 5 $-1 < x < 3$ 6 $-2 < x < 2$
7 $-1 < x < 3$ 8 $-1 < x < 3$ 9 $1.5 < x < 3$

Purposeful practice 3

1 $-3 \leqslant x < -2$ and -3
2 $-3 \leqslant x \leqslant -2$ and $-3, -2$
3 $-2.5 \leqslant x < -1.5$ and -2
4 $-3.5 \leqslant x < -2.5$ and -3
5 $-3.5 \leqslant x < 1.5$ and $-3, -2, -1, 0, 1$
6 $-2.5 \leqslant x < 2.5$ and $-2, -1, 0, 1, 2$

Purposeful practice 4

1 4   2 2 (other answers possible)   3 2
4 4 (other answers possible)   5 3 or 4   6 2

Problem-solving practice

1 $220 < 20x + 80 < 340$ or $220 < y < 340$
2 $90 \leqslant m \leqslant 150$
3 a Yes. $x > 3$ (x must be greater than 3) for the rectangle to have an area greater than 44 cm². $x \leqslant 8$ for the triangle to have an area less than or equal to 38 cm².
  b $6x + 12 \leqslant 12x + 8 \rightarrow x \geqslant \dfrac{4}{6}$
4 Toby has not reversed the inequality or the signs when dividing by a negative number. It should be $-5 \leqslant x < 4$
5 $2.5 \leqslant p \leqslant 3.5$ 6 $12.5 \leqslant d \leqslant 55$ 7 $2 \leqslant n \leqslant 6$

Exam practice

1 $4 \leqslant x < 7$

5.6 Using formulae

Purposeful practice 1

1 3   2 1   3 −1   4 −3   5 −9

Purposeful practice 2

1 3   2 2.5   3 2   4 1.5   5 0

Purposeful practice 3

1 $x = \dfrac{y + 3}{2}$ 2 3

Purposeful practice 4

1 $x = \dfrac{y}{4}$ 2 $I = \dfrac{V}{R}$ 3 $s = ut$
4 $x = y - 3$ 5 $c = f - d$ 6 $a = \dfrac{f}{m}$

Problem-solving practice

1 14 cm
2 a Student A has substituted the value of 48 for x instead of y.
  b Student B has subtracted 4 instead of adding 4.
3 a $F = PA$ b 144 N
4 a 180 km   b 48 mph
5 12 m/s²

Exam practice

1 a $G = 17$ b $T = \dfrac{G - 2}{5}$

5.7 Generating sequences

Purposeful practice 1

1 Add 2
2 Add the two previous terms
3 Double the previous term   4 Add 3
5 Add the two previous terms   6 Multiply by 2

Purposeful practice 2

1 9, 11   2 7, 9   3 −1, 1
4 1, −1   5 −10, −12   6 $\dfrac{9}{2}, \dfrac{11}{2}$
7 $-\dfrac{3}{2}, \dfrac{4}{2}$ 8 $-\dfrac{3}{2}, -2$ 9 3, 3.5

Purposeful practice 3

1 5, 10, 15, 20, 25   2 6, 11, 16, 21, 26
3 7, 12, 17, 22, 27   4 8, 13, 18, 23, 28
5 4, 9, 14, 19, 24   6 3, 8, 13, 18, 23
7 −1, 1, 3, 5, 7   8 −1, 0, 1, 2, 3
9 −1, −1, −1, −1, −1   10 −1, −2, −3, −4, −5
11 −1, −2, −3, −4, −5   12 −1, −3, −5, −7, −9

Problem-solving practice

1 14 more chairs and 4 more tables
2 5 of each
3 a Yes, it will alternate between −2 and 1
  b Start at 3
4 a No, 26 will not appear in the sequence. All of the terms, apart from the starting term, will be odd.
  b No, because doubling any integer and subtracting 1 will give an odd number. Therefore, whatever integer is chosen to start the sequence, the rest of the terms will be odd.
5 2 more terms – using 9 and 11 matchsticks

Exam practice

1 a i 17
  ii Add on three to the previous term
  b 23

5.8 Using the nth term of a sequence

Purposeful practice 1

1 4, 8, 12, 16, 20   2 5, 9, 13, 17, 21
3 6, 10, 14, 18, 22   4 6, 8, 10, 12, 14
5 −2, 0, 2, 4, 6   6 2, 0, −2, −4, −6

Purposeful practice 2

1 $2n$ 2 $2n - 1$ 3 n 4 $n + 1$
5 $2n + 2$ 6 $4n$ 7 $-2n + 17$ 8 $-2n + 22$
9 $-n + 10$ 10 $-5n + 41$ 11 $-3n + 23$ 12 $-4n + 23$

Purposeful practice 3

1 a 50   b 100   c 101   d 150
  e 149   f 24   g −151   h −101
2 a yes, 50th term   b yes, 25th term   c No   d No
  e Yes, 17th term   f Yes, 102nd term   g No   h No

Problem-solving practice

1 The fourth terms of sequence A and B are the same (13). The numbers 23, 33, 43 … appear in both sequences but in different positions.
2 a No, the pattern would need 60 tiles, which would cost £21.
  b Multiple possible student answers that sum to < 50, for example, $3n$ gives 3, 6, 9, 12, which costs $3 \times £3.50$ or £10.50 for the first four terms
3 23, 27 or 31

4 a $4n + 8$

  b No, non-integer result for n.

5 $6n - 1$ **6** $3n - 1$

7 The first four terms of $8n - 3$ have a sum of 68. The first four terms of $5n + 3$ have a sum of 62. After the initial term, all terms of $8n - 3$ are greater than or equal to the equivalent term in $5n + 3$. Therefore any four consecutive terms of $8n - 3$ will have a sum greater than that of the equivalent four consecutive terms in $5n + 3$.

8 D, 10th term.

9 Students' own answers, for example, $-2n + 6$

Exam practice

1 141

6 Angles

6.1 Properties of shapes

Purposeful practice 1

Shape	Equal sides	Pairs of equal opposite sides	Pairs of parallel sides	Angles
	4	2	2	4 equal angles of 90°
	2 pairs, opposite	2	2	4 equal angles of 90°
	2 pairs, opposite	2	2	2 pairs equal, opposite
	4	2	2	2 pairs equal, opposite
	2 pairs, adjacent	0	0	1 pair equal, opposite
	0	0	1	2 equal angles of 90°, adjacent
	2 pairs, opposite	1	1	2 pairs equal, adjacent

Purposeful practice 2

1 a $x = 5\,\text{cm}$

  b $n = 8\,\text{cm}, t = 3\,\text{cm}$

  c $p = 80°, q = 100°, r = 7\,\text{mm}$

  d $j = 80°, k = 120°, l = 20\,\text{mm}, m = 15\,\text{mm}$

  e $u = 110°, v = 70°, w = 2\,\text{cm}$

Problem-solving practice

1 Students' own answers, for example,

a   **b**

2 a Square, rhombus

  b Square – or four right angles
     Rhombus – no right angles

3 Yes, a rhombus has the same properties as a parallelogram, such as two pairs of equal sides, two pairs of opposite parallel sides, opposite angles equal. In addition, a rhombus has an extra property because all of its sides are equal. So, a rhombus is a special type of parallelogram.

4 D = (6, 3)

Exam practice

1 Parallelogram

6.2 Angles in parallel lines

Purposeful practice 1

1 a $a = 110°$ (corresponding angles are equal)

  b $b = 80°$ (alternate angles are equal)
     $c = 100°$ (angles on a straight line add to 180°)

  c $d = 120°$ (alternate angles are equal)
     $e = 60°$ (angles on a straight line add to 180°)

  d $f = 70°$ (corresponding angles are equal)
     $g = 110°$ (angles on a straight line add to 180°)

  e $h = 130°$ (alternate angles are equal)
     $i = 130°$ (corresponding angles are equal OR vertically opposite angles are equal)

  f $j = 130°$ (angles on a straight line add to 180°)
     $k = 130°$ (angles on a straight line add to 180° OR vertically opposite angles are equal)
     $l = 130°$ (alternate angles are equal OR corresponding angles are equal)

Purposeful practice 2

1 Students' reasoning may vary, for example,

  a $a = 60°$ (alternate angles are equal)
     $l = 100°$ (angles in a triangle add to 180°)

  b $n = 55°$ (alternate angles are equal)
     $m = 60°$ (angles on a straight line add to 180°)
     $p = 65°$ (angles in a triangle add to 180°)

  c $s = 50°$ (alternate angles are equal)
     $t = 45°$ (vertically opposite angles are equal)
     $u = 85°$ (angles in a triangle add to 180°)

  d $v = 100°$ (corresponding angles are equal)
     $w = 100°$ (alternate angles are equal)

  e $x = 70°$ (alternate angles are equal)
     $y = 70°$ (corresponding angles are equal)
     $z = 110°$ (angles on a straight line add to 180°)

  f $a + 33 = 125°$ (corresponding angles are equal), so $a = 92°$
     $b = 180 - 125 = 55°$ (corresponding angles are equal; angles on a straight line add to 180°)

Problem-solving practice

1 Students' reasoning may vary, for example,
   Angle $y = 115°$ (alternate angles are equal)
   Angle DBC = 65° (angles on a straight line add to 180°)
   Angle BCD = 40° (vertically opposite angles are equal)
   Angle $x = 75°$ (angles in a triangle add to 180°)

2 a Angles on a straight line add to 180°.

  b Corresponding angles are equal.

  c Vertically opposite angles are equal.

3 Students' own answers, for example,
   $p = 125°$ (corresponding angles are equal)
   $q = 55°$ (angles on a straight line add to 180°)
   So $p + q = 180°$

4 If ABC and DEF were parallel, angle DEB would be 90° (corresponding angles are equal). However, angle DEB is on a straight line with the 85° angle, so it must be 95° (angles on a straight line add to 180°). Therefore, ABC and DEF cannot be parallel.

Exam practice

1 Jamal should have written angle DEB = 119° because alternate angles are equal.

6.3 Angles in triangles

Purposeful practice 1

1 a b and c **b** e and f **c** g and h

  d j and k **e** m and n **f** q and r

Purposeful practice 2

1 a Scalene   **b** Scalene

  c Isosceles   **d** Equilateral

  e Right-angled, scalene   **f** Isosceles

2 a $d = 30°, e = 60°$ **b** $s = 55°, t = 55°$, isosceles

  c $f = 60°, g = 50°$ **d** $x = 30°, y = 75°, z = 75°$, isosceles

Problem-solving practice

1 Angles in a triangle add to 180°. Therefore, triangles can have a maximum of one obtuse angle, so must have at least two acute angles.

2 Angle ACB = 50° (vertically opposite angles are equal)
Angle CAB = 180° − 65° − 50° = 65° (angles in a triangle add to 180°)
Two angles in triangle ABC are equal, so it is isosceles.

3 Angle ZXY = 180° − 110° = 70° (angles on a straight line add to 180°)
Angle XZY + angle XYZ = 180° − 70° = 110° (angles in a triangle add to 180°)
Angle XZY = 110° ÷ 2 = 55° (base angles of an isosceles triangle are equal)

4 Angle PRQ = 38° (vertically opposite angles are equal)
Angle RPQ = 180° − 76° = 104° (angles on a straight line add to 180°)
Angle PQR = 180° − 104° − 38° = 38° (angles in a triangle add to 180°)
Two angles in triangle PQR are equal, so it is isosceles.

5 Students' own answers, for example,
Angle STR = 36° (base angles of an isosceles triangle are equal)
Angle RSU = angle RUS (base angles of an isosceles triangle are equal)
Angle RSU = angle RUS = $\frac{1}{2}$(180° − 36°) = 72° (angles in a triangle add to 180°)
Angle SUT = 180° − 72° = 108° (angles on a straight line add to 180°)
Angle UST = 180° − 36° − 108° = 36° (angles in a triangle add to 180°)
Triangle SUT has two equal angles, so it is isosceles.

Exam practice

1 Angle DBC = 180° − 96° = 84° (angles on a straight line add to 180°)
Angle BDC = 180° − 84° − 48° = 48° (angles in a triangle add to 180°)
Two angles in triangle BCD are equal, so it is isosceles.

6.4 Exterior and interior angles

Purposeful practice 1

1 Angles can be drawn in the 'opposite' direction from that shown, but all sides must be extended in the same way (i.e. clockwise or anticlockwise).

a   b

c   d

Purposeful practice 2

1 a $n = 65°$ b $w = x = 90°$, $y = 110°$
  c $p = r = s = u = 50°$, $t = 80°$

Purposeful practice 3

1 a Exterior angle = 120° b Exterior angle = 90°
    Interior angle = 60°   Interior angle = 90°
  c Exterior angle = 45°   d Exterior angle = 40°
    Interior angle = 135°   Interior angle = 140°

Purposeful practice 4

1 36   2 24   3 18   4 12   5 5

Problem-solving practice

1 $x = \frac{360°}{5} = 72°$ (exterior angle of regular pentagon = $\frac{360°}{\text{number of sides}}$)
$y = 180° − 72° = 108°$ (interior angle and exterior angle add to 180°, all angles in a regular pentagon are equal)
Angle ABF = angle z (symmetry)
$z = \frac{1}{2}$(180° − 108°) = 36° (angles on a straight line add to 180°)

2 square

3 a $a = 45°$ b $b = 135°$

4 For a regular polygon, $\frac{360°}{\text{exterior angle}}$ = number of sides
$\frac{360°}{50°}$ is not a whole number, so Kelly must be wrong.

5 For a regular polygon, $\frac{360°}{\text{number of sides}}$ = exterior angle

Exterior angle of a regular 9-sided polygon = $\frac{360°}{9} = 40°$

Exterior angle of a regular 18-sided polygon = $\frac{360°}{18} = 20°$

40° is double 20°, so the exterior angle of a regular 9-sided polygon is double the exterior angle of a regular 18-sided polygon.

Exterior angle of a regular 9-sided polygon = $\frac{360°}{9} = 40°$

Exterior angle of an equilateral triangle = $\frac{360°}{3} = 120°$
$40 × 3 = 120$
So the exterior angle of an equilateral triangle is 3 times the exterior angle of a regular 9-sided polygon.

6 $x = 120°$, with students' own reasoning, for example,
Exterior angle of regular hexagon is 360° ÷ 6 = 60°
(exterior angle of a regular polygon = 360° ÷ number of sides).
The interior angle of a regular hexagon is 180° − 60° = 120°
(angles on a straight line add to 180°).
Angle HEF = 60° (PEH is a line of symmetry that bisects angle DEF, which is an interior angle).
$x = 120°$ (angles on a straight line add to 180°)

Exam practice

1 Interior angle at C is 60° (angles on a straight line add to 180°)
Interior angle at A is 65° (angles in a triangle add to 180°)
$x = 115°$ (angles on a straight line add to 180°)

6.5 More exterior and interior angles

Purposeful practice 1

1

Polygon	Number of sides	Number of triangles	Angle sum
	3	1	180°
	4	2	2 × 180° = 360°
	5	3	3 × 180° = 540°
	6	4	4 × 180° = 720°
	7	5	5 × 180° = 900°
	8	6	6 × 180° = 1080°

Purposeful practice 2

1 a 1260° b 1440° c 1620°
2 a i 360° ii $x = 150°$ b i 540° ii $y = 80°$
  c i 720° ii $z = 50°$
3 a 108° b 120° c 135°
  d 140° e 144° f 150°

Problem-solving practice

1 11

2 $n = 60°$, with students' own working, for example,
Angle sum of polygon is (number of sides − 2) × 180°
So angle sum of hexagon is (6 − 2) × 180° = 720°
Hexagon is regular, so each interior angle is 720° ÷ 6 = 120°
Horizontal line is line of symmetry, so it bisects an interior 120° angle, therefore $n = 120° ÷ 2 = 60°$

3 $b = 162°$, with students' own working, for example,
Angle sum of polygon is (number of sides − 2) × 180°
So angle sum of pentagon is $(5 − 2) × 180° = 540°$
Pentagon is regular, so each interior angle is 540° ÷ 5 = 108°
Interior angle of square = 90°
Therefore $b = 360° − 108° − 90° = 162°$ (angles around a point add to 360°)

4 Angle sum of polygon is (number of sides − 2) × 180°
So angle sum of nonagon is $(9 − 2) × 180° = 1260°$
Nonagon is regular, so each interior
angle is = 1260° ÷ 9 = 140°. Thus, angle ABC = 140°
Triangle ABC is isosceles because AB = BC
(sides of regular nonagon are equal), so angle BAC = angle BCA
(base angles of an isosceles triangle are equal).
Therefore, angle BAC = $\frac{1}{2}(180° − 140°) = 20°$

5 135°

Exam practice

1 $w = 132°$, with students' own working, for example,
Angle sum of polygon is (number of sides − 2) × 180°
So angle sum of hexagon is $(6 − 2) × 180° = 720°$ and angle sum of pentagon is $(5 − 2) × 180° = 540°$
Hexagon and pentagon are regular, so each interior angle of hexagon is 720° ÷ 6 = 120° and each interior angle of pentagon is 540° ÷ 5 = 108°
Therefore, $w = 360° − 120° − 108° = 132°$ (angles around a point add to 360°)

6.6 Geometrical problems

Purposeful practice 1

1 a $x = 35°$ **b** $y = 105°$
   c $z = 62°$ **d** $n = 130°$
2 a i $a = 40°$ **ii** 80°, 120°, 160°
   b i $b = 36°$ **ii** 36°, 36°, 108°
   c i $c = 36°$ **ii** 36°, 36°, 144°, 144°
   d i $d = 45°$ **ii** 45°, 45°, 90°, 90°, 90°
3 a $e = 60°$, $e + 10° = 70°$, $e − 10° = 50°$
   b $f + 60° = 80°$, $2f = 40°$, $3f = 60°$

Purposeful practice 2

1 angle ACB = 40°, angle CAB = 100°
2 angle DFE = 25°, angle FDE = 75°

Problem-solving practice

1 $m = 70°$, both angles are 110°
2 $x = 60°$
3 45°
4 Angles are 28°, 68°, 84° with students' own working, for example,
Smallest angle = x
Largest angle = $3x$
Other angle = $3x − 16°$
$7x − 16° = 180°$ (angles in a triangle add to 180°)
$7x = 196°$
$x = 28°$
So angles are 28°, 68° and 84°.
5 56°

Exam practice

1 a i $x = 55°$ **ii** Angles in a triangle add to 180°
   b $y = 45°$

7 Averages and range

7.1 Mean and range

Purposeful practice 1

1 10   **2** 8   **3** 6   **4** 6

Purposeful practice 2

1 Route 1 range: 16 mins, Route 2 range: 7 mins
2 Route 1 mean: 9 mins, Route 2 mean: 13 mins

Purposeful practice 3

1 10.64   **2** 10.64

Value, v	Frequency, f	$v \times f$
7	3	21
8	2	16
9	3	27
10	6	60
11	2	22
12	1	12
13	4	52
14	4	56
Total	25	266

Problem-solving practice

1 a The way the calculation is written means that only the 9 is divided by 4. Emir should have found the total of the four numbers, by pressing the equals key, before dividing by 4. Alternatively, he could have used brackets.
   b The mean should lie within the range of the data.
2 18.95 s (2 d.p.)   **3** 3 hours 45 minutes

Exam practice

1 Raj read more consistently. His range of 4 books is smaller than Ellen's range of 12.

7.2 Mode, median and range

Purposeful practice 1

1 Median 12, range 20   **2** Median 12, range 20
3 Median 12, range 15   **4** Median 12, range 15
5 Median 13, range 23   **6** Median 13, range 23
7 Median 12, range 23   **8** Median 13, range 28
9 Median 13, range 23

Purposeful practice 2

1 a 0.6 kg is an outlier.
   b Range, excluding the outlier, is 1.8 kg.
   c Median, excluding the outlier, is 3.6 kg.
2 a Median 23.45, mode 24.6, range 5.5
   b Median 234.5, mode 246, range 55

Problem-solving practice

1 a Any number $\geqslant 10$ **b** Any number $\leqslant 7$
   c 22 is the only extra value that will give a range of 16. Negative 1 would give the required range but is not an acceptable value as the cards display positive numbers.
2 a i Median = 112   **ii** Mode = 112   **iii** Range = 46
   b The manager has only looked at the leaf section of the diagram so has mistakenly taken the highest value as 9 (instead of 139) and the lowest as 3 (instead of 93).
3 a Students' own answers, for example, change 62 to 70, giving a new median of 70.
   b Change 62 to any other integer from 55 to 67 inclusive.

Exam practice

1 137 cm

7.3 Types of average

Purposeful practice 1

Day 1 median: 3 kg, mode: 3 kg   **Day 2** median: 4 kg, mode: 4 kg
Day 3 median: 4 kg, mode: 5 kg   **Day 4** median: 4 kg, mode: 5 kg

Purposeful practice 2

1 10–14 cars (Dev's record); 0–4 cars (Daisy's record)
2 26 (Dev's record); 22 (Daisy's record)
3 10–14 (Dev's record); 5–9 (Daisy's record)

Problem-solving practice

1 Total frequency = 3 + 7 + 8 + 1 = 19
So median = 10th Value.
This lies in the $35 \leqslant x < 40$ height range and so the median height is between 35 and 40 cm.

2 a 1st week: mean = 5.5 minutes, median = 5 minutes
   2nd week: mean = 10.5 minutes, median = 6 minutes
  b Students' own answers, for example, the mean is least useful because it gives a distorted average for week 2 because of the outlier.
3 a The mode
  b Range and mean cannot be calculated, because they can only be calculated from numerical data.

Exam practice

1 a The mean is 15.6 but there is no dress size of 15.6.
  b Students' reasoning may vary, for example, the mode will be the most useful average because it shows Sam that the most frequently bought size is 14.

7.4 Estimating the mean

Purposeful practice 1

1 25.0   **2** 30.0   **3** 25.0   **4** 25.0   **5** 31.7   **6** 131.7

Purposeful practice 2

1 11.875   **2 a** 13.125   **b** 12.1875

Problem-solving practice

1 a Estimated range is 19.   **b** 10 to 14 complaints
  c Estimated mean is $10\frac{1}{2}$ complaints.
2 The missing frequency is 3.

Exam practice

1 a £305
  b Students' reasoning may vary, for example, Terry is correct. The mean may not be the best average to use as there are outliers.

7.5 Sampling

Purposeful practice 1

1 All Year 7 students who are 12 in Julie's school
2 All Year 7 students who are in that class
3 All Year 7 students who are in a Cardiff school
4 All Year 7 students who live in Cardiff
5 All Year 7 students who are in a Lancashire school
6 All Year 7 students who are in a Scottish school

Purposeful practice 2

1 Students' own answers, for example, make a numbered list of all the students in the year group and select numbers using a random number generator.
2 Students' own answers, for example, carrying out a national census is very costly and time-consuming.
3 a Students' own answers, for example, a sample taken at midday may largely involve people who are not working that day so may not be representative. The sample size is too small.
  b Students' own answers, for example, take the survey across a wider range of times. Increase the sample size.
4 Students' own answers, for example, the diet of people at the gym may not be representative of the diet of the rest of the population.

Problem-solving practice

1 a Students' own answers, for example, a sample of 5 is not big enough to be representative. It is not possible to see, from a sample of 5 customers, whether all the different sandwiches need to be ordered.
  b The owner should increase the number of customers in the sample to increase accuracy.
2 Students' own answers, for example, the last 10 beams may be very similar. They should randomly sample from the 100 beams.
3 a Students' own answers, for example, 10 am is early, so people won't have been on many rides. 20 is too small a sample.
  b Students' own answers, for example, take the survey at the park exit. Take a larger sample.
4 Diesel 20, Petrol 25

Exam practice

1 The survey suggests that about 400 people will like rock music. Assumptions made: The sample is representative of the group of people who will be attending the festival. People have one main type of music they like.

8 Perimeter, Area and Volume 1

8.1 Rectangles, parallelograms and triangles

Purposeful practice 1

1 60 cm²   **2** 60 cm²   **3** 60 cm²

Purposeful practice 2

1 30 cm²   **2** 30 cm²   **3** 30 cm²

Purposeful practice 3

1 18 cm²   **2** 9 cm²   **3** 36 cm²
4 36 cm²   **5** 24 cm²   **6** 60 cm²

Problem-solving practice

1 5 cm   **2** 12 cm
3 Students' answers will vary. Length × perpendicular height should be 60 cm².
4 10 cm   **5** 609 cm²

Exam practice

1 8 cm
2 Sketch of a parallelogram with base = 6 cm and height = 3 cm

8.2 Trapezia and changing units

Purposeful practice

1 a 13 cm   **b** 104 cm²   **c** 52 cm²
2 a 60 cm²   **b** 30 cm²
3 42 cm²
4 a 42 cm²   **b** 52.5 cm²   **c** 54.6 cm²

Problem-solving practice

1 7 mm   **2** 3.375 m²   **3** 14 cm   **4** 23.4 cm²

Exam practice

1 Students' answers will vary. Measurements should be clearly labelled with base length and perpendicular height such that $\frac{1}{2}$ base × height = 21 cm².
Example answer:

6 cm

7 cm

8.3 Area of compound shapes

Purposeful practice

1 a 6 cm   **b** 72 cm²   **c** 5 cm by 4 cm   **d** 20 cm²   **e** 92 cm²
2 a Rectangle C is 7 cm by 5 cm and rectangle D is 10 cm by 3 cm.
  b Area of rectangle C = 35 cm² and area of rectangle D = 30 cm².
  c 65 cm²
3 a Area of rectangle E = 36 cm² and area of rectangle F = 45 cm².
  b 81 cm²
4 a 42 cm²   **b** 330 cm²   **c** 70 cm²

Problem-solving practice

1 Shape B has the bigger area, by 4 cm².   **2** 237 cm²
3 Area = (7.5 m × 5.5 m) + (3 m × 4 m) = 53.25 m²
   53.25 m² ÷ 1.75 m² = 30.4, so Caily needs 31 packs.

Exam practice

1 304 cm²

8.4 Surface area of 3D solids

Purposeful practice

1 a and **b**

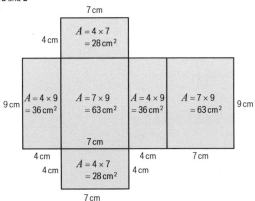

c 254 cm²

2 a 292 cm²   **b** 216 cm²

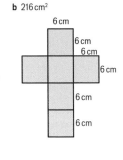

c 636 cm²

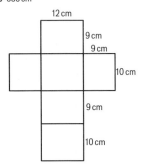

3 a 432 cm²

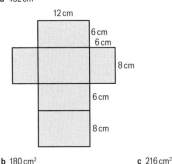

b 180 cm²   **c** 216 cm²

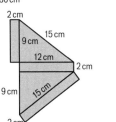

Problem-solving practice

1 7 cm   **2** £1800   **3** 7 cm   **4** 9 cm

Exam practice

1 7 cans

8.5 Volumes of prisms

Purposeful practice 1

1 a 12   **b** 12   **c** 8
2 a 12 cm³   **b** 12 cm³   **c** 8 cm³

Purposeful practice 2

1 a 96 cm³   **b** 90 cm³   **c** 315 cm³
2 a 160 cm³   **b** 54 cm³   **c** 252 cm³

Problem-solving practice

1 95 cm³   **2 a** 3 cm   **b** 27 cm³
3 a 69 m³   **b** £4968

Exam practice

1 512 cm³
2 a Yes, one cube has a volume of 125 cm³, $8 \times 125 = 1000$
  b i Students' answers will vary. Dimensions of cuboid should be 5 cm by 5 cm by 40 cm **or** 10 cm by 10 cm by 10 cm **or** 5 cm by 10 cm by 20 cm.
    ii Students' answers will vary. Surface area of cuboid should be 850 cm² **or** 600 cm² **or** 700 cm².

8.6 More volume and surface area

Purposeful practice 1

1 a 30 cm³   **b** 28 cm³   **c** 0.03 m³   **d** 0.028 m³

Purposeful practice 2

1 a 36 000 mm³   **b** 360 000 mm³
  c 105 000 000 cm³   **d** 378 000 000 cm³

Problem-solving practice

1 a 9 cm   **b** 7 cm   **c** 11 cm
2 225 mm
3 No.
  20 cm ÷ 2 cm = 10, so 10 dice will fit along the width of the box.
  12 cm ÷ 2 cm = 6, so 6 dice will fit along the depth of the box. This means that $10 \times 6 = 60$ dice will be in each layer.
  5 cm ÷ 2 cm = 2.5, so only 2 layers of dice will fit in the box, with a space left at the top.
  Therefore, only 120 dice will fit in the box.

Exam practice

1 32 cm

Mixed exercises B

Mixed problem-solving practice B

1 No, the nth term is $4n - 3$ and when $4n - 3 = 35$, $n = 9.5$
2 8 cm   **3** 12
4 a i 40   **ii** The term-to-term rule is 'add 9'
  b 112
5 $x = 30°$ **6** 12 cm
7 $x = 12$ cm **8** $a = 132°$
9 a Possible answers are 0, 1, 2 or 4   **b** 7, 7, 16
10 Angle BEF = 35°. Students' reasoning may vary, for example, AD and CE are parallel and angle ADF and angle BEF are alternate angles. So, angle BEF = angle ADF = 35° because alternate angles are equal.
11 260
12 a $x = 7$ m   **b** £159.29
13 Jakub, because the range for his scores, 3, is less than Kate's, 7.
14 $91° \leqslant x \leqslant 124°$

Exam practice

15 729 cm³   **16** $7n - 1$
17 Angle DEF = 145°.
  $x = 5 \times 42° = 210°$. The internal angles of a hexagon total 720°.
  Angle DEF = 720° − 138° − 42° − 210° − 95° − 90° = 145°.

18 a 30.6

  b Yes, because the mean is affected by outliers.

19 19°, 66° and 95°

  $x + 5x + 5x - 29 = 180°$, giving $11x - 29 = 180°$. So, $x = 19°$.

  Angles are 19°, $5 \times 19°$ and $(5 \times 19°) - 29°$ i.e. 19°, 95° and 66°.

20 Opposite sides of a rectangle are equal, so $2x + 5 = 4x - 9$.

  Solving these equations gives $x = 7$ cm.

  The length of the rectangle is 19 cm and its area is 95 cm², so $19y = 95$. $y = 5$ cm.

9 Graphs

9.1 Coordinates

Purposeful practice 1

1 Student's own answers, for example, (1, 3), (2, 4), (3, 5)

2 a (−4, −3), (−3, −3), (−2, −3), (−1, −3), (0, −3), (1, −3), (2, −3), (3, −3), (4, −3)

  b (−4, 0), (−3, 0), (−2, 0), (−1, 0), (0, 0), (1, 0), (2, 0), (3, 0), (4, 0)

  c (−4, 3), (−3, 3), (−2, 3), (−1, 3), (0, 3), (1, 3), (2, 3), (3, 3), (4, 3)

  d (−4, −4), (−3, −3), (−2, −2), (−1, −1), (0, 0), (1, 1), (2, 2), (3, 3), (4, 4)

  e (−4, −8), (−3, −6), (−2, −4), (−1, −2), (0, 0), (1, 2), (2, 4), (3, 6), (4, 8)

  f (−4, 8), (−3, 6), (−2, 4), (−1, 2), (0, 0), (1, −2), (2, −4), (3, −6), (4, −8)

3 a (−3, −4), (−3, −3), (−3, −2), (−3, −1), (−3, 0), (−3, 1), (−3, 2), (−3, 3), (−3, 4)

  b (0, −4), (0, −3), (0, −2), (0, −1), (0, 0), (0, 1), (0, 2), (0, 3), (0, 4)

  c (3, −4), (3, −3), (3, −2), (3, −1), (3, 0), (3, 1), (3, 2), (3, 3), (3, 4)

  d (−4, −4), (−3, −3), (−2, −2), (−1, −1), (0, 0), (1, 1), (2, 2), (3, 3), (4, 4)

  e (−2, −4), (−1.5, −3), (−1, −2), (−0.5, −1), (0, 0), (0.5, 1), (1, 2), (1.5, 3), (2, 4)

  f (2, −4), (1.5, −3), (1, −2), (0.5, −1), (0, 0), (−0.5, 1), (−1, 2), (−1.5, 3), (−2, 4)

Purposeful practice 2

1–6

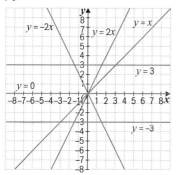

Problem-solving practice

1 (1, −3)

2 $x = 5$ (or $x = −3$)

3 Right-angled triangle

4 a

  b (0, 0)

5 a and b **i**

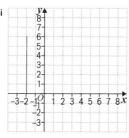

  ii (−2, 3)

c (1, 2)

d

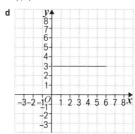

Exam practice

1 a (5, 4)

  b

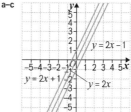

9.2 Linear graphs

Purposeful practice 1

1

x	−2	−1	0	1	2
$y = 2$	2	2	2	2	2
	(−2, 2)	(−1, 2)	(0, 2)	(1, 2)	(2, 2)

2

x	−2	−1	0	1	2
$y = x$	−2	−1	0	1	2
	(−2, −2)	(−1, −1)	(0, 0)	(1, 1)	(2, 2)

3

x	−2	−1	0	1	2
$y = 2x$	−4	−2	0	2	4
	(−2, −4)	(−1, −2)	(0, 0)	(1, 2)	(2, 4)

4

x	−2	−1	0	1	2
$y = 2x + 1$	−3	−1	1	3	5
	(−2, −3)	(−1, −1)	(0, 1)	(1, 3)	(2, 5)

5

x	−2	−1	0	1	2
$y = 2x − 1$	−5	−3	−1	1	3
	(−2, −5)	(−1, −3)	(0, −1)	(1, 1)	(2, 3)

Purposeful practice 2

1 a–c

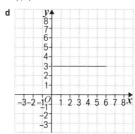

2 a i

x	−2	−1	0	1	2
$y = −2x$	4	2	0	−2	−4

  ii

x	−2	−1	0	1	2
$y = −2x + 1$	5	3	1	−1	−3

  iii

x	−2	−1	0	1	2
$y = −2x − 1$	3	1	−1	−3	−5

b

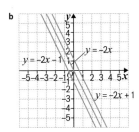

Problem-solving practice

1 a (2, –4) **b** (2, 0) **c** (2, 8) **d** (2, –8)

2 a

x	–2	–1	0	1	2
$y = \frac{1}{2}x$	–1	–0.5	0	0.5	1

b

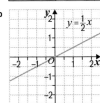

3 A (2, –8); B (2, 8); C (2, 0); D (2, –4)

Exam practice

1 a C **b** A **c** D

9.3 Gradient

Purposeful practice 1

1 A, B, C, D, E, and F have positive gradients.

2 G, H and I have negative gradients.

3 Students' own answers, for example, I and H are parallel.

4 B: 2; C: 1; D: 3; E: 2; F: 1; G: –2; H: –4; I: –4

Purposeful practice 2

1 A: $\frac{1}{3}$; B: 2; C: $\frac{1}{2}$; D: 3

2 D: $y = 3x - 21$
A: $y = \frac{1}{3}x + 4$
B: $y = 2x$
C: $y = \frac{1}{2}x - 1$

Problem-solving practice

1 Line B is steeper because it has a greater gradient (gradient of 4, compared to gradient of 3).

2 Students' own answers, for example,

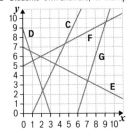

3

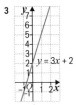

4 a $-\frac{1}{3}$ **b** 2 **c** $\frac{1}{4}$

Exam practice

1 Lines B and E **2** $d = 27$

9.4 $y = mx + c$

Purposeful practice 1

1 The y-intercept of a line is the point where it crosses the y-axis.

2 a (0, 5) **b** (0, –2) **c** (0, –2) **d** (0, –2) **e** (0, –3) **f** (0, 4)
   g (0, –4) **h** (0, 4) **i** (0, 4) **j** (0, –4) **k** (0, –4) **l** (0, 2)

Purposeful practice 2

1 A **a** –3 **b** –2 **c** $y = -3x - 2$
   B **a** 3 **b** 2 **c** $y = 3x + 2$
   C **a** 2 **b** –4 **c** $y = 2x - 4$
   D **a** 0 **b** –4 **c** $y = -4$

Problem-solving practice

1 a $y = x$

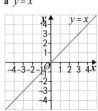

b $y = x + 3$

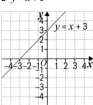

c $y = -x$

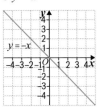

d $y = -x - 1$

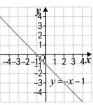

e $y = -2$

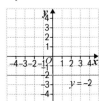

f $y = 2x + 1$

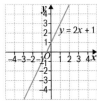

g $y = -3x$

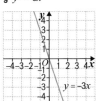

h $y = -3x + 2$

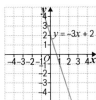

2 A: $y = 2x + 18$ B: $y = x + 9$ C: $y = 2x + 4$
   D: $y = x - 3$ E: $y = -4x + 20$

3 a $y = x - 3$ and $y = x - 4$, $y = -2x + 4$ and $y = -2x - 1$,
   $y = 3x + 1$ and $y = 3x$
   b $y = 2x + 5$ and $y = 5$, $y = 3x + 1$ and $y = -4x + 1$

Exam practice

1 $y = -2x + 4$

9.5 Real-life graphs

Purposeful practice 1

1 Brand A = Line 3, Brand B = Line 2, Brand C = Line 1

2 Brand A = £8/kg, Brand B = £4/kg, Brand C = £2/kg

3 £30

4 No, Brand A and Brand B will cost the same.

Purposeful practice 2

1 a

Strawberries bought (kg)	1	2	3	4	5	6
Cost (£)	1.88	3.76	5.64	7.52	9.40	11.28

b

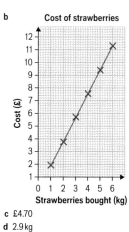

Cost of strawberries

c £4.70

d 2.9 kg

Problem-solving practice

1 a

Electricity used (kWh)	0	200	400	600	800	1000
Brian pays (£)	0.00	30.00	60.00	90.00	120.00	150.00
Tom pays (£)	15.00	39.00	63.00	87.00	111.00	135.00

b

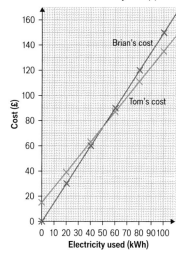

Cost of electricity used (£)

c Brian **d** Tom

2 a

Fuel bought (litres)	2	4	6	8	10	12
Cost (£)	2.60	5.20	7.80	10.40	13.00	15.60

b

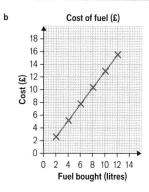

Cost of fuel (£)

c £58.50 **d** Approximately 3.2 litres

Exam practice

1 £0.60

Purposeful practice

1 Red line **2** 40 km **3** Kyle for 2 hours
4 2.30 pm and she stays for 1.5 hours **5** 1.30 pm
6 Approximately 5.30 pm and they are 27.5 km from Bedford
7 Going back to Bedford **8** 9.00 pm
9 a 16 km/hr **b** 8 km/hr **c** 16 km/hr (to 1 d.p.)

Problem-solving practice

1 a

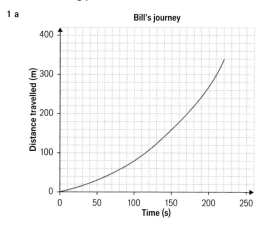

Bill's journey

b Bill's speed is increasing, as the gradient of the distance–time graph becomes steeper.

2 a She has not taken into account the time that Sally was at the service station, stuck in roadworks and buying flowers.

b 48 mph

Exam practice

1 Dalva, with students' own working, for example,
from the graph, Dalva ran 80 metres in 11 seconds.

This is equivalent to $\frac{80}{11} \times 60 \times 60$ metres per hour = 26 200 metres per hour.
(to the nearest 100 m) 26 200 metres per hour = 26.2 km/h.

Dalva's speed is about 26.2 km/h whereas Seb's speed is 22.3 km/h, so Dalva ran faster.

9.7 More real-life graphs

Purposeful practice 1

1 B **2** A **3** A = 3; B = 1; C = 2

Purposeful practice 2

1 a 6.0 cm **b** 3.8 minutes (or 3 minutes and 48 seconds)
c 1.25 cm **d** 1.25
2 a 3.0 cm **b** 7.6 minutes (or 7 minutes and 36 seconds)
c 0.625 cm **d** 0.625

Problem-solving practice

1 a 2002–2012: either by working out the change in each 10-year period, or by noticing that this is the steepest section.

b £1.10 (accept answers between £1.08 and £1.12)

c Students' answers may vary, for example, the price has started to go down and we cannot be sure if it will continue going down, or if it will go up again.

2 a 29

b This is not very reliable because few results lie on the line of best fit. However, most results lie within 10 marks to either side of the line of best fit, so David's score is likely to lie within the range 19–39.

c No other students on the graph scored close to 80 in the history test, so it is not possible to directly predict Sakina's maths score from the graph. However, there is a fairly strong positive correlation between maths and history marks, so it is likely that Sakina scored very highly on the maths test.

Exam practice

1 £80 per hour

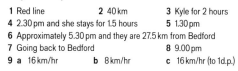

10 Transformations

10.1 Translation

Purposeful practice 1

1 a C **b** H **c** E **d** G **e** B **f** F **g** D

2 a i $\begin{pmatrix} 4 \\ 2 \end{pmatrix}$ **ii** $\begin{pmatrix} 2 \\ -2 \end{pmatrix}$ **iii** $\begin{pmatrix} 6 \\ 0 \end{pmatrix}$

b i $\begin{pmatrix} 2 \\ 2 \end{pmatrix}$ **ii** $\begin{pmatrix} 8 \\ 0 \end{pmatrix}$ **iii** $\begin{pmatrix} 10 \\ 2 \end{pmatrix}$

c i $\begin{pmatrix} 8 \\ 0 \end{pmatrix}$ **ii** $\begin{pmatrix} -4 \\ 8 \end{pmatrix}$ **iii** $\begin{pmatrix} 4 \\ 8 \end{pmatrix}$

Problem-solving practice

1 $y = -2$ **2** C   **3** (56, 26)

4 Q $\begin{pmatrix} 4 \\ 0 \end{pmatrix}$ R $\begin{pmatrix} 4 \\ 3 \end{pmatrix}$ S $\begin{pmatrix} 0 \\ 3 \end{pmatrix}$

Exam practice

1 Translation of 2 units to the left and 4 units down, so $\begin{pmatrix} -2 \\ -4 \end{pmatrix}$.

2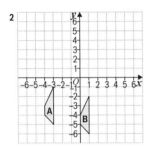

10.2 Reflection

Purposeful practice 1

1 a $x = 2$ **b** $y = 0$ **c** $x = -1$
d $x = 3$ **e** $y = 4$ **f** $y = -2$

Purposeful practice 2

1 a Reflections are labelled A′, B′, C′ and, D′ on the diagram below.

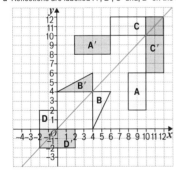

b A: (8, 2), (10, 2), (10, 6), (8, 6)
B: (4, 0), (6, 4), (4, 4)
C: (6, 10), (12, 10), (12, 12), (6, 12)
D: (0, −2), (−2, −2), (−2, 2), (0, 2)
c A: (2, 8), (2, 10), (6, 10), (6, 8)
B: (0, 4), (4, 6), (4, 4)
C: (10, 6), (10, 12), (12, 12), (12, 6)
D: (−2, 0), (−2, −2), (2, −2), (2, 0)

Problem-solving practice

1 a The mirror line is $y = 2$.
b The shape is reflected in the y-axis.
c The mirror line is $x = 4$.
2 a $x = 1$ **b** $y = 4 - x$ **c** $x = -1$
d $y = 4$ **e** $y = 2$

Exam practice

1 Reflection in the x-axis (or the line $y = 0$)
2 Reflection in the y-axis (or the line $x = 0$)

10.3 Rotation

Purposeful practice 1

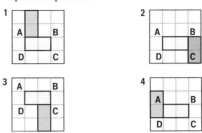

Purposeful practice 2

1 180°   **2** 90° anticlockwise (or 270° clockwise)
3 180°   **4** 90° clockwise (or 270° anticlockwise)

Purposeful practice 3

1 a H   **b** D   **c** G   **d** E   **e** F
2 a R   **b** S   **c** Q   **d** P

Problem-solving practice

1 Alex rotated anticlockwise instead of clockwise.
Alex has labelled the corners incorrectly.
2 a A to C is a rotation 180° around (4, 2).
b C to E is a rotation 90° anticlockwise around (5, 5).
c E to A is a rotation 90° anticlockwise around (7, 1).
3 This is a rotation of 180°. The centre of rotation is the point (1, 0).

Exam practice

1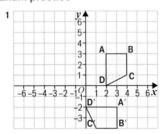

10.4 Enlargement

Purposeful practice 1

1 Shape C   **2** Shape E   **3** Shape B

Purposeful practice 2

1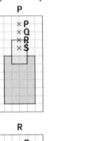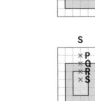

Problem-solving practice

1 a $2\frac{1}{2}$

  b width = 9 cm, height = 6 cm

2 a Scale factor needs to be larger than 1. Check centre of enlargement to ensure the enlarged shape will be in quadrant 1.

  b Scale factor needs to be between 0 and 1. Check centre of enlargement to ensure the enlarged shape will be in quadrant 1.

  c Scale factor needs to be larger than 1. Check centre of enlargement to ensure the enlarged shape will be in quadrant 2.

  d Scale factor needs to be between 0 and 1. Check centre of enlargement to ensure the enlarged shape will be in the same quadrant.

3 Anna: The perimeter should be 36 cm (she has doubled when she should have tripled).

Paul: The difference will triple if the side length triples (i.e. it will become 6 cm not 2 cm).

Charlie: The new area will be 3^2 times larger (54 cm), not 3 times larger.

Exam practice

1 Correct enlargement shown from any centre of enlargement. For example,

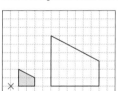

10.5 Describing enlargements

Purposeful practice 1

1 a Scale factor 2   b Scale factor 4

  c Scale factor $\frac{1}{2}$ d Scale factor $\frac{1}{2}$

2 a $\frac{1}{4}$ b 8   c $\frac{1}{8}$ d 2

Purposeful practice 2

1 Centre (1, –1), scale factor 2   2 Centre (1, –1), scale factor $\frac{1}{2}$

3 Centre (0, 8), scale factor 2   4 Centre (0, 8), scale factor $\frac{1}{2}$

Purposeful practice 3

1 Scale factor 2   2 Scale factor 3

Problem-solving practice

1 Centre of enlargement (0, 3), scale factor 2

2 Centre of enlargement (9, 4), scale factor $\frac{1}{2}$

3 An enlargement by scale factor $\frac{1}{3}$, centre (3, 2)

Exam practice

1 Enlargement, scale factor 2, centre of enlargement P

10.6 Combining transformations

Purposeful practice 1

1 a P   b P   c T   d R   e S   f S

2 a Translation of $\begin{pmatrix} 4 \\ 0 \end{pmatrix}$ b Translation of $\begin{pmatrix} 0 \\ -8 \end{pmatrix}$

  c Rotation of 180° about (2, 3)   d Rotation of 180° about (4, –1)

Problem-solving practice

1
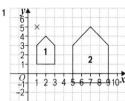

2 a The reflection in the line $y = x$ is labelled (a) on the following diagram; the second reflection in the x-axis is labelled 'End result'

  b The translation is labelled (b) on the following diagram; the final position is the same as (a).

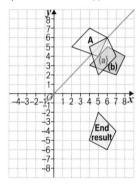

3 After rotation, shape T becomes shape B. This reflects to make shape Q.

Exam practice

1 a and b
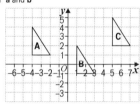

  c $\begin{pmatrix} 9 \\ 1 \end{pmatrix}$

11 Ratio and proportion

11.1 Writing ratios

Purposeful practice 1

1 □ △ △   2 □ □ □ △ △

3 □ □ △ △ △   4 □ □ □ □ △ △ △ △

5 □ □ □ □ △ △ △ △ △   6 □ □ □ □ △ △ △ △

7 □ □ □ □ △ △   8 □ □ △

Purposeful practice 2

1 Yes   2 No   3 No   4 No

5 No   6 Yes   7 No   8 Yes

Purposeful practice 3

1 2 : 3   **2** 2 : 3   **3** 3 : 2   **4** 3 : 2
5 4 : 3   **6** 8 : 3   **7** 4 : 3   **8** 1 : 1
9 2 : 3 : 4   **10** 2 : 4 : 3   **11** 2 : 4 : 3   **12** 2 : 4 : 3
13 1 : 4 : 3   **14** 1 : 8 : 3   **15** 5 : 3   **16** 1 : 7

Problem-solving practice

1 2 : 5   **2** 2 : 3   **3** 1 : 8
4 Harriet is wrong because the ratio 1 : 3 means 3 times as many green marbles as red marbles.
5 4 : 16 : 1
6 a James has not fully simplified, he has just halved the ratio. 8 : 10 simplifies to 4 : 5.
   b Karis has written the ratio back-to-front.
7 The ratio of flour to butter to caster sugar is 9 : 2 : 1
8 No, the ratio 5 : 2 is equivalent to 30 : 12 so the ratio of 30 g : 16 g is not suitable for growing mushrooms.
9 No, 5 adults can only take 60 children, 6 adults are needed for 62 children.

Exam practice

1 1 : 4

11.2 Using ratios 1

Purposeful practice 1

1 16   **2** 4   **3** 8   **4** 2
5 0.5   **6** 1   **7** 10   **8** 40

Purposeful practice 2

1 3 : 4   **2** 3 : 4   **3** 15 : 2   **4** 75 : 1
5 15 : 2   **6** 3 : 4   **7** 3 : 40   **8** 3 : 400

Purposeful practice 3

1 24   **2** 24   **3** 6   **4** 24   **5** 36   **6** 18

Problem-solving practice

1 300 ml   **2 a** 1056   **b** 1200
3 a 24 km   **b** 6 hours
4 a 0.6 m
   b No, the ratio 9 : 2 is equivalent to 1.8 : 0.4 so it should be 0.4 m
5 Daniel is wrong because there are still decimal points in his ratio. It should be 1 : 4.
6 3   **7** 3
8 This year is 7 : 3, so 2 : 1, 9 : 5 and 5 : 3

Exam practice

1 54

11.3 Ratio and measures

Purposeful practice 1

1 a 120 minutes   **b** 30 minutes   **c** 150 minutes
2 a 4.8 km   **b** 8 km   **c** 1.875 miles   **d** 3.125 miles
3 a 6.6 pounds   **b** 11 pounds   **c** 1.36 kg (to 2 d.p.)   **d** 2.27 kg (to 2 d.p.)

Purposeful practice 2

1 €224   **2** $256   **3** £178.57   **4** £156.25

Purposeful practice 3

1 a 1 : 2   **b** 1 : 4   **c** 1 : 8
2 a 1 : 3   **b** 1 : 9   **c** 1 : 27
3 a 1 : 4   **b** 1 : 16   **c** 1 : 64

Problem-solving practice

1 7.92 pounds   **2** 48 km/h   **3** 6.6 pounds or 3 kg
4 2.5 × 1.6 = 4, therefore Nana walks 4 km. Charlie walks 3.5 km, so Nana walks further.
5 America, as $425 = £332.03
6 Callum is incorrect because he should divide by 1.12
7 Ollie gains money, because £300 = ¥42 300, ¥42 300 = £306.52
8 40 cm²

Exam practice

1 204 m

11.4 Using ratios 2

Purposeful practice 1

1 £20 : £80   **2** £20 : £80   **3** £30 : £70
4 £60 : £140   **5** £6 : £14   **6** £6 : £14
7 £9 : £21   **8** £10 : £20   **9** £15 : £15
10 £10 : £9 : £1   **11** £10 : £8 : £2   **12** £15 : £12 : £3
13 £20 : £16 : £4   **14** £25 : £20 : £5   **15** £30 : £24 : £6

Purposeful practice 2

1 60 ml : 100 ml : 40 ml
2 600 ml : 1000 ml : 400 ml
3 0.6 litres : 1 litre : 0.4 litres
4 0.3 litres : 0.5 litres : 0.2 litres
5 150 ml : 250 ml : 100 ml
6 0.15 litres : 0.25 litres : 0.1 litres
7 1.5 litres : 2.5 litres : 1 litre
8 1.8 litres : 3 litres : 1.2 litres

Purposeful practice 3

1 0.8 kg : 1.2 kg   **2** 8 g : 12 g   **3** 80 g : 120 g
4 800 g : 1200 g   **5** 1.6 kg : 2.4 kg   **6** 0.4 kg : 0.6 kg
7 2 kg : 3 kg   **8** 2.4 kg : 3.6 kg

Problem-solving practice

1 100 ml of red paint and 200 ml of yellow paint
2 a Pavlo £12 000, Erik £18 000
   b £9000   **c** Masha £4000, Julia £5000
3 a 252 g silver and 108 g gold   **b** £3327.84
4 Franci should have divided by the total of the ratios, so £60 ÷ 12 = 5. Then she should have multiplied this by her part of the ratio, 5, to give £25.
5 48 jelly beans   **6** 18 cows and 30 sheep
7 400 books

Exam practice

1 72 chocolates

11.5 Comparing using ratios

Purposeful practice 1

1 3 : 1   **2** 1 : 3   **3** 1 : 2   **4** 2 : 4 or 1 : 2

Purposeful practice 2

1 $\frac{2}{3}$ **2** $\frac{2}{3}$ **3** $\frac{1}{3}$ **4** $\frac{3}{10}$ **5** $\frac{3}{10}$

Purposeful practice 3

1 1 : 4   **2** 1 : 2   **3** 1 : 1   **4** 1 : 0.5   **5** 1 : 5
6 1 : 0.2   **7** 1 : 0.3   **8** 1 : 3   **9** 1 : 6   **10** 1 : 0.6

Purposeful practice 4

1 Paint A is 1 : 1.33 blue to yellow.
Paint B is 1 : 0.75 blue to yellow.
So Paint A has more yellow.
2 Paint A is 1 : 1.33 blue to yellow.
Paint B is 1 : 1.25 blue to yellow.
So Paint A has more yellow.

Problem-solving practice

1 2 : 1   **2** $\frac{5}{7}$
3 Louise is not correct. The ratio of sugar to other ingredients is $\frac{3}{10}$ to $\frac{7}{10}$, which is equivalent to 3 : 7.
4 1 : 1.5   **5** 1 : 2.5   **6** $\frac{14}{25}$

Exam practice

1 a $\frac{6}{11}$ **b** 2 : 1

11.6 Using proportion

Purposeful practice 1

1 30 g **2** 60 g **3** 180 g **4** 270 g

Purposeful practice 2

1 7.5 kg **2** 15 kg **3** 45 kg **4** 67.5 kg

Purposeful practice 3

1 £1 : 175 ml **2** £1 : 180 ml **3** £1 : 191.49 ml
4 £1 : 200 ml **5** £1 : 200 ml **6** £1 : 190.22 ml

Purposeful practice 4

1 £0.0057 : 1 ml **2** £0.0055 : 1 ml **3** £0.0052 : 1 ml
4 £0.005 : 1 ml **5** £0.005 : 1 ml **6** £0.0053 : 1 ml

Problem-solving practice

1 330 ÷ 75 = 4.4, so 4.4 ml per pence.
500 ÷ 125 = 4, so 4 ml per pence.
Therefore, the can is better value for money.
2 The 25 kg bag is better value. 11 kg bag is 32p per kg.
25 kg bag is 23p per kg
3 300 ÷ 80 = 3.75, so 3.75p per tea bag.
450 ÷ 160 = 2.8125, so 2.81p per tea bag.
575 ÷ 240 = 2.3958333, so 2.4p per tea bag.
Therefore, the large box at £5.75 is the best value for money.
4 Shop A: 30 ÷ 3 × 1 = £10.
Shop B: 30 ÷ 5 × £1.50 = £9, so shop B is cheaper.

Exam practice

1 For one biscuit: 17.5 g of flour, 5 g butter, 8.75 g brown sugar, 3 g syrup, 0.05 eggs. Matt has only 100 g of syrup so he can make a maximum of 33 biscuits.

11.7 Proportion and graphs

Purposeful practice 1

1 A and **D** show direct proportion

2 a
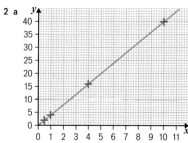

b Yes, the values are in direct proportion as the graph is a straight line passing through the origin.

Purposeful practice 2

1
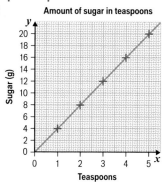
Amount of sugar in teaspoons

2 2.5 teaspoons **3** 25 teaspoons **4** 0 g
5 24 g **6** 240 g

Problem-solving practice

1 a
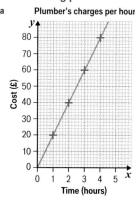
Plumber's charges per hour

b The plumber's charges are in direct proportion to the hours she works because the graph is a straight line which goes through the origin.

2 a
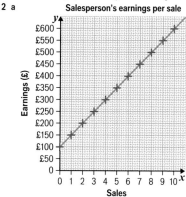
Salesperson's earnings per sale

b This graph does not show direct proportion because the line does not go through the origin.
c They make £560 instead of £500, so they are £60 better off.
3 No, because the graph of the fare compared to the distance travelled would not go through the origin.

Exam practice

1 Approximately 10.5 miles

11.8 Proportion problems

Purposeful practice 1

1 £23.60 **2** 16 chairs **3** £1

Purposeful practice 2

1 £25 **2** 4 hours **3** 300 ml

Purposeful practice 3

1 28 hours
2 a 1.5 days **b** 40 bananas **c** 28 monkeys

Problem-solving practice

1 a No, 4 people would take half as long as 2 people to make the table so the cost would be the same (£115.50).
b $1\frac{3}{4}$ hours
2 It has doubled.
3 a 20 hours **b** 10 hours
4 No, because the temperature has halved, but the number of ice creams sold has not doubled.
5 a 3 surgeons **b** 3 hours **c** 30 patients
6 a £111 **b** £111 **c** 3 people

Exam practice

1 a 7.5 days
b i The rate at which each decorator paints is the same, all the time.
ii If the rate is slower, it will take longer. If the rate is faster, it will take less time.

12 Right-angled triangles

12.1 Pythagoras' theorem 1

Purposeful practice 1
1 a c b b, a 2 a z b x, y
3 a i b g, h 4 a d b e, f

Purposeful practice 2
1 5 cm   2 10 cm   3 20 cm   4 13 cm   5 26 cm   6 25 cm

Purposeful practice 3
1 8.5 cm   2 14.4 cm   3 24.5 cm

Problem-solving practice
1 1.4 m   2 12.8 m
3 It is quicker to travel directly from A to C, by 14.6 minutes
   (or 14 minutes and 36 seconds).
4 a 60.2 cm   b Wall is vertical, shelf is horizontal.

Exam practice
1 21.6 cm^2

12.2 Pythagoras' theorem 2

Purposeful practice 1
1

Coordinates	x length	y length	Length of a line between the points
(0, 0), (3, 4)	3	4	5
(0, 0), (4, 3)	4	3	5
(1, 1), (5, 4)	4	3	5
(1, 2), (5, 5)	4	3	5
(−1, −2), (−5, −5)	4	3	5

Purposeful practice 2
1 a $x^2 + 4^2 = 5^2$ b 3.0 cm   2 a $x^2 + 4^2 = 6^2$ b 4.5 cm
3 a $x^2 + 4^2 = 6^2$ b 4.5 cm   4 a $6^2 + 4^2 = x^2$ b 7.2 cm

Problem-solving practice
1 a Ladder B
  b Using Pythagoras' theorem
    Length of ladder A = 11.4 m (1 d.p.)
    Length of ladder B = 13.6 m (1 d.p.)
    Height ladder A reaches = 12.4 m (1 d.p.)
    Height ladder B reaches = 14.5 m (1 d.p.).
    So ladder B reaches 2.04 m further up the wall.
2 6.6 m (1 d.p.)   3 7.6 cm (1 d.p.)
4 $9^2 + 40^2 = 1681 = 41^2$
5 The hypotenuse of the right-angled triangle is $\sqrt{(7^2 + 3^2)} = 7.6$ cm, so its
   perimeter is 7 cm + 3 cm + 7.6 cm = 17.6 cm.
   Perimeter of the equilateral triangle = 3×6 cm = 18 cm. So the statement
   is incorrect.
6 120.7 cm

Exam practice
1 No, it is not, because Pythagoras' theorem does not hold true.
   AC = 9 cm, but $\sqrt{7^2 + 4^2} = 8.06$ cm.
2 44 cm^2

12.3 Trigonometry: the sine ratio 1

Purposeful practice 1
1 $\sin \theta = \dfrac{a}{c}$ 2 $\sin \theta = \dfrac{b}{c}$ 3 $\sin \theta = \dfrac{r}{t}$ 4 $\sin \theta = \dfrac{s}{t}$

Purposeful practice 2
1 5.0 cm   2 0.5 cm   3 0.9 cm   4 8.7 cm   5 7.1 cm
6 0.7 cm   7 20.0 cm   8 11.5 cm   9 14.1 cm

Problem-solving practice
1 3.83 m   2 3.19 m   3 2.74 cm   4 5.7 m   5 3.95 m

Exam practice
1 9 cm

12.4 Trigonometry: the sine ratio 2

Purposeful practice 1
1 30°   2 30°   3 19.5°

Purposeful practice 2
1 19.5°   2 41.8°   3 75.2°   4 14.5°   5 11.5°   6 9.6°

Problem-solving practice
1 28.1°   2 14.5°   3 a 9.59°   b 10.5°   c 11.5°   4 51.1°

Exam practice
1 43.9°

12.5 Trigonometry: the cosine ratio

Purposeful practice 1
1 $\cos \theta = \dfrac{b}{c}$ 2 $\cos \theta = \dfrac{a}{c}$ 3 $\cos \theta = \dfrac{s}{t}$ 4 $\cos \theta = \dfrac{r}{t}$

Purposeful practice 2
1 8.7 cm   2 5.0 cm   3 7.1 cm   4 11.5 cm
5 20.0 cm   6 14.1 cm   7 15.6 cm   8 6.4 cm

Purposeful practice 3
1 41.4°   2 60.0°   3 75.5°   4 70.5°   5 60.0°   6 48.2°

Problem-solving practice
1 3.46 m   2 0.67 m   3 36.9°   4 41 m

Exam practice
1 33.9°

12.6 Trigonometry: the tangent ratio

Purposeful practice 1
1 $\tan \theta = \dfrac{a}{b}$ 2 $\tan \theta = \dfrac{b}{a}$ 3 $\tan \theta = \dfrac{r}{s}$ 4 $\tan \theta = \dfrac{s}{r}$

Purposeful practice 2
1 5.8 cm   2 17.3 cm   3 10 cm   4 17.3 cm
5 5.8 cm   6 10 cm   7 11.9 cm   8 8.4 cm

Purposeful practice 3
1 63.4°   2 53.1°   3 45°   4 38.7°   5 33.7°   6 56.3°

Problem-solving practice
1 26.6°   2 6.7 m   3 a 8.4 m   b 14.6 m
4 Option B shows the correct calculation.

Exam practice
1 30.7°

12.7 Finding lengths and angles using trigonometry

Purposeful practice 1
1 a $\tan 48° = \dfrac{x}{6}$ b 6.7 cm

2 a $\cos \theta = \dfrac{6}{10}$ b 53.1°

3 a $\sin \theta = \dfrac{6}{10}$ b 36.9°

4 a $\tan \theta = \dfrac{6}{10}$ b 31.0°

5 a $\sin 48° = \dfrac{6}{y}$, $\cos 48° = \dfrac{x}{y}$, $\tan 48° = \dfrac{6}{x}$
  b $x = 5.4$ cm, $y = 8.1$ cm

6 a $\sin 48° = \dfrac{x}{y}$, $\cos 48° = \dfrac{6}{y}$, $\tan 48° = \dfrac{x}{6}$
  b $x = 6.7$ cm, $y = 9.0$ cm

Purposeful practice 2
1 45°   2 2 cm   3 2 cm
4 2 cm   5 3 cm   6 2 cm

Problem-solving practice
1 2
2 $\sin 30°$, $\tan 30°$, $\sin 45°$, $\cos 30°$, $\tan 45°$

3 17.0 cm   **4** 11.7 cm

5 No, it makes an angle of 50.3°.

1 29.4°

Mixed exercises C

Mixed problem-solving practice C

1 **a** and **b**

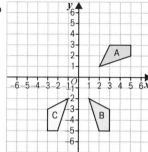

  c A reflection in the line $y = -x$

2 Charlie, because Akram saves 60%, Beth 58% and Charlie 65%

3 £80

4 $325 \div 100 = 3.25$ so Caitlin has enough flour to make $3.25 \times 8 = 26$ pancakes.

  $9 \div 2 = 4.5$ so she has enough eggs to make $4.5 \times 8 = 36$ pancakes. $825 \div 300 = 2.75$ so she has enough milk to make $2.75 \times 8 = 22$ pancakes. The greatest number of pancakes Caitlin can make is 22.

5 Frozen burgers (12 burgers will cost £6.25 compared to £6.39)

6 $y = 2x - 4$

7 **a** 08 20   **b** 8 km

  c

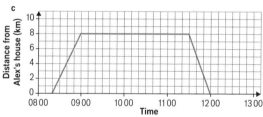

8 24.2 kg   **9** 34.6 cm

10 **a**

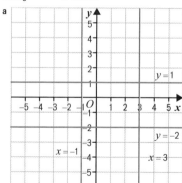

  b 12 squares

11 £42

12

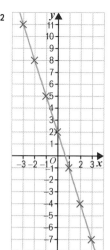

13 A translation by $\begin{pmatrix} -5 \\ 5 \end{pmatrix}$

14 **a** 15.4 pounds (allow answers between 15.2 and 15.6)   **b** 52.3 kg

15 70   **16** 5 : 3

17 Height = 6.42 cm, volume = 360 cm³

18 50.3°

13 Probability

13.1 Calculating probability

Purposeful practice 1

1 $P(R) = \dfrac{2}{3}$ $P(W) = \dfrac{1}{3}$

2 $P(R) = \dfrac{2}{4}$ or $\dfrac{1}{2}$ $P(W) = \dfrac{2}{4}$ or $\dfrac{1}{2}$

3 $P(R) = \dfrac{2}{5}$ $P(W) = \dfrac{3}{5}$

4 $P(R) = \dfrac{2}{6}$ or $\dfrac{1}{3}$ $P(W) = \dfrac{4}{6}$ or $\dfrac{2}{3}$

5 $P(R) = \dfrac{2}{7}$ $P(W) = \dfrac{4}{7}$ $P(B) = \dfrac{1}{7}$

6 $P(R) = \dfrac{2}{8}$ or $\dfrac{1}{4}$ $P(W) = \dfrac{4}{8}$ or $\dfrac{1}{2}$ $P(B) = \dfrac{2}{8}$ or $\dfrac{1}{4}$

Purposeful practice 2

1 $P(B) = \dfrac{1}{6}$ $P(Y) = \dfrac{5}{6}$

2 $P(B) = \dfrac{2}{6}$ or $\dfrac{1}{3}$ $P(Y) = \dfrac{4}{6}$ or $\dfrac{2}{3}$

3 $P(B) = \dfrac{3}{6}$ or $\dfrac{1}{2}$ $P(Y) = \dfrac{3}{6}$ or $\dfrac{1}{2}$

4 $P(B) = \dfrac{4}{6}$ or $\dfrac{2}{3}$ $P(Y) = \dfrac{2}{6}$ or $\dfrac{1}{3}$

5 $P(B) = \dfrac{5}{6}$ $P(Y) = \dfrac{1}{6}$

6 $P(B) = \dfrac{6}{6}$ or 1 $P(Y) = 0$

Purposeful practice 3

1 $\dfrac{1}{10}$ **2** $\dfrac{3}{10}$ **3** $\dfrac{2}{10}$ or $\dfrac{1}{5}$

4 $\dfrac{4}{10}$ or $\dfrac{2}{5}$ **5** $\dfrac{4}{10}$ or $\dfrac{2}{5}$ **6** $\dfrac{3}{10}$

7 $\dfrac{5}{10}$ or $\dfrac{1}{2}$ **8** $\dfrac{6}{10}$ or $\dfrac{3}{5}$ **9** $\dfrac{8}{10}$ or $\dfrac{4}{5}$

10 $\dfrac{9}{10}$ **11** $\dfrac{7}{10}$ **12** $\dfrac{7}{10}$

13 $\frac{8}{10}$ or $\frac{4}{5}$ **14** $\frac{6}{10}$ or $\frac{3}{5}$ **15** $\frac{5}{10}$ or $\frac{1}{2}$

16 $\frac{6}{10}$ or $\frac{3}{5}$ **17** $\frac{3}{10}$ **18** $\frac{4}{10}$ or $\frac{2}{5}$

Problem-solving practice

1 Students' own answers, for example, 4 black and 1 white, or 8 black and 2 white

2 $\frac{3}{8}$ **3** 5%   **4** $\frac{2}{3}$ **5** $\frac{3}{10}$

6 P(1) = P(4) = 0.25

Exam practice

1 $\frac{3}{14}$

13.2 Two events
Purposeful practice 1

1 a 2   **b** 3   **c** HR, HB, HY, TR, TB, TY   **d** 6
2 a 2   **b** 4   **c** HR, HB, HY, HG, TR, TB, TY, TG   **d** 8
3 a 2   **b** 4   **c** H1, H2, H3, H4, T1, T2, T3, T4   **d** 8
4 a 2   **b** 3   **c** HR, HB, HY, TR, TB, TY   **d** 6

Purposeful practice 2

1

		4-sided spinner			
		1	**2**	**4**	**5**
3-sided spinner	**1**	2	3	5	6
	2	3	4	6	7
	3	4	5	7	8

2 a $\frac{2}{12}$ or $\frac{1}{6}$ **b** $\frac{3}{12}$ or $\frac{1}{4}$ **c** $\frac{7}{12}$ **d** $\frac{9}{12}$ or $\frac{3}{4}$ **e** $\frac{5}{12}$

Problem-solving practice

1 a 6   **b** $\frac{1}{18}$

2 $\frac{4}{12}$ or $\frac{1}{3}$ **3** 12   **4** $\frac{9}{18}$ or $\frac{1}{2}$

5 No, it is not fair.
P(more than 6) = $\frac{21}{36}$ and P(6 or less) = $\frac{15}{36}$

Exam practice

1 $\frac{4}{9}$

13.3 Experimental probability
Purposeful practice 1

1 Dice A $\frac{18}{100}$, Dice B $\frac{17}{100}$

No, if the dice were fair the probability of rolling a 6 would be $\frac{1}{6}$

2 Dice A   **a** 2   **b** 9   **c** 36
Dice B   **a** 2   **b** 9   **c** 34

3

	Number of rolls	Money paid to arcade	Estimated prize money paid	Estimated profit
Dice A	200	£200	36 × £3 = £108	£92
Dice B	200	£200	34 × £3 = £102	£98

Purposeful practice 2

1 37   **2** 19   **3** $\frac{19}{37}$ **4** 7   **5** $\frac{7}{37}$ **6** $\frac{7}{19}$ **7** $\frac{5}{17}$

Problem-solving practice

1 a 5   **b** £60 − £30 = £30
c Students' own answers, for example probability is not certainty.
2 a 1 person   **b** 280

3 a

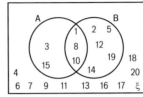

	Milk	Plain	Total
Mint	18	7	25
Orange	14	13	27
Total	32	20	52

b $\frac{18}{52}$ or $\frac{9}{26}$

Exam practice

1 68

13.4 Venn diagrams
Purposeful practice 1

1 a 1, 8, 10

b

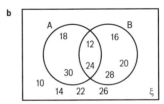

c **i** 1, 2, 3, 5, 8, 10, 12, 14, 15, 19
ii 1, 8, 10
iii 3, 4, 6, 7, 9, 11, 13, 15, 16, 17, 18, 20
iv 4, 6, 7, 9, 11, 13, 16, 17, 18, 20

2 a 12, 24

b

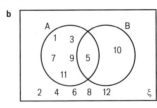

c **i** 12, 16, 18, 20, 24, 28, 30   **ii** 12, 24
iii 10, 14, 18, 22, 26, 30   **iv** 10, 14, 22, 26

3 a 5

b

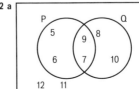

c **i** 1, 3, 5, 7, 9, 10, 11   **ii** 5
iii 1, 2, 3, 4, 6, 7, 8, 9, 11, 12   **iv** 2, 4, 6, 8, 12

Purposeful practice 2

1 11   **2** 2

3 a $\frac{2}{11}$ **b** $\frac{5}{11}$ **c** $\frac{7}{11}$ **d** $\frac{4}{11}$

Problem-solving practice

1 $\frac{2}{9}$

2 a   **b** $\frac{4}{8}$ or $\frac{1}{2}$

3

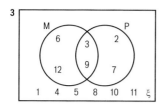

Exam practice

1 a

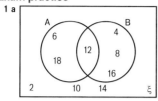

b $\frac{6}{9}$ or $\frac{2}{3}$

13.5 Tree diagrams

Purposeful practice 1

1 40   **2** 19   **3** $\frac{19}{40}$ **4** 23   **5** 11   **6** $\frac{11}{23}$

Purposeful practice 2

1

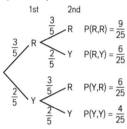

2

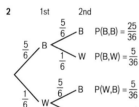

Problem-solving practice

1 a

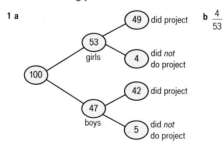

b $\frac{4}{53}$

2 $\frac{15}{39}$

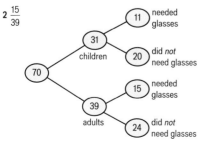

3

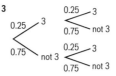

The probability that Nic rolls exactly one 3 is 0.375

Exam practice

1

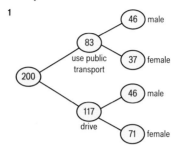

13.6 More tree diagrams

Purposeful practice 1

1 a

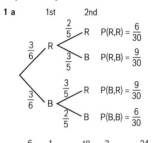

b i $\frac{6}{30}$ or $\frac{1}{5}$ **ii** $\frac{18}{30}$ or $\frac{3}{5}$ **iii** $\frac{24}{30}$ or $\frac{4}{5}$

Purposeful practice 2

1 a

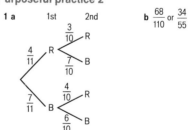

b $\frac{68}{110}$ or $\frac{34}{55}$

2 a

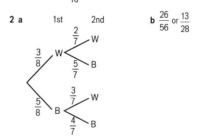

b $\frac{26}{56}$ or $\frac{13}{28}$

Problem-solving practice

1 $\frac{70}{132}$ or $\frac{35}{66}$ **2** $\frac{12}{90}$ or $\frac{4}{30}$

3 a   **b** 0.06

4 0.54

Exam practice

1 The probabilities for the first game do not sum to 1.
  On the second game, the first branch is incorrect as the probabilites are on the wrong branches.

14 Multiplicative reasoning

14.1 Percentages

Purposeful practice 1

1 a £125	b £110	c £105	d £102.50	
2 a £80	b £90.91	c £95.24	d £97.56	
3 a £75	b £90	c £95	d £97.50	
4 a £133.33	b £111.11	c £105.26	d £102.56	

Purposeful practice 2

1 a 10%	b 10%	c −9.1%	d −10%	e 11.1%
f 11.1%	g 11.1%	h −10%	i −99.1%	
2 a 11.1%	b −10%	c 11.1%	d −10%	

Problem-solving practice

1 £11 111.11
2 It is better to buy the small bottle because you get 750 ml for £1.75 instead of £2.50.
3 £266.67
4 a 6923 words   b 16.7% (1 d.p.)
5 With the dessert because it costs £27.12.
6 100%   7 a −4%   b −5%

Exam practice

1 £219.60   2 11.1%

14.2 Growth and decay

Purposeful practice 1

1 £1050   2 £1102.50   3 £1157.63   4 £1340.10

Purposeful practice 2

1 £950   2 £902.50   3 £857.38   4 £735.09

Purposeful practice 3

1 £55.75   2 £1677.14   3 £55.17   4 £1712.06

Purposeful practice 4

1 21%   2 4.5%   3 15.5%   4 −1%

Problem-solving practice

1 Increase of 2% every year for 23 years would give expected price of $12p \times 1.02^{23}$, which is 18.9p (to 1 d.p.). The price has increased to 20p, so the increase in price is more than expected.
2 The first loan (0.2% per day) will involve Chelsea paying back £1586.31 in total. The second loan (2.5% per annum) will involve paying back £1575.94 in total. The 2-year loan is cheaper.
3 2019   4 2008
5 No, Adib will lose £148.40. After the first increase, Adib's shares are worth £968.50. After the second increase, they are worth £1491.49. After the decrease, they are worth £596.60.
6 12.5%

Exam practice

1 £753.91
2 The total amount with Friendly Bank will be £52 000 × 1.021⁴, which is £56 507.53. The total amount with Aspiration Bank after 1 year will be £52 000 × 1.05, which is £54 600 and then after 3 further years will be £54 600 × 1.008³, which is £55 920.91. Monica should use Friendly Bank.

14.3 Compound measures

Purposeful practice 1

1 3 kg/m³	2 6 kg/m³	3 3 kg/m³
4 1.5 kg/m³	5 0.67 kg/m³	6 0.33 kg/m³

Purposeful practice 2

1 a 3 N/m²	b 6 N/m²	c 4 N/m²	d 3 N/m²
2 a 3 litres per minute	b 1.5 litres per minute		
c 0.75 litres per minute	d 0.2 litres per minute		
e 0.1 litres per minute	f 720 litres per minute		

Purposeful practice 3

1 20 kg   2 18 N   3 5 m³   4 2 m²

Problem-solving practice

1 Yes, she is right. The pressure exerted will be 2.45 times greater on Earth.
2 a The second bowl   b 2.9167 litres
3 a £7.74   b £7.29   c Sandra (she is paid £1695).
4 a 246   b 123 sentences and 41 quotes
5 336 kg
6 a 20.98 g   b 3.86 g   c 11.3 g/cm³ (1 d.p.)

Exam practice

1 1.01 g/cm³

14.4 Distance, speed and time

Purposeful practice 1

1 a 2 m/s	b 0.5 m/s	2 a 18 m	b 18 m
3 a 0.5 hrs (or 30 minutes)	b 2 hrs		

Purposeful practice 2

1 a 23 m/s	b 17 m/s	2 a 65 m	b 44 m
3 a 7 m/s	b 7 m/s		

Problem-solving practice

1 54.7 mph (1 d.p.)
2 a 2.04 seconds (2 d.p.)   b 20.41 m (2 d.p.)
3 a 1 hour   b 85 km/hr
4 690 m   5 6.56 m/s
6 No, the car is going faster at 5.6 m/s.

Exam practice

1 70.2 km/h

14.5 Direct and inverse proportion

Purposeful practice 1

1 $4x = y$	2 $x = 4y$	3 $2x = 3y$
4 $3x = 2y$	5 $3x = y$	6 $3x = y$

Purposeful practice 2

1 a i $g = 2.5h$ (or equivalent equation)
   ii 4.8   iii 22.5
  b i $g = 0.4h$ (or equivalent equation)
   ii 30   iii 3.6
2 a i $f = \dfrac{10}{w}$ (or equivalent equation)
   ii 0.83 (2 d.p.)   iii 1.11 (2 d.p.)
  b i $w = \dfrac{10}{f}$ (or equivalent equation)
   ii 0.83 (2 d.p.)   iii 1.11 (2 d.p.)

Problem-solving practice

1 a $c = \dfrac{k}{h}$ b $c = \dfrac{24}{h}$ (or equivalent equation)
  c 6 hours
2 a $w = 6t$ b 60 litres
  c Yes, there will be 90 litres of water.
3 14 books
4 a Inversely proportional   b Neither
  c Directly propotional
5 a 6.7 hours (or 6 hours and 40 minutes)
  b Yes, because the total number of hours of work is fixed; if there are more workers, they will each work fewer hours so the total cost will be the same.

1 a 12 days

b i It is assumed they paint at the same rate.

ii If they paint slower, they will take longer. If they paint faster, they will take a shorter amount of time.

15 Constructions, loci and bearings

15.1 3D solids

Purposeful practice 1

1 a 6 **b** 12 **c** 8   **2 a** 6 **b** 12 **c** 8
3 a 6 **b** 12 **c** 8   **4 a** 6 **b** 12 **c** 8

Purposeful practice 2

1 a cone   **b** cylinder   **c** sphere

Purposeful practice 3

1 a Triangle and square   **b** 5
2 a i 8   **ii** 12   **iii** 18   **b i** 5   **ii** 7   **iii** 10

Problem-solving practice

1 An octagon

2 Each edge of a cube joins two squares together, so two edges from the squares produce only one edge of the cube. The answer is half of 24.

3 Evan is not correct. He has confused edges and vertices. There are 14 faces, 36 edges and 24 vertices.

Exam practice

1 a

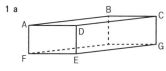

b 6

2 a 7 faces   **b** 12 edges

15.2 Plans and elevations

Purposeful practice 1

1

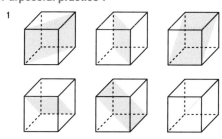

2 a 6 planes of symmetry.
b 5 planes of symmetry.
c 7 planes of symmetry.
d 6 planes of symmetry.

Purposeful practice 2

1 Students' answers may vary, for example
a A cuboid, a rectangular pyramid
b A triangular prism, a pentagonal prism

2 a

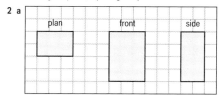

b

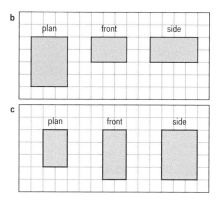

c

Problem-solving practice

1 a Triangular prism   Cuboid

b Side elevation of triangular prism   Side elevation of cuboid

2

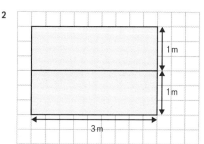

3 a   **b**

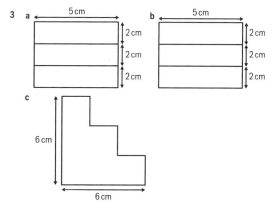

c

Exam practice

1

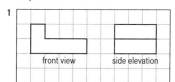

front view   side elevation

2

15.3 Accurate drawings 1
Purposeful practice 1

(These diagrams are not to scale.)

a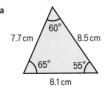
b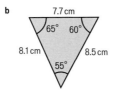

c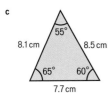

Purposeful practice 2

(These diagrams are not drawn to scale.)

1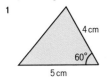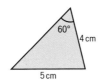

2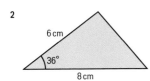

Purposeful practice 3

1 **A** and **C** are congruent (ASA); **B** and **E** are congruent (SAS).

Problem-solving practice

1 a Jamie is incorrect. **A** and **B** are congruent because of the ASA of 50°, 8 cm, 70°. C is not congruent to **A** and **B** because its sides are of different lengths.

2 Abbie has measured angle B instead of angle A. The angle at A is 106°.

3 a RHS   **b** 12 cm   **c** 5 cm   **d** 67.4°

Exam practice

(This diagram is not drawn to scale.)

1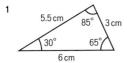

15.4 Scale drawings and maps
Purposeful practice 1

1 a Accurate drawing of a rectangle measuring 18 cm by 12 cm
  b Accurate drawing of a rectangle measuring 9 cm by 6 cm
  c Accurate drawing of a rectangle measuring 6 cm by 4 cm
  d Accurate drawing of a rectangle measuring 4.5 cm by 3 cm
  e Accurate drawing of a rectangle measuring 3 cm by 2 cm
  f Accurate drawing of a rectangle measuring 3.6 cm by 2.4 cm

Purposeful practice 2

1 a i 25 000   **ii** 250   **iii** 0.25   **iv** 4
  b i 2500   **ii** 1250   **iii** 500   **iv** 2000

c i 2.5   **ii** 1.25   **iii** 0.5   **iv** 2
d i 40 cm   **ii** 24 cm   **iii** 7 cm

Purposeful practice 3

1 a 1 cm × 2 cm   **b** 2 cm × 6 cm
  c 1.5 cm × 3 cm   **d** 2 cm × 2.5 cm
  e 1.5 cm × 1 cm

Problem-solving practice

1 a Town A to town B is 20 km; town C to town B is 25 km. So the total distance you travel is 45 km.
  b James is correct. 40 km would be represented by 12 cm on the map. You can quickly try the points that look furthest from town C and discover they are less than 12 cm away.

2 a 150 km = 600 cm; far too large for a printed map
  b 150 km = 150 cm; still too large for a printed map
  c 150 km = 30 cm; a good size for a printed map
  d 150 km = 1.5 cm; too small to be a useful map

3 a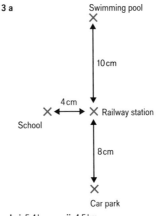

  b i 5.4 km   **ii** 4.5 km

Exam practice

1 7 cm
2 a 8 km

  b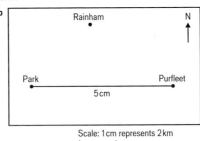

  Scale: 1 cm represents 2 km

15.5 Accurate drawings 2
Purposeful practice 1

1 a Diagram C shows the net of a cube.
  b Students' answers may vary. There are 11 possible nets of a cube.

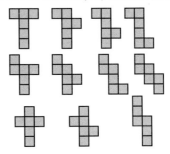

315

2 Students' own answers, with examples shown below. Measurements should be accurate with sides of length 3.5 cm and 5 cm.

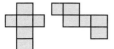

3 Students' own answers, with examples shown below. Measurements should be accurate with sides of length 3.5 cm and 5 cm.

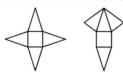

Purposeful practice 2

(These diagrams are not drawn to scale.)

1   **2**

3

Problem-solving practice

1 It is not possible to form a triangle with these side lengths. The third side of a triangle must be smaller than the total of the other two sides. If AB = 8.2 cm and BC = 7.2 cm then AC would have to be smaller than 15.4 cm.

2 30°

3 A scale of 1 cm to 1 m would be appropriate. (This diagram is not drawn to scale.)

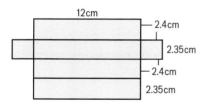

4 a The 8 cm rectangles should alternate between 2 cm and 4 cm tall. The squares on the sides should be rectangles 2 cm wide by 4 cm tall.

b (This diagram is not drawn to scale.)

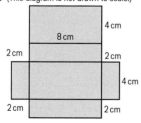

Exam practice

1 Students' diagrams will vary but should show accurate net, for example (diagram not drawn to scale):

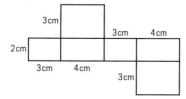

15.6 Constructions

Purposeful practice 1

(These diagrams are not drawn to scale.)

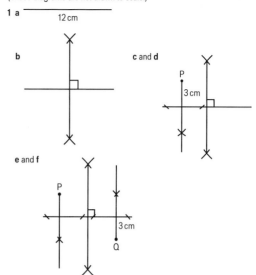

Purposeful practice 2

(This diagram is not drawn to scale.)

1 a and b

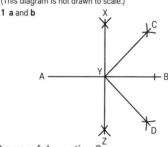

Purposeful practice 3

1 a and b Accurate scalene triangle with three acute angles and angle bisectors accurately constructed

2 a and b Accurate scalene triangle with one obtuse angle and angle bisectors accurately constructed

3 a and b Accurate scalene triangle with three acute angles and perpendicular bisectors accurately constructed

4 a and b Accurate scalene triangle with one obtuse angle and perpendicular bisectors accurately constructed

Problem-solving practice

1 Angle constructed correctly: extend the original line; draw a circle centred on the end of the line; use the diameter of the circle as a new line and construct the perpendicular bisector of this line.

2 Jenna is nearest to the bottom edge of the field. The distance is 75 m.

3 (This diagram is not drawn to scale.)

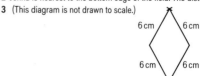

4 Angle constructed correctly (by constructing equilateral triangle, then bisecting one of the angles).

5 Circle with two chords marked. Accurate construction of perpendicular bisector for each chord. Centre of circle is point where perpendicular bisectors intersect.

Exam practice

1 Perpendicular bisector accurately constructed

2 (This diagram is not drawn to scale.)

15.7 Loci and regions

Purposeful practice 1

(These diagrams are not drawn to scale.)

1 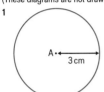 **2**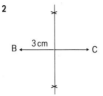

3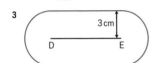

4 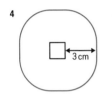 **5**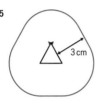

Purposeful practice 2

(These diagrams are not drawn to scale.)

1 **2**

3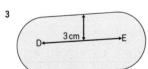

4 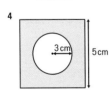 **5**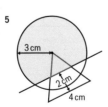

Problem-solving practice

(These diagrams are not drawn to scale.)

1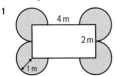

2 a Garden shown by rectangle ACIF.

b Patio shown by rectangle ABGF

c The tree may be planted in the shaded region between line EH and the curve.

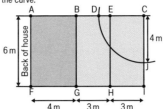

3 a The corners of the locus should be rounded so the outer line is always 2 cm from the rectangle.

b

Exam practice

(These diagrams are not drawn to scale.)

1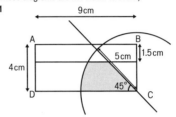

2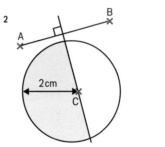

15.8 Bearings

Purposeful practice 1

1 B 025°	**C** 070°	**D** 115°	**E** 160°
F 205°	**G** 250°	**H** 295°	**I** 340°
2 a 220°	**b** 285°	**c** 330°	**d** 195°

Problem-solving practice

1 a and **b** (diagram not drawn to scale)

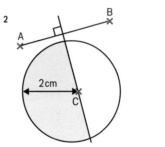

2 a Accurate scale diagram

b 12.8 miles

c 333°

3 a Accurate scale diagram

b Any answer between 252 and 253 km, at a bearing of 206°

Exam practice

1 a 0.6 km   **b** 110°   **c** 235°

2 1 The angle is 50° not 60°.

2 Bearings are always given using three figures, so even if the angle was 60°, the bearing would be written 060°.

16 Quadratic equations and graphs

16.1 Expanding double brackets

Purposeful practice 1

1 $x^2 + 8x + 7$ **2** $x^2 + 8x + 7$ **3** $z^2 - 5z + 6$
4 $z^2 - 5z + 6$ **5** $y^2 + 3y - 4$ **6** $y^2 + 3y - 4$

Purposeful practice 2

2 a 18   **b** $x^2 + 9x + 18$ **3 a** 12   **b** $x^2 + 8x + 12$
4 a 2   **b** $x^2 + 3x + 2$ **5 a** 20   **b** $x^2 + 12x + 20$
6 a −20   **b** $x^2 + 8x - 20$ **7 a** −6   **b** $x^2 + x - 6$
8 a −6   **b** $x^2 - x - 6$ **9 a** −10   **b** $x^2 - 3x - 10$
10 a 4   **b** $x^2 + 4x + 4$ **11 a** 9   **b** $x^2 + 6x + 9$
12 a 9   **b** $x^2 - 6x + 9$ **13 a** 16   **b** $x^2 - 8x + 16$

Purposeful practice 3

1 $x^2 - 1$ **2** $x^2 - 4$ **3** $x^2 - 9$ **4** $x^2 - 16$

Problem-solving practice

1 a A width must be positive, so for $x - 5$ to be more than 0, x must be greater than 5.
   b $x^2 - 25$
2 $x^2 + 8x + 15$
3 a 2   **b** 2   **c** 6   **d** 1   **e** 4
4 $(y - 1)(y + 4) = y^2 + 3y - 4$ and $(y + 1)(y - 4) = y^2 - 3y - 4$;
Rowan is wrong because the two expansions have different y terms.
5 Area = length × width
$$= (x + 2)(x - 3)$$
$$= x^2 + 2x - 3x - 6$$
$$= x^2 - x - 6$$
So the width must be $x - 3$
6 $6x + 8$ or $2(3x + 4)$
7 $a = 17$

Exam practice

1 $n^2 + 9n + 14$

16.2 Plotting quadratic graphs

Purposeful practice 1

1 a

x	−3	−2	−1	0	1	2	3
$y = x^2$	9	4	1	0	1	4	9
$y = x^2 + 1$	10	5	2	1	2	5	10
$y = x^2 - 2$	7	2	−1	−2	−1	2	7
$y = 2 + x^2$	11	6	3	2	3	6	11

b
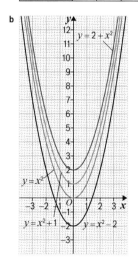

2 a

x	−3	−2	−1	0	1	2	3
$y = -x^2$	−9	−4	−1	0	−1	−4	−9
$y = -x^2 + 5$	−4	1	4	5	4	1	−4
$y = 4 - x^2$	−5	0	3	4	3	0	−5
$y = -x^2 - 1$	−10	−5	−2	−1	−2	−5	−10

b
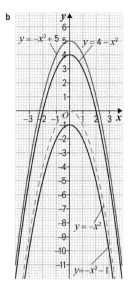

Purposeful practice 2

1 a

x	−3	−2	−1	0	1	2
x^2	9	4	1	0	1	4
$x^2 + x$	6	2	0	0	2	6

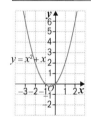

b

x	−4	−3	−2	−1	0	1	2
x^2	16	9	4	1	0	1	4
$2x$	−8	−6	−4	−2	0	2	4
$x^2 + 2x + 1$	9	4	1	0	1	4	9

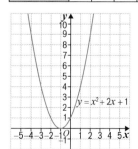

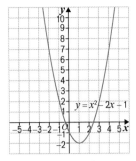

c

x	-2	-1	0	1	2	3	4
x^2	4	1	0	1	4	9	16
$-2x$	4	2	0	-2	-4	-6	-8
$x^2 - 2x - 1$	7	2	-1	-2	-1	2	7

$y = x^2 - 2x - 1$

Problem-solving practice

1 B and C

2 a

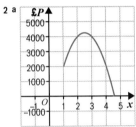

b Between £4100 and £4400 (exact answer is £4250).

3 a Graph is not symmetrical, and is not a parabola or a ∪-shaped curve. Pat has wrongly calculated $(-3)^2$ as -9, and so on.

b

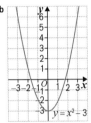

$y = x^2 - 3$

c $(0, -3)$ is a minimum.

Exam practice

1 Olivia has used straight lines between the points instead of drawing a smooth curve.

16.3 Using quadratic graphs

Purposeful practice 1

1 a $x = -2, x = -3$ **b** $x = 1$

Purposeful practice 2

1 a $x = 0.37, x = -5.37$ (accept answers between $x = 0.35$ and $x = 0.4$, $x = -5.35$ and $x = -5.4$)

b $x = -6, x = 1$

c $x = -4.56, x = -0.44$ (accept answers between $x = -4.5$ and $x = -4.6$, and between $x = -0.3$ and $x = -0.5$)

Problem-solving practice

1 a

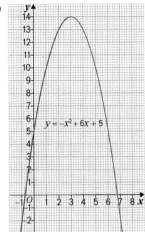

$y = -x^2 + 6x + 5$

b $x = -0.7, x = 6.7$ (approximately)

c Line at $y = 14$ only touches the graph at one point. Solution is $x = 3$

d $x = 0, x = 6$

2 a $x = 3.7$ (accept between 3.6 and 3.8) and $x = 0.3$ (accept between 0.2 and 0.4)

b $x = 2$ (repeated root)

c $x = 0$ and $x = 4$

Exam practice

1 a

x	-3	-2	-1	0	1	2	3
y	5	1	-1	-1	1	5	11

b

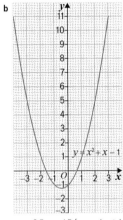

$y = x^2 + x - 1$

c $x = -2.5, x = 1.5$ (approximately)

16.4 Factorising quadratic expressions

Purposeful practice 1

1 $(x+1)(x+7)$ **2** $(x-1)(x+7)$ **3** $(x+1)(x-7)$
4 $(x-1)(x-7)$ **5** $(x+1)(x-5)$ **6** $(x+1)(x+5)$
7 $(x-1)(x+5)$ **8** $(x-1)(x-5)$

Purposeful practice 2

1 a $(x+1)(x+4)$ **b** $(x-1)(x-4)$ **c** $(x+2)(x+2)$
d $(x-2)(x-2)$ **e** $(x-1)(x+4)$ **f** $(x+1)(x-4)$

2 a $(x+1)(x-6)$ **b** $(x+1)(x+6)$ **c** $(x+2)(x+3)$
d $(x-2)(x+3)$ **e** $(x-1)(x+6)$ **f** $(x+2)(x-3)$
g $(x-1)(x-6)$ **h** $(x-2)(x-3)$

3 a $(x+3)(x-6)$ **b** $(x-2)(x+9)$ **c** $(x-3)(x-6)$
d $(x+1)(x+18)$ **e** $(x+2)(x+9)$ **f** $(x+2)(x-9)$
g $(x-1)(x+18)$ **h** $(x+3)(x+6)$ **i** $(x-2)(x-9)$
j $(x+1)(x-18)$ **k** $(x-3)(x+6)$ **l** $(x-1)(x-18)$

Problem-solving practice

1 The two answers are equivalent, as the order of two brackets multiplied together is not important. Alternatively, students may give working to show both Ben and Jill's answers expand to the original quadratic expression.

2 a $(x-3)(x+5)$

   b Desi has taken the x out of the first two terms as a common factor, but has not factorised all three terms in the expression.

3 a $(x-3)$ and $(x-5)$

   b $(x-7)$ and $(x-5)$

   c $(x-7)$ and $(x-4)$

4 Students' answers may vary,

   a of form $x^2 \pm a$ **b** of form $x^2 - a^2$

5 a $(x+2)(x-6) = x^2 - 4x - 12$

   b $(x-3)(x+7) = x^2 + 4x - 21$

   c $(x-5)(x-1) = x^2 - 6x + 5$

Exam practice

1 $(x-3)(x-3)$

2 $(x+3)(x+2)$

16.5 Solving quadratic equations algebraically

Purposeful practice 1

1 $x = 7, x = -7$ **2** $x = 7, x = -7$ **3** $x = 7, x = -7$

4 $x = 8, x = -8$ **5** $x = 8, x = -8$ **6** $x = 8, x = -8$

Purposeful practice 2

1 a 0   **b** 0   **c** 0   **d** 0

   e 0   **f** 0   **g** 0   **h** 0

2 a One of a or b or both are zero.

   b One of a or $(x-3)$ or both are zero.

   c One of $(x+4)$ or $(x-3)$ is zero.

3 a $x = 0$ **b** $x = 5$ **c** $x = -3$

   d $x = 5$ **e** $x = 0, x = 5$ **f** $x = 0, x = -3$

   g $x = -3, x = 5$ **h** $x = -3, x = 3$

Purposeful practice 3

1 a $x = -4, x = -3$ **b** $x = 4, x = -3$ **c** $x = 4, x = 3$

   d $x = 4, x = 3$ **e** $x = -4, x = 6$ **f** $x = 4, x = -6$

   g $x = 4, x = 6$ **h** $x = -4, x = -6$ **i** $x = 3, x = 5$

   j $x = 3, x = -5$ **k** $x = -3, x = -5$ **l** $x = -3, x = 5$

2 a $x = -2, x = -2$ **b** $x = 2, x = 2$ **c** $x = 3, x = 3$

   d $x = -3, x = -3$ **e** $x = -1, x = -1$ **f** $x = 5, x = 5$

   g $x = -7, x = -7$ **h** $x = 10, x = 10$

Problem-solving practice

1 Every quadratic equation has two solutions. The square root of any number has a positive and negative value, as the product of two negative numbers is positive.

2 a $x(x+3)$ **b** $x = 0, x = -3$ **c** $x = -1, x = -2$

3 a $x^2 - 16 = 0$ or $x^2 = 16$

   b $x^2 + 17x + 72 = 0$

   c $x^2 + 10x + 25 = 0$

   d $x(x+7) = 0$ or $x^2 + 7x = 0$

4 a Either substitute $x = -2$ into $x^2 - 3x - 10$ to show it gives zero or factorise to find both solutions and show that one is $x = -2$

   b $x = 5$

5 a $x = -13, x = 13$

   b $x = -19, x = 19$

   c $x = -25, x = 25$

6 $x = -15, x = -15$

7 Solutions are $x = -2$ and $x = 4$. Positive solution is $x = 4$

8 $x = 10$

9

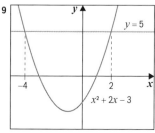

The x-coordinates are 2 and −4.

Exam practice

1 a $x = 4, x = -9$ **b** $x = 4, x = 8$

Mixed exercises D

Mixed problem-solving practice D

1 a

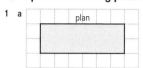

   b 60 cm³

2 $\dfrac{1}{16}$

3 a 0.29   **b** 116   **c** 156

4 a

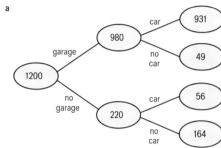

   b $\dfrac{56}{220}$ or $\dfrac{14}{55}$

5 PQ on the map is 3.7 cm. 3.7×100 km $= 370$ km, so the distance between the ports in real life is 370 km. $370 \div 40 = 9.25$, so the journey will take $9\frac{1}{4}$ hours or 9 hours and 15 minutes.

6 Accurate drawing of net. See example below (not drawn to scale).

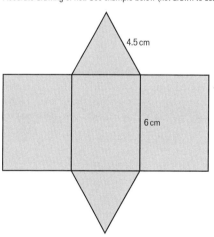

7 (This diagram is not drawn to scale.)

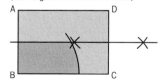

8 $x^2 + 6x + 9$

9 a $-3, -4, 0, 5$

b

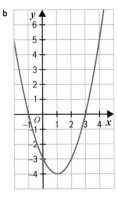

c −0.7 and 2.7 (approximately)

10 The branches for the first spin total 0.9, not 1, P(not red) should be 0.45
The 0.45 and 0.55 on the first two branches of the second spin are the wrong way around.

11 $p = 17.5$

Exam practice

12 Jenny has joined the points with straight lines instead of a smooth curve.

13 360 m   **14** 48   **15** £9

16 Bank A, as Bank A gives £2048.43 interest and Bank B gives £2040.28 interest

17 $x = 3$

17 Perimeter, area and volume 2

17.1 Circumference of a circle 1

Purposeful practice 1

1 a 37.68 cm   **b** 37.68 m   **c** 75.36 cm
d 75.36 cm   **e** 15.70 m   **f** 15.70 m
g 1.57 m   **h** 1.57 m   **i** 157.00 cm
2 a 37.70 cm   **b** 37.70 m   **c** 75.40 cm
d 75.40 cm   **e** 15.71 m   **f** 15.71 m
g 1.57 m   **h** 1.57 m   **i** 157.08 cm

Purposeful practice 2

1 6.28 cm   **2** 12.57 cm   **3** 25.13 cm
4 125.66 cm   **5** 29.53 m   **6** 20.14 km

Problem-solving practice

1 7.96 cm
2 Kasia needs to type $2\pi \times 6$; she has missed out the multiplication sign.
3 9.42 m   **4** 433 complete revolutions

Exam practice

1 31.42 (to 2 d.p.)

17.2 Circumference of a circle 2

Purposeful practice 1

1 a $3495 \leqslant 3500 < 3505$ **b** $3499.5 \leqslant 3500 < 3500.5$
c $349\,500 \leqslant 350\,000 < 350\,500$ **d** $349\,950 \leqslant 350\,000 < 350\,050$
e $349\,995 \leqslant 350\,000 < 350\,005$ **f** $349\,999.5 \leqslant 350\,000 < 350\,000.5$
2 Answers should be given to 2 decimal places. You should use the same level of accuracy in your answers as in the information in the question.

Purposeful practice 2

1 a 2000   **b** 2400   **c** 2400
d 2396   **e** 2396.3   **f** 2396.35
g 2396.3   **h** 2396.35   **i** 2396.346
2 a $2500 \leqslant 3000 < 3500$ **b** $3495 \leqslant 3500 < 3505$
c $34.5 \leqslant 35 < 35.5$ **d** $3.45 \leqslant 3.5 < 3.55$
e $0.345 \leqslant 0.35 < 0.355$
3 a Rounded to the nearest 1000
b Rounded to the nearest 10
c Rounded to the nearest unit
d Rounded to the nearest tenth
e Rounded to the nearest hundredth

Problem-solving practice

1 a 810   **b** 14 000   **c** 8565
d 182 125   **e** 24 097 500   **f** 11.8125
2 79.3 m
3 a 6650 km ⩽ radius < 6750 km   **b** 42 000 km
4 6500 km   **5** 9.95 m or 995 cm
6 a 0.75 m ⩽ side length < 0.85 m   **b** 0.421875 m³   **c** 3.375 m²

Exam practice

1 a £17 500   **b** £18 499.99

17.3 Area of a circle

Purposeful practice

1 a 28.27 cm²   **b** 113.10 cm²   **c** 113.10 cm²
d 0.09 km²   **e** 2.54 m²   **f** 0.64 m²
2 a 256π cm²   **b** 0.64π m²   **c** $\frac{1}{36}\pi$ m²   **d** $\frac{1}{144}\pi$ m²
3 a 3.99 cm   **b** 5.64 cm   **c** 7.98 cm   **d** 0.89 m
4 a 3 cm   **b** 9 cm   **c** 2.5 m   **d** $\frac{1}{4}$ km

Problem-solving practice

1 25 cm   **2** 3.39 m   **3** 18.75π cm²
4 Hoorain should have worked out the area of each circle separately, then subtracted the smaller area from the larger area. This would give 36π cm².

Exam practice

1 Area = 36π m² ≈ 113 m². 113 ÷ 23 ≈ 4.9, so Jo must buy 5 boxes.

17.4 Semicircles and sectors

Purposeful practice 1

1 $\frac{1}{8}$ **2** $\frac{3}{8}$ **3** $\frac{5}{8}$ **4** $\frac{8}{9}$ **5** $\frac{7}{9}$ **6** $\frac{5}{9}$

Purposeful practice 2

1 a 4.36 cm²   **b** 1.75 cm
2 a 8.73 cm²   **b** 3.49 cm
3 a 34.9 cm²   **b** 6.98 cm
4 a 56.5 m²   **b** 18.8 m
5 a 339 mm²   **b** 56.5 mm
6 a 0.885 m²   **b** 1.36 m
7 a 3.54 m²   **b** 2.72 m
8 a 1.77 m²   **b** 2.72 m

Problem-solving practice

1 36.54 cm   **2** 8.02 m
3 a 3180 cm²   **b** 411 cm
c Work out the area of the whole circle and divide by 2.
4 a 110 cm   **b** 6.54 cm
5 0.691 m²

Exam practice

1 8.02 cm²

17.5 Composite 2D shapes and cylinders

Purposeful practice 1

1 2260 cm³   **2** 9050 cm³   **3** 18 100 cm³
4 0.339 m³   **5** 1.36 m³   **6** 2.71 m³

Purposeful practice 2

1 4.08 m²   **2** 0.589 m²   **3** 4.52 m²

Purposeful practice 3

1 942 cm²   **2** 4360 cm²   **3** 12 700 cm² or 1.27 m²   **4** 1.75 m²

Problem-solving practice

1 11 300 m²   **2** 6706 cm²   **3** 392 cm²   **4** 7540 m²   **5** 5 tins

Exam practice

1 339 cm³ (to nearest whole cm³)

17.6 Pyramids and cones

Purposeful practice 1

1 $18\,000\,\text{cm}^3$ or $0.018\,\text{m}^3$ 2 $128\,000\,\text{cm}^3$ or $0.128\,\text{m}^3$

3 $1.5\,\text{m}^3$ 4 $120\,000\,\text{cm}^3$ or $0.12\,\text{m}^3$

Purposeful practice 2

1 $20\,900\,\text{cm}^3$ 2 $83\,800\,\text{cm}^3$ 3 $41\,900\,\text{cm}^3$

4 $168\,000\,\text{cm}^3$

Purposeful practice 3

1 $0.146\pi\,\text{m}^2$ 2 $0.15\pi\,\text{m}^2$ 3 $65\pi\,\text{m}^2$

Problem-solving practice

1 $260\,\text{cm}^2$ 2 a $1395\,\text{cm}^2$ b £20.92   3 $6\frac{2}{3}\,\text{cm}^3$

Exam practice

1 A has the greater volume.
Volume of A = $30.8\,\text{cm}^3$.
Volume of B = $29.3\,\text{cm}^3$.

17.7 Spheres and composite solids

Purposeful practice 1

1 a $36\pi\,\text{cm}^3$ b $36\pi\,\text{cm}^2$

2 a $288\pi\,\text{cm}^3$ b $144\pi\,\text{cm}^2$

3 a $972\pi\,\text{cm}^3$ b $324\pi\,\text{cm}^2$

4 a $2304\pi\,\text{cm}^3$ b $576\pi\,\text{cm}^2$

Purposeful practice 2

1 a $1436.76\,\text{cm}^3$ b $615.75\,\text{cm}^2$

2 a $7696.90\,\text{cm}^3$ b $2507.00\,\text{cm}^2$

3 a $9133.66\,\text{cm}^3$ b $2814.87\,\text{cm}^2$

4 a $2565.63\,\text{cm}^3$ b $1264.22\,\text{cm}^2$

Problem-solving practice

1 a $24\,200\,\text{cm}^3$ b $5660\,\text{cm}^2$

2 $3811\,\text{cm}^3$ 3 $1767\,\text{cm}^3$

4 a $244\,\text{cm}^3$ b $214\,\text{cm}^2$

Exam practice

1 $603.2\,\text{cm}^2$

18 Fractions, indices and standard form

18.1 Multiplying and dividing fractions

Purposeful practice 1

1 a $\frac{21}{4}$ b $\frac{16}{3}$ c $\frac{10}{3}$ d $\frac{11}{3}$

2

×	$3\frac{2}{3}$	$5\frac{1}{4}$
$3\frac{2}{3}$	$\frac{121}{9}=13\frac{4}{9}$	$\frac{231}{12}=19\frac{1}{4}$
$5\frac{1}{4}$	$\frac{231}{12}=19\frac{1}{4}$	$\frac{441}{16}=27\frac{9}{16}$

Purposeful practice 2

1 a $\frac{1}{4}$ b $\frac{1}{4}$ c 4   d 4

2 a 9   b 6   c 16   d 10

3 a $3\frac{1}{3}$ b $3\frac{7}{9}$ c $9\frac{9}{35}$ d $1\frac{11}{24}$

4

÷	$3\frac{2}{3}$	$5\frac{1}{4}$
$3\frac{2}{3}$	1	$\frac{44}{63}$
$5\frac{1}{4}$	$1\frac{19}{44}$	1

Problem-solving practice

1 $18\frac{2}{15}$ 2 a 3   b 5   c 7   d 11

3 $4\frac{3}{5}\,\text{cm}$ 4 a $\frac{2}{5}$ b $\frac{2}{7}$ c $\frac{2}{13}$

5 a 40 Egyptian pounds   b $\frac{27}{4}=6\frac{3}{4}$ pounds

Exam practice

1 Students' reasoning may vary, for example, Tim has calculated
2×6 and $\frac{3}{7}\times\frac{1}{2}$ but has forgotten to calculate $\frac{3}{7}\times 6$ and $2\times\frac{1}{2}$.

18.2 The laws of indices

Purposeful practice 1

1 a 2^6 b 2^6 c 2^0 d 2^{15} e 2^{15} f 2^0

   g 2^0 h 2^{12} i 2^{4a} j 2^0 k 2^{10a} l 2^{10a}

2 a 2^{10} b 2^4 c 2^6 d 2^8 e 2^0 f 2^3

   g 2^6 h 2^9

Purposeful practice 2

1 $\frac{1}{3}$ 2 $\frac{1}{5}$ 3 3   4 5   5 $\frac{5}{2}$ 6 $\frac{1}{9}$

7 $\frac{1}{16}$ 8 $\frac{1}{25}$ 9 9   10 25   11 $\frac{25}{4}$ 12 $\frac{125}{8}$

Purposeful practice 3

1 a 1 b 1   2 a $\frac{1}{8}$ b $\frac{1}{8}$ 3 a $\frac{1}{9}$ b $\frac{1}{9}$

Purposeful practice 4

1 m^3 2 m^6 3 m^0 4 m^4 5 m^4

6 m^4 7 m^4 8 m^{10} 9 m^{-4}

Problem-solving practice

1 a Tina has calculated the reciprocals of the whole number and the fraction parts of the mixed number separately and then added these reciprocals together.

   b $\frac{2}{9}$

2 a 2^3 b 2^{-3} c 2^5 d 2^{-5} e 2^{15} f 2^{-15}

3 3^8

4 a −3   b 2   c 9   d 0

5 a $y=6$ b $y=-1$ c $y=10$ d $y=4$

Exam practice

1 a $\frac{1}{9}$ b 1

18.3 Writing large numbers in standard form

Purposeful practice 1

1 a 5.2×10^1 b 5.2×10^2 c 5.2×10^3

   d 5.2×10^4 e 5.2×10^7

2 a 1.01×10^2 b 1.1×10^2 c 1.01×10^4

   d 1.1×10^3 e 1.001×10^5 f 1.001×10^3

Purposeful practice 2

1 a 3010   b 3 010 000   c 301   d 30 100   e 30.1

2 a 2050   b 2500   c 2005

   d 5 210 000   e 5 020 100   f 5 021 000

Purposeful practice 3

1 507, 570, 5007, 5070, 5700

2 5.07×10^2, 5.7×10^2, 5.007×10^3, 5.07×10^3, 5.7×10^3

Problem-solving practice

1

Country	Poupulation
Canada	$3.628\,64\times 10^7$
India	1.339×10^9
Thailand	6.7959×10^7
Monaco	3.84×10^4

2 a 2900 kg   **b** 3400 kg   **c** 4300 kg
    d 82 000 kg   **e** 25 000 kg
3 a 5×10^6 **b** 4.8×10^8 **c** 2.5×10^4
    d 2.5×10^5 **e** 3.2×10^9
4 a 3×10^{14} **b** 3×10^{16} **c** 4×10^{10} **d** 6.5×10^7
5 a 1.64×10^4 kg   **b** 5.1×10^5 kg   **c** 7.48×10^4 kg
    d 8.36×10^1 kg   **e** 4.725×10^3 kg
6 2.5×10^7, 250 000, 2.5×10^4, 2.5×10^3, 250

Exam practice

1 a 25 630   **b** 8093
2 a 4.3×10^7 **b** 4.0506×10^4

18.4 Writing small numbers in standard form

Purposeful practice 1

1 a 5.2×10^{-1} **b** 5.2×10^{-2} **c** 5.2×10^{-4} **d** 5.2×10^{-7}
2 a 1.025×10^{-3} **b** 1.025×10^{-4} **c** 9.52×10^{-2} **d** 9.52×10^{-1}
3 a 4.04×10^{-3} **b** 4.4×10^{-4} **c** 4.04×10^{-1} **d** 4.4×10^{-1}

Purposeful practice 2

1 a 0.0035   **b** 0.35   **c** 0.000 000 35   **d** 0.035
    e 0.0109   **f** 0.109   **g** 0.000 000 2508   **h** 0.02508
    i 0.0103   **j** 0.13   **k** 0.000 000 1003   **l** 0.01003
2 As an ordinary number: 0.00031, 0.0031, 0.000 301, 0.0032
    In order (smallest first): 0.00031, 0.000 301, 0.0031, 0.0032
3 As an ordinary number: 0.651, 0.006 15, 0.0651, 0.006 14
    In order (largest first): 0.651, 0.0651, 0.006 15, 0.006 14
4 In standard form: 1.02×10^{-4}, 1.2×10^{-5}, 1.002×10^{-4}, 1.2×10^{-4}
    In order (smallest first): 1.2×10^{-5}, 1.002×10^{-4}, 1.02×10^{-4}, 1.2×10^{-4}
5 In standard form: 7.008×10^{-4}, 7.8×10^{-5}, 7.08×10^{-4}, 7.8×10^{-4}
    In order (largest first): 7.8×10^{-4}, 7.08×10^{-4}, 7.008×10^{-4}, 7.8×10^{-5}

Problem-solving practice

1 a 2.5×10^0 litres   **b** 5.0×10^{-1} litres   **c** 1.2×10^1 litres
    d 3.5×10^{-1} litres   **e** 1.5×10^{-2} litres
2 Students could correct either side of the equals sign.
    a $500 = 5 \times 10^2$ or $0.05 = 5 \times 10^{-2}$
    b $0.0021 = 2.1 \times 10^{-3}$ or $0.002\,01 = 2.01 \times 10^{-3}$
    c $0.000\,02 = 2 \times 10^{-5}$ or $0.05 = 5 \times 10^{-2}$
    d Robyn is already correct.
    e $0.000\,012 = 1.2 \times 10^{-5}$ or $0.001\,024 = 1.024 \times 10^{-3}$
3 a 4×10^{-6} **b** 1.5×10^{-4} **c** 6.5×10^{-5}
    d 4.1×10^{-4} **e** 7.6×10^{-4} **f** 2.3×10^{-9}
4 a James: The power should be -4 not 4.
    Hannah: The initial number should be 4.06 not 4.6.
    Katy: The initial number 40.6 in standard form should be between 1 and 10 so should be 4.06 and so the power needs to be -4.
    b 4.06×10^{-4}

Exam practice

1 a 0.017   **b** 0.007 34
2 a 2.5×10^{-2} **b** 5×10^{-1}

18.5 Calculating with standard form

Purposeful practice 1

1 a and **b** are both 7×10^5 **c** and **d** are both 7×10^3
2 All answers are 9.8×10^5

Purposeful practice 2

Answers to **Q1–3** are the same:
1 1.6×10^{12} **2** 1.6×10^{12} **3** 1.6×10^{12}

Purposeful practice 3

1 a 3×10^{-2} **b** 3×10^{-2} **c** 3×10^2
    d 3×10^2 **e** 1.2×10^3
2 a 4×10^1 **b** 4×10^2 **c** 4×10^{-2} **d** 4×10^{-2}
    e 4×10^{-2} **f** 4×10^{-2}
3 a 1600   **b** 16 000   **c** 160

Problem-solving practice

1 a Alpha Centauri is 3.78×10^{13} km away
    b Procyon is 1.026×10^{14} km away
2 a 2.3×10^{-10} kg   **b** 1.15×10^{-13} kg
3 3.01×10^{25}

4 a 3×10^{-2} m^3 **b** $400 = 4 \times 10^2$
5 Students' working may vary, for example,
    a time for light to reach Earth from the Sun $= (1.496 \times 10^{11}) \div (3 \times 10^8)$
    $\approx 0.5 \times 10^3 = 500$ seconds
    500 seconds $= (500 \div 60)$ minutes ≈ 8.3 minutes.
    So, light takes about 8 minutes to reach Earth from the Sun.
    b The distance from the Moon to Earth is about $\dfrac{1}{400}$ of the distance from the Sun to Earth, so the time light takes to travel from the Moon to Earth $\approx 500 \div 400$ seconds ≈ 1.25 seconds

Exam practice

1 8×10^{-2} **2** 7.452×10^{-3} **3** 3.7×10^4

19 Congruence, similarity and vectors

19.1 Similarity and enlargement

Purposeful practice 1

1 Set 1 a $1 : 2, 2$ **b** $1 : 4, 4$ **c** $2 : 1, \dfrac{1}{2}$ **d** $4 : 1, \dfrac{1}{4}$

    Set 2 a $1 : 2, 2$ **b** $1 : 4, 4$ **c** $2 : 1, \dfrac{1}{2}$ **d** $4 : 1, \dfrac{1}{4}$

Purposeful practice 2

1 Corresponding angles: angle BAC and angle EFD, angle ABC and angle FDE, angle ACB and angle FED
    Corresponding sides: AB and FD, AC and FE, BC and DE
2 Corresponding angles: angle PMN and angle QTR, angle MNP and angle TRQ, angle MPN and angle TQR
    Corresponding sides: MP and TQ, NP and RQ, MN and TR
3 Corresponding angles: angle VUW and angle XZY, angle UWV and angle ZYX, angle UVW and angle ZXY
    Corresponding sides: UV and ZX, UW and ZY, VW and XY

Problem-solving practice

1 A and C are similar rectangles because they have corresponding sides in a ratio of $2 : 3 \left(\dfrac{2}{3}\right)$

2 B and D are similar triangles because they have corresponding angles and sides in a ratio of $1 : 3 \left(\dfrac{1}{3}\right)$
    A and D are also similar triangles because they have corresponding angles and sides in a ratio of $2 : 3 \left(\dfrac{2}{3}\right)$

3 Q1 ratio of corresponding sides is $2 : 3 \left(\dfrac{2}{3}\right)$
    Q2 ratio of corresponding sides is $1 : 3 \left(\dfrac{1}{3}\right)$

Exam practice

1 All sides correspond in a ratio of $9 : 2 \left(\dfrac{9}{2}\right)$

19.2 More similarity

Purposeful practice 1

1 Scale factor = 2, $a = 6$ cm   **2** Scale factor = 2, $b = 4$ cm
3 Scale factor = 1.5, $c = 7.5$ cm   **4** Scale factor = 0.5, $d = 4.5$ cm
5 Scale factor = 0.4, $e = 1.6$ cm

Purposeful practice 2

1 angle CED   **2** angle CDE   **3** angle ECD
4 CE   **5** CD   **6** DE
7 a 2   **b** 2   **c** 2   **8** 2

Problem-solving practice

1 6 cm   **2** 1 cm

Exam practice

1 a 2.88 cm   **b** 9.5 cm

19.3 Using similarity

Purposeful practice 1

1 Yes   **2** No   **3** No   **4** Yes
5 No   **6** Yes   **7** Yes

Purposeful practice 2

1 $1:3\left(\dfrac{1}{3}\right)$ **2** 48 mm   **3** 144 mm   **4** $1:3\left(\dfrac{1}{3}\right)$

Problem-solving practice

1 a 24 cm   **b** 24 cm   **c** 40.5 cm
2 33 cm   **3** 48 cm   **4** 80 cm

Exam practice

1 a 15.5 cm   **b** 4.6 cm

19.4 Congruence 1

Purposeful practice

1 a SAS   **b** RHS   **c** ASA
2 Yes. BC = DE, AC = FE, AB = FD
3 A and C

Problem-solving practice

1 Yes, by RHS. XY = XZ. Angle XMY = angle XMZ = 90°, XM shared.

2 $x = 30°$, $y = 55°$

3 $x = 40°$. Students' working may vary, for example, the two triangles are congruent (SSS), so the two unmarked angles in the bottom triangle are 120° and 20°. Angles in a triangle add up to 180°, so $x = 180° - 120° - 20° = 40°$

Exam practice

1 a 3 cm   **b i** 30°   **ii** 80°

19.5 Congruence 2

Purposeful practice

1 a

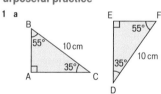

   i Angles are 90°, 35° and 55°.
   ii AB = EF, AC = ED, BC = FD

b

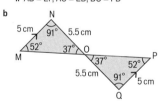

   i Angle MNO = 91°, angle QPO = 52°
   ii MN = PQ, NO = QO, MO = PO

2 a AB = ZY, BC = YX, angle ABC = angle ZYX, congruent by SAS

   b PR = MN, PQ = MO, angle PQR = angle MON = 90°, congruent by RHS

   c GI = LK, angle HGI = angle JLK, angle GIH = angle LKJ, congruent by ASA

Problem-solving practice

1 Students' own answers, for example, BD is a common side, AD = CB (opposite sides in a rectangle are equal), angle BAD = angle BCD = 90° (angles in a rectangle are 90° degrees), so triangles are congruent by RHS.

2 Students' own answers, for example, FH is a common side, EF = GH (opposite sides in a parallelogram are equal), FG = HE (opposite sides in a parallelogram are equal), so triangles are congruent by SSS.

3 a Students' own answers, for example, XW = ZY (given), angle WXV = angle YZV (alternate angles are equal), angle XWV = angle ZYV (alternate angles are equal), so triangles are congruent by ASA.

   b 6 cm   **c** 5 cm

Exam practice

1 Angle BAC = 50° because it is an isosceles triangle.
Angle ACB = 80° because angles in a triangle sum to 180°.
Side PQ is 3 cm because it is an isosceles triangle.
SAS: triangles must be congruent.

19.6 Vectors 1

Purposeful practice 1

1 $\begin{pmatrix} 3 \\ 2 \end{pmatrix}$ **2** $\begin{pmatrix} -2 \\ 3 \end{pmatrix}$ **3** $\begin{pmatrix} -2 \\ -3 \end{pmatrix}$ **4** $\begin{pmatrix} 2 \\ -3 \end{pmatrix}$ **5** $\begin{pmatrix} -3 \\ 2 \end{pmatrix}$

Purposeful practice 2

1 a $\begin{pmatrix} 3 \\ 8 \end{pmatrix}$ **b** $\begin{pmatrix} -1 \\ -2 \end{pmatrix}$ **c** $\begin{pmatrix} 1 \\ 2 \end{pmatrix}$ **d** $\begin{pmatrix} 3 \\ -8 \end{pmatrix}$ **e** $\begin{pmatrix} -3 \\ 8 \end{pmatrix}$ **f** $\begin{pmatrix} -3 \\ -8 \end{pmatrix}$

2 a $\overrightarrow{AC}$ **b** $\overrightarrow{AB}$ **c** $\overrightarrow{BD}$ **d** $\overrightarrow{OE}$ **e** $\overrightarrow{XZ}$ **f** $\overrightarrow{OY}$

Problem-solving practice

1 a $\begin{pmatrix} 4 \\ 1 \end{pmatrix}$ **b** $\begin{pmatrix} -1 \\ 6 \end{pmatrix}$ **c** $\begin{pmatrix} 3 \\ 2 \end{pmatrix}$ **d** $\begin{pmatrix} 4 \\ 4 \end{pmatrix}$

2 a $x = 5$ **b** $x = 2, y = 7$
   c $x = 4, y = -9$ **d** $x = 5, y = 14$

3 $\begin{pmatrix} 2m+1 \\ 3n+8 \end{pmatrix}$ **4** $\overrightarrow{AB} = \begin{pmatrix} -7 \\ -9 \end{pmatrix}$ **5** $x = 4, y = -1$

Exam practice

1 $\begin{pmatrix} 9 \\ 5 \end{pmatrix}$

19.7 Vectors 2

Purposeful practice 1

1 $\begin{pmatrix} 1 \\ 5 \end{pmatrix}$ **2** $\begin{pmatrix} 2 \\ 4 \end{pmatrix}$ **3** $\begin{pmatrix} -1 \\ -5 \end{pmatrix}$ **4** $\begin{pmatrix} -2 \\ -4 \end{pmatrix}$ **5** $\begin{pmatrix} 10 \\ 2 \end{pmatrix}$

6 $\begin{pmatrix} -4 \\ -2 \end{pmatrix}$ **7** $\begin{pmatrix} 1 \\ -4 \end{pmatrix}$ **8** $\begin{pmatrix} -1 \\ 4 \end{pmatrix}$ **9** $\begin{pmatrix} -1 \\ 4 \end{pmatrix}$

Purposeful practice 2

1 a $\begin{pmatrix} -6 \\ 10 \end{pmatrix}$ **b** $\begin{pmatrix} -9 \\ 15 \end{pmatrix}$ **c** $\begin{pmatrix} 3 \\ -5 \end{pmatrix}$ **d** $\begin{pmatrix} -4 \\ 1 \end{pmatrix}$

   e $\begin{pmatrix} -8 \\ 2 \end{pmatrix}$ **f** $\begin{pmatrix} -16 \\ 4 \end{pmatrix}$

2 a $\begin{pmatrix} -3 \\ 2 \end{pmatrix}$ **b** $\begin{pmatrix} 1 \\ -4 \end{pmatrix}$ **c** $\begin{pmatrix} 6 \\ -4 \end{pmatrix}$ **d** $\begin{pmatrix} -2 \\ 8 \end{pmatrix}$

   e $\begin{pmatrix} 5 \\ 0 \end{pmatrix}$ **f** $\begin{pmatrix} 11 \\ -14 \end{pmatrix}$

3 a $\begin{pmatrix} 8 \\ 12 \end{pmatrix}$ **b** $\begin{pmatrix} 16 \\ 24 \end{pmatrix}$ **c** $\begin{pmatrix} -12 \\ -18 \end{pmatrix}$ **d** $\begin{pmatrix} 2 \\ -3 \end{pmatrix}$

Problem-solving practice

1

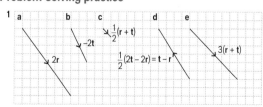

2 a $x = 3, y = 2$ **b** $y = 4$
3 $x = 8, y = 5$
4 $x = -2, y = 2$
5 $p = 4, q = 1$

Exam practice

1 $\begin{pmatrix} 9 \\ -2 \end{pmatrix}$

20 More algebra

20.1 Graphs of cubic and reciprocal functions

Purposeful practice 1

1 a $y = x^3 + 1$

x	–3	–2	–1	0	1	2	3
$x^3 + 1$	–26	–7	0	1	2	9	28

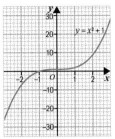

b $y = x^3 - x + 1$

x	–3	–2	–1	0	1	2	3
$x^3 - x + 1$	–23	–5	1	1	1	7	25

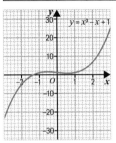

c $y = x^3 + x^2 - x + 1$

x	–3	–2	–1	0	1	2	3
$x^3 + x^2 - x + 1$	–14	–1	2	1	2	11	34

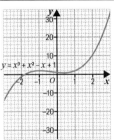

d $y = x^3 + x^2 - x - 1$

x	–3	–2	–1	0	1	2	3
$x^3 + x^2 - x - 1$	–16	–3	0	–1	0	9	32

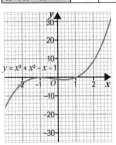

e $y = -x^3 + 1$

x	–3	–2	–1	0	1	2	3
$-x^3 + 1$	28	9	2	1	0	–7	–26

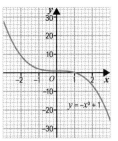

f $y = -x^3 + 2x + 1$

x	–3	–2	–1	0	1	2	3
$-x^3 + 2x + 1$	22	5	0	1	2	–3	–20

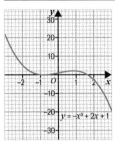

g $y = -x^3 - x^2 + 2x + 1$

x	–3	–2	–1	0	1	2	3
$-x^3 - x^2 + 2x + 1$	13	1	–1	1	1	–7	–29

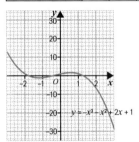

h $y = -x^3 - x^2 + 2x - 3$

x	–3	–2	–1	0	1	2	3
$-x^3 - x^2 + 2x - 3$	9	–3	–5	–3	–3	–11	–33

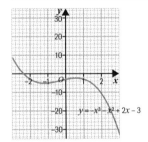

Purposeful practice 2

1 a $y = \dfrac{2}{x}$

x	0.25	0.5	1	2	4	5	10
$y = \dfrac{2}{x}$	8	4	2	1	0.5	0.4	0.2

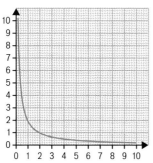

b $y = \dfrac{3}{x}$

x	0.5	1	2	3	4	5	10
$y = \dfrac{3}{x}$	6	3	1.5	1	0.75	0.6	0.3

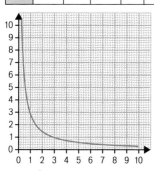

c $y = \dfrac{4}{x}$

x	0.5	1	2	4	5	8	10
$y = \dfrac{4}{x}$	8	4	2	1	0.8	0.5	0.4

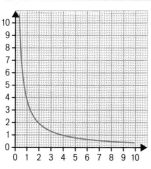

Problem-solving practice

1 a Graph ii shows $y = \dfrac{5}{x}$ **b** Graph i shows $y = \dfrac{8}{x}$

2 a Graph iii   **b** Graph iv   **c** Graph i   **d** Graph ii

Exam practice

1 a

x	0.5	1	1.5	2	3	4	5	6
y	**6**	3	**2**	1.5	1	0.75	**0.6**	**0.5**

b

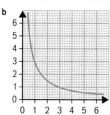

20.2 Non-linear graphs

Purposeful practice 1

1 a 100 ants   **b** 200 ants   **c** Month 5

2 a 100°C   **b** 22°C   **c** 3 minutes and 48 seconds   **d** 56°C

3 a Initial/starting height is 40 cm.   **b** Initial distance is 40 km.

    c Initial balance/amount saved is £40.   **d** Initial temperature is 40°C.

Problem-solving practice

1 a Approximately $3\frac{1}{4}$ hours   **b** 60

2 a 3.6 kg   **b** Week 6 and week 7

3 31 m

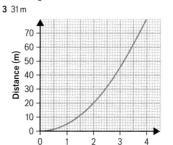

Exam practice

1 a 13 m/s   **b** 20 m/s   **c** 7 seconds and 15 seconds

20.3 Solving simultaneous equations graphically

Purposeful practice 1

1 a

x	−2	−1	0	2	3.5	4
y	11	9	7	3	0	−1

b Students' own answers, for example, $x = 1$, $y = 5$ and $x = 5$, $y = -3$

c $x = 2$ and $y = 3$

d

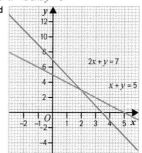

e $x = 2$ and $y = 3$. This is the same as the answer to **Q1c**. The point at which the two lines intersect is the only point where both equations are satisfied.

f Students' own answers, for example, I found eight pairs of values but the line extends beyond the graph I have drawn so there are infinite possible pairs.

g There are infinite possible solutions to $2x + y = 7$ but only one that also satisfies $x + y = 5$.

Purposeful practice 2

1 a

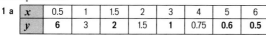

$x = 4$, $y = 2$

b

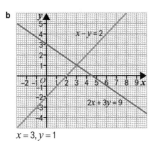

$x = 3, y = 1$

c

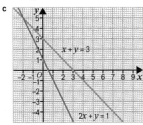

$x = -2, y = 5$

d

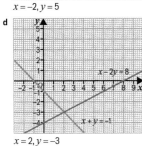

$x = 2, y = -3$

e

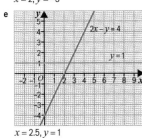

$x = 2.5, y = 1$

f

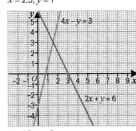

$x = 1.5, y = 3$

g

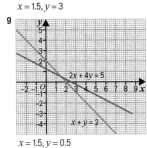

$x = 1.5, y = 0.5$

h

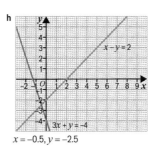

$x = -0.5, y = -2.5$

Problem-solving practice

1 Students' own answers – any two graphs that intersect at $(4, 1)$, for example, graphs to show equations $x + y = 5$ and $x - y = 3$

2 $x = -3, y = 4$. Students may or may not draw a graph.

3 -0.5 and 9.5. Students may or may not draw graphs of $x + y = 9$ and $x - y = 10$

4 $x = 7, y = 5$. Students may or may not draw a graph showing $2x - 3y = -1$ and $3x - 2y = 11$

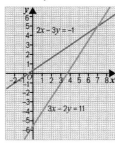

5 Students may or may not draw a graph showing $2x + y = 4.30$ **and** $3x + 5y = 9.25$

   a £1.75   **b** 80p

Exam practice

1 **a**

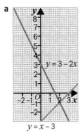

$y = x - 3$

b $x = 2, y = -1$

20.4 Solving simultaneous equations algebraically

Purposeful practice 1

1 **a** $3x = 6, x = 2$ **b** $5x + 2y = 16$ **c** $-2y = 4, y = -2$

2 **a** $3x = 6, x = 2$ **b** $-4y = -24, y = 6$ **c** $x - 2y = 0$

Purposeful practice 2

1 **a** $4x + 8y = 16$ **b** $3x + y = 8$ **c** $2x - 3y = 7$
    $4x + y = 9$ $3x - 6y = -6$ $2x + 2y = 12$

2 **a** $x + 2y = 4$ **b** $6x + 2y = 16$ **c** $2x - 3y = 7$
    $8x + 2y = 18$ $x - 2y = -2$ $3x + 3y = 18$

3 **a** $6x - 2y = 2$ **b** $10x + 5y = 25$ **c** $21x + 7y = 21$
    $6x + 3y = 27$ $10x + 4y = 28$ $21x + 6y = 15$

4 **a** $2x + 6y = 24$ **b** $5x + 10y = 55$ **c** $5x - 20y = 55$
    $3x - 6y = 6$ $8x + 10y = 70$ $16x + 20y = 40$

Problem-solving practice

1 $x = 4, y = 3$

2 **a** Danny has not multiplied the total of (2) by 3
  b Correct working to give $x = 7$ and $y = 2$

3 Students' own answers, for example, $2x - y = 8$ and $x + 3y = 11$.

4 Solution from graph is $x = -1, y = 5$
Students' own working to show solution algebraically is $x = -1, y = 5$. The answers should be the same.

5 317 and 586

6 Using simultaneous equations, adult ticket and child ticket is £6. So, adult ticket costs twice as much as child ticket. Students may use another method.

Exam practice

1 $x = -0.5, y = -3$

20.5 Rearranging formulae

Purposeful practice

1 a $t = \dfrac{m}{3}$ b $t = 2p$ or $t = \dfrac{p}{0.5}$ c $t = \dfrac{q}{n}$ d $t = \dfrac{r}{4n}$ e $t = \dfrac{v}{x}$

f $t = \dfrac{w}{2x}$ g $t = \dfrac{z}{nx}$ h $t = \dfrac{2y}{x}$ i $t = \dfrac{2s}{n}$

2 a $h = 3c$ b $h = 10d$ c $h = as$ d $h = abf$

e $h = \dfrac{1}{g}$ f $h = \dfrac{2}{m}$ g $h = \dfrac{r}{n}$ h $h = \dfrac{4s}{p}$

i $h = \dfrac{t}{4r}$ j $h = \dfrac{sv}{a}$ k $h = \dfrac{uw}{a}$ l $h = \dfrac{vwx}{a}$

3 a $x = y - 2$ b $x = a - b$ c $x = v + b$ d $x = \dfrac{w - a}{2}$

e $x = \dfrac{c + a}{2}$ f $x = \dfrac{g - a}{3}$ g $x = \dfrac{h + a}{3}$ h $x = \dfrac{k - 3}{b}$

i $x = 2(z - 3)$ j $x = 2(f - c)$ k $x = a(m - c)$ l $x = a(m + d)$

4 a $y = \dfrac{t}{2x}$ b $y = \dfrac{n}{az}$ c $y = \dfrac{10p}{a}$ d $y = \dfrac{10q}{z}$

e $y = \dfrac{2r}{z}$ f $y = \dfrac{2s}{az}$ g $y = \sqrt{t}$ h $y = \sqrt{\dfrac{u}{3}}$

i $y = \sqrt{\dfrac{v}{5}}$ j $y = \sqrt{\dfrac{x}{b}}$ k $y = \dfrac{\sqrt{z}}{2}$ l $y = \dfrac{b}{3}$

Problem-solving practice

1 a distance = speed × time   b time = $\dfrac{\text{distance}}{\text{speed}}$

2 9 seconds

3 a She has divided by 2 first, instead of adding 3 to both sides first. She has not divided all terms by 2.

b $y = \dfrac{x + 3}{2}$

4 $y = 5x + 3$ and $5x - y = -3$

5 a $r = \dfrac{C}{2\pi}$ b $r = \sqrt{\dfrac{A}{\pi}}$

Exam practice

1 $n = \dfrac{D - 5}{3}$ 2 $x = 2(y + 3z)$

20.6 Proof

Purposeful practice 1

1 Ensure students have expanded and simplified correctly.

2 a $x^2 + 3x + 2 - x^2 = 3x + 2$

b $x^2 + 3x + 2 - x = 2x + 2 = 2(x + 1)$

Purposeful practice 2

1 Even number: $2n$
Odd number: $2n + 1$
Multiple of 3: $3n$
3 consecutive integers: $n + n + 1 + n + 2$

2 a $n + n + 1 = 2n + 1$. $2n$ is even, so $2n + 1$ is odd.

b $2m - 2n = 2(m - n)$ which is a multiple of 2, so even.

c $2n + 1 - (2m + 1) = 2n + 1 - 2m - 1 = 2n - 2m = 2(n - m)$ which is a multiple of 2, so even.

d $2n + 1 - 2m = 2n - 2m + 1 = 2(n - m) + 1$ which is a multiple of 2, plus 1, so odd.

Problem-solving practice

1 a Students' answers will vary, for example, $1 + 2 + 3 = 6$, which is a multiple of 3.

b Three consecutive integers are $a, a + 1, a + 2$
$a + a + 1 + a + 2 = 3a + 3 = 3(a + 1)$, which is a multiple of 3.

2 a Perimeter $P = 3a + b + 3a + b + 3a + b + 3a + b = 12a + 4b$

b Yes, Bella is correct. $12a + 4b = 4(3a + b)$, which is a multiple of 4.

3 a Students' answers will vary, for example, $1 + 2 = 3$, which is not even.

b $2m + 2n + 1 = 2(m + n) + 1$, which is 1 more than an even number, so is odd.

Exam practice

1 Area $(x + 2)^2 = x^2 + 4x + 4 = 9$. Therefore, $x^2 + 4x = 5$

Mixed exercises E

Mixed problem-solving practice E

1 a A and iii, B and v, C and viii, D and vii, E and ii, F and iv

b

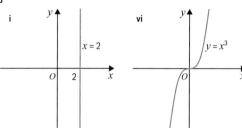

2 Jane has ordered the digits at the start of each distance and has not looked at the place value of the digits. The order should be Mercury, Earth, Jupiter, Saturn.

3 79.6 cm

4 Total area = $\pi \times 12^2 = 144\pi$;
Shaded area = $144\pi - \pi \times 6^2 = 144\pi - 36\pi = 108\pi$;
108π is not half of 144π, so Farrah is not correct.

5 $4\dfrac{15}{32}$

6 Students' estimates may vary. For example, $5 \times 10^7 \div 5 \times 10^4 = 1 \times 10^3$ hours

7 For the second triangle, use Pythagoras' theorem to find the missing side: $\sqrt{60^2 + 11^2} = 61$ cm. Both triangles have a right angle, a hypotenuse of 61 cm and a side of 60 cm and so are congruent (RHS).

8 $x = -\dfrac{1}{2}$ and $y = -5$

9 a Students' own answers, for example, $3 \times (1 + 3) = 3 \times 4 = 12$

b An odd number plus an odd number is always an even number, so $m + n$ is always even.
3 multiplied by an even number is always an even multiple of 3, which is also a multiple of 6. Therefore, the value of $3(m + n)$ will always be a multiple of 6.

10 Angle AMB = angle CMD because opposite angles are equal, AM = CM because M is the midpoint of AC and angle MAB = angle MCD because alternate angles are equal. Therefore, triangles ABM and CDM are congruent (ASA).

11 Squaring both sides gives $A^2 = x + y$ and then subtracting x from both sides gives $A^2 - x = y$ or $y = A^2 - x$

12 $\left(\dfrac{p}{q}\right)^{-2} = \dfrac{1}{\left(\dfrac{p}{q}\right)^2} = 1 \times \left(\dfrac{q}{p}\right)^2 = \dfrac{q^2}{p^2}$

13 36.1 cm

Exam practice

14 $\begin{pmatrix} 12 \\ 5 \end{pmatrix}$

15 1.4×10^{-4} 16 £2588.84

17 a 9.5 cm   b 10.4 cm

18 The equation of the line L_2 rearranges to give $y = 4x + \dfrac{7}{3}$.
The gradient of both L_1 and L_2 is 4 so the lines are parallel.

19 $(x + 4)(x + 5) = 30, x^2 + 9x + 20 = 30, x^2 + 9x = 10$

Index